THE DIOCESE OF ELPHIN

Edited by Francis Beirne

The Diocese of Elphin
People, Places and Pilgrimage

the columba press

First published in 2000 by

the columba press

55a Spruce Avenue, Stillorgan Industrial Park, Blackrock, Co Dublin

Cover by Bill Bolger
Origination by The Columba Press
Maps by Fiona Gallagher

ISBN 1 85607 299 1

Acknowledgements

The publisher and editor gratefully acknowledge the kind assistance and co-operation of Athlone Library, The National Architectural Archive, The National Library of Ireland, The National Millennium Committee, The National Museum of Ireland, Roscommon County Library, Sligo County Library, The Vatican Archives.

Contents

The Editorial Board

Back (left to right): John McTernan, Fiona Gallagher, Eamonn Bolger. Front: Brendan Nelson, William Gacquin, Very Rev Francis Beirne PP, John Brady. Inset: Sr Gabrielle McManus

FRANCIS BEIRNE is a native of Elphin and parish priest of Ballyforan, Dysart and Tisrara. He has pioneered many cultural projects in both counties Roscommon and Sligo and is author and contributor to various local histories.

JOHN BRADY is a native of the parish of Ballymoe and Ballintubber. He is principal of St Bride's NS, Ballintubber, and holds a Masters Degree in history from NUI Maynooth.

EAMONN BOLGER, born in Clontarf, Dublin, but resident for most of his life in Cloontuskert, Ballyleague, is a librarian at Roscommon County Library.

WILLIAM GACQUIN, a native of Kiltoom and Cam parish, teaches at the Christian Brothers School, Roscommon. He holds an MA in local history from NUI Maynooth, and has published material on the history of south Roscommon.

FIONA GALLAGHER, a native of Sligo town, has worked as researcher for the County Sligo Heritage and Genealogical Society for the last twelve years and has an abiding interest in local history, placenames and maps.

SR GABRIELLE MCMANUS, M Ed (Man), is a native of Roscommon town. As a Sister of Mercy she has worked in the education and health services in Sligo and at St Joseph's College, Summerhill, Athlone, for the past number of years.

JOHN C. MCTERNAN, a native of Riverstown parish, is a former County Librarian of Kilkenny and Sligo, and the author of a number of publications on the history of Sligo. He is currently secretary of the County Sligo Heritage and Genealogical Society.

BRENDAN NELSON, of Sligo Cathedral parish, spent his formative years in Calry parish. He retired from banking in 1990 and came to live in Sligo.

Preface

In this Jubilee year 2000AD we celebrate our Christian faith through the centuries going back to Christ and through Christ to its roots in the Old Testament. The light of faith helps us discover who God is, who we are and what we are called to be. The story of our faith in God is the story of our people in this diocese through the centuries. The more we reflect on the story of our people the more we discover who we are.

The ruins of ancient churches, monasteries and cemeteries, together with so many sacred shrines and holy wells, are very rugged reminders of our peoples' faith and trust in God. We also have many artifacts and written records which give us invaluable insight into the story of our past.

It is a great source of joy and gratitude for me and for the diocese of Elphin that we have now, for the first time, a history of our diocese. This publication will give our people, and especially our youth, a sense of pride in our past and a determination to face the future with great faith and trust in God.

On behalf of the diocese I wish to put on record our sincerest gratitude and congratulations to the Elphin Diocesan Heritage Society, under the guidance of Fr Francis Beirne, PP Ballyforan, Dysart and Tisrara, for presenting us with this scholarly publication. Over the past three years the Society has met regularly for entire days as it co-ordinated the fruits of much research and compiled this history.

The Heritage Society has also provided us with excellent maps, photographic records and a bibliography of historical sources that will be invaluable to Elphin historians of the future. It is a spectacular achievement for a very small group of volunteers driven by faith, knowledge, expertise and above all by an abiding love of history.

I sincerely hope that this publication will be used in every first and second level school of this diocese as a means of giving the students of our day a great appreciation of our people who persevered in their faith through centuries of oppression, famine and poverty. It was the only light of hope in those very dark days. I hope also that, inspired by the story of our past, young people will be motivated to build a better world for our people in the future – a world where God is very much at the centre of hearts, homes and communities.

Cuireann an leabhar tráthúil seo saibhreas ár n-oidhreachta Críostaí i ndeoise

Ailfinne ós ár gcomhair. Tá súil agam go mbeidh sé mar lochrann dóibh siúd atá le teacht. Go raibh Muire gan Smál agus Naomh Aiseach mar idirghuítheoirí ag gach duine a léann é.

✠ *Christopher Jones*
Bishop of Elphin.

Bishop Jones in private audience with Pope John Paul II
during his *ad limina* visit to Rome in 1999

Introduction

The history of any church, diocese, or parish entails people, places and pilgrimage. The story of the Diocese of Elphin is no different – it is an account of a pilgrim people in county Roscommon and parts of Sligo and east Galway. The pilgrim journey covers centuries of a believing and worshipping people who have ernestly tried to live the gospel message in their own time, place and circumstances. It recalls the strengths and struggles of the church during various and sometimes hostile periods of Irish history. It is a commendable statement about Christian people bearing testimony to Christ often under pain of persecution and death.

Our story in Elphin begins with the arrival of St Patrick in the fifth century when, tradition tells us, he made his historic crossing of the Shannon into Connacht and began the process of evangelisation. Since that time generation after generation have kept the light of faith burning over a period of fifteen hundred years. This honoured task has been the responsibility of bishops, priests, religious, communities and families alike. They have all, in their own way, shouldered the responsibility of ensuring that the Christian faith has been passed on to succeeding generations. Every period of history reflects difficulties in transmitting the gospel message, either because of poverty, division, persecution, affluence or indifference.

However, despite the inherent obstacles, the church in the Diocese of Elphin has had a remarkable influence on the way of life of the people, communities and families in this region. The survival of elements of the earliest traditions, in our Holy Wells, the remains of monastic settlements, and numerous medieval church ruins dotted throughout the diocese, indicates the pivotal role played by the faith in the initiation and fostering of a common bond of charity among all classes of people and communities. The remnants of Christian works of art, in the wooden carved statue of St Molaise, the ninth- and tenth-century inscribed grave-slabs in many parts of the diocese, the eighth-century crucifixion plaque from Rindoon, the twelfth-century crozier of St Barry, the Cross of Cong, Drumcliff High Cross, all in their own unique way remind us of the golden years of Celtic Christian art.

Several examples of romanesque and gothic architecture, which were spared the ravages and turbulence of war, stand out. One has only to visit Boyle Abbey, or any of the ruined churches, to see what was achieved by the work of human hands, without the wonderful facilities of a technological age.

The twelfth century saw the re-organisation of the diocesan structure with the Synods of Rath Breasail and Kells, in IIII and 1152 respectively. The Diocese of Elphin as constituted today dates from 1152, and was followed by the establishment of a parochial structure. It was during this time also that we saw the arrival from the continent of the contemplative and mendicant orders in the twelfth, thirteenth, and fourteenth centuries. These Orders included the Cistercians, Premonstratensians, Canons Regular of St Augustine, Cluniacs, Knight Hospitallers, the Dominicans, Franciscans, Carmelites and Augustinians. They each contributed towards the spiritual enrichment and pastoral care of the Catholic population of the diocese.

However, the sixteenth century signalled the arrival of the Reformation, the Cromwellian invasion and the subsequent penal laws. This was a particularly cruel time for the Catholic population. The reports to Rome in the seventeenth and eighteenth centuries bear this out, as do the list of martyrs and the *Report on the State of Popery* in 1731. This period was the bleakest and most painful in the history of the diocese. However, the unremitting fidelity to the faith, and the persistent and undaunted desire of the people to practise it and to worship God, ensured that the church prevailed through the almost insurmountable opposition of that era.

The securing of Catholic Emancipation in 1829 was an important milestone in religious freedom for the diocese, and once again saw the building of churches and the return of public Catholic worship. It was shortly after this period, in 1858, that the newly-appointed Bishop Laurence Gillooly initiated long overdue change and reform and heralded a new chapter of development and re-organisation in the diocese. The arrival of men and women religious in the aftermath of the Great Famine brought new opportunities and hope to the diocese at a time when poverty and social deprivation were rampant and education and medical care were dire needs.

It is important to remember that the clergy and religious were instrumental in establishing many of the infrastructural services and care which are now state-owned and funded from the national exchequer. The Sisters of Mercy, Ursulines, Poor Sisters of Nazareth, Presentation, Augustinians, Franciscan Sisters of Mary, La Sagesse, Sisters of the Divine Master, St Joseph of the Apparition, as well as the Marist Brothers, Christian Brothers, De La Salle Brothers and others, established institutional care throughout the diocese, setting up schools and hospitals, together with social and community care for all sections, but primarily for the disadvantaged.

The twentieth century, and more particularly the second half thereof, saw revolutionary changes in the church worldwide, which percolated down to every diocese, parish and individual Catholic. The Second Vatican Council (1962-65) introduced much revision and change which helped to equip the present day Catholic to deal more effectively with the challenges of a new technological and liberal age. The diocese experienced rapid re-ordering of its churches in order to facilitate and implement the new liturgical norms of the council, which was daunting and challenging for both priests and people.

In the post-conciliar era, the promotion of renewal, scripture and prayer groups, coupled with greater involvement and participation in the administration, pastoral activity and liturgical life of the church, has engendered a renewed spirit of commitment among people to live and practise the faith in these transitional times. These reforms have necessitated vast changes and challenges at all levels, and no doubt place enormous demands on the pastoral ministers and carers committed to the welfare of the post-conciliar church in Elphin.

The arrival of the third millennium is an opportune time to glance back over the centuries of the church in the Diocese of Elphin. We are fortunate to have access to well-documented accounts of the early period, which are described in the *Tripartite Life of Saint Patrick,* as well as the *Book of Armagh,* Patrician documents, and the various annals. The early Christian sites and ruined churches in every parish relate their own stories, as do the inscribed stones and other relics all around us.

This book has been made possible from a combination of sources, compiled by various authors over the years. These are listed in the extensive Bibliography at the end of this book, which we hope will provide the basis for ongoing research and motivate present and future generations to undertake parish and diocesan historical projects. In particular, we are grateful to the late Fr Canice Mooney OFM, who has chronicled the history of Elphin Diocese from the early years. It is published here with the invaluable assistance of Fr Ignatius Fennessy OFM, of Dún Mhuire, Killiney, Dublin, who edited the original text for publication. We also rely on a number of well-researched historical accounts compiled by the late Mgr James J. Kelly of Athlone. These include the succession of bishops in the diocese, patron saints, martyrs of the diocese, and others, which have all been published in the *Irish Ecclesiastical Record.* The late Archdeacon Michael Connellan of Aughrim, county Roscommon, devoted years to researching the origin and derivation of place-names, and his work also provided us with vital material. Fr Hugh Fenning OP, Tallaght, Dublin, has done trojan work in researching bishops, clergy and religious of Elphin. There are several other well-known sources and authors which were extremely useful and deserve grateful mention. They are acknowledged in the Bibliography.

The special features of this book include the colour section and the indexed diocesan and parish maps, with accompanying townland lists, which have been meticulously researched and drawn by Fiona Gallagher of Sligo, funded by FÁS and sponsored by the County Sligo Heritage and Genealogical Society. There are also numerous illustrations throughout from late eighteenth-century publications, including Grosse's *Antiquities of Ireland,* as well as drawings by the nineteenth-century illustrator, W. F. Wakeman. The majority of the illustrations have been drawn by Albert Siggins of Roscommon, Fiona Gallagher of Sligo, Berna Chapman of Strokestown, and Marian Moffat of Sligo. Many of the photographs were taken by Brendan Nelson of Sligo, Josie Hannon of Ballygar, as well as Christy Regan of Boyle, Jimmy McHugh of Sligo and Fr Liam Devine.

The short parish histories should have a special appeal to every community and hopefully will prompt historians and communities to undertake their own local parish history projects, if they haven't already done so. We wish to acknowledge the kind assistance of many clergy, people and parishes in the compilation of these accounts. In particular we would like to thank the Elphin Diocesan Archives, St Mary's Sligo, the County Libraries of Roscommon, Sligo and Galway, and especially Mrs Anne Lohan of Four Roads, county Roscommon, who spent many months researching provincial papers in Roscommon County Library.

Several others provided much valued help and we owe them a great deal of gratitude: Mgr Gerard Dolan of Sligo, Mgr Charles Travers of Roscommon, the Sisters of Mercy Boyle, the CBS Roscommon, and the Church of Ireland communities in counties Roscommon and Sligo. In a special way we would like to thank Peter Dunne, Manager of Community Services, FÁS, Sligo, and Joe Quinn, Senior Development Officer, FÁS, Sligo, who provided the project with funding and secretarial services under their FÁS youth training scheme.

This book was the idea of Bishop Christopher Jones and is part of a series of diocesan events organised to celebrate the Jubilee Year 2000. We are deeply grateful to him for his continued support, encouragement and sustained commitment during the entire project.

The Elphin Diocesan Heritage Society, consisting of Fr Francis M. Beirne (Chairperson), John McTernan (Vice-Chairperson), Sister Gabrielle McManus (Secretary), William Gacquin (Treasurer), and committee members, John Brady, Brian Curran, Edward Egan, Fiona Gallagher, Helen Kilcline, Eileen McGowan, James Mulcahy (RIP), and Brendan Nelson, initiated the project. However, the main responsibility of researching, compiling and editing was undertaken by the members of the Society's editorial board, details of which are given on page 6.

This book is not meant to be a definitive history of the diocese. It is our fervent wish that somebody in the future will compile a more comprehensive and detailed historical account of the diocese, and thus record for posterity the Christian endeavours of a pilgrim people.

I salute the memory of so many outstanding Catholic people who have contributed to the Christian heritage of our diocese. I also express my sincere gratitude and appreciation to all who have assisted in any way towards ensuring that a history of the diocese is finally put between covers. Like living the faith itself, the compilation of this book has been both a joy and a challenge.

Go mba fíor-chuimhneachán é seo orthu sin go léir, in ár nDeoise, a thug a saol ar son an Chreidimh Chaitlicí. Go mba foinse feabhais agus eolais é do Chríostaithe an lae inniú, chomh maith le bheith ina údar ionspioráide agus dóchais do na glúnta atá le teacht.

Francis M. Beirne
4 October 2000
Feast of St Francis of Assisi

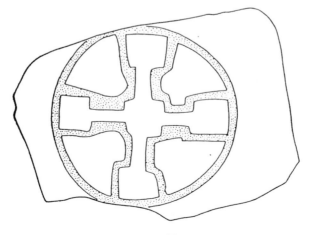

A cross-inscribed slab from Cloontuskert

The parishes of Elphin, showing the county boundaries
and adjoining parishes in county Roscommon.

PART I

The Diocese

The Diocesan Map
The Parishes of Elphin

The map on page 19 shows the civil parishes as representing the medieval parishes of the diocese of Elphin, overlaid by the modern parish boundaries. It is evident from this map that huge changes have occurred in the geographical structure of the parishes since the Reformation, and more especially since the post-Famine years.

The parish is an ecclesiastical administrative unit of great antiquity whose origins are traced back to the early monastic structure. These monasteries were presided over by an abbot-bishop. In many instances the medieval churches were founded by particular families, such as the O'Conors or McDermots in Connacht, and were usually patronised by them.

After the synods of Rathbreasail (1111) and Kells (1152), much reform took place which resulted in the establishment of new diocesan and parochial structures and the replacement of the old monastic system. The arrival of the Normans greatly expedited this process with the building of churches and the introduction of religious orders from the continent. One of the legacies of the Norman influence is the number of churches that were dedicated to the universal saints, rather than native Irish ones, especially St John the Baptist to whom they had great devotion.

With the major conflicts of the sixteenth and seventeenth centuries, the church was forced underground and Catholic worship suppressed. It became more difficult for the church to operate in public or to administer its diocesan and parochial affairs. However, the spiritual welfare of the people was not neglected as bishops and clergy carried out an effective pastoral care of the people. The parochial structures became somewhat irrelevant for church administration during the penal era.

Pettys' 'Downs' Survey of the 1650s recorded the boundaries of these ancient parishes for the first time, and they were used as civil administrative divisions. The new Anglican Church adopted the old parishes and dioceses as their own church structure, but the absence of a substantial Protestant community over the greater part of the country resulted in the neglect of the old parochial centres, and their eventual demise. This is evident today in the large number of ruined Protestant churches, located in isolated areas, often situated beside or near a ruined medieval church. The majority Catholic population lived in the rural areas, which were to see huge increases in population in the eighteenth and early nineteenth centuries.

Many new market towns grew up, often on the boundaries of two or more ancient parishes, as rivers had frequently been used as boundaries, and these towns became the new focus of social administration in the eighteenth century. There are 2,445 civil or ancient parishes in Ireland today.

There was a significant change in the pastoral life of the church after the Reformation when the church was deprived of its temporal goods and places of worship. At the height of the penal laws there was a shortage of clergy and this, combined with the extreme poverty of the people, initiated a process of re-organisation of parish boundaries. Also to be borne in mind is that in the period spanning the Great Famine, the enormous decrease in the population density and distribution hastened the amalgamation of some of the older parishes to form unions. The composition of these unions varied from time to time until they finally settled into their current form around the 1880s. For instance, in 1839 Croghan and Ballinameen formed one parish stretching from Carrick-on-Shannon to Lough Gara. Kilbride, Kilgefin and Cloontuskert were united until 1861, when Cloontuskert separated; the other two parishes remain united until 1880, when Kilgefin joined Cloontuskert, and Kilbride annexed Oran. Kilbride finally became a unitary parish in 1890. The ancient Cathedral Parish of Elphin is in actual fact much smaller than the modern parish of the same name, and part of it lies within the boundaries of the present parish of Tulsk. The large union of Tibohine, corresponding to the ancient territory of Airteach, which in 1839 had three chapels located at Tibohine, Frenchpark and Loughglynn, had by 1843 broken up into three parishes. Frenchpark, which had been attached to Tibohine again for a period after the Famine, finally united with Ballinagare (Kilcorkey) in 1869. The carving-up of Lissonuffy and Bumlin parishes has a more logical reason: the new western boundary of Strokestown parish would now run along the crest of the Sliabh Bán mountain, a natural division.

The public re-emergence of the Catholic Church after Catholic Emancipation in 1829, combined with the change in the population structure, has ensured that some modern parishes bear only minimal resemblance to the medieval parishes whose names and patrons they often retain. However, for most of county Roscommon, these new parishes have taken the form of unions of two or more ancient parishes, maintaining some sense of continuity, with the exception of the northeast of the county, where major re-structuring has taken place. Since the civil parish boundaries are based on the medieval church parish, they often break or cross county boundaries, which for the most part are a sixteenth-century composition.

Today, the parish has become the focal point of Irish life, the ultimate place of belonging, a fact re-enforced by many cultural, sporting and social organisations.

The Parishes of the Diocese of Elphin in the year 2000.

This map shows the boundaries of the civil or ancient parishes of Elphin, overlaid by the boundaries of the modern Catholic parishes. The names given are those of the civil parishes. The present parishes often contain parts of several of the older parishes.

Interior of the Cathedral of the Immaculate Conception, Sligo, before the sanctuary alterations in 1974.

IN LOVING MEMORY OF JAMES CONNAUGHTON
ERECTED BY HIS WIFE ANNE CONNAUGHTON

The Flight into Egypt, a stained glass window by Harry Clarke (1889-1931) from the Church of the Good Shepherd, Tisrara. Some of Clarke's best ecclesiastical works of art are to be seen in churches in the diocese, as are the works of other distinguished stained glass artists including Alfred Ernest Child (1875-1939), Michael Healy (1873-1941), Ethel Rhind (c.1879-1952), Catherine O'Brien (1881-1963), Evie Hone (1894-1955) and Hubert McGoldrick (1897-1967).

Bishop Egan's Chalice, 1634.
The chalice, 25cm high, is made of nine sections of spun silver, recently regilded. There is no maker's mark, but it may have been made in a Galway workshop. The inscription on the cup reads: 'Calicem salutaris accipiam et nomen Domini invocabo. Pro conventu ff: min: regul: obser:ae de Elphin anno Domini 1634.' (For the friary of the Friars Minor of the Regular Observance at Elphin, the year of the Lord 1634.) Around the lower part of the foot is the following inscription: 'Frater Boetius Eganus Episcopus Elphinensis me fieri fecit 1634.' (Friar Boetius Egan, Bishop of Elphin, had me made, 1634.)

Seal of Thomas Barrett, Bishop of Elphin (1372-1404). The matrix is bronze and measures 6.58cm x 3.81cm. It has a pierced handle at the back, is pointed oval and is very finely cut. It represents the Blessed Virgin Mary enthroned in a niche beneath a pinnacled gothic canopy with screen work at the sides; the background of the niche is decorated with sprigs of foliage. The Virgin wears a crown and carries a sceptre ending in a trefoil. She is holding the child Jesus standing on her left knee. Beneath, in a round-arched niche, is a demi-figure with mitre, amice and chasuble, his hands clasped in prayer and his crozier resting over his right shoulder. On the canopy is a shield of arms with three mitres. This diocesan coat of arms is quite different from that now used by the diocese (see page 73). The Seal bears the following Latin inscription: 'Sigillum dni thome dei gracia elphinensis epi.' (Seal of Lord Thomas, by the grace of God Bishop of Elphin.) The Barrett Seal was acquired by the Royal Irish Academy in 1831, and is now part of their collection in the National Museum, Dublin.

The Cross of Cong is a twelfth-century reliquary made in 1123 by Mael Isu at Clooncraff in the parish of Roscommon/Kilteevan at the behest of Turlough O'Conor, King of Connacht. It enshrines a fragment of the True Cross which was presented to the king by Pope Callistus II (1119-1124) at the close of the Lateran Council. The Cross is made of wood covered in bronze plates decorated in openwork interlaced animal designs in the Irish Urnes style, and measures 76cm x 47.9cm (2′ 6″ x 1′ 6″). It disappeared for many centuries and was re-discovered in the nineteenth century at Cong, Co Mayo, and it has since been called the Cross of Cong. It was presented in 1839 to the Royal Irish Academy whose collection is now in the National Museum, Dublin. A replica of the Cross was presented to the parish of Roscommon, its original home, in 1903.

Rinnegan eighth-century crucifixion plaque (Knockcroghery parish). See note on back cover.

23

St Asicus
Patron of the Diocese

St Asicus depicted in a stained glass window in the Cathedral of the Immaculate Conception, Sligo.

St Patrick came to Elphin in 435 on his missionary tour through Connacht, crossing the Shannon at Drumboylan in the parish of Ardcarne. He came to the territory of Corcoghlan in which was situated the place now called Elphin. The prince or chief of that territory, a noble druid named Ona or Ono, or Hono, of the royal Connacian race of Hy-Briuin, gave land and afterwards his fort to St Patrick to found a church and monastery.

St Patrick appointed Asicus as first abbot-bishop of this church in the fifth century. St Asicus was a worker in metal, and is described in the Book of Armagh as a *cérd*, or wright. He made altars, chalices and patens, and metal book-covers for the newly founded churches. He was instrumental in establishing a school of art, which produced most beautiful objects of Celtic workmanship in the diocese. His artisanship inspired many of the great Christian works of art, such as the Cross of Cong, the Ardagh Chalice, and many other Celtic works which are treasured for their beauty and antiquity.

One of the remarkable images of Asicus is that he is always portrayed as both a craftsman and a bishop. He preached the word of God through his work. His work, which was a prayer and his craftsmanship, gave praise and glory to God.

Asicus left Elphin seven years before his death to lead a more penitential life and lived in solitude on the island of Rathlin O'Beirne off the coast of Donegal. Some of the monks at Elphin pleaded with him to return, and on the way he died at a place called Rathcung near Ballintra in county Donegal, where he is buried. The diocese erected a memorial over his grave in 1957, and an annual diocesan pilgrimage takes place there on or near 27 April, which is his feastday.

The saint is also commemorated by a carved wooden statue, which was discovered in London in 1960, and is now enshrined in the Cathedral. There are several churches throughout Elphin which also feature the saint in their stained-glass windows. St Asicus will always be honoured as the patronal saint of the diocese, and 'father of our faith'.

A Short History of the Diocese of Elphin
by Canice Mooney OFM*

Reverend Canice Mooney, OFM, MA, Lic Sc Hist, B Ph, was born in Drumshanbo, Co Leitrim in 1911 and was educated at St Louis' College, Multyfarnham. He attended the Catholic University of Louvain, St Isidore's College in Rome and the Athenaeum Antonianum, Rome. He was the Superior of the Franciscan House of Studies, Killiney from 1948 to 1954. He held the position of Assistant Research Professor in the Dublin Institute for Advanced Studies from 1945 to 1950 and was also a member of the Royal Irish Academy. Father Mooney died on 19 December 1963.

This Irish diocese was called *Ail-finn* or *Oil-find,* and in Latin, *Elphinum, Elphinium, Alfinnia, Elphinensis, Oilefinensis,* and *Saxum lucidi fontis* (the rock of the clear spring). A suffragan of the Archdiocese of Tuam, its area was 3,200 square kilometres, corresponding approximately with the present Co Roscommon, but excluding small portions of the south and west of the county, and including the northern and eastern portion of Co Sligo and some of the north eastern part of Co Galway.

The ancient designations of the chief territories comprising the diocese, going from north to south, were Cairbre (Carbery) and Tír-Ailealla (Tirerill) in Co Sligo; Maigh-luirg and Maigh-aoí or Machaire Chonnacht in Co Roscommon; and the north eastern portion of Uí Máine in Co Galway. In this diocese was situated Cruacha (often called Cruacha-maighe-aoí to distinguish it from other placenames with the same first element) now Rathcroghan, which was the ancient residence of the kings of Connacht. In medieval times the chief families were the O'Connors (Ó Conchubhair), O'Hanleys (Ó hAinlighe), Mac Dermotts (Mac Diarmada), Mac Donaghs (Mac Donnchadha), Connellans (Ó Conalláin), O'Murrays (Ó Muireadhaigh), O'Beirnes (Ó Birn), Brennans (Mac Branáin), Geraghtys (Mág Oireachtaigh), and Conrys (Ó Maolchonaire).

---

* The original English text, written c. 1958, which was translated verbatim into French for the *Dictionnaire d'histoire et de géographie ecclésiatiques (DHGE)*, xv, 1963, col. 269-292, the year in which Fr Mooney died, and is edited here by Ignatius Fennessy OFM.

FROM THE COMING OF CHRISTIANITY TO THE ANGLO-NORMANS

St Patrick and St Asicus

St Patrick visited the territory during each of his evangelising tours of Connacht. He concentrated on the northern portion of the diocese. A druid named Ono of the race of the Uí Briúin gave him a site for a church and monastery, which from its owner had been known as Imleach-Ono or Imleach-Ónonn, but soon came to be known as Ail-finn, Elphin, meaning, according to some, the white rock or, according to others, the rock of the clear spring. The church was called Teampall Pádraic, St Patrick's Church.

Patrick left at Elphin his smith (Ir. *ceard*, L. *faber aeris*), Asicus, along with Bite or Betheus, who was a nephew of Asicus, and Cipia (or Copia?) who was Bite's mother. Asicus had been employed by Patrick in making altars, altar-plate, and metal book-covers. We are not informed at what stage he was consecrated bishop, and are not even certain whether it was during the lifetime of St Patrick. He has been identified with Tassach, Bishop of Rath-colptha in Co Down (feastday, 14 April), who administered viaticum to the dying Patrick, but the identification is unlikely. Tassach, it was explained, was a hypocoristic [or pet] form of Asicus/Assicus (Assach, T'Assach), and it was pointed out that Tassach, also, in some medieval writings was described as Patrick's smith or artisan. Nor is the other suggested identification with St Assanus likely either (feastday, 27 April). Asicus is very probably the same as the saint Isaac or Isac, who is commemorated at 26 April in the martyrologies of Tallaght and Gorman. (Today the feast of St Asicus, the patron of the diocese of Elphin, is celebrated on 27 April; see bibliography below, John O'Hanlon and J. J. Kelly.– *ed.*)

As a result of a lie told either by him or about him in Elphin, he retired as a recluse to south-west Donegal and spent seven years on Rathlin O'Byrne Island (Rochuil) until his monks found him and tried to prevail on him to return with them to Elphin; but he refused. He is buried at Racoon (Ráith-cunga) in the parish of Drumhome in Co Donegal. Also buried there is his nephew Bite. The local chieftain made a grant of some land and a monastery was established there. A few years ago the diocese of Elphin erected a monument on the site to St Asicus. Examples of his metal-work were preserved for centuries in the churches of Armagh, Elphin, and Domhnach-mór-maighe-seola.

Other foundations

Of the other churches founded by Patrick in what is now the diocese of Elphin, one can mention Aghanagh (Each-eanach), Tawnagh (Tamhnach), Caiseal-Iorra, near Strandhill, and Shancough (Sean-chua), all in Co Sligo; and the following, which are all in Co Roscommon: Kilmore (Cill-mór), Baslick (L. *Basilica Sanctorum*), Shankill (Sean-chill Dumhaighe), Ard-sean-lios now Kildalloge near Strokestown, Fuerty

(Fiodharta), Oran (Cill-Garad), and perhaps Tibohine (Teach-Baoithine-Airtigh), Cloonshanville (Cluain-Seanmhaoil), Kilnamanagh (Cill-na-manach, Cluain-na-manach), and Emlagh (Imleach-Brocadha).

In order to continue the good work in his absence, Patrick put different disciples in charge of the different churches he founded. Some of those were bishops, some were priests, some were monks. He placed St Soicheall or Sachell (feastday, 1 August?) as bishop at Baslick; St Brocaidh (feastday, 9 July) as bishop of Emlagh, St Máine (feastday, 24 November?), son of Eichean or of Eoghan, as bishop in the territory of the Uí Earalla (Tirerill), probably at Aghanagh, where he is buried; the nun, St Lallóc at Ard-sean-lios; the deacon Caomhán at Sean-domhnach; the monks Conleng (Conlang) and Ercleng (Erclang) at Kilmore. St Ceitheach (L. *Cethacus;* feastday, 16 June), who is buried at Oran and who was a bishop, was probably put in charge of that place by Patrick. At Tawnagh he left St Caireall (feastday, 13 June?), who had been consecrated bishop by Bishops Brón and Bite. He left four people at Shankill: Maichet and Cetchen and Rodán a priest and Mathona (Mo-Chonna?) a nun. He appointed St Brón (feastday, 8 June) to Caiseal-Iorra, and the church consequently became known as Cill-easpaig-Brón (in English, Killaspugbrone); but we find also mention of a certain Bite of Caiseal-Iorra who was a bishop and a contemporary of Patrick. Since Brón, according to the *Annals of Ulster,* did not die until 512, it can hardly be a question of Bite succeeding him. It is not certain that he is the same as Bite of Elphin who was a nephew of Asicus.

The *Tripartite Life* describes several occurrences during Patrick's visits to this region: his dramatic conversion of Eithne and Feidhelm, the two daughters of King Laoghaire; his encounters with two pairs of brothers who were druids, Id and Ono, Maol and Caplaid; his formation of a well at Elphin an another at Oran; the stealing of his horses in Moylurg by the descendants of Erc (moccu Eirc); his falling into the Boyle River at Áth-carpaid; the strange incident in which Patrick, after he had ordained Ailbhe at Dumha-Gráidh, directed him to a place in the hills (Sliabh Ua nAilealla) where he would find a subterranean stone altar with four chalices at its four angles. Ailbhe is buried at Shancough, and may have been placed in charge of that church by Patrick.

Other saints

There were several saints prominent in the region during the first few centuries after the introduction of Christianity. In the case of some of them one account implies that they were contemporaries of Patrick who lived in the middle of the fifth century, another account implies that they lived in the second half of the sixth century since they are brought into contact with St Colmcille (died, 597) and his contemporaries. One solution of such cases that suggests itself is that in reality it is a question of two different persons whose *acta* (deeds) have been confused. Another is either that the advocates of Patrician claims push back the *floruit* (lifespan) of certain popular local saints in order to represent them as dependent on Patrick for their reception and baptism, ordination, consecration, or the veil of virginity; or else that the partisans of Colmcille bring forward their *floruit* in order to claim their churches as part of the *paruchia* (sphere of influence) of Colmcille. A third solution, which definitely explains several of the cases, is that the accounts on which we depend were written too long after the events to be of any historical value.

St Attracta

An example of such confusion is St Attracta (Athracht, Ethracht), a virgin, with feastday on 11 August. Tíreachán's notes and the *Tripartite Life of St Patrick* tell of a woman of this name who was a daughter of Talan and received the veil of virginity from Patrick. According to the *Tripartite Life,* Patrick founded her church, Cill Athrachta (Killaraght in the present Co Sligo and diocese of Achonry), and left with her a chalice and paten. It also tells us that she was a sister of Caomhán of Airdne-Caomháin. This St Caomhán will be found commemorated in the *Martyrology of Tallaght* at 7 June and 12 June. According to another account, her father was Tighearnach, and according to another, Saran. Even those accounts that agree on the name of her father disagree on the name of her father's father. She is said to have fled from Cill-sáile in Críoch Conaill southwards into Connacht in order to escape being forced into marriage by her father, and in order to consecrate her virginity to God. She was accompanied only by her handmaiden Miotáin, and by her servant Mocháin. She founded a hospice for travellers at a place where seven roads met (Killaraght?). She hoped to found another convent near Drum in the vicinity of Boyle, but St Conall, her brother or half-brother, sent St Mo-Chonna to dissuade her. This Mo-Chonna (also written Da-Chonna and Conna, with feastday on 8 March) would seem to be the person who, according to other accounts, was placed by St Colmcille in charge of the monastery of Eas-mic-nEirc (see below, under St Molaise).

St Attracta's Well in the townland of Clogher

The life of Attracta published by John Colgan OFM in his *Acta Sanctorum Hiberniae* (pp 277-282), and reprinted by the Bollandists, is practically worthless. It was probably compiled by a Cistercian monk of Boyle in the latter half of the twelfth century or in the course of the thirteenth century. See the mention of the construction of a monastery of monks (a veiled reference to Boyle?) between the monasteries of Conall and Mo-Chonna as the fulfilment of an alleged prophecy of Attracta when she cursed those two saints for refusing to allow her to found a nunnery in their district. Although there is much historical confusion about this saint, devotion to her is widespread, and her feast is celebrated liturgically throughout Ireland.

St Beoadh and others

Beoadh (also Beo-Aodh, and in Latin *Aidus* and *Beatus*), son of Olc, son of Comán, was bishop of Ardcarne (probably its first bishop) and died 8 March 524. The *Martyrology of Tallaght* is incorrect in giving his feastday as 7 March. He was noted for his generosity and hospitality. St Barry (Bearach, Beirreach, L. *Barachius, Berachius,* feast on 15 February), was abbot of Cluain-Cairpthe, i.e. Kilbarry, Termonbarry, Co Roscommon. His father was Neamhnann, son of Aimhirgin, of the race of Dobhtha, and his mother was Fionmhaith, sister of Cruimhthear Fraoich of Cloone (Cluain-Chonmaicne), Co Leitrim. St Comán, the hypocoristic form of whose name (pet-name) was Mo-Chommóg (literally, 'my young Com'), feastday 26 December, was the son of Faolchú, son of Dreathlan, son of Connla, and gave his name to the town (and consequently the county) of Roscommon (Ros Comáin, Comán's grove), where he founded a monastery. St Éadaoin (Etáin, virgin, feastday 5 July) is buried at Tumna on the river Boyle, of which place she is patron. St Muadhnat, also a virgin whose feastday is on 6 January, was associated with Caille (Drumcliff, Co Sligo); and St Altene or Eltene, son of Maolán (feastday, 11 January), is venerated at Shancough.

St Molaisse

St Molaisse or Laisréan (feastday, 12 August), son of Declan, co-operated with St Colmcille in the founding of a monastery on Inishmurray (Inis-Muireadhaigh), an island off the coast of Sligo where there are still considerable remains. The tradition that it was St Molaisse (Molaisse of Inishmurray, according to some; Molaisse of Devenish or Daimh-Inis according to others) who imposed the penance of exile on Colmcille is late and unreliable.

St Molaisse's statue and house on Inishmurray

Several writers mention a St Dicholla of Inishmurray, but his claims to canonisation are doubtful. The son of Menida, he was, however, abbot there and died in 752 (*Annals of Ulster,* i, p. 214, ad an. 751; and *Annals of the Four Masters,* i, p. 350, ad an. 747).

Apart from Inishmurray, a few other churches and monasteries in the region (Drumcliff, Assylin, and Inis-mac-nErnán) belonged to the *paruchia* of Colmcille; and it was claimed for them that they were founded either directly by him or by his disciples. Drumcliff (Druim-cliabh), Co Sligo, had as first abbot and patron Tarannán (Mo-Thorannán; feastday, 12 June). Assylin (Eas-Uí-Fhloinn, but originally Eas-mic-nEirc), on the north bank of the Boyle River about a mile west of the town of

Boyle, was placed under the charge of St Mo-Chonna (Da-Chonna, Conna; feastday 8 March). Inis-mac-nErnin, now Church Island on Loch Cé, is also believed to have been a Columban monastery.

St Brigit

It is generally claimed that St Brigid of Kildare also visited this territory, founding convents and cells there and blessing wells. The claim can be neither substantiated nor disproved, but some of the churches (and wells) that bear her name were in all probablility merely dedicated to her, not founded or discovered by her. On the other hand, there is no doubt that, as with St Colmcille in the northern portion of the diocese, so in the southern portion, several churches belonged to the *paruchia* of St Brigid and owed allegiance to her house at Kildare. Her influence and her cult is evidenced by the churches dedicated to her at Drum (Druim-Dreastain), Kilbride, Kilmore, Dysart, Camma or Cam (Cammach Brighde), Kilsellagh, Kilteevan, and by the holy wells dedicated to her at Brideswell (Tobair-Brighde), Kilbride, Kilsellagh, Kilteevan, and Cloonourn.

Monasteries

The eleventh, twelfth and thirteenth centuries saw the transfer of some of the ancient monastic foundations to the Canons Regular of St Augustine. We find them established at Inis-mac-nErnán, Roscommon, Derrane, Cloontuskert, Ardcarne, and Kilmore. It is also stated that a convent of nuns at Ardcarne at an unspecified date attached themselves as a cell to the convent of Kilcreevanty (Cill-Chraobhnata, L. *Casta Silva*) in Co Galway. However that may be, certainly in a papal document of about the year 1220 which is quoted in another papal document of April 1400 (*Calendar...papal letters, 1396-1404*, v, p. 335), St Mary's, Ardcarne, and also St Mary's Roscommon, St Mary's Derrane, and St Mary's Drumcliff, are included among the

R. J. King's design for a stamp to commemorate the Four Masters in 1944.

appurtenances of Kilcreevanty; and in the deed of surrender of April 1543, at the time of the dissolution of the monasteries, the abbess of Kilcreevanty, Dervaile O'Connor, is found to be in possession of the rectory of Ardcarne. Ware (*Whole works*, ed. Harris, II, p. 274) followed by Archdall, Lanigan, and several other historians, states that Kilcreevanty was a Benedictine convent. This does not seem to be strictly correct. From its foundation in the thirteenth century until the dissolution it appears to have remained a house of Augustinian Canonesses of the congregation of Arrouaise except for a short period around 1220 when the community followed the Cistercian rule.

Boyle
Cistercian
Abbey

A community of Cistercian monks from Mellifont, Co Louth, after temporary residence in three other places in the district during the years 1148-62, finally settled at Boyle about the year 1162. Their church, which was dedicated to the Blessed Virgin Mary, was consecrated in 1219. Considerable ruins of the building still stand. See the article on Boyle in *DHGE*, x, col. 315-316.

A Benedictine priory under the invocation of Saints Peter and Paul was established on the Connacht side of Athlone sometime during the latter half of the twelfth or during the early years of the thirteenth century. It was also known as Prioratus de Innocentia, but never attained the status of an abbey. Although certain Benedictine houses are known to have been wrongly described as Cluniac foundations, even in papal documents, yet, Athlone is so frequently referred to as Cluniac, that it probably did belong to the Cluniac reformed branch of the Benedictines; it has sometimes been wrongly described as Cistercian.

Vikings

In the year 845, Turgéis or Turgesius, one of the most ruthless of the Scandinavian leaders, established a base (some of the annals say a fleet) on Lough Ree (Loch Rí) from which he sent plundering expeditions into Connacht and Meath. Again in 932 there was a fleet of Scandinavians on the lake. In 807 they raided and burned Inishmurray and attacked Roscommon. Apart from that, the region with which we are dealing escaped comparatively lightly during the period of the Scandinavian invasions, AD 795-1014. Inevitably, however, as a result of the disruption caused throughout Ireland, this area also shared in the subsequent decline of monastic discipline and religious fervour.

Early dioceses

Siadhal, abbot and bishop of Roscommon, died in 817; and Aodh, son of Fianghus, bishop and scribe of Roscommon, died in 874. No doubt, other places in the present diocese also had bishops of their own, at least from time to time, but nearly all of those were either abbot bishops or monastic functionaries with no territorial jurisdiction. The whole church in Ireland from the sixth or seventh century onwards had come to be organised mainly around the monastic settlements. The monasteries became the centres of ecclesiastical jurisdiction, and, from the point of view of administration, the abbot was more important than the bishop. The synod of Rathbreasil (Raith-Breasail), held in the year 1111, sought to bring Ireland into line with continental Europe by reducing the number of bishops, and allocating territories to each.

Connacht, which at that period embraced parts of the present counties of Longford and Cavan, was divided by the synod into five dioceses: Tuam, Clonfert, Cong, Killala, and Ardcarne or Ardagh. The Connacht clergy were allowed to alter the divisions but not to exceed five dioceses. Elphin was not named. The two dioceses in the list that included its territory were Tuam and Ardcarne; the latter was allowed to choose the alternative name of Ardagh, if it so wished. Tuam is not to be confused with the present diocese of that name; nor are the episcopal sees that gave present dioceses their names identical with them. The Tuam named in the synod of Rathbreasail embraced the southern part of the present diocese of Elphin as well as parts of the present dioceses of Tuam and Clonfert. Ardcarne or Ardagh covered the northern portion of the present diocese of Elphin, and seemingly most of the present diocese of Ardagh and part of the present diocese of Kilmore as well. It did not include the most northerly portion of the present diocese of Elphin, that is, the north-eastern part of Co Sligo, because that was allocated to Killala.

Tuam, as arranged by the synod, extended from the River Suck to Ardcarne and from Áth-an-tearmainn (perhaps at Termon Keelin near Castlereagh) to the River Shannon. Ardcarne or Ardagh was described as extending from Ardcarne to Slieve-an-erin (Sliabh-an-iarainn, a mountain a few miles north of Drumshanbo in Co Leitrim), and from Keshcorran (Céis-Chorainn, a mountain a few miles south-east of Ballymote) to Ur-choilltéin, an unidentified place which was probably near the boundary between the present dioceses of Ardagh and Meath.

This division did not meet with general agreement, and at a synod held in Kells in 1152, and presided over by Cardinal John Papara as papal legate, drastic changes were made. Elphin does not appear by name, but the diocese of Roscommon, which does, evidently corresponds substantially to the present diocese of Elphin. The name Ardcarne is omitted, but a diocese of Ardagh is formed and made a suffragan not of Tuam but of Armagh. Achonry appears, or re-appears. Roscommon becomes a suffragan see of Tuam, which in turn at this synod is raised to archiepiscopal status, and the archbishop received the pallium from the cardinal. The diocese of Roscommon received the eastern portion of the old diocese of Tuam, the western portion of the old diocese of Ardcarne or Ardagh, and, probably about the same time, a corridor to the sea at Sligo which had formerly belonged to the old diocese of Killala.

Elphin's first bishop

Among the bishops present at the synod of Kells was Maol-Íosa O'Connaghton (Ó Connachtáin), who is described as Bishop of East Connacht. He may have been the first bishop of the diocese of Elphin as we know it today; but there is also a probability that the synod merely sanctioned divisions of dioceses agreed upon by the Connacht clergy soon after the synod of Rathbreasail. In that case, Donal O'Duffy (Domhnall Ó Dubhthaigh), who is described in the *Annals of Clonmacnoise* (pp 194-195) as Archbishop of Connacht, but in the *Annals of Loch Cé* (i, p.138) as *Elefinensis episcopus* (Bishop of Elphin), may have been the first of the series. He died about 1137; and it was he who caused the exquisite cross of Cong, now preserved in the National Museum, Dublin, to be made as a reliquary for a portion of the true cross.

The diocese of Elphin, in anything corresponding to its present territorial boundaries, cannot be traced to a date anterior to the synod of Rathbreasail (1111); but from the time of that synod or of the one held in Kells (1152) to our own day, although occasionally in the early stages referred to as Roscommon, or Síol Muireadhaigh, or Oirthear Chonnacht (East Connacht), the diocese has maintained its essential identity, with at most only minor alterations. We do not know for certain when the small territories south-east of Lough Gill and south-west of Lough Allen (that is, the parishes of Killenummery and Killerry and Kilronan) were assigned to Ardagh. They are west of the Shannon, and from the point of view of geography, belong rather to Elphin, but their incorporation in Ardagh is no doubt due to the political framework of the period, and probably dates from the synod of Kells (1152).

Flanagan O'Duffy (Ó Dubhthaigh), who died in 1168 and is highly praised in the *Annals of the Four Masters,* is described in some manuscript copies of the *Annals of Ulster* as Bishop of Síol Muireadhaigh, a territory which corresponds approximately with the present diocese of Elphin, yet it is doubtful whether he can be considered as Bishop of Elphin in the present accepted sense of the term. He may have been one of the bishops of the old diocese of Tuam as established by the synod of Raithbreasail; but more probably he was either one of the former monastic bishops or one of the bishops of small sees that became mere deaneries in the new diocese of Elphin.

FROM THE COMING OF THE ANGLO-NORMANS TO THE REFORMATION

Four gallowglasses: detail from the tomb of King Felim in the Dominican Abbey Roscommon

The first Anglo-Norman expedition reached Ireland in 1167, to be followed in 1169 and 1170 by more powerful forces. The chief opponent of the invaders was Rory O'Conor (Ruaidhrí Ó Conchubhair) of our territory, who was then acknowledged as *ard-rí* or supreme king of Ireland. The Irish failed to impede the Anglo-Norman advance, with the result that Rory and his successor, Cathal Crobhdearg, had to content themselves with the lesser status of provincial kings of Connacht. Cathal's successor, Aodh, had to submit to the further humiliation in 1227 of seeing his kingdom taken away from him, and of being left with a territory corresponding approximately with the present diocese of Elphin. Despite several attempts at winning back some of what was lost, the power of the O'Conors continued to decline and, with it, the fortunes of the native Irish of the diocese. In the internecine wars that resulted, churches and monasteries were burned, pulled down, or pillaged. Elphin, Roscommon, Boyle and other places all suffered in turn. The decline of the old Irish monasteries was accelerated and new orders under Anglo-Norman patronage were introduced.

More bishops

At least from the first half of the thirteenth century onwards, we find the King of England, whenever a see falls vacant, insisting on his right to grant the *congé d'élire* (permission to elect) and to confirm the elected or appointed candidate in office. Yet this diocese suffered less than most in the matter of the attempts by English kings to impose or intrude their own nominees as bishops and abbots, nominees who were often Englishmen with no knowledge of the language or customs of the people over whom they were placed. It is only in the fifteenth and sixteenth centuries that we find Englishmen being appointed to Elphin, for example, Thomas Colley and Robert Foston in the fifteenth century, and Christopher Fisher, Thomas Walsh and John Maxey in the sixteenth.

Six or possibly more of the bishops down to the time of the Reformation belonged to the dominant family of the O'Conors, and some of these were near kinsmen of the O'Conor chieftains. Many others belonged to prominent local families, such as the Mac Dermotts, the Flanagans and the Rooneys or Ó Maolruanaidh.

Donagh O'Flanagan, who was abbot of the Cistercian abbey at Boyle for five years and Bishop of Elphin for three and a half years, is praised in the *Annals of Loch Cé* (I, p. 538) for his piety, hospitality, generosity, wisdom, shrewdness, amiability and gentleness. He died on 22 June 1307 after an illness of five months. See also the *Annals of the Four Masters,* II, p. 1166.

The Four Masters (iv, p. 778), in recording the death of Bishop Thomas Barrett who died in 1404, describe him as 'saoi Éireann', one of the most learned men in the Ireland of his time, who was proficient in both the profane and sacred sciences. The *Annals of Connacht* (ad an. 1404, 2) also give him the same title. His bronze seal is preserved in the National Museum in Dublin.

On the other hand, the same *Annals* (ad an. 1530, 16) have what seems to be an uncomplimentary reference to George Brana, known as the Greek bishop: 'Ní hoilbéim don daonacht ant ecc-sin', (humanity – or generosity? – suffered no loss from his death). He had been procurator of indulgences for the hospital of the Holy Ghost at Rome, and his financial exactions may have rendered him odious to the Irish people. (See more on Georgius de Brana under 'Later bishops' below. – *ed.*)

Bishop Thomas Colby or Colley (1412-1414), was a Carmelite of Norwich, who was a graduate of Oxford and Cambridge and the author of a number of theological and devotional tracts. Christopher Fisher had been Henry VIII's agent at Rome and was a friend of Erasmus, whom he entertained at Paris in 1505. John Maxey, who was appointed bishop in 1525, had been abbot of the Premonstratensian abbey of Welbeck in England. He does not seem ever to have visited his diocese. There were several occasions on which unseemly contentions for the see occurred, and there were rival claimants to the office.

In 1244 a large section of the chapter of Elphin elected Thomas O'Quinn, OFM, as bishop; but the two archdeacons, the dean, and the sacristan objected that a member of the chapter should have been chosen. The junior canons then elected O'Connor, coarb of Roscommon, but the four seniors mentioned, at a synod in Athlone, elected John O'Horan (Eoin Ó hUghráin), referred to as John the Archdeacon. Eoin set out for Lyon where the Pope was then in exile, and obtained papal provision although he had been elected by a minority of the chapter. The Archbishop of Tuam at first refused to consecrate him, because he had not received the royal consent, but this was afterwards granted, as well as the restoration of the temporalities.

In 1260 Mellaghlin O'Connor, son of Tadhg, was elected by a majority of the chapter, consecrated at Dundalk by the Archbishop of Armagh, and restored to the temporalities by the king. But some of the senior members of the chapter declared the election irregular, prevailed on the Archbishop of Tuam to annul it, and presented Thomas MacDermott as the rightful candidate; Thomas also appealed to the Pope against Mellaghlin; the death of Mellaghlin in 1262 put an end to the dispute.

In 1296 Marianus O'Donnaver (Ó Donnabair), a Dominican, was elected bishop by the chapter, but the Archbishop of Tuam refused to confirm the election. Mellaghlin MacBrien (son of Brian MacDermott?) was then elected, and Marianus went to Rome in person to present his case. The Pope confirmed him in office, but he died on the homeward journey.

Eubel (*Hierarchia Catholica*, i, p. 237) has erroneously made a single bishop of the two: Malachias (Marianus) MacBrien, 1296; while the Four Masters incorrectly state that they both went to Rome to present their claims.

There was further contention in 1308 after the election of Mellaghlin Mac Aodha. Salamon, dean of Elphin, refused to recognise him and caused Charles O'Conor (Conchubhair), abbot of the Premonstratensian abbey on Loch Cé, to be elected instead. The election of Charles was confirmed by Reginald, official of the court of Armagh, in the absence of the archbishop, and Charles was consecrated at Armagh. Neglecting to answer a summons to appear before the papal court, he was deprived by the Pope in June 1310 of all rights deriving from such election, confirmation, and consecration, and all his acts as bishop were declared null and void. He retired to his abbey on Loch Cé, where he died in 1343.

In 1312 Mellaghlin was transferred to Tuam. On or before the death of Seán Ó Fionnachta in 1354, Pope Innocent VI reserved the right of appointment of his successor to himself *ea vice* (on that occasion); and in 1357 appointed Gregory, whom in 1353, under the misapprehension that that see was vacant, he had appointed to Down. The canons of the chapter appear to have been unaware of such a reservation, for they elected Carolus (Cathal?), archdeacon of the diocese, who was duly consecrated and proceeded to fulfil the usual episcopal functions. In 1372 Gregory was transferred to Tuam, and Pope Gregory XI proceeded to provide Thomas Barrett to Elphin, '*que antea dispositioni apostolice generaliter fuerat reservata*' (which provision had usually been left before to the disposition of the apostolic see; see the text in Augustinus Theiner, *Vetera monumenta Hibernorum et Scotorum*, p. 363); but that was a claim which could hardly be substantiated. In August 1377 the Pope sent a mandate to the Bishop of Kilmacduagh to protect Thomas against the intrusions of Carolus.

Phantom bishops

A few phantom bishops have found their way into the episcopal lists. The inclusion of Tomhaltach or Thomas O'Connor about 1172-1181 seems to be due to confusion of a bishop of Elphin with this name (1246-1258), with a namesake who was Archbishop of Armagh 1181-1201. Harris's edition of Ware, followed by Gams, etc., lists Dionysius Ó Maolchiaráin as bishop in 1224, but he was merely erenagh of Ardcarne; see *Annals of Ulster*, II, p. 274, ad an. 1225. Cornelius Rufus, son of the coarb of St Molua, according to Ware, Cotton, Powicke, etc., was bishop in 1246, but this is probably due to a misreading of the entry in the annals about Eoin Ó hUghráin, son of the coarb of St Mochua. The *Annals of the Four Masters* incorrectly give Tomás Ó Congaláin (d. 1508), Bishop of Achonry as Bishop of Elphin. There was no such bishop of Elphin as Demetrius Healy, who is listed by Powicke and given, though with a question mark, by Brady. The error can be traced back to a report made to Propaganda Fide in 1623 by Eugene Matthews, Archbishop of Dublin, in which he speaks of Demetrius Healy, Bishop of Elphin, a Franciscan and martyr for the faith, when he really had in mind Patrick Healy or O'Healy, Bishop of Mayo, Franciscan, who was killed by the English in 1579 (and beatified in September 1992 – *ed.*). The inclusion of Raymundus Galvirus (see below) would also seem to be an error. Lawrence O'Lachtnan, who was Bishop of Elphin from 1313 to 1326, is to be distinguished from the person of the same name, one-time abbot of the Cistercian abbey of Boyle, who was Bishop of Kilmacduagh from 1290 to 1307. The two have been confused by Cotton.

Taxes

The fiscal list of 1302-06 (*Calendar of documents relating to Ireland,* v, pp 223-25) gives eighty-eight taxable churches for the diocese, including two at Elphin itself – St Mary's and St Patrick's. St Mary's was the cathedral and is at present the Protestant church. St Patrick's was the parish church, the old Teampall Pádraig, which in the fifteenth century was handed over to the Franciscans. Four churches, including Kilglass and Kiltullagh, although taxed, are stated to be deserted. Five others are named but not taxed because destroyed, burned down, or deserted. The total amount which the diocese was taxed for was £69 7s. 4d. in the money of the time. Boyle (presumably the Cistercian monastery there) was taxed at £10, but under the diocese of Achonry (*Calendar ... Ireland,* v, p. 218) we find a further tax of 22s on the temporalities and spiritualities of the abbot and monks of Boyle. The Elphin list makes no mention of the bishop, the dean, or the members of the chapter.

In 1525 the See was taxed at sixty-six florins in the books of the Camera Apostolica in Rome. During the reigns of Henry VIII and Elizabeth I all the church property passed into Protestant hands and the Catholic clergy had to depend from that onwards on the voluntary contributions of the faithful. The value of the various benefices (all then in Protestant hands) in the twenty-eighth year of Queen Elizabeth I (1585-6) was as follows: the bishop's, £103 18s. od.; the dean's, £13 6s. 8d.; the archdeacon's, £2 13s. od.; the provost's £1 10s. od.

The thirteen prebends were estimated at values varying from 6s. 8d. to £4 (Cotton, *Fasti,* IV, p. 117). Sometime before 1638 the Church of Ireland reduced the number of prebends from thirteen to eight.

Religious houses

Apart from the houses of Canons Regular already mentioned, there was an abbey of Premonstratensian canons on the island of Holy Trinity on Loch Cé. It was founded about 1225 by Clarus Mac Maoilín (Ó Maolchonaire), archdeacon of Elphin, and received a considerable endowment of land on the mainland in 1237 from Donnchadh Mac Diarmada during the single month in which he ruled as prince over Moylurg (Maigh-Luirg). In 1466 the abbey was burned down through the negligence of a woman. Two of its abbots were elected bishops of Elphin.

A hospital of St John the Baptist of the Crutched Friars (Cruciferi) of Jerusalem was founded in the thirteenth century at Rindown (Rinn-dúin) on the west shore of Lough Ree; it was also known as Teach-Eoin. There were no houses of the Hermits of St Augustine in the diocese in pre-Reformation times, but the other three orders of friars were represented.

About the year 1377, owing to some extraordinary phenomenon by which the sign of the cross was found on the site, the people erected a little oratory at Slew or Slewshancough. This place, which has been wrongly identified by W. H. Grattan Flood with a place near Geevagh, Co Sligo, was the present Eglish in Co Galway. Bishop William O'Hetigan (1429–1449), handed over the oratory to the care of the Carmelites; the local chieftain granted them some lands, and in 1437 they received papal permission to erect a church and convent there. They dedicated the place to the Holy Cross. The Carmelites also had a house at Caltra-na-pallice (sometimes referred to as Caltra, sometimes as Pallice), Co Galway. Some have thought this house belonged to the Franciscan tertiaries. There are references to a house of friars at Knockmore, Co Sligo, which according to some was Dominican, but which was more probably a Carmelite foundation.

The Franciscans founded a house at Roscommon in 1269. It was burned with the town in the wars between the Irish and English the following year, and we are not sure whether it was ever rebuilt. In 1453, Bishop Cornelius O'Mulally, with the consent of clergy and laity, granted the parish church of St Patrick in the town of Elphin to his fellow-Franciscans. The place was declared free from any obligation of the cure of souls and from all cess and exaction.

The Dominicans were particularly strong in this diocese. They founded a house at Sligo in 1252 or 1253; at Ballindoon, Co Sligo, in 1507; at Cloonshanville, Co Roscommon, in the fourteenth or fifteenth century; at Tulsk in 1448 and at Roscommon in 1253. Sligo priory was accidentally burned in 1414 but was re-built two years later. Roscommon was badly damaged by lightning around Christmas 1308. Ware, who was followed by other writers, says there was a convent of Dominican nuns at Ballindoon which was founded in 1427.

The Franciscan Third Order Regular for men had several houses, some of which have not yet been satisfactorily identified. They were Caldragh (Ceall-braighe-ual-laighe), Clonrahan, Toomona, Toberelly (Tobair Ailbhe?), and there is also reference to one at Knockvicar. The dates of foundation or transfer are unknown, but it is to be presumed that they date from the second half of the fifteenth or the beginning of the sixteenth century.

FROM THE PROTESTANT REFORMATION TO THE PRESENT

Little information

An anonymous writer in the *Irish Ecclesiastical Record* (*IER*), II (1866), 151-2, who was probably Cardinal P. F. Moran, states that after John Maxey the next three bishops of Elphin that we meet with are Ludovicus, Hubert and O'Donnell. Ludovicus or Louis was translated from Elphin to the See of Gaudatensis in 1539 and his successor was Hubert Iseranen, Cistercian, of the diocese of Rouen. On 3 June 1541 Hubert was translated from Elphin to Ferns, and Bernard O'Donnell, who had been appointed to Ferns only a few months before, was translated to Elphin. This writer, like Eubel and his collaborators, claims to be quoting the consistorial acts, but it is hard to reconcile his data and Eubel's (*Hier. Cath.*, III, p. 191). Eubel gives William Magin, canon of Dromore, as having been appointed (with a dispensation) Bishop of Elphin on 16 June 1539, and as having been succeeded on his death by Gabriel de S. Serio, prior of Bousnes, OSB, in the diocese of Amiens, who was appointed on 27 August 1539. According to Gams, Gabriel was transferred to Ferns 3 June 1541 (*ibidem*, p. 195).

Bernard O'Higgins, who succeeded in 1542, was not a Dominican, as some state, but a Hermit of St Augustine. He had been vicar general of his order in Ireland and continued to hold that post for some time after becoming a bishop. In 1545 he was forced to surrender the temporalities of the See into the hands of a nominee of Henry VIII, to whom we shall refer presently.

John O'Heyne was provided to the See of Elphin in February 1545. He had formerly been a canon of the diocese of Elphin, but at the time of this appointment, he was bishop of Cork and Cloyne, though unable because of the power of the Protestants in that territory to take possession of his Sees. He was given permission to retain the regimen of the three dioceses for a maximum of six months from the date on which he entered into peaceful possession either of Elphin or of the united dioceses of Cork and Cloyne. Since Bernard O'Higgins was still alive in Spain at this time, and since the provision of O'Heyne mentions that the See was vacant through the death of George Bran (Brana), it would appear as if O'Heyne's provi-

sion was made in error. When Andrew O'Crean, Dominican, was appointed in January 1562, it was stated that the vacancy had occurred through the resignation of
O'Higgins. (For this section see *A New History of Ireland*, IX (1984), pp 328, 384:
Georgius de Brana died in 1529; John O'Heyne was Bishop of Cork and Cloyne,
1540-1556, and administrator of Elphin from February 1545 to c. 1553/4. – *ed.*) O'Crean
lived chiefly at Sligo and was left comparatively free by the reformers. In 1566, he
together with Raymond O'Gallagher, Bishop of Killala, and Eugene O'Hart, Bishop
of Achonry, held a provincial synod at which they solemnly promulgated the
decrees of the Council of Trent. O'Crean had such devotion to St Ursula and her
companions in martyrdom that he used to recite 11,000 Pater Nosters and Ave
Marias in their honour each year, under the influence of the medieval legend that
said that was the number of the martyred.

From his death in 1594 until the appointment of Boetius MacEgan in 1625 the
diocese was ruled by vicars, and again from about 1653 until the appointment of
Dominick Burke in 1671. In the provision of MacEgan the See was stated to be vacant after the death *'pro Christi fide'* of Raymundus Galvirius (W. Maziere Brady,
Episcopal succession, II, p. 201). On the strength of this, Brady himself, J. J. Kelly (in
Cath. Encyc., V, p. 395), Powicke (in *Handbook of Brit. Chron.*, p. 287), Eubel (IV, p. 182)
and others, include Raymundus Galvirius or Galvinus among the bishops of Elphin.
But the mention of his name seems to be due merely to lack of accurate information at Rome. The person the Roman authorities had in mind is almost certainly
Raymond O'Gallagher, who was Bishop of Killala and later of Derry, and for whom
see Derry in *DHGE*, XIV, col. 323-5. There is no evidence that he was ever Bishop of
Elphin, but, in his capacity either as Bishop of Killala or as vice-primate of Ireland,
he may occasionally have taken a hand in the administration of Elphin during the
vacancy of the See. In 1613 the diocese was being administered by Eoghan
MacBreen as vicar general, and in August 1620 Nicholas a Sancto Patritio was appointed vicar apostolic. Cardinal Moran, (*Spicilegium Ossoriense*, I, p. 128), quoting
from the archives of the Secretaria Brevium, calls him a Carmelite. Eubel (IV, p. 182,
n. 2) says he was minister provincial of the Irish Hermits of St Augustine.

Reformation bishops
It was only in the seventeenth century that Protestantism succeeded in making any
headway in Elphin. Although the monasteries were legally dissolved under King
Henry VIII, many of the regulars continued to minister to the spiritual needs of the
people. Some of the orders, like the Dominicans and Franciscans, when expelled
from their original foundations, established little communities in the neighbourhood in what came to be known as places of refuge (L. *loci refugii*). Some of the regulars and diocesan clergy paid the supreme penalty for their fidelity to their religious
principles. On 21 November 1584 Gelasius O'Cullenan, abbot of the Cistercian
abbey of Boyle was hanged in Dublin along with John O'Mulkeeran (Ó Maol-

Chiaráin), abbot of the Premonstratensian abbey of Loch Cé. According to some writers two other Cistercians of Boyle, Patrick O'Connor and Malachy O'Kelly were hanged about the year 1585.

The first schismatic bishop of the diocese was Connacht O'Shiel (Ó Siaghail), who had been prior in Ballisodare and Aughris, two houses of the Canons of St Augustine which are situated in the diocese of Achonry and the county of Sligo. He had been chaplain to Manus O'Donnell, chieftain of Tyreconnell (Tír Chonaill), within whose claimed sphere of influence the northern part of the diocese fell; and Manus, at a period during which he was friendly with King Henry VIII, had recommended him for the post. The dean and chapter of Elphin refused to elect him, so Henry appointed him on his own authority. There is no evidence that he was ever consecrated. In 1552 Roland Burke, Catholic Bishop of Clonfert, obtained from King Edward VI, without any reference to the Pope, possession of the See of Elphin 'in commendam' (for safekeeping), although there was already a Catholic bishop of the diocese. For this, he must be listed among the schismatic bishops of Elphin, although he afterwards obtained a pardon during the reign of Queen Mary. In 1582, Andrew O'Crean OP, who, as we have seen, was legitimate Catholic bishop, was also appointed by the Council of Ireland but, since he continued to yield spiritual allegiance to the Pope only, he was set aside. Thomas Chester, a native of London, was appointed in 1582, but he does not seem to have been ordained or consecrated.

In 1584 Queen Elizabeth issued a mandate to have John Fitzjames Lynch, that is John Lynch, son of James, a native of Galway, consecrated bishop of the diocese; but from the point of view of the Protestants, this appointment was as unfortunate as those that preceded it; he wasted and alienated the property of the See. He resigned in August 1611 and was reputed to have died a Catholic. The next two Protestant bishops, King and Tilson, were Englishmen. King repaired the cathedral, recovered some of the ecclesiastical property alienated by Lynch, and built an episcopal residence at Elphin, using for the purpose the stones of the Franciscan friary. Tilson had to flee for safety to England when the rebellion of 1641 broke out.

Parker, a native of Dublin, had been chaplain to the marquis of Ormond and had suffered imprisonment under the Cromwellian regime. He repaired the cathedral at Elphin which had again fallen into disrepair. He became Archbishop of Tuam in 1667 and of Dublin in 1668. John Hodson's special interests were the education of the poor and the maintenance of the cathedral in a worthy state. Robert Howard, who was transferred from Killala to Elphin by patent dated 13 January 1729 (old style), was ancestor of the Earls of Wicklow, of whom the present holder of the title (1958), a distinguished Irish writer and publisher is a convert to Catholicism (William C. J. Howard, Clonmore & Reynolds). About 1757 the cathedral of Elphin was in such a ruinous condition that it had to be re-built almost in its entirety.

An act of parliament in 1834 directed that the See be united with Kilmore upon the next vacancy, and on the death of George de la Poer Beresford, Bishop of Kilmore, 15 October 1841, John Leslie, who was Bishop of Elphin at the time, became bishop of the united dioceses of Kilmore, Elphin, and Ardagh. Kilmore and Ardagh had already been united since 1839; (in fact they had been held by one bishop on several occasions before that. – *ed.*). The present Protestant bishop of the united dioceses is the Right Rev Edward Francis Butler Moore, formerly archdeacon of Glendalough, who was elected 28 November 1958 and is due to be consecrated at Armagh on 6 January 1959. (He died in 1981, and was succeeded by William Gilbert Wilson in June of that year. Michael Mayes was appointed on 29 April 1993. – *ed.*)

Outside the towns, the Protestants have never been numerous in the diocese, and from the first half of the eighteenth century onwards their numbers in the diocese as a whole have been constantly declining. According to *Annuario Pontificio* for 1958 the number of non-Catholics in the diocese is 1,895. The great majority of those are members of the Church of Ireland, that is Episcopalians. Presbyterians number not more than a few hundred, Methodists less than two hundred. There are at most only a few Baptists, Jews, and members of other religions and sects. (The *Annuario Pontificio* for 1998 gives the extent of the diocese as 3,100 square kilometres, the population in round numbers as 70,000, Catholics 68,000. – *ed.*)

Bishop Boetius MacEgan

To return to the Catholic prelates. On 3 January 1637 Boetius MacEgan (or Egan) sent a report on the state of the diocese to Dr Edmond Dwyer, his procurator at Rome, for presentation to Pope Urban VIII. It is printed in Moran's *Spicilegium Ossoriense,* I, pp 214-17. The Catholics were in a majority in the diocese as a whole, but the town of Elphin was inhabited exclusively by Scottish and English Protestants. In fact, no Catholic was permitted to reside there. There were forty-two priests in the diocese. The prescriptions of the Council of Trent were being followed as far as the circumstances of the time allowed. For fear of the Protestants, the clergy were unable to come together in chapter, but in each deanery *(decanatus)* the priests assembled in some solitary place once a year. In olden times, the diocese, he says, was divided into seven deaneries. Each pastor teaches the Christian Doctrine to his flock, at least on each Sunday, but this has to be done, like the celebration of Mass, in secluded places, such as in the woods. The bishop has no fixed abode, and has often to flee from house to house, from mountain to wood. We know that in 1635 he had petitioned Rome for permission to reside outside his diocese because of the persecution. When MacEgan was appointed there were no religious houses in the diocese and he was not aware that there had been any since the monasteries had been suppressed, but he re-introduced the Dominicans and Franciscans, who, he says, living in caves and woods, labour strenuously in the vineyard of the Lord. He gives a list of the pre-Reformation religious houses but says they are all in Protestant hands.

In a previous report of his (printed in *Archivium Hibernicum*, III, p. 359-65) which was presented to Propaganda Fide on 24 June 1631 by his procurator in Rome, James Fallon, he mentioned that there were some old friars in the diocese who had been acting as parish priests but without the requisite authority. He states that there were formerly sixty-five parish churches in the diocese but at the period of writing all were destroyed except five and those five were being used by the Protestants. The cathedral church was still standing but all the altars, chapels. and images in it had been destroyed. It was being used by the Protestants. There was only one Catholic in the town of Elphin. There were a few in Boyle. There were some in Sligo, but the Protestant minister there was so zealous in arresting priests as usurpers of ecclesiastical authority that it was only with difficulty that they could succeed in entering the town and visiting the Catholics there. There were many Catholics in Athlone (that is, the part of it on the west of the Shannon). MacEgan then enumerates the measures he has adopted for the better governance of the diocese since he became bishop. He tells that while on visitation in his diocese he has to go around disguised as a merchant, under a false name, and limiting his travelling to after sunset or early morning and sometimes moving from place to place by night to avoid detection.

We are told by John Lynch, archdeacon of Tuam, in his *De Praesulibus Hiberniae*, II, pp 293-4) that even after becoming a bishop, MacEgan tried to observe as far as possible the precepts and spirit of the rule of St Francis, even in the matter of clothing and fasting, and that whatever funds he could spare were spent not on himself but on good and charitable causes. He died in the Franciscan friary of Kilconnell, Co Galway, in April 1650. About three weeks later died a contemporary namesake with whom he is sometimes confused – Boetius MacEgan, Bishop of Ross, also a Franciscan who was hanged by the Cromwellians at Carrigadrohid, Co Cork.

His successors
According to Lynch, the next bishop was Charles Kelly (Ceallach Ó Ceallaigh), but he is not listed by Eubel, Brady, or Powicke. He was of noble birth, a doctor of theology of the university of Seville, and had formerly been dean of Tuam. He died in exile in Spain, where he was a chaplain with the Irish soldiers, about the year 1653, before he had an opportunity of being consecrated. (He is not on the succession list in *A New History of Ireland*, IX (1984), pp 384-6, which says that between 1650 and 1671 Elphin was ruled by vicars: William Burgat (1665), Thomas Higgins (1666), and James Farrell (1669). – *ed.*)

After a long vacancy the See was filled in 1671 by the appointment of Dominick Burke, or de Burgo. A native of Co Galway, he had become a Dominican in the priory of Athenry. On his way to Spain to continue his studies he was captured by the Cromwellians but escaped from prison at Kinsale, and after two years again set out for Spain. The rest of his life until his consecration was spent in Spain and Italy. On the very day of his consecration, which took place in Ghent in Belgium, he set out for his diocese via Calais, London, and Dublin. He visited every parish in the diocese and administered confirmation. He ordained several candidates as priests, and in 1672 he held a diocesan synod. A reward of £200 was offered by the government for his capture. Driven into exile after the Williamite revolution, he spent his last years in Louvain and is buried in St Anthony's, the Irish Franciscan college there. His report on the state of his diocese in 1675 can be found in *Archiv. Hib.*, xv, pp 62-5. His successor was a fellow-Dominican, Ambrose MacDermott, who was consecrated at Rome in March 1707. Arrested in London on his way home, he was deported, but later managed to return secretly to his diocese.

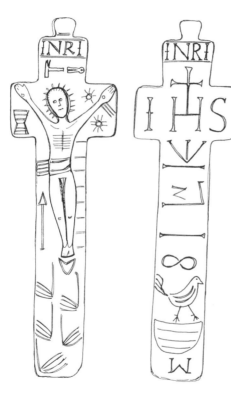

Penal Cross acquired by the National Museum of Ireland from Mrs Mai Murphy, Cootehall in 1970.

Penal times

During the latter half of the seventeenth century and the early part of the eighteenth, many priests suffered for the faith. Fr Felix O'Connor OP, prior of the convent of Sligo, was arrested and died in prison in 1679. In 1703 Patrick O'Connor OP, also of Sligo, was ordered to be detained in jail until he could be transported. About January 1693 five priests were arrested in Co Roscommon. In March 1712 eight priests of Co Roscommon were thrown into prison, and the search was being continued for the others in the county. Towards the end of October 1715 a sensation was caused when James Kilkenny, a Franciscan friar who was being conveyed to jail in Roscommon, was rescued by a group of men and women. A proclamation was issued in which £100 was offered for the apprehension of Kilkenny and £20 for the apprehension of each of his rescuers. The friar eluded re-capture, but some of his rescuers were apprehended and fined.

In 1731, the government, alarmed by rumours about the growth of popery despite all attempts at suppression, ordered enquiries to be made throughout the country about bishops, priests, friars, chapels, nunneries, etc. The report for the diocese of Elphin (printed in *Archiv. Hib.,* III, pp 136-40) lists about forty-four Mass Houses or huts used for the saying of Mass. An attempt was made by the Catholics to build a Mass House in the town of Elphin but it was pulled down, while another was begun in Drumcliff, Co Sligo, but the Protestant bishop ordered it to be demolished. The number of parish priests is given and their assistants, and in many cases their names also. There was a friary about two miles from Sligo, another at Drinane, and another at Kilbegnet. The one at Drinane was the place of refuge of the Franciscans of Elphin. The other two were evidently the places of refuge of the Dominicans of the convents of Sligo and Roscommon, respectively. There were besides several individual friars scattered throughout the diocese. On particular festivals pilgrims assembled in large numbers at St Bride's (Brigit's) Well in the parish of Cam, Co Roscommon. The 1731 report noted eighteen 'popish' or Catholic schools.

Various reports

On 9 March 1744 Ambrose Gilligan OP, of Sligo, was subjected to a close examination by government Protestant officials. He revealed that the Bishop of Elphin at the time was Patrick French, his vicar general was Patrick Gaffney, and his dean was Brian Geraghty. The prior of the Dominicans of Sligo was Michael Harte, the subprior was Michael Kilhawly, and the names of eight other friars in the community were given. The prior of Ballindoon was Dominick Harte, and two other Dominicans of that community were named. An enquiry held the same day by Gilbert King, high sheriff of Co Sligo, established that Patrick French, the Catholic bishop, was then residing at Cloonyquin, Co Roscommon; he was a Franciscan.

Bishop James O'Fallon, in his report to Rome dated 1770, revealed that there was still danger of renewed outbreaks of persecution. He could not risk holding a synod, and the pastors were afraid to risk the keeping of parish registers. A Sr Susanna O'Fallon, who had died twenty-two years before that, had made an attempt to found a house of her order in Athlone, but no trace of it remained; in fact, there was no house of female religious in the diocese. The bishop met many, old as well as young, who were ignorant of the elements of their faith; and servile work on holidays of obligation was common (*Archiv. Hib.*, v, pp 143-8). (For this period see 'The diocese of Elphin, 1747-1802: documents from Roman archives' by Fr Hugh Fenning OP, in *Collectanea Hibernica, 36/37* (1994-95). – ed.)

By the year 1800 relations between the government and the Catholic hierarchy had become more friendly, and in that year Bishop Edmund French submitted a report to the government on the state of the diocese (See *Memoirs & Correspondence of Viscount Castlereagh*, ed. Charles Vance, IV, 1849, pp 166-8, under the year 1801). The income of the bishop, 'arising from proxies, &c., paid by his clergy, and other dues … may amount to £450 per annum', he said. The revenues of the different parishes varied from £140 for St John's, Sligo, to £336 for Kilmacowen. The income from St Peter's, Athlone, which was held 'in commendam' by the bishop, amounted to £130. There were fifty-nine parishes. There were twenty-two curates, of whom six were regulars. The towns of Athlone and Sligo, as well as a few other parishes, were in need of more assistant priests, but they were not available. (Compare this with the summary of the report, dated 1802, given by Fr Fenning in *Collect. Hib.* (as above), pp 170-1. – *ed.*) There were six houses of regulars in the diocese, of which three were Dominican, namely Sligo, Cloonshanville, and Roscommon. There was a Franciscan house at Elphin, a Carmelite house at Toghergar, and a house of Augustinian friars at a place specified merely as The Hermitage. The average numbers of members in each of those six houses were two, two, six, one, three, and four respectively. Tohergar, which is in the barony of Killian, Co Galway, was probably the place of refuge for one of the original foundations of the Carmelites at Slew (Eglish) or Caltra.

The Augustinian house was the place of refuge of the original foundation of Dunmore in the county of Galway and diocese of Tuam, which had been founded about the year 1423. At the end of the eighteenth century the community was living at the Hermitage, Mayfield, Dunmore; but Bishop Edmund French's report shows they were living within his diocese in 1800. We do know that they purchased a small house, garden, and store on the Connacht side of Athlone in 1809 and opened a small church. The two subsequent bishops queried their canonical right to found a house there. The case was referred to the Holy See, and in 1837 a decision was given in favour of the Augustinians, the house being approved and confirmed then, as if it had been erected with proper permission. But it did not prove very successful and the Augustinians finally withdrew from the place about 1873.

The government report on the regulars in Ireland in 1829 (see *Archiv. Hib.,* III, pp 78-9) lists one Augustinian, who lived at Athlone, and four Dominicans, of whom two lived in a house at Sligo, another at Castleivicogue Co Roscommon, and the fourth at Castlecoote, Co Roscommon. In 1841 there were forty-three parishes. Of seventy-two chapels in the diocese, fifty-eight were slated, and of those, twenty-six had been erected since the year 1825. The only houses of regulars were that of the Dominicans at Sligo, that of the Augustinians at Athlone, and that of the Carmelites at Toghergar. The Dominicans of Sligo are the only one of the three that have survived as a community until the present day. The Carmelite priory of Toghergar ceased to exist soon after the middle of the century. Anthony Garrahan, the last of the Franciscans of Elphin had died in 1835.

According to the *Irish Catholic Directory* for the year 1864, (pp 205-07), there were then forty-one parishes, eighty-four chapels, one college, and one seminary; also thirty-nine pastors, fifty curates, and five religious priests. There were three convents of men, including the Carmelite house of Tohergar, which, however, according to other authorities had ceased to exist before this date. There were two communities of teaching brothers, the Marists at Sligo and the Franciscan Tertiaries Regular at Oran (Farragher), Co Roscommon. There were four convents of teaching sisters, the Ursulines at Sligo, and the Sisters of Mercy at Athlone, Sligo, and

Roscommon. The diocesan college mentioned in the *Directory* was that of the Immaculate Conception at Summerhill, a few miles from Athlone, and the seminary was St John's, Sligo.

According to the *Annuario Pontificio* for 1958 (p. 227) the diocese now has 88 churches, 33 parishes, 112 diocesan clergy, 10 regular priests, 7 houses of male religious, 16 houses of female religious. There are seven educational institutions and four charitable institutions under church authority. (The figures given for 1998 are: parishes 37, clergy 85, religious priests 1, other religious (male) 11, seminarians 5, female religious 150, schools 148, charitable institutes 18; no numbers given for churches and deacons. – *ed.*)

The facts and statistics given in the *Directory* for 1958 (pp 270-7) do not always correspond with those in the *Annuario,* and sometimes the figures given in different parts of the directory are mutually contradictory. It gives 33 parishes, 31 pastors or parish priests, 79 administrators, curates and others, 9 regular priests, 87 parochial and other churches, 2 communities of regular clergy (Dominicans at Sligo and Society of the Divine Word (SVD) for Foreign Missions at Donamon Castle (founded 1939), 5 communities of brothers (Marists at Sligo, Castlerea, and Strokestown; Irish Christian Brothers at Roscommon; Franciscan Tertiaries at Farragher), 14 communities of sisters (Ursulines at Sligo, Sisters of Mercy in various towns, Franciscan Missionaries of Mary at Loughglynn, Sisters of Nazareth at Sligo, Filles de la Sagesse at Sligo), 7 schools for secondary education, one combined diocesan seminary, and one college for boys at Sligo. On page 276 the parochial primary schools under secular teachers exceed 320 in number; but on page 277, the number of primary schools given for 1958 is 224. The chapter consists of a dean, archdeacon, precentor, treasurer, chancellor, theologian, and penitentiary, as well as of the five prebendaries of Tirebrine, Kilgoghlin, Tibohine, Kilmacallane and Oran. According to the *Annuario* for 1958, there are 82,948 Catholics out of a total population of 84,843. According to the *Irish Catholic Directory* for 1958 (whose latest returns are based on the census of 1946) the Catholics numbered 94,659 out of a total population of 97,484. (The *Directory* for the year 2000 (p. 197) says: 'The seventy-seven original parishes of the diocese have been to a great extent amalgamated because of a shift in population, and today they form thirty-eight parishes … The Catholic population of the diocese now stands at 68,000 and is served by 88 diocesan priests.' – *ed.*)

Episcopal residence

During the era of persecution, the bishops of Elphin had to change their abode frequently to avoid capture by the enemies of their religion. Some like Dominick Burke had to live in exile on the continent. Others, like Boetius MacEgan, sought permission from Rome to reside outside their dioceses. From the time of their expulsion in the sixteenth century, none of them was able to reside in the town of Elphin. During the course of the nineteenth century the different bishops had different places of residence. For instance, Patrick Burke was living at Sligo in 1839 but at Turlough Co Galway in 1842. George Browne lived at Athlone in 1845 and at Roscommon in 1857. His successor, Laurence Gillooly remained for a time at Roscommon, but about 1860 he transferred the episcopal residence to Sligo, where it still is.

The old cathedral of St Mary's at Elphin has remained in Protestant hands since the sixteenth century and now serves as a parish church for the members of the Church of Ireland. Bishop Gillooly erected a new cathedral in neo-romanesque style in Sligo town; the architect was George Goldie, it was completed in 1882, and it was the bishop's successor who consecrated it in 1897. Bishop Gillooly is also responsible for the building of the present episcopal residence and presbytery of St Mary's in Sligo, and also for the present diocesan college and seminary of the Immaculate Conception there (it was transferred from old Summerhill, Athlone, in 1879), and for numerous other churches. In fact, it was said of him that in a sense he reversed the miracle of Joshua of old, at whose word the walls of Jerusalem came tumbling down; at the bishop's command buildings sprang up all over the diocese. He died at Sligo on 15 January 1895 and was succeeded by John Joseph Clancy, who had been appointed his coadjutor a few days before he died, and who was consecrated on 24 March that year. Bishop Clancy continued the building policies of his predecessor, and died on 23 October 1912.

The next two bishops, Bernard Coyne, who died on 17 July 1926, and Edward Doorly, who died on 4 April 1950 at the age of eighty-one, were men of quiet, retiring dispositions who were very popular with their flocks. Their successor, Dr Vincent Hanly, was consecrated at Sligo, on 24 September 1950, in the presence of seven bishops, the President of the State, His Excellency Seán T. Ó Ceallaigh, the head of the government or Taoiseach, Mr Éamon de Valera, and many other dignitaries of church and state. It was a far cry from the long night of persecution when the Catholic bishops of Elphin were outlaws with a price on their heads. Immediately after his consecration the bishop was proclaimed a free man of the borough of Sligo. He was the first Catholic bishop to receive that honour. (After his death, Dominic Conway became bishop of Elphin on 15 March 1971, having been Dr Hanly's auxiliary from 17 October 1970. He resigned the burden of office in 1994, and the present incumbent, Bishop Christopher Jones, was consecrated on 15 August that year. – *ed.*)*

*: Fr Mooney's lists of the Elphin bishops, Catholic and Protestant, placed here in the text, have been omitted since they have been superseded by the more up-to-date lists in *A New History of Ireland*, IX (Oxford, 1984), 326-8, 384-5, 435-6, and by the notes on the bishops published in this book. A list of guardians of the Elphin friary has been inserted instead. – *ed.*

FRANCISCAN GUARDIANS OF ELPHIN FRIARY

cm = capitular meeting; dm = definitorial meeting (meeting of the definitors or provincial councillors); mc = middle chapter; pc = provincial chapter; vacant = no guardian appointed

pc, Limerick, 15 August 1629: vacant.[1]

pc, Armagh, 15 August 1635: George Dillon was guardian at the chapter.

mc, Kildare, 14 October 1639: Anthony Caron.

mc, Kilconnell, 8 February 1645: Fr Bernard/Brian [?Ward] continues.[2]

pc, Ros Riala (Rosserily), 5 September 1647: Francis O'Connor, junior.

mc, Cavan, 4 February 1648: Francis O'Connor, junior, continues.

pc, Kilconnell, 17 August 1650: Francis O'Connor, junior, continues.[3]

pc, Ballinasaggart, 9 October 1658: Laurence Dillon.

mc, Jamestown, 26/29 February 1659: Francis Reynolds.

pc, Jamestown, 8 September 1661: Francis Magranell.[4]

cm, Meelick, 18 October 1669: Francis Beirne.[5]

mc, Athlone, 5 March 1670: Francis Beirne continues.

pc, Elphin, 21 November 1672: Anthony O'Connor.[6]

pc, Athlone, 23 August 1675: Francis Beirne.

mc, Killeigh, 23 January 1676: Francis Flanagan.

pc, Athlone, 24 August 1678: Anthony Beirne.

mc, place of refuge, 28 April 1680: Francis Beirne.[7]

cm, place of refuge, 14 March 1681: Bonaventure McGeraghty.

mc, place of refuge, 13 June 1683: Francis Beirne.

pc, Athlone, 23 August 1684: Francis Beirne.

mc, Kilnalahan, 27 January 1685: Francis Hanly.

pc, Ros Riala (Rosserilly), 15 August 1687: Bonaventure McGeraghty.[8]

mc, Kilconnell, 5 May 1689: Eugene (Eoghan?) O'Rourke.

pc, Galway, 24 August 1690: Eugene O'Rourke continues.

pc, Dublin, 18 February 1693: John Hanly continues.

pc, Dublin, 25 July 1697: Paul Flanagan.

mc, Louvain, 26 July 1699: John O'Hanly.

pc, Louvain, 17 October 1700: John Hanly.

mc, Cavan, 9 June 1702: Patrick Donnellan.

pc, refuge of Dublin friars, 13 November 1703: Francis O'Connor.

mc, the same, 9 June 1705: Peter Donnellan.

pc, the same, 13 November 1706: Francis O'Connor.

mc, the same, 12 May 1708: Francis O'Connor.

pc, the same, 12 October 1709: Patrick Donnellan.

pc, the same, 7 June 1711: Michael Flanagan.

cm, the same, 13 October 1714: John Hanly.

mc, refuge of Kilconnell friars, 10 May 1716: John Hanly.

pc, refuge of Dublin friars, 16 October 1717: Francis O'Connor.

mc, the same, 30 May 1719: Francis O'Connor.

pc, the same, 3 September 1720: John Hanly.

pc, the same, 22 July 1724: Patrick French, STL.

pc, the same, 16 August 1727: Antony Flaherty.

mc, the same, 17 November 1729: Francis Flaherty.

pc, the same, 5 September 1733: Francis O Cahan.[9]

mc, the same, 5 March 1735: Francis O'Kane.

pc, the same, 6 September 1736: Antony Hanly.

mc, the same, 6 March 1738: Antony Hanly.

pc, the same, 24 July 1739: Luke Donnellan.

mc, the same, 25 May 1741: Charles MacDermott.

pc, the same, 16 August 1742: Charles MacDermott.

mc, the same, 16 April 1744: Antony Flaherty.

pc, the same, 12 August 1745: Antony Flaherty.

mc, the same, 12 February 1746: Christopher French, STL, ex-custos.

pc, the same, 22 August 1748: Antony Hanly.

mc, refuge of Athlone friars, 16 February 1751: Antony Hanly.

pc, refuge of Dublin friars, 26 August 1751: Francis O'Rourke.[10]

mc, the same, 26 February 1753: Charles MacDermott.

pc, the same, 26 August 1754: Charles MacDermott.

mc, the same, 24 September 1755: Francis Brookes.

pc, the same, 29 August 1757: Antony Hanly.

mc, the same, 19 February 1759: Antony Hanly.

pc, the same, 18 August 1760: Eugene (?Eoghan) Hanly.

mc, refuge of Athlone friars, 19 October 1761: Eugene Hanly.

pc, refuge of Dublin friars, 22 August 1763: Francis O'Rourke.

mc, refuge of Athlone friars, 17 April 1765: Francis O'Rourke.

mc, the same, 12 November 1767: Patrick Pettit, STL[11]

mc, the same, 8 October 1770: Roger O'Connor.

pc, refuge of Dublin friars, 31 August 1772: Roger O'Connor.

mc, refuge of Athlone friars, 13 November 1773: Patrick Pettit.

pc, refuge of Dublin friars, 1 July 1776: Roger O'Connor.

mc, refuge of Athlone friars, 30 April 1778: Roger O'Connor.

pc, refuge of Dublin friars, 19 July 1779: Patrick Pettit, STL emeritus, ex-custos.

mc, refuge of Athlone friars, 29 May 1781: Patrick Pettit, ex-custos.[12]

pc, refuge of Dublin friars, 22 July 1782: Roger O'Connor.

mc, refuge of Athlone friars, 12 May 1784: Roger O'Connor.

pc, refuge of Dublin friars, 25 July 1785: James Farrell.

mc, refuge of Athlone friars, 9 May 1787: James Farrell.

pc, refuge of Dublin friars, 14 July 1788: James Farrell.

mc, refuge of Athlone friars, 18 May 1790: James Farrell.

pc, refuge of Dublin friars, 11 July 1791: James Farrell.

mc, refuge of Athlone friars, 23 July 1793: Patrick Brady.

pc, refuge of Dublin friars, 14 July 1794: Patrick Brady.

mc, refuge of Athlone friars, 6 June 1796: Michael McCormick STL[13]

mc, the same, 22 September 1800: Antony Garrahan.[14]

pc, refuge of Dublin friars, 13 July 1801: Antony Garrahan.

mc, the same, 13 July 1803: Antony Garrahan.

pc, the same, 16 July 1804: Antony Garrahan.

mc, Kilkenny, 14 July 1806: Antony Garrahan.

pc, refuge of Dublin friars, 12 July 1815: James McQuinn.

pc, the same, 14 July 1819: Antony Garrahan, ex-provincial.

pc, the same, 15 July 1822: Antony Garrahan, ex-pro.

mc, refuge of Athlone friars, 14 Jan 1824: Antony Garrahan, ex-pro.

pc, refuge of Dublin friars, 13 July 1825: Antony Garrahan, ex-pro.

mc, refuge of Athlone friars, 26 September 1827: Antony Garrahan, ex-pro.

pc, refuge of Dublin friars, 16 July 1828: Antony Garrahan, ex-pro.

mc, refuge of Athlone friars, 28 April 1830: Antony Garrahan, ex-pro.

pc, refuge of Dublin friars, 14 July 1831: Antony Garrahan, ex-pro.

mc, refuge of Athlone friars, 11 November 1832: Antony Garrahan, ex-pro.

pc, Waterford, 23 July 1834: Antony Garrahan, ex-pro.[15]

mc, Athlone, 13 January 1836: Francis McLaughlin.

pc, Dublin, 19 July 1837: Francis McLaughlin.

dm, the same, 19 August 1840: vacant.

mc, the same, 30 March 1842: John Magrath.

pc, the same, 25 October 1843: John Francis.

mc, Cork, 29 January 1845: Patrick Burke.

pc, Dublin, 26 August 1846: John Magrath.

mc, the same, 18 January 1848: vacant.

pc, the same, 18 July 1849: John Magrath, ex-definitor.

mc, the same, 23 January 1851: Michael Jennings.

pc, the same, 13 October 1852: [Michael] Magrath

mc, the same, 21 September 1853: Michael McGrath.

pc, the same, 18 July 1855: Michael McGrath.

mc, the same, 14 January 1857: Michael McEvoy.

pc, the same, 20 April 1858: Laurence McEvoy.[16]

mc, the same, 24 January 1860: Laurence McEvoy.

pc, the same, 9 April 1861: Patrick McAuley.

mc, the same, 8 April 1863: Patrick McAuley.

dm, the same, 6 October 1864: Laurence Steen.

mc, the same, 7 Jume 1866: Laurence Steen.

pc, the same, 26 November 1867: Laurence Steen.

mc, the same, 13 April 1869: Laurence Steen.

pc, the same, 26/29 October 1870: Francis Antony Walshe.

mc, the same, 23 April 1872: Francis Anthony Walshe.

From the end of the 1780s the guardians appointed were titular only, that is, not resident in Elphin. Some may at times have been in Drinane and Kilcorkery, where Anthony Garrahan died in 1835. Titular guardianships were abolished before the chapter of November 1873.

Footnotes

1. This chapter asked for the prayers of the friars for the bishop of Elphin, Boetius MacEgan, who had been consecrated in 1626.

2. The surname is faded, but looks brief, possibly with the letters V, r, s (?Vardeus). A Bernard Ward appears only once in the chapter bills, elected guardian of Kilnalahan friary in Co Galway in 1629.

3. The chapter asked for the prayers of the friars for Bishop Boetius MacEgan, who had died in April that year.

4. The chapter due in 1664 was cancelled because of persecution; at the 1666 chapter the mode of procedure was challenged, and no list of appointments has been found.

5. Francis Beirne was appointed guardian of Elphin friary six times in the years 1669-1684, and may have been there earlier. On a list of Franciscans, c.1668, thought suitable for the episcopal dignity he is described as professor of theology in Prague and guardian of Elphin (*Collect. Hib.,* 6/7, 1963-64, p. 110); in 1657 he was teaching theology in Prague, and hearing confessions there in Spanish (*Collect. Hib.,* 36/37, 1994-95, p. 62).

6. Antony O'Connor is on the list mentioned in footnote 5 as professor of theology and guardian of Prague.

7. The place of refuge could have been that of the Athlone friars (as later), but may have been elsewhere. Usually it was some miles from a vacated friary but retained its name.

8. At the chapter of 1687 twenty-one friaries were designated novitiates, including Elphin, where Francis Hanly was appointed novice master; he was perhaps identical with John.

9. The surname in Irish (in a Latin document) reminds us that it was necessary for priests in Elphin diocese then and later to be able to speak the language of the people; see Hugh Fenning OP, 'The journey of James Lyons from Rome to Sligo, 1763-65' in *Collect. Hib.*, 11, 1968.

10. The middle chapter between the provincial chapters of August 1748 and 1751 was delayed, giving rise to two chapters in the latter year.

11. The middle chapters were held at the Athlone friars' place of refuge up to 1800, and again between 1824 and 1832, alternating usually with the Dublin refuge.

12. A custos was originally in charge of a subdivision of a province, called a custody; later he was the minister provincial's vicar, acting in his absence.

13. Michael McCormick was living in Naples in 1796; he was a native of Athlone, perhaps on the Elphin diocese side of the river Shannon. As titular guardian of Elphin friary he could vote at a provincial chapter in Ireland.

14. See C. Giblin, 'The Franciscans in Elphin' (in bibliography) for Edward Anthony Garrahan's special relationship with Elphin; he was appointed titular guardian fifteen times.

15. 'Place of refuge' no longer used on the chapter lists. Religious in Ireland, even if still legally non-existent, did not have to hide any longer.

16. Michael McEvoy may have been named Laurence in religion. In 1860 he was one of three appointed examiners of candidates for the order.

Church of Ireland eighteenth-century episcopal residence at Elphin. It was partly destroyed by fire in 1911 and is now derelict. *(Photo courtesy of The Irish Architectural Archive.)*

BIBLIOGRAPHY[*]

General: sources

Annála Rioghachta Éireann: Annals of the Kingdom of Ireland by the Four Masters, ed. John O'Donovan (Dublin 1856), 7 volumes, see vol. II and III.

Annála Uladh: Annals of Ulster, ed. W. M. Hennessy (Dublin 1887-1901), 4 volumes, see vol. I and II.

The Annals of Clonmacnoise, ed. D. Murphy (Dublin, 1896).

General: works

W. G. Wood-Martin, *History of Sligo, county and town,* 3 volumes (Dublin, 1882-1892).

T O'Rorke, *The history of Sligo: town and county,* 2 volumes (Dublin, 1890).

F. Burke, *Loch Cé and its Annals: North Roscommon and the diocese of Elphin in times of old* (Dublin, 1895).

J. J. Kelly, 'Elphin', *The Catholic Encyclopedia,* v (New York, 1909).

P. A. Sharkey, *The heart of Ireland* (Boyle 1927).

Ordnance Survey letters, 1837: Roscommon, 2 volumes, reproduced by Michael O'Flanagan (Bray, 1927); also Sligo, one volume (Bray, 1928).

T. Hurley, *St Patrick and the parish of Kilkeevan,* vol. I (Dublin 1943).

M. Connellan, 'Elphin parish', in *College of the Immaculate Conception, Sligo, Annual* (1947), pp 23-7.

From St Patrick to the Normans

J. Colgan OFM, *Acta sanctorum ... Hiberniae* (Louvain 1645); and *Triadis thaumaturgae ... acta* (Louvain 1647).

The martyrology of Donegal, ed. J. H. Todd & W. Reeves (Dublin, 1864).

J. O'Hanlon, *Lives of the Irish saints,* IV (after 1875), under April 27.

J. J. Kelly, 'St Columba at Boyle', *Irish Ecclesiastical Record (IER)* 1880.

The tripartite life of St Patrick, ed. W. Stokes, 2 volumes (London, 1887).

P. Fabre and L. Duchesne, *Le 'Liber censuum' de l'Eglise Romaine,* I (Paris, 1889).

W. F. Wakeman, *A survey of the antiquarian remains on the Island of Inismurray* (London, 1893).

Félire hUí Gormáin: the martyrology of Gorman, ed. W. Stokes (London, 1895).

J. J. Kelly, 'St Assicus: first bishop and patron of the diocese of Elphin', *IER,* XI (1902), pp 289f, 400f; and XII (1903), pp 71f and 355f – correspondence with W. H. Grattan Flood.

J. J. Kelly, 'Patron saints of the parishes of the dioceses of Elphin', *IER,* XVI (1904), pp 43f.

Félire Oengusso Céli Dé: the martyrology of Oengus the Culdee, ed. W. Stokes (London, 1905).

J. B. Bury, *The life of St Patrick* (London, 1905).

E. Hogan, *Onomasticon Goedelicum* (Dublin, 1910).

Liber Ardmachanus: the book of Armagh, ed. J. Gwynn (Dublin, 1913).

The Four Masters, 'Genealogiae regum et sanctorum Hiberniae', ed. Paul Walsh, *Archivium Hibernicum (Archiv. Hib.),* v (1916), and separately (Maynooth, 1918).

H. J. Lawlor, 'A fresh authority for the synod of Kells, 1152', *Proceedings of RIA,* xxxvi (1922 c).

The Martyrology of Tallaght, ed. R. I. Best & H. J. Lawlor (London, 1931).

Bethu Phátraic: The tripartite life of St Patrick (Dublin, 1939).

M. Connellan, 'The implications of Rath Breasail synod', *Jn. Ardagh & Clonmacnaoise Ant. Soc.,* II, 9 (1943); 'St Muadhnat of Kill Muadhnat', *Jn. Galway Arch. & Hist. Soc.,* xxi (1944-45); 'St Brocaidh of Imliuch Brocadha', the same, xxiii (1948); 'The see of Tuaim in Raith Breasail synod', the same, xxiv (1950-51); 'Sliabh Ua nAilealla and Bearnas Ua nAilealla', *Jn. Royal Soc. Antiq. Ireland (JRSAI),* lxxx (1950); 'St Patrick's two crossings of the Shannon', *Jn. Ardagh & Clonmacnoise Antiq. Soc.,* II, 12 (1951).

J. J. Namee, *History of the diocese of Ardagh* (Dublin, 1954).

From the Normans to the Reformation: sources

A. Theiner, *Vetera monumenta Hibernorum et Scotorum* (Rome, 1864).

The Annals of Lough Cé, ed. W. H. Hennessy, 2 volumes (London, 1871).

'Ecclesiastical taxation of Ireland', *Calendar of documents relating to Ireland,* ed. H. Sweetman, & others, v (London, 1886).

Calendar of entries in the papal registers relating to Great Britain and Ireland. Papal letters, ed. W. H. Bliss, & others, 13 volumes (London, 1893f).

Annála Connacht: The annals of Connacht, ed. A. M. Freeman (Dublin, 1970).

'Obligationes pro annatibus' ed. G. Mac Niocaill, *Archv. Hib.,* xxii (1959).

From the Normans to the Reformation: works

The whole works of Sir James Ware concerning Ireland, I, ed. W. Harris (Dublin, 1739).

H. Cotton, *Fasti ecclesiae Hibernicae,* iv and v (Dublin, 1850).

W. H. Grattan Flood, 'The episcopal succession in Elphin, 1216–1539', *IER* (1914).

M. H. MacInerny, *A history of the Irish Dominicans,* I (Dublin, 1916), pp 271-84, 477-93, two bishops.

From the Reformation: sources

Manuscript in State Archives Ireland, Royal Commission transcript, Regal Visitation Book, vol. 4: Report of Visitation in 1615; also manuscript on the diocesan census, Elphin, 1749 (Breandán Mac Giolla Choille has prepared this for publication.)

National Library of Ireland, MSS 1543-1547: M. J. Moran, Records of Athlone and district, 4 volumes.

C. Vane, *Correspondence of Viscount Castlereagh* (London, 1849).

Calendar of State papers relating to Ireland, 1509-1573, ed. H. C. Hamilton (London, 1860).

Calendar of the patent and close rolls of Chancery in Ireland, ed. J. Morrin (Dublin, 1861).

P. F. Moran, *Spicilegium Ossoriense,* I (Dublin, 1874) and II (1878).

R. E. Matheson, *Census of Ireland, 1901. General topographical index* (Dublin, 1904).

Reginald Walsh, 'A list of the regulars registered in Ireland ... 1829', *Archiv. Hib.,* III (1914).

Anon., 'Report on the state of popery in Ireland, 1731', *Archiv. Hib.,* III (1914).

J. Hagan, 'Miscellanea Vaticano-Hibernica, 1580-1631', *Archiv. Hib.,* III (1914); v (1916).

J. Linchaeus (Lynch), *De praesulibus Hiberniae,* ed. J. F. O'Doherty, II (Dublin, 1944).

Brendan Jennings OFM, 'Miscellaneous documents III, 1602-1715', *Archiv. Hib.,* xv (1950), pp 62-4.

Hugh Fenning OP, 'The diocese of Elphin, 1747-1802: documents from Roman archives', *Collectanea Hibernica,* 36/37 (1994-95), 159-73.

From the Reformation: works

P. Osullevanus Bearrus (Philip O'Sullivan Beare) *Historiae Catholicae Iberniae compendium* (Lisbon, 1621); (also, ed. Matthew Kelly, Dublin, 1850).

Anon., 'The see of Elphin in the sixteenth century', *IER* (1866).

J. J. Kelly, 'The diocese of Elphin 1671-1717', *IER* (1893); and 'Episcopal succession in the diocese of Elphin during the Reformation period', *IER* (1907).

W. P. Burke, *The Irish priests in the penal times* (Waterford, 1914).

Canice Mooney OFM, 'Bishop Boetius MacEgan of Elphin', *Franciscan College Annual* (Multyfarnham, 1952).

Cathaldus Giblin OFM, 'The Franciscans in Elphin', *Roscommon Hist. & Arch. Soc. Jn.,* II (1988).

H. Fenning, 'Clergy of Elphin diocese 1810-12', *Collect. Hib.,* xxxiv-xxxv (1992-93).

H. Fenning, 'Clergy lists of Elphin, 1731-1818', *Collect. Hib.,* xxxviii (1996).

Religious Orders

T. de Burgo (Burke OP), *Hibernia Dominicana* (Cologne?, 1762).

M. Archdall, *Monasticon Hibernicum* (Dublin, 1786).

(W. J. Battersby), *A history of all the abbeys, convents, churches ... of St Augustine in Ireland* (Dublin, 1856).

P. Mannion, 'The Franciscans in Elphin', *The Roscommon Journal* (3 Jan 1903).

W. H. Grattan Flood, 'The Cluniacs in Ireland', *IER* (1913).

Reginald Walsh, as above, *Archiv. Hib.*, III (1914).

A. H. Thompson, & others, 'The Cistercian Order in Ireland', *The Archaeological Journal*, LXXXVIII (1931).

M. J. Connellan, 'Caldragh', *Assisi*, XV (1943), 132-4; and 'Eglish monastery', *Jn. R. Soc. Ant. Ireland*, LXXIII (1943).

H. J. de Varebeke, 'The Benedictines in medieval Ireland', *JRSAI*, LXXX (1950).

Liber Lovaniensis. A collection of Irish Franciscan documents, ed. C. Giblin OFM (Dublin, 1956).

Liber Dubliniensis. Chapter documents of the Irish Franciscans, 1719-1875, ed. Anselm Faulkner OFM (Killiney, 1978).

B. Millett, 'Elphin and Ross seek Franciscans as bishops, 1649-51' (Boetius Mac Egan), *Collect. Hib.*, XXXIV-XXXV (1992-93).

See under Bishops and Periodicals below.

Bishops

P. B. Gams, *Series episcoporum ecclesiae catholicae* (Ratisbon, 1873).

W. Maziere Brady, *The episcopal succession in England, Scotland and Ireland AD 1400 to 1875*, II (Rome, 1876).

C. Eubel & others, *Hierarchia catholica medii aevi*, I-V (1898-1935).

C. Giblin, 'Ten documents relating to Irish diocesan affairs 1740-84, from Franciscan Library, Killiney' (incl. statement by Bishop James Fallon), *Collect. Hib.*, XX (1978).

F. M. Powicke, *Handbook of British Chronology* (3rd edn., ed. E. B. Fryde & others, London, 1986).

M. Robson, 'Franciscan bishops of Irish dioceses active in medieval England', *Collect. Hib.*, 38 (1996) – especially for Bishop Robert Foston.

See also the Irish annals and the works given above by Ware, Lynch, Cotton, MacInerny, Kelly and Grattan Flood.

See Dictionary of National Biography, under names of bishops.

Periodicals

W. J. B. (Battersby) & others, *Irish Catholic Directory* (1836f).

Irish Church Directory & Yearbook (1862f).

Annuario Pontificio (1898f).

Collectanea Hibernica (1958f).

Taxation List of 1306 under Pope Clement V
Diocese of Elphin

The Taxation List of 1306 for the Diocese of Elphin is based on a valuation roll believed to have been drawn up in the reign of Edward I, King of England (1272-1307), to regulate the collection of ecclesiastical revenues. A tenth of ecclesiastical benefices had been temporarily granted to the King by the See of Rome, to defray the expenses of a crusade.

The listing below is the earliest available index to the diocese within its present geographical limits and is derived from two published sources:
1. Hurley, Very Rev Timothy Canon DD PP, *St Patrick and the Parish of Kilkeevan*, Vol I (Dublin, 1943).
2. Topographical Notes of the Late Archdeacon Michael J Connellan, *The Angelus* (Sligo, June, 1984).

Many modern parishes can be identified from these lists, showing their continuity over the past seven hundred years. The origin of the names of other parishes is more obscure, some using an ancient form of the name while others may have been copied incorrectly, with syllables having benn added or omitted.

	1306 List	*Place of Worship*	*Present Parish*
1	St Mary's of Elphin	Elphin	Elphin
2	Kilquenmora?		
3	St Patrick's of Elphin	Elphin	Elphin
4	Clonorenma	Clooncraff?	Aughrim
5	Kilglasse (deserted)	Kilglass	Kilglass
6	Cloncardi	Kilbarry	Tarmonbarry
7	Bunillng	Bumlin	Strokestown
8	Clonagaleg?		
9	Cuff	Creeve	Elphin
10	Kilmire Comsig	Kilmacumsey	Elphin
11	Schevrill	Shankill	Elphin
12	Kiltoulach (deserted)	Kilcola	Croghan
13	Kilnamban??		
14	Kilnecayr	Killynagh	Tulsk

1306 List	Place of Worship	Present Parish
15 Elionfynlacte	Cloonfinlough	Strokestown
16 Lissomtyg	Lissonuffy	Strokestown
17 Kildlog	Kildalog	Strokestown
18 Clonyn In Bernan (deserted)	Kilverdon	Strokestown
19 Kilcurcumagy	Kilorkey?	Frenchpark
20 Oclolf	Ogulla	Tulsk
21 Kiliculy	Kilcooley	Tulsk
22 Tulach	Tulsk	Tulsk
23 Kilbriada	Kilbride	Kilbride
24 Doryn	Derrane	Kilbride
25 Athblor	Aclare	Oran
26 Baslick	Baslick	Tulsk
27 Ternumkrum	Tarmon	Castlerea
28 Killafry (deserted)	Kilfree	Achonry Diocese
29 Kilnaroonanak?		Tulsk?
30 Clonkasa	Clooncoose	Castlerea
31 Imletford	Emlagh	Castlerea
32 Toberbrig	Ballintubber	Ballintubber
33 Foran	Oran	Oran
34 Inigan	Dunamon	Kilbegnet
35 Luylesbrith??		
36 Kilmcangyn	Ballinakill	Kilbegnet
37 Kilcurvan	Kilcroan	Ballintober
38 Kilbegnata	Kilbegnet	Kilbegnet
39 Fidard	Fuerty	Athleague
40 Insedun	Teampall Inenan	Roscommon
41 Roscoman	Roscommon	Roscommon
42 Kilmedan	Kilmaine	Knockcroghery
43 Kilfuymegy	Killinvoy	Knockcroghery
44 Randon	Rindoon	Knockcroghery
45 Kiloma	Kiltoom	Kiltoom & Cam
46 Canach	Cam	Kiltoom & Cam
47 Rathfard	Rahara	Knockcroghery
48 Checkfrate	Tisrara	Ballyforan
49 Techfrick	Taghboy	Ballyforan
50 Athag	Athleague	Athleague

1306 List	Place of Worship	Present Parish
51 Kilcum'acan	Kilcomman	Knockcroghery
52 Kilgorland	Killeroran	Ballygar
53 Bathalle	Boughill	Ballyforan
54 Killethean	Killyan	Ballygar
55 Kilosadilan	Killosolan	Ahascragh
56 Athesgrach	Ahascragh	Ahascragh
57 Disert	Dysart	Ballyforan
58 Colmacarmacan	Cloonigormican	Oran
59 Kilmore	Kilmore	Aughrim
60 Ethdrum	Eachdruim	Aughrim
61 Ardcarna	Ardcarne	Ardcarne
62 Kilankyn	Killukin	Croghan
63 Killaunagh	Killumod	Croghan
64 Kilseisyn	Kilteasheen	Ardcarne
65 Kilsilum	Killeelin	Ardcarne
66 Thuanna	Tumna	Ardcarne
67 Drum	Drum	Boyle
68 Disertmyda	Estersnow	Croghan
69 Esmakirk	Assylinn	Boyle
70 Killinamanach	Killnamanagh	Ballinameen
71 Glynsennul	Cloonshanville	Frenchpark
72 Techbithirn	Tibohine	Fairymount
73 Kilredan	Kilroddan	Loughglynn
74 Clonard	Cloonard	Loughglynn
75 Kilnardan	Kilrooane	Loughglynn
76 Atanagh	Aughannagh	Aghanagh
77 Kilmactrena (wasted)	Kilmactranny	Geevagh
78 Kilmachita??		
79 Kilmactalun	Kilmacallan	Riverstown
80 Hildega	Coolea	Riverstown
81 Drumduliand	Drumcolum	Riverstown
82 Kilrass	Kilross	Riverstown
83 Inismore	Church Is, Lough Gill	St Joseph's, Calry
84 Drumclief	Drumcliff	Drumcliff
85 Athymglas	Ahamlish	Ahamlish
86 De Buello	Boyle	Boyle
87 Locque Cononicoriem	Trinity Is, Loch Cé	Boyle

Many of the places listed have been amalgamated to form the present parishes of the Diocese of Elphin. However, the following parochial areas are not listed:

Cloontuskert	Shancough	Kilmacowen
Kilgefin	Kilbryan	Killadoon
Killukin (South)	Ballysummaghan	Sligo
Kilteevan	Taughnagh	Cloonkeen
St Peter's	Coolera	Killaspugbrone

Kilmacowen medieval church, a typical thirteenth-century religious foundation

Bishops of Elphin 1111-2000

THIS LIST OF BISHOPS of Elphin is based primarily on the list found in T. W. Moody, F. X. Martin, F .J. Byrne (Editors), *A New History of Ireland*, IX, (Oxford, 1984). Other sources used are W. M. Brady, *The Episcopal Succession in England, Scotland and Ireland 1400-1875*, vol II (Rome, 1876), and the bishops listed in the Cathedral in Sligo. The biographical notes are from various sources recorded in the bibliography which is to be found at the end of this book.

Donaldus (Domnall) Ua Dubhthaigh 1111-1136
He was abbot of Roscommon and Bishop of Clonmacnoise before being appointed the first bishop of the new enlarged diocese of Elphin. He died on 17 March 1136.

Muireadacus Ua Dubhthaigh 1137-

Flannacán Ua Dubhthaigh 1150-1152
He reigned the See in 1152 and died in 1168.

Maél Íosa Ua Connachtáin 1152-1174
He was appointed in March 1152 and died in 1174.

Thomas Ua Conchúir 1175-1180
He was translated to Armagh in 1180.

Floirint Ua Maolruaidh, O Cist 1180-1195
He was abbot of the Cistercian abbey of Boyle.

Ardgall Ua Conchúir 1206-1214
He was appointed on 14 February 1206. He died in 1215.

Dionysius Ó Maolchiaráin 1214

Dionysius Ó Mordha 1226-1229
He resigned the See in 1229 and died on 15 December 1231.

Alanus c. 1230
He probably did not get possession of the See.

Donatus (Donnchad) Ó Conchúir 1231-1244
He was consecrated in 1232 and died on 24 April 1244.

Ionnes (Eoin) Ó hUghroin 1244-1246
He was archdeacon of Elphin before becoming bishop.

Thomas Ó Conchúir 1246-1259
He was appointed Bishop of Elphin on 21 August 1246 and translated to Tuam on 23 March 1259.

Milo (Máel Seachlainn) Ó Conchúir 1260-1262
He was archdeacon of Clonmacnoise before being appointed Bishop of Elphin in November 1260. He died on 9 January 1262.

Thomas Mac Diarmada, O Cist 1262-1265
He was abbot of the Cistercian abbey of Boyle before being appointed bishop.

Maurice Mac Néill Ó Conchúir, OP 1266-1284
He was the first Dominican to be Bishop of Elphin and was appointed in Spring of 1266. There was much unrest in Connacht at this time as the English tried to make advances into the west. In 1274 Bishop Ó Conchúir was one of only three Irish bishops to attend the Ecumenical Council of Lyons. This Council effected a short lived union of the Eastern Church with Rome. His seal as Bishop of Elphin is preserved in the Vatican Archives. He died on 5 December 1284.

Fragment of the episcopal seal of Maurice MacNéill Ó Conchúir OP, preserved in the Vatican Archives.

Auliffre (Amlaím) Ó Tumaltaigh 1285
He was appointed bishop but died before he was consecrated.

Gelasius (Gilla Íosa) Ó Conchúir, O Pream 1285-1296
He was abbot of the Premonstratensian abbey of Loch Cé before being appointed bishop. He died in September 1296.

Marianus Ó Donnachair, OP 1296-1297

Malachias (Máel Seachlainn) Mac Briain, O Cist 1297-1303
He died in March 1303.

Donatus (Donnchad) Ó Flanagáin, O Cist 1303-1307
He was abbot of the Cistercian abbey of Boyle before being appointed bishop in June 1303. He died on 22 June 1307.

Cathal Ó Conchúir, O Praem 1307-1310
He was abbot of the Premonstratensian abbey of Loch Cé before being appointed bishop in September 1307. He resigned the diocese in 1310 and died in 1343.

Malachias Mac Áeda 1310-1312
He was a canon of Elphin when appointed bishop in September 1307. He was translated to Tuam on 19 December 1312.

Laurentius Ó Lachtnáin 1313-1326
A canon of Elphin, he was appointed bishop in January 1313 and died in 1326.

Ionnes (Seoán) Ó Finnachta 1326-1354
He was consecrated bishop in 1326 and died in 1354.

Carolus 1355-1357
Appointed in 1355, he died in 1357.

Gregorius Ó Mocháin 1357-1372
He was from Killala Diocese and was appointed bishop on 27 February 1357. He was translated to Tuam on 7 May 1372.

Thomas Bairéad 1372-1404
He was archdeacon of Annaghdown before being appointed bishop on 16 June 1372. His seal as Bishop of Elphin still survives and is preserved in the National Museum. He died in 1404.

Ionnes (Seoán) Ó Mocháin 1383-1394
Possibly a priest of Achonry Diocese, he was appointed in January 1383 while his predecessor was still living. He was probably translated to Derry in 1394.

Ioannes (Seaán) Ó Gráda 1407-1417
He was appointed Bishop of Elphin on 12 October 1407. He died in 1417.

Thomas Colby 1412-1414
He was appointed by John XXII on 18 March 1412 but he was translated to Waterford and Lismore in 1414.

Robert Fosten, OFM 1418-1430
He was appointed as Bishop of Elphin on 16 February 1418 and died in 1430.

Lawrence Ó Beolain 1429
A canon of Elphin, he was appointed in January 1429 but died in December of the same year.

William Ó hEidigheain 1429-1449
Appointed Bishop of Elphin on 2 December 1429, he was translated to Emly in 1499.

Cornelius Ó Maolalaidh, OFM 1449-1468
He had been Bishop of Emly and was appointed to Elphin on 20 October 1449. He died in 1468.

Nicholas Ó Flanagáin, OP 1469-1494

A Dominican, he was appointed Bishop of Elphin on 7 June 1458. He resigned in September 1494 requesting that George Brana, Bishop of Dromore, be appointed in his place. A Bishop John is mentioned in his Provision as having been his predecessor.

Hugo Mac a Bhaird 1487-?1495

He was appointed Bishop of Elphin in January 1487 while his predecessor was still living. There are no further references to him.

Richard Mac Brien, OP 1492-

A Dominican, he was appointed on 22 June 1492 while his predecessor was still living. There are no further references to him. A Bishop Cornelius is mentioned in his Provision as having been his predecessor.

George Brana 1499-1529

Born near Athens, Greece. He moved to Rome following the fall of Constantinople in 1453. He was briefly in Ireland before being appointed Bishop of Dromore in 1483 and he visited Ulster in July 1489. He was translated to Elphin on 15 April 1499 but did not visit the diocese. He died in 1529, probably in Edinburgh where he had lived for some time.

Christopher Fisher 1508-

He was appointed Bishop of Elphin on 12 December 1508. He had been *custos* of the English hospice at Rome. He did not exercise authority in Elphin and his appointment probably lapsed when it became known that his predecessor was still living.

John Maxey, O Praem 1525-?1534

Born in England, he became abbot of the Premonstratensian Abbey of Welbeck in 1519. He was appointed Bishop of Elphin in 1525 while his predecessor was still alive. His appointment probably did not take affect until 1529. He did not leave England at any time and accepted the Reformation in 1534. He was the first Anglican Bishop of Elphin. He died on 15 August 1536.

William Maginn 1539

He was a canon of Dromore Diocese. He was appointed Bishop of Elphin on 16 June 1539. There is no further mention of him for Elphin. There may be confusion with a Eugene Magennis, appointed Bishop of Down and Connor on the same day. In this year also two Frenchmen, Louis Lemendaut and Hubert Iserand O Cist, are mentioned in Roman records as being bishops of Elphin.

Gabriel de S. Serio, OSB 1539-1541

He was Benedictine prior of the abbey of Bousnes. He was appointed Bishop of Elphin on 27 August 1539 but was translated to Ferns in 1541.

Bernard O'Donnell, OFM 1541

He was connected to the O'Donnell family of Tír Chonaill. He was already Bishop of Ferns when he was appointed Bishop of Elphin on 3 June 1541. However, he died shortly afterwards and probably never reached Elphin.

Bernard O'Higgins, OSA 1542-1561

Born probably in the barony of Leyney, county Sligo. He joined the Augustinian Observant Friars who had a priory at Banada from 1423. He was appointed Bishop of Elphin while in Rome on 5 May 1542. His appointment was part of an early papal effort to counteract the Henrician Reformation. He had considerable success in reorganising the Augustinian Order in Ireland in the years 1542-3. He returned to Elphin, then in a very disorganised state, but was unable to take control of the diocese due mostly to local political conditions. He returned to the continent where he remained until early 1553. However he was again forced to leave and went first to Lisbon and then to Spain. He resigned as Bishop of Elphin in 1561. He died at Villaviciosa, Portugal, in 1563 and was buried in the Augustinian monastery there.

John O'Heyne 1545 Apostolic Administrator

He was Bishop of Cork and Cloyne and came to Elphin for six months in 1545 as Bishop O'Higgins had failed to secure possession of the See. He returned to his old diocese.

Andrew O'Crean, OP 1562-1594

A native of Sligo, he was Prior of the Dominican abbey in Sligo in 1561. He was appointed Bishop of Elphin on 28 January 1562 while on his way to Rome. He was able to administer his diocese in relative freedom until 1584. He received the decrees of the Council of Trent in 1566 on behalf of Tuam Province with other bishops from the province. He was a very popular bishop, particularly in the north of the diocese. He lived his latter years in the Dominican abbey in Sligo until his death in 1594. He was buried in Sligo.

Dermot O'Healy, OFM

The only reference to him as Bishop of Elphin is in a report to Rome in 1623. He was martyred for the faith in 1579.

Raymond Galvin ?- c. 1600

He is named in the appointment of his successor. He was martyred for the faith, c. 1600, although little information survives on his life.

Dermot McGrath, OSA was Vicar Apostolic of Elphin in 1620.

Nicholas of St Patrick, OSA was Vicar Apostolic of Elphin from August 1620.

Boetius Egan, OFM 1625-1650

Born at Park, county Galway, about 1580, he entered the Franciscan Order at St Anthony's, Louvain in 1611. He was appointed Bishop of Elphin in 1625 at a time of persecution for the church in Ireland. His episcopate coincided with the turbulent years of the 1641 rebellion and the consequent Cromwellan invasion of Ireland. After his consecration he came secretly to his diocese and was the only bishop in Connacht for much of his time there. He was co-signatory to many documents forwarded to Rome in the name of the Connacht bishops. He administered the diocese mostly in secret, disguised as a merchant, travelling on foot and staying wherever he could find shelter. His chief place of refuge was at Glinsk castle where the Burke family lived. His report on the diocese, written in 1637, gives a deep insight into the plight of the Catholics of that period. For a short time after 1641 he was able to reside in the episcopal palace at Elphin. This did not last long and soon the bishop was again living the life of a fugitive as he faithfully carried out his duties. He died on 19 April 1650 and was buried in the Franciscan Friary at Kilconnell in the Diocese of Clonfert.

1650-1671

During this period the diocese was administered by Vicars Apostolic.
Thomas Higgins Vicar General up to 1668
James Finaghty Vicar General 1668 (d. 1683)

Dominic Burke, OP 1671-1704

Born in 1629 of a noble family near Craughwell, county Galway, he was professed a Dominican in 1648 at Athenry. While on his way to Spain he was arrested and imprisoned at Kinsale. He escaped and spent a number of years in Spain and Italy before being appointed bishop in May 1671. His life on his return to Elphin was difficult and much of the time he was obliged to remain in hiding. He lived in extreme poverty and had little means of support. A reward of £200 was offered by the government of the day for his capture. Consequently he was forced to travel disguised and by night. During his time in prison St Oliver Plunkett, Archbishop of Armagh, corresponded regularly with Bishop Burke. It was with great difficulty that he fulfilled his duties as a bishop. Following the victory of King William in 1691 he retired to Louvain. He died on 1 January 1704 in Louvain and is buried in the Franciscan church there.

Ambrose McDermott, OP 1707-1717

Born at Boyle in 1654, or a little earlier, he made his profession as a Dominican at Roscommon in 1668. He completed his studies in Spain and went to teach in Rome. He was appointed Bishop of Elphin in March 1707 at a time when there were only a handful of bishops left in Ireland. He was arrested and imprisoned in London in 1708 on his way to Elphin. Later that year he was released and returned to the continent. He again tried to reach Ireland and did so in September 1709. For a time he was left in relative peace to carry out the functions of his office. However, from 1714 on he was forced to live in hiding as many priests were being imprisoned. He died in September 1717 and was buried near the abbey of Cloontuskert.

Carbery O'Kelly 1718-1731

Born c. 1661, he was ordained in Caltra, county Galway, in 1680. He continued his education in Paris following his ordination, receiving a doctorate in theology in 1701. He was parish priest of Ballinakill in 1704. He was still parish priest of Ballinakill in 1712, when he refused to take the oath of abjuration and went into hiding. He went to France in 1713 taking with him two young Burkes of the Clanrickard family to be educated there. He was appointed Bishop of Elphin in March 1718 having been Vicar General of the diocese for the previous seventeen years. He was consecrated on 8 June 1718 in Glinsk. He died on 4 August 1731 and local tradition says he was buried in Ballinakill cemetery.

Patrick French, OFM 1731-1748

He was the son of Arthur French of Clonyquinn, county Roscommon. He was probably educated in Spain and was appointed bishop on 23 November 1731. He was described by the priests of the diocese as an upright man of great learning. Prior to being bishop he had been guardian of the Franciscan friary of Elphin in 1724 and was appointed provincial definitor (advisor to the provincial) in 1727. He was again guardian of Elphin in 1731. His brother, Fr Bonaventure French OFM, was guardian of Galway friary in 1729. In 1747 he approved the founding of a convent of Augustinian nuns at Athlone for the education of girls. He resided at Foxborough, near Elphin, county Roscommon, while he was bishop. His will, which still survives, was written at Foxborough and is dated 14 June 1748. He died in June 1748.

John Brett, OP 1748-1756

Born at Ballymote, county Sligo, in 1698, he joined the Dominican Order in Sligo and then went to Italy to study. He went on to teach at a number of Roman colleges. He was consecrated Bishop of Killala on 8 September 1743 and was translated to Elphin in 1748. His report to Rome on his diocese in 1753 gives a good indication of conditions at that time. There were forty-five parishes, being amalgamations of seventy-seven old parishes. There were forty-five parish priests and seventeen curates. Some forty friars lived in five friaries through out the diocese. He died 22 June 1756 and was buried in the Franciscan abbey in Ballymote, county Sligo.

James O'Fallon 1756-1786

Born in Taughboy parish c. 1709, he was educated on the continent, probably at Nantes in France. Prior to his appointment as bishop on 14 August 1756, he was parish priest of Dysart. He administered the diocese from his brother's residence at

Cloonagh House in Taughboy parish. During his episcopate Catholics were slowly emerging from the full rigours of the Penal Laws and Bishop O'Fallon took a keen interest in the political changes of his day. His report on the diocese in 1770 gives a good insight into conditions of the time. There were forty-five parish priests in 1770 but most chalices in use were made of tin. He was a good friend of the regular clergy in his own diocese and the rest of Connacht. He founded a clerical seminary in Athlone in 1786. He died at Cloonagh on 1 December 1786 and was probably buried in Dysart cemetery, the traditional burial place of the O'Fallons.

Edmund French 1787-1810
He was parish priest of St Peter's and Drum, Athlone, when appointed Bishop of Elphin in February 1787. He continued to live in Athlone while bishop. His first *relatio status* sent to Rome in 1792 gives some information on the conditions of the time. There were forty-one parish priests for seventy-two parishes. There were seven houses of male religious but no convents. His lenten pastoral of 1797 condemned the outrages of the French Revolution. He reported to Rome again in 1802 that there were less than sixty parish priests for seventy-four parishes. The number of monasteries of men in the diocese was reduced to four. In 1809 he invited the Augustinians to open a house in Athlone. He died, in Paris, on 29 April 1810 and was buried in Oran cemetery.

George Thomas Plunkett 1814-1827
Born at Bothar, Drumlion, in 1756. His family emigrated to Belgium and he joined the Dominican Order at Louvain in c. 1780 and was ordained there in 1788. He became a secular priest and canon of Ghent Cathedral about 1792. He returned to Elphin diocese in 1795 and served in his native parish. He was later parish priest of Croghan and then Roscommon in 1803. He was elected Vicar Capitular of the diocese in 1810 and was appointed bishop on 4 October 1814 and was ordained bishop together with Dr Peter Waldron, Bishop of Killala, on 24 February 1815. In 1818 Dr Patrick Burke was appointed as coadjutor bishop to Bishop Plunkett. In 1821 the bishop moved his residence from Roscommon to Athlone. He died in Versailles on 28 April 1827, probably on his way to Rome, and was buried in Versailles.

Patrick Burke 1827-1843
He was born at Lisnageera in the parish of Kilcroan (Ballymoe) in 1779. He was educated at St Patrick's College Maynooth, where he was ordained in 1803. He ministered in his native parish before being appointed Coadjutor Bishop of Elphin on 6 December 1818. He succeeded as Bishop of Elphin in 1827. He witnessed the granting of Catholic Emancipation in 1829 and was outstanding in his leadership during the cholera epidemic in 1832. At first he lived at Finisklin, Sligo, but later in 1840 he moved to his native Ballymoe where he remained until his death on 16 September 1843. He was buried in the family vault in Kilcroan cemetery.

George Joseph Plunkett Browne 1844-1858

From a portrait in the Ursuline Convent, Sligo

Born in 1795 at Cloonfad, Aughrim parish, he was educated at Maynooth and ordained there in 1818. He was for many years administrator of St Peter's Athlone. In 1831 he was appointed the first bishop of the new diocese of Galway. He was highly regarded in Galway and took an interest in political as well ecclesiastical affairs. He was translated to Elphin on 10 March 1844. He lived in Sligo, Athlone and finally at Roscommon while bishop. He was a man of singularly mild temperament and was universally and fondly known as 'the dove of Elphin'. He introduced the Ursuline Sisters to the diocese, first in Athlone and later in Sligo. In September 1856 Rev Laurence Gillooly was appointed Coadjutor Bishop of Elphin to assist Dr Browne. He died on 1 December 1858 and was buried in the parish church, Roscommon, then in the town square. He was later re-interred at the western apse of the Sacred Heart Church, Roscommon.

Laurence Gillooly 1858-1895

Born near Roscommon on 18 May 1819, he was educated locally and in Paris. He joined the Vincentian Congregation in 1844 and was ordained in 1847. He was appointed Coadjutor Bishop of Elphin in 1856. He became bishop of the diocese on 1 December 1858. His thirty seven years as bishop were years of expansion for the church. He was aptly titled the 'Borromeo' of the west because like St Charles Borromeo (1538-84) he was the great reformer of the nineteenth century, initiating numerous changes for the good of the church of Elphin. Many new churches and schools were built during his episcopate. The Diocesan College and the present Cathedral were built in Sligo. He took a keen interest in all national issues, particularly education. He attended the First Vatican Council 1869-70, where he was an outstanding spokesman for the Irish Episcopal Conference. He died on 5 January 1895 and was interred in the crypt beneath the high altar in the Cathedral in Sligo, which he built.

John Clancy 1895-1912

Born at Sooey, Riverstown, county Sligo, on 23 December 1856, he was educated in Summerhill, Athlone and St Patrick's College Maynooth. He was ordained in Maynooth on 25 June 1882. From 1882 to 1887 he taught at Summerhill College and was Professor of English at St Patrick's Maynooth from 1887 to 1895. He was appointed Bishop of Elphin on 4 February 1895. He was a renowned preacher and spoke eloquently on many subjects. His motto was 'Charity in all things' and this he fulfilled many times, especially in the manner in which he championed the cause of the oppressed. He brought the Nazareth Sisters to Sligo and built the Gillooly Temperance Hall in Sligo. He also invited the Redemptorists to Elphin Diocese in 1899 but they later moved to Esker in Clonfert Diocese. A strong nationalist, he took no part in politics except to condemn agrarian unrest which he did his best to discourage. He died in Sligo on 19 October 1912 and was interred in the Cathedral crypt.

Bernard Coyne 1913-1926

Born at Sandfield, in Knockcroghery Parish in 1854, he was educated in Summerhill College Athlone and St Patrick's Maynooth. He was ordained in Maynooth in 1880. He served in a number of parishes throughout the diocese and was parish priest of Boyle before being appointed Bishop of Elphin on 18 January 1913. He was essentially a shy man of retiring disposition but his love for the poor was phenomenal. He worked tirelessly for peace during the troubled years of the

War of Independence and the Civil War period. For some years prior to his death he was in ill health and he was granted a coadjutor-bishop from 1923. He died in Sligo on 17 July 1926 and is interred in the crypt of Sligo Cathedral.

Edward Doorly 1926-1950

Born on 23 November 1868 in Oran, county Roscommon, he was educated at Summerhill College Sligo and St Patrick's College Maynooth. He was ordained in Maynooth on 23 June 1895 and served in a number of parishes in the diocese. He was appointed Coadjutor Bishop of Elphin and titular Bishop of Sarepta on 16 March 1923. He succeeded as bishop of Elphin on 17 July 1926. He took a keen interest in the welfare of Summerhill College. He was affectionately known as *pastor populi,* the people's bishop and this was borne out in his final request to be buried

among his people. He died on 5 April 1950 and is buried in Sligo cemetery.

Vincent Hanly 1950-1970

Born at Smith Hill House, Elphin, on 22 April 1899, he was educated in Summerhill College Sligo and St Patrick's College Maynooth. He was ordained in Maynooth on 17 June 1923. He taught in Summerhill College from 1925 to 1926 and again from 1930 to 1944. He served in the Cathedral parish from 1926 to 1930 and as administrator there from 1944-50. He was also secretary to Bishop Doorly from 1926-1950. He was appointed Bishop of Elphin on 19 July 1950. During his episcopate he took a keen interest in the educational needs of the diocese, establishing a number of post-primary schools. He was instrumental in the development of many other educational facilities, particularly in the expansion of Summerhill College. He attended the Second Vatican Council (1962-1965). He was granted a coadjutor bishop in October 1970 and he died on 9 November 1970. He is buried in Sligo Cathedral grounds.

Dominic Joseph Conway 1971-1994

Born in Longford in 1918, he was ordained for Elphin Diocese in Rome in 1941 where he had studied for the priesthood. He ministered from 1943 to 1948 in Nigeria. From 1948 to 1951 he was professor first at All Hallows College Dublin, and then in Summerhill College Sligo. He returned to the Irish College Rome, first as Spiritual Director from 1951-1965 and then as Rector from 1965-1968. From 1968 to 1970 he was Secretary General at Propaganda Fide in Rome. On 17 October he was appointed Titular Bishop of Ros Cré and Auxiliary Bishop of Elphin. He was ordained bishop on 8 November 1970 and was installed as Bishop of Elphin on 15 March 1971. He was deeply committed to the missionary apostolate of the church and enthusiastically promoted a mission awareness during his twenty-three years as bishop of the diocese. He introduced many renewal movements to the diocese, especially at a time of transition and change for the church worldwide. He resigned in accordance with Canon Law on 24 May 1994. He died in Sligo on 22 August 1996 and is buried in the Cathedral grounds.

Christopher Jones 1994-
Born in Rathcroghan, Tulsk, county Roscommon in 1936, he was educated at Summerhill College Sligo and at St Patrick's College Maynooth. He was ordained on 21 June 1962. From 1962 to 1963 he taught at St Muredach's College Ballina, and subsequently at Summerhill College Sligo, from 1965 to 1971. He was Director of Sligo Social Services from 1973 to 1987 and for a time curate in Rosses Point. He served for many years as Chairperson of the National Council for Travelling People and has persistently pursued the rights of the underprivileged at every opportunity. From 1987 he was administrator of St Mary's Parish Sligo. He was appointed Bishop of Elphin on 24 May 1994 and was ordained bishop on 15 August of the same year.

His appointment signals a time of hope as we herald the arrival of a new millennium of Christianity.

The diocesan coat of arms

The Cathedrals of Elphin

Cathedral of St Mary the Virgin, Elphin
St John's Pro-Cathedral, Sligo
Cathedral of the Immaculate Conception, Sligo

The Diocese of Elphin dates from the Synod of Kells in 1152. It was during this synod that the diocesan boundaries of Elphin were finally constituted and have remained unaltered to the present day. The location of the diocesan seat was a more contentious matter and the diocese for a time was referred to as the Diocese of Roscommon. However, by 1174 Elphin was clearly the established centre and the episcopal church was erected by 1200. The Cathedral church stood at the eastern end of the town of Elphin adjacent to the ancient church of St Patrick where the Canons Regulars of St Augustine ministered.

Throughout the pre-Tudor ages, the Elphin Cathedral stood so magnificently that the Four Masters, under the date 1235 distinguished it amongst the cathedrals of the country as 'the great church'. It was dedicated to Blessed Mary the Virgin, a title that was retained by both Catholic and Anglican for their respective Cathedrals. This was prompted by a deep devotion to the Virgin Mary from Patrician times. In 1306 the Cathedral is again listed as St Mary's, and in 1377 the diocesan seal bears the name of the Blessed Virgin Mary.

The Cathedral was to a great extent destroyed in 1433 and Pope Eugene IV granted privileges to those who would contribute to its repair and restoration. The Cathedral continued to be the Catholic place of worship until the sixteenth century. In the mid 1500s the first Anglican bishop was appointed to Elphin.

During the thirteenth, fourteenth and fifteenth centuries, the Diocese of Elphin witnessed the appointment of some very distinguished and learned bishops. Murris Mac Neill Ó Conchobhaire OP, (1266-1284), represented the Irish church, together with the Archbishop of Armagh and Bishop of Clonfert, at the Second Council of Lyons in 1274. Thomas Barrett (1372-1404), whose episcopal seal is preserved in the National Museum, administered the diocese for thirty years. Thomas Colby (1412-1414) a Carmelite of Norwich and a graduate of Oxford, was transferred to the diocese of Waterford. He was the author of several works. He is described as a man of acute mind, of singular eloquence, and of widespread fame for his preaching. Dr George Brana, who transferred from Dromore in 1499, was born in Athens and when he died in 1530, the Four Masters, when registering his death simply stated: 'The Greek Bishop of Elphin died in 1530.'

John Maxey was appointed bishop of the diocese in 1525 and was described as

The Cathedral of
St Mary the Virgin
in Elphin, which
marks the site of
the first Cathedral
in the diocese, built
C. 1200 AD.

abbot of a Premonstratensian monastery in the diocese of York. Andrew O'Crean,
a prior of the Dominicans in Sligo, became bishop in 1562. He was unable to assist
at the session of the Council of Trent, but hastened back to guard the fold entrusted to his care. In 1566 he assembled in synod with the Bishops of Killala and
Achonry to solemnly promulgate the decrees of the Council of Trent. In 1584 he
was deprived of his See when the Anglican bishop took over the Cathedral. He be-
took himself to the Friary of Sligo until his death in 1594, but remained faithful to
his flock through a difficult period for the Irish church. Demetreius O'Healy, a late
sixteenth-century bishop of the diocese, is recognised as one of the martyrs of the
Irish church.

Dr Boetius Egan's period as Bishop (1626-1650) coincides almost with that of the
Stuart King, Charles I. He experienced the intermittent persecution of the church.
When Boetius Egan became bishop in 1626, he was for some time the only Catholic
bishop in the province of Connacht. His chief place of refuge was in the Burke Castle of Glinsk from where he sent his historic report of the diocese in 1637. In 1641 he
took up residence for a few years in the episcopal palace of Elphin. Bishop Egan
was singularly remarkable as a scholar and a patron of learning, a linguist and a lover
of the Gaelic language. On his death in 1650, the dark days of persecution returned
and were to continue for many years. The diocese was administered by vicars and
administrators from 1650 until 1671. Bishop Egan was the last Catholic bishop to reside in Elphin.

In the 1631 report on the diocese to Rome, we learn that Elphin Cathedral was by then used as a place of worship for the Anglican Church and no Catholic public worship was allowed. The medieval Cathedral was extensively damaged in 1641 and rebuilt during the Anglican episcopate of Bishop Parkes in 1660. It was again completely rebuilt in 1757-58 and the existing remains of the tower dates from that time. The nave of the Cathedral was rebuilt in 1823 and an apse in semi-medieval style was added in 1872.

Elphin Cathedral ceased to be the Anglican place of worship on 25 October 1961, when the diocesan See was moved to Sligo. The Cathedral was demolished in 1964, but its titular of St Mary the Virgin, was bestowed on the Church of St John the Baptist in Sligo, thus ensuring continuity with the ancient See.

For seven hundred years Elphin was the Cathedral town for the diocese. The Catholic Pro-Cathedral of St John was established in Sligo in 1830, and was in use until the present Cathedral of the Immaculate Conception was opened for divine worship on 26 July 1874. While Elphin has been stripped of all its former glory as a Cathedral town, nevertheless, its contribution to the spread of the faith in these parts can never be underestimated. The many distinguished bishops who administered the diocese over the centuries may now be consigned to history, but their mortal remains await the resurrection from the dead, from the precincts of the ruined Cathedral church, which they lovingly served in former centuries.

ST JOHN'S PRO-CATHEDRAL, SLIGO

For over three hundred years, the Diocese of Elphin was bereft of a Cathedral; in the meanwhile, the bishops administered the diocese from their respective places of residence. Shortly after the appointment of Bishop Burke in 1827, St John's Parish Chapel in Sligo was recognised as the Pro-Cathedral of Elphin.

There are no records of when the first parish chapel was erected in Sligo, but it appears to have been around the early eighteenth century. In 1712, Thomas Corkran, a local merchant, confessed to a local Court of Inquiry that he had heard Mass two weeks earlier at the 'Chappel or Mass-house in Sligo', with the celebrant being Peter Feighney, a registered priest for the parish of Killadoon. In 1731 a House of Lords committee noted the existence of both a Friary and Mass-house (the parish chapel) in Sligo. A deed dated February 1776, records that William Burton … leased to Thomas Corkran of Sligo Esq., 'the Mass-house situated lying and being in the Abbey Quarter and Parish of St Johns, with the small enclosure thereto belonging', to hold for a term of thirty-one years at an annual rent of £1.10s. This Thomas Corkran was the descendant of the Corkran mention in the 1712 deposition. The chapel was located on a lane subsequently called Mass Lane or Chapel Lane. The site is presently occupied by the Cheshire Home, at the bottom of Chapel Hill.

Fr John O'Flynn was appointed parish priest of Sligo in 1775, and commenced a

St John's Pro-Cathedral, Sligo (1830-1874) Sketched from a photograph taken before its demolition.

campaign to erect a larger church to accommodate a growing population. Tradition has it that the new edifice was erected around the old building, thus ensured the continuation of worship on the site. The church, dedicated to St John, was large and commodious, with balconies and galleries. The Select Vestry of the Protestant Church of St John, made a contribution towards the cost of the new building. Fr O'Flynn was subsequently dean and vicar general of the diocese, and Bishop of Achonry 1809-1817. His consecration to that See took place in St John's parish chapel in November 1809. He is buried in an uncommemorated grave in the eastern cloister of Sligo Abbey.

The French consul, Coquebert de Montbret, visited the parish chapel during his tour of Ireland in 1791, and penned the following: 'Not far from the Abbey is a Catholic church. Service in the church is conducted in Irish, and judging by the loud manner in which they express their devotion, certain passages in the service rouse the emotions of those present …'

The Liberator, Daniel O'Connell, worshipped at its altar during the Repeal rallies of 1837 and 1843. In 1840, Fr Mathew, leader of the temperance movement, preached to a large congregation there. On many occasions throughout the 1830s, the chapel was used as a meeting place for the local Liberal Party, whose membership was composed not only of Catholics, but also liberal-minded Protestants, all of whom favoured reform and the fair representation of their fellow citizens in Parliament, irrespective of their faith. According to the *Sligo Journal* of January 1836, Sir James Crofton, a local Protestant landlord, chairing a meeting of the Liberal Club, sat beside Bishop Burke on a specially constructed rostrum in front of the high altar.

Daniel O'Connell (1775-1847) , who campaigned for Catholic Emancipation, which he achieved in 1829. He then became Ireland's first Catholic MP and was hailed as 'The Liberator'.

Patrick Burke (1779-1843), elevated to bishop in 1827, was the first holder of that office to make Sligo his place of residence, living at a thatched cottage in Finisklin, just outside the town. However, in 1840, he decided to reside in Kilcroan parish in county Galway. Despite the petitions of a large number of the town's merchants and citizens – both Catholic and Protestant – he left Sligo, and died at Turla, near Ballymoe, county Galway, in 1843. Bishop Browne (1844-1858) resided for a short period in Sligo, at Marino House, Finisklin, before taking up residence in Athlone. Sligo was not to become the permanent episcopal seat of Elphin until 1858, with the appointment of Dr Gillooly as bishop.

In June 1845, Bishop Browne convened a meeting to organise the raising of funds for a new building, more fitting for the title of Cathedral, and 'both suitable to the wants of the area, and worthy of the diocese'. A management committee was formed, composed for the most part of the leading Catholic merchants of the town. Almost £1,000 was guaranteed at the first meeting. Three diocesan clergymen travelled to England and Scotland to collect funds there, and by the end of the summer, the fund had grown enormously. However, the grim intervention of the Great Famine forced the postponement of all these plans as the country was plunged into horrendous poverty.

The Chapel of St John was extended immediately after the Famine at substantial cost, but in 1852 a section of archway in the building collapsed during Mass. Panic ensued as the congregation thought the chapel was about to fall in on them, and there was a mad rush through the doors and ground floor windows. Eventually, calm was restored by the celebrant, Fr Andrew Quinn, and fortunately nobody was hurt. The fund for the building of a new Cathedral had to be used instead to restore and enlarge St John's, and by 1855, the parish was in debt, owing to the cost of maintaining the much-altered parish chapel. By 1859, the Renovation Fund was still £500 in debt, a considerable sum by the standards of the day.

In 1858, with the appointment of Dr Laurence Gillooly as bishop, the plans for a new Cathedral were re-examined. Dr Gillooly had decided to move his place of residence from Athlone to Sligo, and he reasoned that the building of a new Cathedral there would result in a permanent centre of administration, something which the diocese had not had since the Reformation.

CATHEDRAL OF THE IMMACULATE CONCEPTION, SLIGO

In August 1859 Bishop Gillooly secured a renewable lease from Sir Gilbert King of two adjacent properties close to The Lungy, described as Edward Stephen's plot, and Eubule Ormsby's large garden, known as the 'Bowling Green'. This was to be the site for the new Cathedral in Sligo.

The foundation stone was laid on 6 October 1868, and work commenced in earnest in 1869, by Joseph Clarence of Ballisodare. Charles Kilgallin had laid the original foundations, but resigned his contract after a difficulty with the sub-contractors. The architect was George Goldie of London, designer of many of the churches in the diocese. The exterior of the Cathedral was built in cut limestone, and a contemporary picture shows the wooden scaffolding

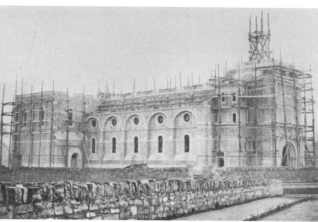

The Cathedral in the course of construction, 1873

used during the building work. Peter O'Connor of Cairnsfoot House, a leading Catholic merchant in the town, was a generous benefactor towards ensuring the completion of the Cathedral, including the donation of a clock and chimes.

The Cathedral was modelled on a Normano-Romano-Byzantine style and acclaimed by an eminent architect as a 'poem in stone'. It is the only example of a Romanesque style cathedral built in the nineteenth century. Designed in the shape of a basilica, the church has a square, pyramid-capped tower, which reaches a height of 70 metres, and supporting turrets at the west end. The tower incorporates the main entrance to the building. The cruciform Cathedral is sixty-nine metres long, twenty metres wide at the nave and aisles, and nineteen metres in height to the apex of the nave roof. It is a very spacious building with side galleries and choir loft, and can accommodate up to 4,000 people. Arches, supported by eighteen massive stone pillars of finely chiselled limestone, connect the nave and aisles.

The arch over the main entrance has a series of scriptural figures sculpted in 'alto rellevo'. The three-faced clock tower, designed by Gillet & Bland of London in 1877, is one of the finest examples of a nineteenth-century turret clock, and the carillon, comprising nine bells, has few comparable to it in Ireland. Each of the nine bells is named after one of the great saints and has the appropriate figure embossed on it. The largest weighs 208 stone (1,456 kg), and is dedicated to Our Lady. All the bells are beautifully decorated with the harp and shamrock and the chimes are a familiar sound to all Sligonians.

The original high altar was considered one of the finest in the country, surmounted by a brass baldachino and reached by six marble steps. The tabernacle was flanked by two carved panels depicting the sacrifices of Abraham and Melchisidech. The baldachino and high altar recall, in beaten brass, the artisanship of Asicus, the first Abbot-Bishop of Elphin and Patron of the Diocese, whose wood carved statue is enshrined in the Cathedral. There are two side altars in the transepts, one dedicated to the Sacred Heart and the other to St Joseph.

The circular baptistry, incorporated in the apse with its five lancet windows behind the high altar, was originally designed as a mortuary chapel. The Cathedral crypt lies immediately beneath the baptistry, where the remains of Bishops Gillooly, Clancy and Coyne were laid to rest and now await the resurrection.

One of the chief attractions of the building is its stained-glass windows supplied by Loblin of Tours in France, and executed by some of the renowned stained-glass artists in Europe during the nineteenth century.

Cardinal Paul Cullen of Dublin solemnly opened the Cathedral on 26 July 1874, although the tower was not yet complete, and it wasn't until 1882 that all construction works, including the sacristy, were finished. The Cathedral was finally consecrated on 1 July 1897 and dedicated in honour of the Immaculate Conception of the Blessed Virgin Mary, as indeed the first Cathedral church at Elphin was likewise dedicated in honour of the Blessed Virgin Mary, reflecting the long Christian devotion to the Mother of God in this diocese. The French-designed alabaster statue of the Immaculate Conception of the Blessed Virgin, standing above the high altar, bears testimony to the titular protector of the Cathedral and its diocese.

The throne occupying a prominent place in the sanctuary is set against the double pilaster and the corresponding pilaster on the other side of the sanctuary displays the diocesan coat of arms executed in marble. The throne or bishop's chair is synonymous with Cathedrals and expresses the continuity of episcopal succession and the apostolic foundations as well as the universality of the faith.

The Cathedral c. 1900

The Cathedral has undergone extensive renovations on two occasions since it was erected. The remodelling of the sanctuary in 1974-75, to comply with the revised liturgical norms, was expertly carried out ensuring a sensitive blend between old and new, and thus safeguarding its aesthetic appearance as well as the many exquisite interior Christian works of art. It is a fine example of nineteenth-century architecture being adapted to facilitate contemporary twenty-first-century Catholic worship while at the same time preserving its devotional appeal.

The sanctuary was extended at the level of the high altar, and provided access to the baptistry in the apse. A new altar, which occupies a central position on a raised dais, is of cut limestone and complimented by a matching ambo. The original high altar has been beautifully preserved, along with the brass baldachino. The architects added a brass screen, worked in a clover pattern, through which the original tabernacle is visible. The brass screen is reminiscent of the rood-screen common in medieval churches.

This much admired Cathedral, with its picturesque Ben Bulben backdrop, stands as a memorial to the faith of generations of Catholics in this diocese. This edifice, with its old world of architecture, provides a reflective and prayerful environment for Christian people in every age, and an oasis of hope for those who strive to love and serve God.

The interior
of the Cathedral
c. 1900

PART II

The Church under Duress

Bishops' Reports to Rome
1600-1800

In the seventeenth and eighteenth centuries, due to the prevailing conditions, bishops could not undertake the traditional *ad limina* visit to Rome. Instead, they forwarded written reports, or *relationes status,* as they were technically called, which are to be found in the archives of Propaganda Fide. These documents provide us with a good overview of conditions in the various dioceses between 1600 and 1800, relevant extracts from which are printed below.

The earliest extant report the Diocese of Elphin was presented by James Fallon, VG, on behalf of Bishop Boetius Egan of January 1631. It went as follows:

The Bishop of Elphin, Boetius Egan, consecrated four years previously, has laboured assiduously ever since and, disguised as a merchant, has visited his diocese and has found desolation and sorrow everywhere.

- The City of Elphin occupied by the Protestant bishop, his family and friends.
- Only one Catholic allowed to reside there.
- The Cathedral still stands, but all its altars, chapels and images have been destroyed, and a Protestant altar erected in the centre of the edifice in Protestant fashion.
- The Franciscan friary pulled down to provide building material for a place for the Protestant bishop.
- At Boyle, eight miles distant, there was a Cistercian monastery, now in ruins. A few Catholics live there. The local minister cruelly, and with impunity, oppresses priests and people. No priest can venture to appear openly there.
- The Premonstratensian monastery of Irishcrinin, a mile away, levelled to the ground.
- At Sligo, twenty miles distant, another minister with authority from the Crown to punish offenders is very severe on Catholics and supporters of the clergy, whom he arrests and imprisons on the charge of usurping ecclesiastical authority.
- There are some Catholics there, but priests experience great difficulty in visiting them.
- The Dominican priory is now in ruins, except the chapel, which is used by the Protestants as a courthouse.

- There are many Protestants in the neighbourhood in possession of confiscated church property, and these are filled with hatred towards the priests.
- To the west is Thulsk, where there was a monastery of the Canons Regular now in ruins.
- Eight miles from Thulsk, is Roscommon, with a Dominican priory partly in ruins. It is used as a courthouse, and the private residence of a Lutheran.
- Athlone, twelve miles distant, on the eastern borders of the diocese, is inhabited by many Catholics, and can be visited with comparative ease …

Formerly there were sixty-five churches in the diocese: only five of these remain and are used by the Protestants. In many cases not even a trace of them is to be found. Forty priests minister to the faithful …

… The decrees of the Council of Trent were published but whether duly or not, is uncertain. There were some old friars acting as parish priests without any authority, together with some priests not belonging to the diocese. Having examined the parish priests, the bishop found them competent to discharge their sacred duties. The old parishes were badly arranged and divided.

Steps taken by the Bishop since his consecration:

1. Appointment of deans, archdeacons and pastors in and around the towns, according to merit;
2. Publication of decrees of Trent in every parish, to remove all uncertainty;
3. Renewal of consent by those who had been married by the friars referred to, or by Protestant ministers;
4. Better division of parishes;
5. Regular holding of synod, but with the utmost secrecy so as to avoid persecution;
6. Transactions at such synods;
7. Regular theological conferences in each deanery once a month;
8. A vicar foran appointed over each deanery;
9. Preaching;
10. Regular visitation of diocese.

In conclusion, Bishop Egan sought confirmation of his appointments and of the division of parishes. In its response, the Propaganda Congregation commended the bishop's diligence and advised him that approval was not necessary for dividing the parishes.

BISHOP EGAN'S REPORT 1637

Six years later in 1637, Bishop Egan himself made a report to Rome on the state of his diocese. The fruits of his organisation were already visible, especially in the regular meetings of priests and in the pastoral care exercised by his forty two diocesan priests. The bishop wrote:

English and Scottish Protestants have complete possession of the town of Elphin and no Catholic is permitted to live there among them. Outside this town both Catholics and Protestants are found scattered throughout the entire diocese, but the Catholics are numerically the stronger. In so far as the present evil times permit it, we follow in all things the norms prescribed by the Council of Trent.

At present, God be praised, we have, in addition to some others, forty-two priests of this diocese in which, before my appointment to it, there were only thirteen parish priests. We see to it that our priests, with the help of Almighty, carry out to the letter the statutes, diocesan and provincial, which have recently been approved by the Apostolic See. We have synodal witnesses. For fear of the Protestants we dare not summon all our priests together to one Chapter as the Canon Law prescribes, but, instead, we manage each year to summon the priests of each deanery to some remote place, and there carry out the visitation demanded by law. From of old this diocese of ours has been divided into seven small deaneries.

Each parish priest instructs his people in Christian doctrine – at least, on each Sunday – and this is done in secret and secluded places. In such places also Mass is celebrated, and the priest's sole support is derived from the alms of our faithful Catholics, there being no income derived from ecclesiastical levy. In this way I also am supported, relying for my sustenance on the devoted loyalty of my Catholic people, having no ecclesiastical revenue, enduring, God be praised, the burden of the day and the heat, flying from house to house and from the hills to the woods. Following in the footsteps of our Saviour, guided by His Spirit and having here no lasting city where I might rest my head.

Bishop Egan's
signature

BISHOP MAC DERMOTT'S REPORT 1709

Seventy years later, Bishop Ambrose Mac Dermott, who had been appointed Bishop of Elphin in 1707, with difficulty made his way back to his diocese two years later, having been imprisoned for a time on London. Shortly after his arrival he made the following report to Rome, which highlighted conditions in the diocese at the height of the Penal Laws.

Most Illustrious and most Reverend Patron,

God knows that immediately upon my arrival I would have informed you of my arrival if circumstances of time and place had permitted, and only God knows if this letter will arrive (but I will try by every means possible). I will find someone in London who will bring it safely to Count Bianchi in Venice. After thirty-four days at sea I arrived miraculously, it can be said, at this country.

I have visited and consoled not alone my diocesan priests, but many others almost fed up and disgusted with life, harassed not alone in temporal matters but, which is worse, in spiritual matters and in conscience. Unheard of and horrible things, false accusations, sly suggestions and craftiness evermore resorted to in

A typical penal chapel from the mid 1700s

order to completely uproot our holy religion. In every diocese the taking of the *iuramenti iniqui* (the evil oath) is strictly ordered under pain of terrible penalties. I have used all possible means, explaining the gravity of sin, the penalty for perjury on the one hand and on the other hand the denial of the faith inherent in the said oath. I hope in the Lord I have been successful and I have sent my companion in religion to many far off places where he has prevented many who were well-disposed from taking the said oath. And with all that I fear that unless God prevents it, the Catholic religion will be totally destroyed. The few missionaries who are here are doing a lot of good but they will be forced to leave if things don't change, because they cannot live. I know for certain that they cannot spend two nights in the one place (on my arrival I too was unable to spend two nights in the same place), each one fearing the rigour of the law. I have withdrawn to a mountain, God knows to a hovel. Milk is available, but no beer. A little light beer would be a gift! When I need water I have to send a messenger a distance of half a mile from here to fetch it, and pay him. I can say in truth we drink our water with money. I am too old to travel on foot and I have not sufficient money left to buy a horse nor am I able to keep a servant.

I ask your Excellency to bring all to the knowledge of His Holiness, and if ever there is peace I hope His Holiness will do everything possible to have the present severity alleviated. Otherwise we will all be ruined … I have very many things to write and communicate, but I will have to wait and see if this letter arrives.

I remain, etc., + *Bishop of Elphin*.

BISHOP BRETT'S REPORT 1753

Almost half a century later, in September 1753, Bishop John Brett (1748-1756) made a report to Rome on the spiritual state of his diocese. The following is an extract:

Apart from the bishop, the diocese of Elphin has three dignitaries – a dean, an archdeacon and a precentor. The Chapter is composed of these and sixteen canons. None of them take part in choir chant nor could they since the Cathedral and everything appertaining to it are in the hands of the Protestants. The priests are scattered throughout the diocese and when it is necessary to consult them, by edict of the bishop or the dean, they are assembled in some named place.

There are seventy-seven parishes but during the past fifty years or so many have been amalgamated so that there are now only forty-five. Each of these has a PP and in the case of seventeen there is also a curate who assists the PP if he is old or in poor health. A third of the stipends of the parish are given to him for services rendered.

In the age in which we live we need not be surprised at the amalgamation of the parishes since our PPs have no tithe or other resources and depend on the people for their upkeep. With a falling population the number of priests must naturally be decreased. During the past fifty years numbers have fallen since the most fertile lands have been taken over by the landlords. As a result, where in the past one parish gave a good living for a PP, today two give a very meagre living for the same.

Apart from the priests ministering to the faithful there are five houses of mendicant religious in the diocese. The spiritual sons of St Dominic had formerly one house in Sligo, another in Ballindoon, a third in Cloonshanville, a fourth in Roscommon. The Friars Minor have a house in Elphin. These houses, as is evident from their ruins, were stately but are now in a dilapidated state. The religious belonging to these houses now live in remote places on account of the evils of the day. In the whole diocese we have not a single convent of nuns. There are no hospitals, confraternities nor retreat houses in the diocese. As regards the state of the laity, if heads be counted, only one in twenty will be found to be Protestant whereas in rural areas hardly one in thirty is a Protestant. The common run of shopkeepers, farmers, tradesmen, shepherds, servants and those who earn their bread by their labour adhere to the truth faith ... The diocese is divided into five deaneries and monthly conferences are held in each. All the PPs and curates attend, and causes of conscience, points of faith, gospel difficulties and other points that arise are debated. The bishop in person presides at one of these meetings, vicars general and vicars forane take charge of the others. The bishop visits each part of the diocese at least once a year.

The above is the spiritual state of the Diocese of Elphin which I, its unworthy bishop, submit to the judgement and approval of your Holiness.

Signed Fr John Brett,
Order of St Dominic,
Bishop of Elphin.

BISHOP O'FALLON'S REPORT 1770

In January 1770 Bishop James O'Fallon, who was writing from Mantua, Elphin, gave a detailed report on the state of his diocese which, in some respects, was a repeat of what Bishop Brett had written less than two decades earlier. It was delivered in person to the Sacred Congregation by Father Charles O'Reilly OP. In the course of his report the bishop stated that the income of the priests was so slender that in most of the parishes the chalices were made of tin. The Mendicant Orders had six houses in the diocese – four Dominican, one Franciscan minor, one Calced Carmelite, and one Hermits of St Augustine, but no house of nuns. The bishop visited the deaneries yearly, where he received a report on the state of his parish from each PP. However, it was not possible to hold a synod, owing to the size of the diocese, the poverty of the priests, and the fact that there was no building capable of holding a crowd 'with proper hospitality'.

All of the parish priests reside in their parishes with one exception. He left his parish some years ago without informing his bishop and went to the East Indies to labour there. As a result, since his parish was vacant, another priest was installed there. Another priest with permission went to France, where he remained longer than allowed, but without fault since, owing to the severity of the winter, he could not sail without danger to his life …

… Recently the parish priests have books for marriage, baptisms and deaths. It was not easy to procure such according to the Roman Rite. Many feared at a time of persecution these books would be definite proof of the administration of the sacraments. It goes without saying that their fears were well grounded. Even if all is calm and peaceful at the moment, who can tell if such will last? What is important in this matter is the ruling of the Holy See …

… Priests and others having the care of souls apply the Mass on Sundays and holydays for the welfare of those under their care. Conferences are held in all the deaneries at the beginning of the month from spring to September inclusive. The exposition of the gospel of the day, the problems of the faith between us and non-Catholics are aired, and questions on moral theology are discussed. Great benefits are drawn from those conferences. The morals of the clergy are normally excellent, but if some fall, which seldom happens, having been admonished by the bishop, amend their ways. The regular clergy no less than the diocesan deserve the greater credit for the efficient manner in which they carry out their duties …

… The impious and awful habit of swearing is rampant every place. To put a stop to this the clergy were strictly obliged to speak out strongly on the first Sunday of the month, to persuade people to enter a pact that anyone hearing another swearing should admonish him with great charity, and ask him to be on his guard in future. The priests obeyed the injunction immediately, and many people have made the pact and keep it from a motive of religion.

There is another matter the remedy for which is reserved to the Holy See. Benedict XIV now reigning has granted permission to do servile work on holydays of obligation but with the clause that they must hear Mass. This, however, is not and cannot be observed in this diocese. The country people for the most part live three or four miles from the church where the parish Mass is said.

A great part of the day is spent in travelling that distance. For the rest of the day the amount of work they can do is negligible. As a result neither Catholic or Protestant master will employ them for the short time remaining after they have returned from Mass. This clause is not observed and work is done every place on holydays of obligation. It follows that the parish priest remains alone in his house waiting for some one to save his Mass.

The bishop greatly desires and humbly seeks from the Sacred Office a remedy for such a great evil for which not he alone but all the spiritual rulers of the kingdom would be most grateful.

If it is allowed that he should give more consideration to the matter and deem it expedient to transfer the holydays to the following Sunday this would have some advantages …

To the judgement, correction, and censure of the Holy See, the bishop reverently and with filial submission begs the blessing of the Vicar of Jesus Christ.

Mantua, near Elphin 20 January 1770
James O'Fallon, Bishop of Elphin in Ireland
(*Translated from the Latin by Br O'Donoghue CFC, Christian Brothers, Roscommon.*)

BISHOP EDMUND FRENCH'S REPORT 1792

The following is the present state of the diocese:
I have not seen any documents dealing with the foundation of the diocese, and I cannot even work out its boundary with any accuracy. The diocese has no temporal privileges; its authority is purely spiritual.

We have no Cathedral, but we do have a Chapter, comprising an archdeacon, a precentor, and fifteen canons. None of them are in the receipt of stipends even though they are called stipendaries … there are seventy-two parishes and only forty-one PPs. The parish churches in many places, owing to the position of the Irish church and the poverty of the people, are very small, and poorly furnished. They are gradually becoming more spacious due to the zeal of the PPs and the amelioration of the law. There are no convents of women. We have seven for men, namely four for Dominicans, one for the Franciscans, and for Carmelities.

All are subject to the bishop ... there are six deaneries in the diocese with a vicar forane in charge of each. In each of these, conferences on moral and dogmatic theology are held yearly. All the priests having the care of souls take part in them and confessors are appointed. By the grace of God the clergy in general, by their lives, manners and zeal for souls, are excellent ...

I have conferred sacred orders in the diocese. I have administered the Sacrament of Confirmation in all the parishes with the exception of five or six, as some were not prepared and others I could not reach ... All the PPs reside in their own parishes ... I have done my utmost to see to it that the PP himself, or through others if there is a legitimate excuse, that the word of God is preached especially on the Lord's Day, and that the faith is explained according to the time of year.

There is no seminary or religious house of strict observance in the diocese. After mature deliberation on my part, and on those of my clergy, we have decided to found a school where those aspiring to the clerical state, and those who after serious thought have given up their former way of living, may be educated ... When the severity of the Penal Laws was relaxed, my predecessor of happy memory, undertook the same work, but died before he could complete it. Following in his footsteps I have found the clergy to be favourable to it. It has been of great help and produced excellent fruits.

In general the faithful are religious. Some abuses and scandals are evident, but this is not to be wondered at since they and their pastors are deprived of all human aid. In the case of the church I have laid down what is to be done and what is to be avoided for the past five since I became bishop ... thanks to God, I do my utmost to carry out my obligations in such a manner that both your opinion and that of the Sacred Congregation may find me worthy of commendation.

Given on the 1st May 1792
Edward, Bishop of Elphin

PENAL LAWS IN OPERATION

In 1691, shortly after the signing of the Articles of Limerick, an Act of Parliament was promulgated which excluded Catholics from Parliament, from municipal corporations and from civil and military offices. In 1695 another Act banished all papists exercising ecclesiastical jurisdiction under the penalty of high treason if they returned. The first Act to 'Prevent the further Growth of Popery' was passed in 1703 in the reign of Queen Anne. In addition to renewing the prohibitions and penalties of 1695, it directed that all popish priests be registered at the Quarter Sessions to be held after St John the Baptist Day in 1704.

The resulting registration casts considerable light on the state of the Catholic

Church in Elphin at the beginning of the eighteenth century. It gives the names of the parish priests, the parishes which they served, their ages, their residences, the dates of their ordination, and the names of the ordaining bishops. The names of two sureties are also given, bound each in the penal sum of £50 sterling to guarantee 'that every such popish priest, shall be of peaceable behaviour, and not remove out of such county, where his or their place of abode lies, into any other part of the Kingdom'.

Five years later in 1709 a second Act to 'Prevent the further Growth of Popery' became law, and this imposed the oath of abjuration on the priests whose names, residences and parishes had already been ascertained. While the parish priests came freely forward and complied with the requirements of the law at the general registration in 1704, they shrank with horror, and refused to comply with the penal terms of the 1709 Act. As a result, local Justices of the Peace held courts of enquiry to ascertain the whereabouts of the non-complying clergy, the proceedings of which were duly reported to Dublin Castle. These reports are singularly interesting as they give us a truer picture than any narrative account could of the actual workings of the Penal Laws and proof of the actual imprisonment, once apprehended, of the priests who failed to comply with the terms of the 1709 Act.

In Sligo, as elsewhere in the diocese, priests were regarded as the root cause of the agrarian troubles of 1711-12, and instructions were issued by Secretary of State Dawson to have them put under arrest. The High Sheriff complied, and the county magistrates issued warrants against them. This was followed on 4 March by further directions to commit them to jail. A week later, Col Edward Wingfield replied as follows: 'Most of the popish priests are fled from their dwelling houses and their normal places of abode.'

The following are extracts from the said reports emanating from the Justices of the Peace/Magistrates in the counties of Roscommon, Sligo and Galway, as they pertain to the Diocese of Elphin.

STATE REPORTS

County Roscommon

Roscommon 5 March 1711-2

Sir – This is to acquaint his Excellency and the Lords justices that in obedience to their commands in your letter of the 26th ultimo, I have on Tuesday the 4th instant secured and delivered into the Gaoler's custody the under-named popish priests. Their names and what parishes are as follows:

Hugh Dermott priest of the parish of Ardcarna.
Charles Cahan priest of the parish of Killiroly.
William Keogh priest of the parish of Roscommon.
Edmund Keely priest of the parish of fuerty.

Edmund Conry priest of the parish of Killbride.

Thady McGreah priest of the parish of Lisonuffy.

Patrick Duigenan priest of the parish of Rumlin and Killtrustan.

John Egan priest of the parish of Clunfinlagh.

These are all, with one Terence Rory, priest of the parish of Killeglasse who has been for several years past confyned to his bedd, that I could by this time secure, the county being large and the popish priests living very remote one from another. As for Rory, being by noe means able to come to Gaole by reason of his infirmities, he gave sufficient security for his good behaviour. I hope in my next to be able to give you an account of having in my Custody, a good part of the rest, having given most of the Justices of the Peace of this County Notice of the Government's pleasure. I am always ready to receive and execute.

The enclosed [missing] is the Gaoler's certificate of his having received in to his custodey the above named popish priests. Yours

JOHN KELLY

Tobervady October 13 1712

(Athleague)

Sir – We summoned the principal Popish inhabitants of the parish of Athleague on the 7th instant and they being sworn acknowledged that they had heard mass on Michaelmass duly celebrated by ffather Philip Higgins, registered priest of the said parish. They refused the Oath of Abjuration but one, whose name is Edmund Corr, alledges he had taken it before. Whereupon we asked him whether he since had not confessed it as a sin to his priest. By his evasive answers we judge he did confess it and received absolution, and it is a general report that all the Papists who formerly took the Oath have done in like manner. Which occasions in us the melancholy reflection of living amongst men, whom neither oath can bind nor justice and lenity oblige to fidelity. The priests and regular clergy are all absconded so that we can't take them. We are informed of multitudes lately coming into the kingdom and their Superiors turning out the Registered priests as dull, inactive sort of people and placeing others who will be more subservient to their purpose.

GILBERT ORMSBY

The Examination of Charles Feeny, Constable of the Parish of ffuerty, taken before Sir Edward Crofton Bart., Sir Arthur Shaen Bart., Gilbert Ormsby and William Caulfield Esquires, four of her Majesties Justices of the Peace for the said County.

This Examinate being duly sworn saith, that he was present on or about the 28 of February last when ffather Edmund Kelly Parish Priest of the Parish of Fuerty celebrated mass according to the usage and custom of the Church of Rome at a place called Kinmully in the Parish aforesaid. And further saith that one Richard Corr of the said Parish about three weeks before being very sicke and indisposed and he sent for the said Edmund Kelly to attend him in his sickness and the day he sent for him happening to be on a Sunday he was personally present when ffather Kelly a regular ffryer did officiate and celebrate mass according to the use of the Church of Rome at and in the place and parish afforesaid in the stead of the said Father Edmund Kelly. And saith he doth believe in his conscience that the said Father Edmund never did take the Oath of Abjuration as required by an Act entitled, 'An Act for Explaining and Amending an Act for the Preventing the Further Growth of Popery', and further saith that on or about the latter end of the month of May last past he went to the buriall of one Daniell Rowen dyed in the parish of Ballinakill in the County of Galway and as the Corps of the said Daniell Rowen was carried to be buried there he saw three fryers one of whom they call ffather Burke; and further saith that on or about a month since at a place called Aghagower in the parish of ffuerty and county of Roscommon he saw one ffather Francis Hurly a fryer and also saith that within these six months last past he has often heard and was present when the said ffather Hurly celebrated mass according to the usage of the Church of Rome in the parish of ffuerty.

… He saith that Father Edmund Kelly's place of abode is at Aghagower in the parish of ffuerty and county aforesaid. This Examinat further saith that he was personally present on or about the month of June last when one ffather Philip Higgins officiated and celebrated mass according to the usage of the church of Rome at a place called Araghty in the parish of Athleague and County of Roscommon and further saith that he believes the said ffather Phillip was never registered for the said Parish , and alsoe believes in his conscience he never took the Oath of Abjuration.

Jurat coram nobis Octb. 21 1712

GILBERT ORMSBY, EDWARD CROFTON,
ARTHUR SHAEN, W. CAULFIELD.

In June 1714 the Magistrates of Roscommon addressed their Excellencies, the Lords Justices, as follows:

We take leave to lay before your Lordships that we have heretofore committed severall popish priests to Gaole who have appeared at the General Assizes and been there discharged without any further prosecution or orders, and that persons have been bound over to prosecute some popish priests who could not be apprehended, and upon which recognizances we have not heard of any further prosecution.

The Humble answer of the Grand Jury of the County of Roscommon at a General Assizes held the 25 March 1715.

It appears to us that Francis Dillon popish priest of Kilredoon parish is dead as also Edmund Kelly of the parish of ffuerty, Bryan Doyle of Killaloone parish, Daniel Concannon of Canneo parish, Owen Connor of Kilroneen parish, William Hanley of Cloonyormason parish, Daniel Gannon of Crew parish, Edmund Gormally of Clontoskert and Killevan parishes, James Muldoon of Baslisk parish, Thady Mulrehine Kelltullagh parish, Terence Nary of the parish of Kellglass succeded by one Gebolan, in the parish of ffuerty succeeded one Bartholemew Croghan popish priest to Edmund Kelly deceased. Terence Gannon made a priest since the Registery.

We know of no priests in the County of Roscommon who have taken the Oath though they were summoned, but we will use our utmost endeavours to putt the law in Execution against them and the regulars.

County Galway

Sirs – In obedience to the late proclamation we summonded Carbery Kelly a registered popish priest for the parish of Ballinakill to take the Oath of Abjuration. He refused to appear, the summons been left in his chamber and is a person generally supposed to be qualifyed for conferring holy orders and exercising ecclesiasticall jurisdiction though as yett we could not find any legal evidence. But on all occasion he absconds though between times of searching for him he is daring to a fault, and depends on the shelter he has under the roof of Mr Feogh Burke at Glinsk.

We summoned also Roger Moore registered popish priest of the parish of Kilbegnet who did not appear but is removed from his usuall place of abode. He is an ignorant though we can't say an innocent man of his persuasion though not as dangerous as the others.

We think it our duty to inform you we summoned Sir John Burke of Milford, Baronet, and his sons Henry and Richard, to take the Oath of Abjuration. But these gentlemen have refused to appear before us. We also left a summons at the dwelling house of Teig Burk but for the greate part of the year he usually goes by the name of John Griffin, one Bryan Mcalleghany who goes by the name of Mr Lyon, one Bryan Comn and one James McKillcumy all Regular popish Clergy came into this County.

Sir – The above information was given in this day which we believe to be our duty to have laid before their Excellencies the lords Justices and desire you will be pleased to lay it before them.

Nov 29 1712

CHR. COOTE, JOHN FRENCH

County Sligo

The depositions of Owen Devanny of Sligo, and other of the Popish inhabitants of the Town and County of Sligo, taken before Percy Gethin, William Ormsby, and William Smith, three of her Majesty's Justices of the Peace for the said County, this 28th day of October 1712

Owen Devanny, of Sligoe, merchant, being duly sworne upon the Holy Evangelists, and examined, saith, that some time within a month be heard Mass at the Chappell or Mass-house of Sligoe, celebrated by Peter Feighney, Registered Popish Priest of the Parish of Killadoone, in this county, who is a non-juror, and this examinant saith that within these six months past he heard Mass from Dennis Kerrigan, his registered Parish Priest, who is also a non-juror, and this examinant saith also that he knoweth one Father James Feighney, a Regular of the Order of St Dominick, whom he heareth is or is to be Prior of the Convent of Sligoe, and he saith that he knows of no other Regulars or Dignitarys of the Church of Roome, neither does he know of any popish schoolmasters, tutors, or ushers in this county, and further this Deponent saith not.

William Bourke of Doonamurray being duly sworne upon the Holy Evangelists, and examined, saith, that on Sunday last was sennight he heard Mass at Castlecarragh, in the parish of Kill McTrany, by one Bryan McDermott Roe, alias Smith, and saith that the said McDermott Roe disguises his name to cloake his Power in the church; this Deponent also saith that he heard one Bryan Higgins say Mass within the space of two months in the parish of Killross; and that the said Bryan Higgins dwells at Dunmore in the parish of Ballysummahan, being Registered non-juring Popish Priest of the said parish, in this county; this Deponent also saith be heard one Denis McDermott celebrate Mass in the parish of Kill McTrany, in this county, the said Denis McDermott being registered non-juring Popish Priest of the parishes of Kill McTrany and Shancough, in the said county, and this Deponent also saith that he saw one Garrett Cullican, a fryar, proceed at Guievagh, in said parish of Kill Mc Trany aforesaid, and this Deponent saith also that he did see one Gallagher, an Ittenerant fryar, at Longa, in the parish of Ballysummahan aforesaid, and this Deponent saith also be did see one Thomas Rutledge, a fryar, and heard him say mass at Longa aforesaid, in the parish aforesaid, and this Deponent saith be did see one Rourke, who is reputed to be Bishop of Killala, travelling on the roads in the barony of Corran, and this Deponent further saith, he heard that there was one McDermott, Bishop of Elphin, some time ago in the upper part of the Barony of Tirerrill, in this county.

Bryan Hart, being duly sworn etc., saith that abouth the beginning of August last, being at the funeral of one Mr Conmy about twelve miles from Sligoe, he heard severall masses from three or four priests that he knows not; and firther saith that he saw at the said funerall one McDermott, reputed to be the Titular Bishop of Elphin, and this examinant saith that he has heard that the siad Bishop has been in this kingdom five years but he knows not his place of abode.

Ju co. nobis.

W. ORMSBY, WM. SMITH

The hunt for priests continued apace over the following years. At the Sligo Summer Assizes, 1719, a direction was issued from Dublin Castle to the effect that any Popish Priests 'who are come into this kingdom from Foreign parts be proceeded against according to law.'

A quarter of a century later, in March 1743-44 at an enquiry at Sligo before Gilbert King, High Sheriff, it was found that the persons named hereunder did 'exercise Popish Ecclesiastical Jurisdiction in this County' namely:

Patrick French, Titular Bishop of Elphin, whose place.of abode is at Clonaquin in the County of Roscommon; James Fieghney, Ambrose Gilligan, Michael Kill-hawley, James Scanlan and John Gildea, all belonging to the Friery in the town of Sligoe; Michael Mc Donough and Mathew (O) Coner, priests in the union of St John's in Sligoe. Thomas Brennan, Frier at Cloghermore in said union; David Flynn, priest of the parishes of KillmacOwer and Killaspickbrown in said union; James Banaghan, parish priest in the parishes of Killross and Ballysinighan; Thady McMurra and Phelim Knofin, friers in the parish Drumcliffe.

The only memorial of the troublous year 1744 in Roscommon is the following:

Tulsk March 14 1743-4

Sir – Within the limits of the Corporation of Tulsk, the place is mostly waste save a few poor Cabbins and one Inn all inhabited by Papists. The Corporation lies in the parishes of Kilcooly and Ragala of which parishes one Bryan O'Connor is the official popish priest and as I am credibly informed his place of residence is att one Mr Daniel Kelly's of Carrigins. I am likewise informed that joining the limits of this Corporation att Foxborough there lives one Patrick Frinch who is said to be the Titular Bishop of Elfin, and am assured the said Frinch had lately intelligence of some disturbance intended him and thereupon left his house and this County about the 23 of February last.

JAMES BARLONG, Portrieve.

To John Lyons Esq. at H. M. Castle of Dublin.

Sources: Burke, William P., *Irish Priests in the Penal Times (1660-1760)*, Waterford, 1914.
O'Rorke, Rev T., *History of Sligo*, Vol I, pp 226-232, Sligo, 1889. Reprinted 1986.

The Martyrs*
(1579-1707)

1579   John O'Dowd OSF, a monk of the Franciscan Convent of Elphin, was put to death because he refused to break the confessional seal.

1580   On 21 November: Gelasius Ó Cullenan, Abbot of Boyle, a Cistercian, with Eugene Cronin, priest, and John Kieran, Abbot of the Premonstratensian monastery on Trinity Island, Loch Cé, were tried in Dublin, before John O Garwin or Garvey, and hanged. Their martyrdom is attested

Ó Cullenan's Rosary, preserved in Mount St Joseph Abbey, Roscrea

---

*Extracts from an article written by Dean J. J. Kelly of Athlone, c. 1890, and published in the *Summerhill College Annual,* 1953-54.

Right Rev Mgr James J. Kelly, DD, PP, VG, MRIA (1840-1917)
Born at Roscommon in November 1840, and educated at Summerhill College, Athlone, and St Malachy's College Belfast, he studied for the priesthood at St Patrick's College Maynooth and was ordained at Athlone on 13 July 1866.

He was parish priest of Tulsk from 1879-1888, and of Athlone from 1888-1917. He was made a papal prelate of honour and at the time of his death he was Dean of the Diocese. He died on 17 June 1917, and is interred in the church grounds of Ss Peter's and Paul's, Athlone.

He was nephew of Very Rev Patrick Canon Kelly PP VF of Strokestown (1866-1898), and grand nephew of Rev James Kelly PP VG Strokestown (1770-1818), as well as a relative of Carberry O'Kelly, Bishop of Elphin 1718-1731.

Mgr Kelly was a distinguished scholar, and a frequent contributor of verse to *The Nation*, under the pen-name 'Coman'. He was also author of *The Haunts of Goldsmith* and *Youthful Verses,* and several articles on the history of the diocese which are listed in the bibliographical section of this book.

to by the learned David Rothe, Bishop of Ossory, a contemporary, in his *Anelecta,* who styles Cronin a priest.

1585   19 May: Two monks of the Cistercian Monastery of Boyle, Patrick O'Conor and Malachy O'Kelly, were seized by soldiers of Elizabeth I, and hanged and quartered.

1593   28 June: Edmund Magauran, Archbishop of Armagh and Primate of All Ireland, while hearing confession, received a deadly wound from a soldier. He was put to death at a place called Sgiath na bhFeart, now called Skea, near Elphin.

1642   Hillary Conmy, a native of the county of Roscommon OSF of the Franciscan convent of Elphin, was seized on the road by Sir Charles Coote and taken to Castle Coote, and hanged there.

1642   Raymond Keoghy OP and Cormac Mac Egan OP, of the Friars of Roscommon monastery, were seized and put to death.

1645   23 October: Malachy Ó Queely, Archbishop of Tuam, was captured at Cleveragh, near Sligo, and although he had been promised that his life would be spared, he was cruelly put to death. His companion, Thaddeus O'Conell OSA, of the Canons of St Augustine, was also seized at the same time and put to death.

1648   At Roscommon: Donald O'Neaghten OP, laybrother of Roscommon Dominican Convent was murdered. Fr John O'Heyne OP writes in 1706 that 'Brother Donald O'Naghten, a laybrother of the same community (Roscommon) most observant of his rule of never from his reception using linen next his skin, and always openly wearing the habit of the Order in the midst of the persecution, most devoted to his rosary which he always carried in his hands, after receiving many blows, was slain with a sword in 1648.'

1651   At Athlone: Hugh McKeon OSF. He was seized by the priest-hunters and cast into prison at Athlone, where 'worn out by the filth and foulness of the place, he died in 1651'.

1652   At Boyle: Thaddeus O'Conor, Sligo, 'descended from the stock of the ancient monarchs of Ireland, was a man of wonderful innocence and kindliness'. After an amnesty given to the whole kingdom, he however was hanged at Boyle, county Roscommon.

1652   Anthony O Ferrall OSF was seized by the Cromwellians as he was preaching in the pulpit at Tulsk, county Roscommon, and put to death.

1653   At Galway: Bernard O'Kelly OP, a laybrother of the convent of Roscommon, after a long term of imprisonment was condemned to death at Galway. He was publicly executed and manfully laid down his life for his faith.

1679   At Sligo: Felix O'Conor OP. He taught in Louvain, and was at one time prior of Roscommon. He died a prisoner in Sligo, in the cruel persecution at the time of the Shaftsbury plot. Fr MacDonagh, writing in Bilbao in 1703, thus refers to him: 'It is most sure when ye R Fa Mr Felix O'Conor was Prior of Sligoe, and died a prisoner in Sligoe in ye … year 1679. There was a cruel and vigorous persecution in those days, yt none of ye fathers of our Convent cud assist him nor come near him, nor get any satisfactory account of our goods and effects at the time.'

1707:   At Dublin, on February 3rd: Father Felix MacDowel OP, of St Patrick's Priory, Tulsk, county Roscommon. He was of the family of the founder of the priory, Mac Dowel of Mantua, near Elphin. The walls of the church and the ruins of the monastery still stand. The tomb of the Mac Dowel family, with a Latin inscription, is still to be seen. Felix, having received his early training in Tulsk, finished his studies at Valladolid. He afterwards taught philosophy in Sardinia. Transferred to Rome he was one of the seven Dominicans who received possession for the Order of the Churches of St Sixtus and St Clement's. These churches with their respective houses were united into one priory, intended to supply priests to the Irish mission. In 1680, Father Felix was appointed prior of this house, and by his zeal and example brought it to the most exact standard of regular observance. He returned to Ireland, then sorely in need of such missioners. In the war between James and William, he was chaplain in one of the Irish regiments. After the defeat of the Jacobite cause, he went abroad and lived for a time in England, watching his opportunity to return to Ireland. He succeeded at length, but had scarcely reached Dublin when he was cast into a dungeon and held in the closest confinement. Here he died a martyr for his faith, after nearly two years imprisonment, on 3 February 1707.

St Oliver Plunkett 1625-1681 Archbishop of Armagh 1669-1681. The last of the Irish martyrs who was executed at Tyburn, London, on 1 July 1681. His mother, Thomassina Dillon, was related to the Dillon families of county Roscommon. While in prison he corresponded regularly with Bishop Dominic Burke.

Footnote:

This footnote was written by the Editor of the *Summerhill Annual* 1953, who had obtained it from the Cistercian Community in Roscrea:

(1) The Gelasius O'Cullenan mentioned was born in 1554, the probable place of his birth being Ballyshannon, county Donegal. He studied in Louvain and Rome. Ordained in the Holy City, he entered the Cistercians on his return to Ireland and was almost immediately appointed Abbot of Boyle by Pope Gregory XIII. For a while, he succeeded in securing the agreement of the British authorities and local landowners to the reinstation of the scattered Cistercian Community in Boyle. The success attending his work drew down on him the hatred of John Garvey, afterwards Protestant Primate. At the solicitation of the latter, he was arrested in Dublin. Garvey offered him his choice of the bishoprics of Connacht on condition that he renounced the Catholic faith. On the abbot's spurning the offer, he was tortured by fire and had his limbs crushed with hammers. But nothing could break his spirit. He was hanged in Dublin on 21 November 1580.

It is interesting to note that the martyred abbot had six brothers, all of whom consecrated themselves to the service of God. One, Bernard, was the last Abbot of Boyle of whom we have any record. He died in London on his way to Ireland in 1639. Another brother, Eugene, died abbot of a monastery in Rome. A third, James, was Abbot of Asseroe, while a fourth, John, became Bishop of Raphoe and ruled from 1626 to 1655. With the abbot also suffered, on 21 November 1580, Eugene Mulkeirin, who belonged to the Boyle community but who was also, in accordance with the custom of the time, titular abbot of a neighbouring Benedictine monastery. As they approached the scaffold. Mulkerin's courage began to falter and he begged and was allowed to die first that he might be sustained to the end by the abbot's encouragement. The latter was only 26 years old when he suffered martyrdom.

(2) The Patrick O'Connor and Malachy O'Kelly mentioned were hanged and quartered by British soldiery, not in the abbey, itself, but in a wood nearby.

List of Registered Clergy 1704

Parish	Surname	First Name	Age	Place of Abode	Year Ordained	Place Ordained	By Whom Ordained	Sureties' Names
Boyle	Sercoyd	Miles	53	Abbyboyle	1676	Cloonsellit	Dom Burke Bishop of Elphin	Wm Cummins, Ballymore; Chas Carey, Carrick
Kilnamangh & part of Tibohine	M'Gragh	Terence	54	Callow	1673	Athleague	Dom Burke Bishop of Elphin	Fergus Naughton, Athlone; William Higgins, Cartron
Killridane	M'Morris	Manus	48	Tibilime	1671	Cloonsellit	Dom Burke Bishop of Elphin	David Stewart, Kilridane; Denis Croghan, Roscommon
Killbrine	Dignane	Fargus	49	Dromdee	1677	Belleeck	Pat Plunket Tit Bp of Meath	Arthur Lawless, Ballybryan; Robert Lawless, Clonca
Killrodane	Dillion	Francis	45	Clootowart	1684	Ahaster	Dom Burk Bishop of Elphin	Toby Dillon, Cloontowart; Redmond Follone, Killmeverane
Ardcarne	M'Dermott	Hugh	52	Knocknacarew	1675	Cloonsellagh	Dom Burk Bishop of Elphin	Fergus Naughton, Athlone; Christopher Kirwane, Rahevin
No Parish	Higgins	Phillip	35	Athleague	1697	Ballyluoge	Dominick Donnellan Bishop of Clonfert	James Donnell, Roscommon; John Kely, Athleague
Tumna	Murry	Thady	50	Glory	1684	Caltragh	Dom Burke Bishop of Elphin	Charles Cary, Carrick; William Higgins, Cartron
Killcola & Estersnow	Berne	Farrel	56	Knockroe	1673	Navan	Pat Plunket Bishop of Meath	William Cummins, Ballymore; Denis Croghan, Roscommon
Roscommon	Keogh	William	45	Roscommon	1685	Caltragh	Dom Burke Bishop of Elphin	Denis Croghan, Roscommon; Hector Ross, Roscommon

Parish	Surname	First Name	Age	Place of Abode	Year Ordained	Place Ordained	By Whom Ordained	Sureties' Names
St John's & Kilanvoy	Geraghty	Lawrence	47	St John's	1685	Caltragh	Dom Burk, Bishop of Elphin	Denis Croghan, Roscommon / Edward Geraghty, Roscommon
Fuerty	Kelly	Edmond	46	Aghaour	1683	Caltragh	Dom Burk, Bishop of Elphin	Stephen Ropper, Castlecoote / Edward Walker, Castlecoote
Kilutume	Doyle	Bryan	55	Faghamore	1673	Dublin	Patrick Plunket, Archbp of Dublin	Francis Fallon, Lisgreaghan / Hugh Naughtin, Carrick
Disert & Taughboy	Lea	Nicholas	50	Cloonagh	1676	Logorea	Dom Bourk, Bishop of Elphin	Redmond Fallon, Ballinaban / Patrick Hyne, Erickmore
Tescarta	Fallon	Ambrose	32	Clondenagh	1694	Killconnell	Murtagh Donnellan, Bp of Meath	Redmond Fallon, Ballinaban / Patrick Hyne, Erickmore
Canu	Concannon	Dan.	48	Grange	1674	Cong	James Lynch Titl, Archbp of Tuam	Bartholemew Bryan, Killmore / Laughlin Lea, Kilnagralta
St Peter's & Drome	Flyn	Patrick	48	Drome	1674	Killtiscaell	Dom Bourk, Bishop of Elphin	Francis Naughton, Athlone / Ths Naughton, Thomastown
Athleague	Croghan	Barthw.	49	Eraghty	1674	Coraghbegg	Dom Bourk, Bishop of Elphin	Darby Darcy, Ballybrackbegg / John Croghan, Ballyboghan
Killcorkey	Keirne	Darby	28	Cloone	1701	Ballylooge	James Donnellan, Bishop of Clonfert	Neale M'Laughlin, Lismacola / Charles Carey, Carrick
Kilruane	Conner	Owen	50	Teagh	1676	Spain	Bishop Inadis	John Flemming, Roscommon / David Stewart, Kilridane
Rahara & Killminne	Cornelly	Teige	63	Coraghnevine	1673	Athleague	Dom Bourk, Bishop of Elphin	Richard Geraghty, Roscommon / Daniel Carty, Kilcost

Parish	Surname	First Name	Age	Place of Abode	Year Ordained	Place Ordained	By Whom Ordained	Sureties' Names
Killickin	Berne	Nicholas	41	Ardmore	1686	Galway	James Lynch Titl Archbp of Tuam	Daniel Caarty, Kilcost William Higgins, Cartron
Cloonagormagon	Hanley	William	60	Kiltonghagh	1684	Clonbarne	James Lynch Titl Archbp of Tuam	Patrick Balfe, Carkon Bryan Teige, Clonoraine
Creife & halfe Clongranfe	Gunan	Daniel	53	Creifevollin	1677	Athleague	Dom Bourk Bishop of Elphin	Patrick Balfe, Carkon Bryan Teige, Clonoraine
Clontoscart & Killtivane	Goromolly	Edmond	56	Killtivine	1670	Cong	James Lynch Titl Archbp of Tuam	Patrick Balfe, Carkon Denis Croghan, Lisemacoole
Shankill & Kilmacumsey	Brennan	Roger	38	Montagh	1696	Ballyloagh	Murtagh Donnellan Bishop of Clonfert	George Hynes, Roscommon Neale M'Reighlin, Lisemacoole
Elphin	Higgin	Irill	53	Killinacarr	1673	Athleague	Dom Bourk Bishop of Elphin	William Higgins, Cartron Bryan Teigue, Cloonreane
Aughrim	Berne	John	33	Lackan	1696	Ballyluogh	Murtagh Donnellan Bishop of Clonfert	Charles Cary, Carrick Bryan Teige, Cloonrean
Killcooly, Killukin & Ogilly	Keane	Cormuck	48	Srugh	1676	Clonsellagh	Dom Bourk Bishop of Elphin	Thomas Charletin, Dromdalph Edmond Kelly, Ballunesoligh
Killtrustan & Dumblin	Digginan	Patrick	45	Cotterglasse	1684	Derrycrauffe	Dom Bourk Bishop of Elphin	William Divinish, Corry Coll. Keogh, Colmin

Parish	Surname	First Name	Age	Place of Abode	Year Ordained	Place Ordained	By Whom Ordained	Sureties' Names
Listinufy	Gneale	Thady	55	Cullagh	1676	Dublin	Aurthur Plunket, Titl Archbp of Dublin	George Hynes, Roscommon William Pitcher, Strokestown
Cloonfinlagh	Fagon	John	44	Cluneagh	1687	Athleage	Dom Bourk Bishop of Elphin	Robert Lawleses, Clooneagh Thomas Carleton, Drumduffie
Killglass	Nary	Terence	50	Ruane	1672	Madesorle	Dom Bourk Bishop of Elphin	Edmond Kelly, Ranelogh John Hegon, Killaghnamore
Killgessin	Higgin	Farrell	55	Cloonsee	1696	Ballyleague	Murtagh Donnellan Bp of Clonfert	Darby Darcy, Ballybridgebegg Richard Geraghty, Roscommon
Killbride & Killgessine	Conry	Edmond	41	Boyanagh	1686	Ahaskeragh	Dom Bourk Bishop of Elphin	Denis Croghan, Roscommon Thomas Carleton, Drumdalph
Kilmore, halfe Clooncrauffe	Reynolds	Patrick	34	Cloonshamber	1696	Ballyleagh	Murtagh Donnellan Bp of Clonfert	Thomas Carleton, Drumdalph Edmond Kelly, Ranelagh
Kilkevine	M'Donagh	Teige	54	Cloonefada	1685	Athleag	Dom Bourk Bishop mof Elphin	George Hynes, Roscommon Edmond Kelly, Ranelagh
Horan & Cloongorman	Dillon	Chris	37	Slevine	1689	Galway	James Lynch Titl Archbp of Tuam	Thomas Pillsworth, Roscommon Toby Dillon, Clontowart
Balslick	Mulrine	James	60	Castleplunket	1679	Dublin	Patrick Plunket Primate of Armagh	Daniel Carrby, Kilcost William Croghau, Rathbreany
Ballintobber & Dromtemple	M'Donnagh	Logh	45	Fohannagh	1685	Ahaskeragh	Dom Bourk Titl Bishop mof Elphin	Thomas Naughtin, Thomastown Chris Keirwane, Raheverine

Parish	Surname	First Name	Age	Place of Abode	Year Ordained	Place Ordained	By Whom Ordained	Sureties' Names
Tarminbarry	Kelly	Bryan	57	Kilbarry	1673	Dublin	Patrick Plunket, Titl Archbp of Dublin	Thomas Cumpton, Carrowroagh; Christopher Kiervane, Rahaverine
Kilronane	Muloghry	Neh.	57	Dromore	1671	Lowth	Oliver Plunkett, Bishop of Armagh	William Cumins, Ballymore; Lawerence Muloghry, Dromore
Killmore	Kelly	Carbry	49	Clondea	1676	Clonsellitt	Dom Bourk, Titl Bishop of Elphin	Denis Croghan, Roscommon; Toby Dillon, Clontowart
Killerdoon	M'Dermottroe	Dmk.	54	Killbranaght	1676	Clonsellitt	Dom Bourk, Titl Bishop of Elphin	Hugh M'Dermottroe, Grange; William Cumins, Balymore
Augainlis	Collin	Lawrence	42	Carne	1685	Kilkenny	James Whelan, Titl Bishop of Ossary	Charles Phillips, Ogtrain; Miles Phillips, Ballendune
St John's & Calry	Kerrigan	Denis	45	Sligoe	1685	Caldrahh Pallice, Co Galway	Dom Bourk, Titl Bishop of Elphin	John Maley, Sligoe; Humphrey Griffith, Calgach
Drumcliffe, Kilmacowen & Kilaspickbrown	Ternane	Hugh	56	Ballentemple	1672	Poolsillan, County Roscommon	Dom Bourk, Titl Bishop of Elphin	John Crean, Sligo; John Matley, do.
	Dugan	John	53	Kilmacowen	1673	Athleage, County Galway	Dom Bourk, Bishop of Elphin	William Smyth, Sligoe; Nich. Smyth, Knocknashammer
Dromcliffe	Teeny	Cormack	31	Millinenane	1697	Clonfert, County Galway	Donnellan, Titl Bishop of Clonfert	Charles Parks, Lislatily; Lawrence Comnylan, Ballincar
Anghamlish	Heart	Bryan	48	Cashelgall	1684	Ballafforin, County Galway	Dom Bourk, Bishop of Elphin	Matthew Dugan, Mullaghmore; John Crean, Sligo

Parish	Surname	First Name	Age	Place of Abode	Year Ordained	Place Ordained	By Whom Ordained	Sureties' Names
Ballishumahane	Higgin	Braya	48	Levally	1685	Calltragh, County Galway	Dom Bourk, Titl Bishop of Elphin	Cn. Connor O'Clery, Rballpatrick William Burke, Dunymanrah
Kil Mac Tranny & Shancoogh	Dermott	Dennis	60	Derrylea	1699	Dublin	Plunket, Tit Bishop of Meath	Capt Francis King, Ballindune Bryan M'Donagh, Farnadarah
Tawnagh	Brehune	Morish	29	Ballinascarvah	1699	City of Cork	Slane, Tit Bishop of Cork	John Dod, Cams James Clifford, Cloonlorig
Kil Mac Callen & Ballenakill	Brehune	Laughlen	75	Ardvanagh	1699	Dublin	Patrick Plunkett, Tit Bishop of Meath	Ct. Connor O'Clery, Rhatpatrick Bryan M'Donagh, Behy
Aughanna	Conmy alias Knouhan	Owen	31	Millofforne	1701	Clonfert	Donnellan, Titl Bishop of Clonfert	Robert Johnson, Balleneffed William Bourk, Dunymarrah
Killadune	Feighny	Peter	31	Carrowglass	1697	City of Cork	John Slane, Tit Bishop of Cork	Charles Phillips, Oghan Bryan M'Donnagh, Ballindoragh

The State of Popery in the Diocese of Elphin 1731

Parishes	Mass Houses	Parish Priests	Convent of ffryars or Nuns	Popish Schools	Mass Houses, when Built
Union of Sligo	1	Michael McDonnagh Thomas Brennan William McDonnagh	One Friery, the Fryars are dispersed about ye Country not above 3 or 4 known		Before George ye 1st These 2, 2 miles from the town.
Drumcliffe	1	— Feeny		2 but Little known	Another Mass House begun, but ordered to be pulled down by the Bishop
Kilmacallan Tawna Aughana	1	Morris Brahany		4 in these 8 parishes	
Killmctranny Shanko Killrickdown Ballysumahon Kilross	No Mass House, But hutts	Two Popish priests		↓	
Boyle	1	Charles McDermot Peter Connoghton	1 Regular, sometimes in the Country	2 kept very privately	Built before the 1st of George ye 1st
Kilnemanah	1	Terence McGrah Edmund Lavin			
Tibohin	3	Terence McGrah Reg. Edmond Timoty Edward Lavin	Antony Ternan a Fryar Chaplain in a Gentlemans House	1 Vast Concourse at Cloonshawille on St Dominicks day formerly a Friery there	

Parishes	Mass Houses	Parish Priests	Convent of ffryars or Nuns	Popish Schools	Mass Houses, when Built
Killukin	1	Mathias Forester, Curate to Nicholas Byrn Registered		1	Built before the 1st of George ye 1st
Ardcarn	1	Connor Rogers		1	
Elphin	1 three miles from Elphin, a Masshouse begun in Elphin, but pulled down	Terence Ganan Owen Birn, a Fryar Officiates in Elphin	Friary at Drinane about 3 miles from Elphin, about 15 said to belong to it	1	
Ogilla		Cormach McDonnagh		1	
Creeve	1	Con. Groork			Since George 1st
Killcoola Eastersnow	1	Miles Branan			
Killmccumpsy	1	1 Priest			
Shankil		1 Priest			
Agharim		John Beirn			
Killumod		Nicholas Beirn			
Clooncraff		Patrick Reynolds			
Castlereah	1	Tague McDonnagh			
Cloongormagon	1	Patrick Keen			
Baslick	Mass houses or Hutts	Richard Prendergast			
Ballintober		Cormík McDonnagh			
Killsolan	1	Edward Flynn			
Killrorane	1	1 Priest			
Ahamplish	1	1 Priest			

Parishes	Mass Houses	Parish Priests	Convent of ffryars or Nuns	Popish Schools	Mass Houses, when Built
Ahaskeragh	1	1 Priest			
Killion	1	1 Priest			
Killcorkey		1 Priest, Friar Assistant			
Killcooly Killoocan	1	1 Priest			Before George 1st
Kilmore	1	Patrick Reynolds		1	Before George 1st
Termonbarry	1	Hugh Cox		1	
Killglass	1	1 Priest		1	
Bumlin Killtrustan	1	1 Priest			
Lissonuffy	1	1 Priest			Before George 1st
Cloonfinlogh	1	1 Priest			Before George 1st
Cloontuscart	1	1 Priest			
Killgefin	1				
Oran Drumtemple		Served by Priests of other Parishes			
Roscommon Kilteevan	1	Peter Conry Michael Feely			
Kilbride	1	John Conry			
Killmyon		Teige Kirrily Reg'd			
St Johns		John Naughton Laurence Geraghty, Reg'd. Andrew Egan	Dominick Doyle, Resident Friar		
Athleague	1	1 priest with assist.			Ruinous but now rebuilding

Parishes	Mass Houses	Parish Priests	Convent of ffryars or Nuns	Popish Schools	Mass Houses, when Built
Fuerty	1	Popish Priest old assisted by another			Mass House rebuilding
Killbegnet Dunamon	1	Priest old assisted by a young Friar	Some Friars 2 or 3 said to belong to ye abby of Roscomon		
Ballynakill	1	Dr Kelly reputed Tit. Bishop of Elphin lately dead assisted by a young Priest.		1	
Killeroan	1, lately erected	1 Priest			
Taussarara	1	1 Priest		1	
Disert Taughboy	1	Priest old, assisted by a young Priest			
Killtome	1	1 priest			
Killenvoy	1	1 Priest			
Raharrow	1	1 Priest			Since George 1st
Camm	1	1 Priest	At particular times great numbers assemble here at St. Brides Well		

Is iad is ábhar glóirithe dom
Peadar Ó Láimhín

'Ina luí anseo mar ba mhian leis féin é tá an Dr Sár-Oirmhinneach Dominic de Burgo. Ba de shliocht uasal é agus sagart d'Ord na nDoiminiceánach a bhí ann. Bhí sé ina Easpag ar Ailfíonn in Éirinn. Níor bheag a d'fhulaing sé ar son a Rí is ar son a Dhé. Ar deoraíocht dó fuair sé bás sa choláiste seo, Coláiste San Antóin de Padua le Bráithre Mionúr na hÉireann ar an gcéad lá den bhliain 1704 agus é in aois a cúig bliana is seachtó. R.I.P.A.' Leac uaigh sa Lobháin agus é scríofa as Laidin a thugann an scéal seo dúinn.

De Burgo Óg

Rugadh Doiminic de Burgo sa bhliain 1629. Ba de Chlann Riocaird é. Glacadh leis in Ord na nDoiminiceánach i mBaile Átha an Rí sa bhliain 1648. Agus é ar a bhealach go dtí an Spáinn ghabh na Sasanaigh an long ar a raibh sé. Baineadh de a raibh aige agus caitheadh é isteach i bpríosún. Fuair sé deis éalaithe lá agus léim sé den fhalla isteach sa láib a fágadh ag an taoille tráite. Le linn dó bheith ar a choimeád sna coillte chaith sé dhá lá gan bia gan deoch. Cé gur bhocht an feic é agus é millte ó bhaithis go bonn ag an bpuiteach, ní ligfeadh an faitíos dó dul amach agus é féin a ní. Faoi dheireadh tháinig Caitliceach air, fear de bhunadh uasal darbh ainm de Róiste, agus thug sé bia is lóistín dó agus chuidigh sé leis filleadh ar a mháthair. Nuair a chuala a mháthair faoin ngabh a ndeachaigh sé tríd, bhí an oiread sin imní uirthi go ndeachaigh sí go bog is go crua air gan tabhairt faoi dhul thar sáile arís. Níor ghéill sé di ach d'imigh sé leis. Sheol sé amach ó chuan na Gaillimhe agus an uair seo bhain sé an Spáinn amach go slán sábhailte. Chaith sé sé bliana i Sagovia san tír sin. Ina dhiaidh sin chuaigh sé go dtí an Iodáil. Chaith sé tréimhsí i mainistreacha i Milan, san Venéis agus i mBosco agus ins na mainistreacha seo bhí sé ina mháistir ar na n-oibhisigh. Ar chomhthionóil na nDoiminiceanach sa Róimh sa bhliain 1670 eisean a bhí ina *definitor*. An bhliain dar gcionn, d'ainmigh an Pápa Clement x é ina Easpag ar Ailfíonn. I nGhent a h-oirníodh ina easpag é.

Easpag in Éirinn

B'ainnis an bhail a bhí ar Éirinn ar fhilleadh dó. 'The poor,' arsa R. Sheridan san *Intellingencer,* 'were reduced to the lowest level of poverty and misery, their houses were dunghills, their victuals the blood of cattle, or the herbs of the fields.' Mar bharr ar an donas bhí dian thóir ar easpaig is ar shagairt. Tugann sliocht as seanmóir

Dopping, easpag Protastúnach na Mí, dearcadh an Rialtais dúinn: 'Nobody should hold faith with the Catholics, their insolence should be curbed and they should be treated like the vanquished race they are.' Ní raibh lá nach raibh an teaspag i mbaol. Faoi dhó thairg an Tiarna-lefteanant agus an Rí-chomhairle céad punt d'éinne a sceithfeadh air. I ndorchadas na hoíche a rinne sé a chuid taistil. Babhta amháin chaith sé ceithre mhí as a chéile i bhfolach i dteach gan bogadh as. Ar fhágáil an tí sin dó rinne sé turas dhá scór míle san aon oíche amháin ionas go mbeadh sé in ann na holaí beannaithe a choisriceadh ar Dhéardaoin Choirp Chríost. Maolaíodh ar na péindlithe ar feadh tamaillín agus chaith an teaspag an tréimhse sin ar eastát bheag a bhí ar chíos aige óna fhear gaoil, an tIarla Clann Riocaird. Nuair a bhris cogadh an dá Rí amach, bhí air dul agus cónaí i gcathair na Gaillimhe. I ndiaidh an chogaidh b'éigean dó dul ar a theitheadh arís agus an Mhór-roinn a thabairt air féin.

Easpag ar deoraíocht
Cothrom an ama seo scríobhann S. Eustace chuig an Cairdineal Cibo, rúnaí Propaganda Fide, agus déir sé go bhfuil seisear easpag agus céad sagart leo i bParis agus go bhfuil dhá chéad sagart eile thréis teacht i dtír ag Brest. I mainistir na Croise Naofa lena ord féin a bhí an tEaspag de Burgo. Ar 7 Lúnasa 1695 chuir sé litir uaidh chuig an Róimh. An ghéarleanúint atá á dhéanamh ar na Caitlicigh in Éirinn príomhábhar na litreach seo. Molann sé don Phápa iarraidh ar chomghuaillithe an Phrionsa Oráistigh impí air maolú ar an ngéarleanúint atá á dheanamh ar na sagairt. 'Baint ar bith níl againn le polaitíocht,' a deir sé, 'cé gur breá leo siúd atá in ár n-aghaidh bréaga a chur amach orainn chun go mbeidh leithscéal polaitíochta acu go leor d'ár sagairt a chur chun báis. Ar chúis bhréagach dá leithéid a crochadh an Príomháidh, Oilibhéar Pluincéid. Agus na h-eiricigh féin anois, admhaíonn siad nach raibh sé ciontach.' Sa litir seo leis insíonn sé faoi na hiarrachtaí a rinne sé ar dhul arais go hAilfionn agus insíonn sé mar a theip ar gach iarracht acu.

An dara litir uaidh
Sé mhí ina dhiaidh sin tagann litir eile uaidh chuig an Róimh. An chontúirt atá ann go gcaillfear an creideamh ar fad atá ag déanamh imní dó an uair seo. Insíonn sé faoi na hiarrachtaí nua atá á ndéanamh ag an Rialtas chun é a dhíothú ar fad. 'Le déanaí cuireadh dlí níos géire trí Phairlimint Bhaile Átha Cliath a choscann ar dhuine dul thar lear le staidéar a dhéanamh. Na daoine a fhágáil in aineolas ar airteagail a gcréidimh, nó eiricigh a dhéanamh astu, an t-aon chuspóir amháin atá leis seo.' Mar a rinne sé sa chéad litir, impíonn sé ar an bPápa áiteamh ar na prionsaí Caitliceacha dul crua ar an bPrionsa Oráisteach faoiseamh a thabhairt dos na Caitlicigh. 'Tá an chontúirt ann go bhfeicfimid an tír agus an creideamh caillte inti.' B'shin é a bhreith dheireannach ar chás na hÉireann. Agus ní dhearna an Róimh faillí i gcás an tseaneaspaig bhoicht seo: sa litir chéanna gabhann sé buíochas leo as céad

scudi a chur chuige. Cúig bliana déag a bhí caite aige ar deoraíocht agus é beo bocht nuair a fuair sé bás sa bhliain 1704.

An teaspag nua

De thoradh dlithe 1696-97 bhí an Phairlimint sásta go raibh na hOird briste acu. Ní raibh le déanamh acu mar sin ach tabhairt níos déine faoin ngnáthchléir. Chuaigh na péindlithe i ndéine agus ba ghéire iad na spiairí. Ardaíodh tuarastal an spiaire agus tugadh £50 don duine a tháinig ar easpag. Sa bhliain 1708 ainmníodh Ambros Mac Diarmada ina Easpag ar Ailfionn. Ar eagla go bhfaigheadh spiairí gaoth an fhocail coinníodh an tainmniúchán faoi rún agus is go príobháideach a h-oirníodh é sa Róimh ag duine des na cairdinéil. De shliocht ársa Gael ab ea an teaspag nua. Oileadh é i Mainistir na nDoiminiceánach ag Tuilsc, Co Ros Cómáin. Bhí sé ina Mháistir le Diacht agus chaith sé blianta ag múineadh diagachta i gcoláiste Ss. Sixtus agus Clement sa Róimh. Bhí sé ina phrior ar an mainistir sin ó 1686 go 1689. Ina dhiaidh sin chaith sé tamall in Eaglais S. Maria Maggiore.

An turas abhaile

Ag teacht tré Londain dó agus é ar a bhealach abhaile gabhadh é. Lig sé air gurbh lodálach é agus bhí pas aige a dúirt gurbh é Fillipo Gherardini é. Sagart a shéan a chreideamh a bhí ina theangaire ag muintir Londain ach níor sceith an fear seo ar an easpag. Agus é réidh leis an teangaire cuireadh fios air ag duine des na hoifigigh. Thug an fear seo gach eolas dó ar a shaol ó rinneadh sagart de. D'inis sé dó an lá is an áit a ndearnadh easpag de. Agus bhí ainm an chairdineil a d'oirnigh é aige freisin. Caitheadh isteach i bpriosún é ar an bpointe. Rinne taidhleoir na Venéise idirghuí ar a shon leis na húdarais. Ceithre mhí ina dhiaidh sin chuir an taidhleoir litir chuig Grimaldi, an Nuncio sa Bhruiséal – is faoi siúd a bhí cúram na heaglaise in Éirinn. 'Tá Gherardini slán i mo theach féin agam,' a deir sé. 'Tá mé ag iarraidh bealach abhaile a fháil dó chomh luath agus is féidir mar tá sé thar a bheith contúirteach dó féin agus dá chompánaigh anseo. Cheana féin tá pas faighte agam dóibh agus beidh mé ag cuidiú leo go bhfágann siad an tír.' Ligeadh an teaspag saor ar choinníoll go bhfágfadh sé an Ríocht taobh istigh de sé lá.

An díbirt

Le linn samradh agus fómhar na bliana 1708 bhí tréimhsí síochána ann agus ní raibh na dlithe chomh géar agus a bhí. Rug an tInternuncio ar an bhfaill seo le sagairt a chur abhaile ón Mór-roinn. Tá dhá rud spéisiúla le hinsint ag an Nuncio faoin bhfeachtas seo aige. Agus é ag cur ina luí ar na sagairt an dualgas a bhí orthu dul arais go hÉirinn, deir sé go bhfuair sé an-chabhair ó Easpag Ailfinne, Ambros Mac Diarmada. Bhí an oiread sin sagart toilteanach filleadh ar a dtír de bharr na bolscaireachta seo nach raibh táille an bháid aige do go leor acu. Bhí an teaspag sa

Lobháin faoin am seo. Leis na Doiminiceánaigh a d'fhan sé. Ach bhí siadsan chomh bocht sin nár bheag orthu aon duine amháin eile sa mbreis. Mar sin nuair a thug na Premonstratensigh i dTongerloot cuireadh dó teacht agus fanacht leo ghlac sé leis an gcuireadh uathu. Ardtreas a gcuirfí ina leith dá dtabharfadh sé faoi dhul arais don dara huair ach bhí sé socraithe aige cheana féin gabháil siar thar na farraigí arís agus Ailfionn a bhaint amach. Mar sin d'fhan sé i dTongerloot fad is a bhí sé ag feitheamh ar phas nua, ón Impire.

Siar arís
Chuir an Nuncio Grimaldi litir chuig an Róimh, 26 Meán Fómhair 1709, agus dhealródh sé ón litir sin gur fhág an teaspag an Ollainn ar long. Ar an dturas dóibh ba mhinic a thug foghlaithe mara leis an bhFrainc fúthu. Chaill an teaspag a raibh de bhagáiste aige agus ba é deireadh an scéil é go raibh air a pháipéir féin a chaitheamh isteach sa bhfarraige. Agus dhá lá is tríocha caite ar an bhfarraige aige, bhain sé Corcaigh amach. I 1710 scríobhann sé faoin ainm de Witt. Bhí go leor daoine as an Mór-roinn agus sa Róimh féin ar an dtuairim nár cheart easpaig nua a oirniú nuair nach raibh sé ar a gcumas fáil isteach sa tír. Ba leor, dar leo, easpag in aghaidh na cúige. Bhí Mac Diarmada go tréan in aghaidh na tuairime sin. Ar 15 Samhain 1714 chuir sé litir chuig an Róimh. Gabhann sé buíochas leis an Róimh as na heaspaig nua a h-oirníodh. Ba iad na heaspaig a thug na Caitlicigh slán tríd an ghéarleanúint, déir sé, agus molann sé iad an sár-obair atá déanta acu. Sa bhliain sin crochadh fiche duine i mBaile Átha Cliath. 'Coireanna in aghaidh an stáit' a cuireadh ina leith. Bhí an ghéar-leanúint as siúl arís. 'Ní abróidh mé ach an méid seo: má chuireann siad na dlithe i bhfeidhm atá á mbagairt acu orainn, níl i ndán dúinn ach an priosún fad a mhairimid. Cheana féin tá go leor d'ár misnéirí sa phriosún acu.' Sin mar a chonaic sé an ghéarleanúint úr seo in iarthar na hÉireann.

Cúram easpaig
I mí Mhárta sa bhliain dár gcionn scríobhann sé chuig Vincenzo Santini, an Nuncio nua sa Bhruiséal. I dtosach deir sé go bhfuil géarleanúint 1714 thart – bhí an Bhanríon Áine básaithe faoi seo. Ansin tugann sé cuntas ar a dheoise ó tháinig sé ann seacht mbliana roimhe sin. Na sagairt a bhí sa deoise aige, bhí siad ar fheabhas cé is móite de dhuine amháin acu. Agus an pobal, thug siad a raibh ar a gcumas dos na sagairt. Beirt fhear is tríocha a d'oirnigh sé i rith na seacht mbliana. Chuaigh a leath acu seo le deoise Ailfinne. Ach ina ainneoin sin, agus na sagairt a tháinig anoir thar farraige chuige a chur san áireamh, duirt sé nach raibh a dhóthain sagart aige le cúram ceart a thabairt dá phobal. Ag féachaint dó ar na fir óga a chuaigh leis an sagartóireacht, mhol sé go mbainfí níos mó úsáide as choláistí eaglasta na Mór-roinne. Níl raibh sé sásta leis an gcoláiste i bParis. 'B'fhearr,' deir sé, 'cuid des na micléinn a aistriú ó Pharis mar gur mhór an cathú a bhí ar na fir seo fanacht ansin tréis iad a oirniú.'

Agus sagairt Pharis, nuair a d'fhill siad, níor shocraigh siad síos riamh ach iad ag iarraidh dhul arais. Níorbh amhlaidh d'fhormhór na sagart a tháinig ó cholaistí eile.'

I 1717 fuair an tEaspag Mac Diarmada bás in aice le Cluain Tuaiscirt, Co Ros Comáin. Meitheamh na bliana sin oirníodh Cabritius Ó Ceallaigh i nGlinsce, ag Éamonn, Easpag Chluain Fearta. Bhí ré ba ghéire na bpéindlithe thart.

Glinsk Castle, a place of refuge for some of the bishops of Elphin during the penal era.

PART III

Clergy and Religious

Priests of Elphin 1661-1835

CLERGY LISTS for Catholic priests are very difficult to construct until the start of the publication of the *Irish Catholic Directory* in 1836. The following lists are based on a number of already published lists, mostly in various issues of *Collectanea Hibernica* and *Archivium Hibernicum* and other sources, most of which are listed in the bibliography at the end of this book. Much of the research on these lists was done by Fr Hugh Fenning OP, St Mary's, Tallaght, Dublin. We owe him a great debt of gratitude for his work on the eighteenth century period in particular.

The lists here are arranged on a parish basis which hopefully will be of interest to the reader, but which results in the same clergy names being repeated in various parishes. Each individual parish is listed (seventy-nine in all) but these were sometimes grouped to form unions, the constituent parishes of which changed over time. Two parishes have the same name, Ballinakill, one in county Sligo and the other in county Galway. This makes it difficult, when examining some clergy lists, to be certain which parish a particular priest was assigned to. A similar problem exists for two county Roscommon parishes, Killukin and Killucan. In some of the clergy lists used as sources, priests are named without any parish. These are listed at the end of the parishes with the dates as available.

Throughout the lists different titles were used for the priest in charge of a parish and these are abbreviated here as follows:
adm = administrator, cc = curate, co = coadjutor, pa = pastor, per v = perpetual vicar, preb = prebbendary, pro v = pro vicar, pp = parish priest, r = rector, v = vicar.

Aghanagh: Thadeus McDonnogh OP pro v 1668 (with Tawnagh, Kilmacallan and Killadoon). Malachy Brehoane pa 1683. Owen Conmy (alias Knuohan), pp 1704. Morish Brahany 1731 (with Killmacallan and Tawnagh). Michael Reynolds OP 1760-?1785. Roger O'Connor 1785. Terence M'Sweeny pp 1835. Thomas O'Connor cc 1835.

Ahamlish: Patrick O'Hohy v 1661, pp 1668. Bryan Heart pp 1704. Roger O'Connor 1786. Roger Birne 1796-1814. Stephen Fallon 1814-1818. Patrick Bligh v 1812. John Hanly pa 1818-1826. John McHugh pp 1826-1836. Dominick Noon cc 1835.

Ahascragh: Edmund O'Teige r 1661. Thady Kerelly pa 1683. Dermot Gately v 1683. Richard Betagh pp 1704 (with Killian). Hugh Morgan 1749. Denis Naughten 1756. James Chapman pa 1779, 1786. John Brennan 1810. James O'Connor pp 1835. John Geraghty cc 1835.

Ardcarne: Bernard Beirne per v 1668 (with Tumna and Kilbryan). Hugh Tiernane pa 1683. Hugh McDermott pp 1704, 1711. Conor Rogers pp 1731. Martin Talbot 1786. Thady Conry 1810, 1812. Bernard McManus v 1812. Thomas Conry pa 1818. Patrick O'Gara pp 1835. Patrick Kelly cc 1835.

Athleague: Bernard O'Murily v 1661, per v 1668. Daniel Ceogra v 1683. Bartholomew Croghan listed as priest in 1683 no parish, pp 1704. Philip Higgins 1704 (no parish, living in Athleague), pp 1712. Thady McDermott r 1739, 1748. Bernard McDermott OP pp 1756, pp 1762. Eugene Kilcommon pa 1779, pp 1786. Eugeen Tristan OSA 1805, 1810, 1812, 1818, 1835 (d 1837). John Kine cc 1835.

Aughrim: Constantine O'Dubhilly v 1661, per v 1668. Terentius Connor cc 1683. John Berne pp 1704, 1731. Patrick Beirn 1749 (will dated 1776, residing in Aughrim). John Green pa 1779, 1786. Nicholas Green 1810. James Green 1812. Michael Cahill adm 1818. Thomas King pp 1835.

Ballinakill (Sligo): Cornelius O'Sumaghan acting pp 1668 (with Ballysumaghan, Drumcolumb and Kilross). Cornelius Brehane pa 1683. Malachy Brehune pp 1704 (with Kilmacallan). Eugene O'Connor pa 1739, 1748. James Phegny (Fegny) 1749.

Ballinakill (Galway): Roger Noone pp 1683. Carbery Kelly pp 1704, 1731, (d 1731). Dominic Kelly pp 1756, 1762. Luke Reiney pa 1779, 1786, 1790. Bernard Kelly 1786. Patrick Burke 1810, 1812. James Quinn adm 1812. Peter O'Connor adm 1818. Patrick Grehan pp, Andrew Egan cc, Patrick McDermott cc 1835 (with Kilcroan).

Ballintubber: William O'Mulrennin r 1661. Dermot Hanly preb 1668. Logh McDonnagh pp 1704 (with Drumatemple). Cormac McDonagh pp 1731 (with Ogulla) 1748, 1749. Michael O'Connor 1748. Eugeen Flynn pa 1810. Thomas Dillon pp 1835.

Ballysumaghan: Cornelius O'Sumaghan acting pp 1668 (with Ballinakill, Drumcolumb and Kilross). Henry Haert pa 1683 (with Kilross). Bryan Higgins pp 1704, 1712 (with Kilross). Ó. Gallagher friar 1712. Thomas Rutledge friar 1712. James Banaghan 1743 (with Kilross).

Baslick: Thady O'Mulrenin per v 1668 (with Kilkeevan). James Mulruine (Renyn) pp 1704, died before 1715. Richard Prendergast pp 1731, 1748, 1756. Michael Gorman pa 1779. John O'Callaghan pa 1810, 1812, pp 1835. Michael Flood cc 1835.

Boyle: John O'Sarcoide (Sherkott) pp 1661, v 1668 (since c. 1640), listed 1683. Milerus Sarcoide (pa Alilane 1683) pp 1704. Charles McDermott OFM pp 1731. Peter Connoghton 1731. Andrew O'Beirn pa 1739, 1749, listed 1756 (will dated 1773). Michael O'Connor 1748. James Tyrrell pa 1784, pp 1786. Francis Kelly co 1784, (d. 1784). James Bradley pa 1810, 1812. Michael Nerhney 1812. Michael Devine pp 1835. Edward Feeny cc 1835.

Bumlin: Edmund Hanly pp 1683 (with Kiltrustan). Pat Digginnan pp 1704 (with Kiltrustan), 1711 (with Kiltrustan). Carby O'Beirne 1748 (with Kiltrustan). James Kelly pp (Strokestown) pa 1779, 1786, pa 1810. John Hurly co 1779. William Dolan pa 1818 (Strokestown) (will dated 1833). Michael McDermott pp 1835 (Strokestown). Michael Walker cc 1835.

Calry: Malachy Conry preb 1668 (with Drumcliff). Roger Hart per v 1668 (with Minbrisg), pa (of Carbry) 1683. Denis Kerrigan pp 1704 (with Sligo). Thomas Brennan friar 1743 (with Sligo).

Cam: Nicholas McLea MD v 1661, per v 1668. Daniel Concannon pp 1704, died before 1715. Patrick Coniffe OSA 1749. John Glennon O Carm (d. 1773). Michael Garvey 1810, 1812, 1818 (with Kiltoom). Terrence G. O'Neill cc 1830. Michael McLoughlin cc 1835.

Clonard: Magonius Morishy (M'Morris) per v 1683 (with Kilrudane).

Clooncraf: Roger O'Flancy [Glancy] procurator of the prebendary 1661. Dermot Cahan preb 1668. Donaldus Gunane pp 1704 (with Creeve). Patrick Reynolds pp 1704 (half with Kilmore), 1731 (with Kilmore). Francis Rorke 1749.

Cloonfinlogh: Hugh Mac Egan v 1661. Thadaeus Gneale pp 1683 (with Lissonuffy). John Fagon pp 1704. John Egan 1711. Patrick Duffy 1748 (with Lissonuffy) (d. 1763).

Cloonigormican: William Hanly per v 1683, pp 1704, died before 1715. Chris Dillon pp 1704 (with Oran). Patrick Keen pp 1731. Patrick Conry 1748 (with Oran).

Cloontuskert: Cormacus Cahane (Keane) pa 1683 (with Kilgefin). Edmund Gormley (priest 1683, no parish) pp 1704 (with Kilteevan), died before 1715. Boetius Egan 1748, pp 1756. Thomas Charleton pa 1779. Richard Rorke OSA 1810.

Corraghlan: Edmund O'Hanly r 1661.

Creeve: Donaldus Gunane pp 1683, pp 1704 (with Clooncraff), died before 1715. Con Groork pp 1731. Patrick Bligh 1812 (will dated 1829). Henry Brennan pp 1835.

Donamon: Roger Noone pp 1704 (with Kilbegnet).

Drum: Theadeus Naghten snr substitute 1668. James Killian per v 1668. Hugh Gaffy pp d 1703. Patrick Flyn pp 1704 (with St Peter's). William Keogh cc 1741, pp (with St Peter's).

Drumatemple: Logh McDonnagh pp 1704 (with Ballintubber).

Drumcliff: Malachy Conry per v 1668 (with Calry). Brian King co. Daniel Lydaw (possibly Liddane, ord 1668) c. 1698. Hugh Ternane pp 1704. Philip Costello pp 1760-1767 (d 1767). Cormack Teeny (Feeny) pp 1704, 1731. Thady McMurra friar 1743. James

Lyons 1765, 1786. Bernard O'Berne pp 1766, 1782, 1786, 1810, pa 1812 (d 1814). Thomas O'Flynn cc (d 1810). John Barry v 1812. Roger Burn pp 1818, (d 1832). M Feeny cc 1832. Michael O'Callaghan pp 1832-1842. Thomas Walker cc 1835. (Malachy Brenan pp Magheron 1835.)

Drumcolumb: Cornelius O'Sumaghan acting pp 1668 (with Ballysumaghan, Balli-nakill and Kilross). Darby Brennan pp 1755-1782 (with Kilmacallan). Bryan Kelly pp 1782-1803 (with Kilmacallan). James Hester 1803-1836 (with Kilmacallan).

Dysart: Theadeus Naghten jnr pp 1668 (with Rahara). Malachy Fallon pa 1683. Nicholas Lea pp 1704 (with Taughboy). James O'Fallon pa 1756. Peter Coniffe pp 1776-1821. Michael McDermott 1821-1826. Andrew M'Cann pp 1826-1850.

Eastersnow: Dermot O'Lenaghan per v 1668 (with Killummod). Fergal Berne per v 1683, pp 1704 (with Killcola). Miles Brennan pp 1731 (with Killcola). John Morris pa 1784 (with Killcola), 1812.

Elphin: Eurialius Higgins v (St Mary's) 1683, pp 1704. ? Walter Burke 1683. Owen Birn friar, Terence Ganan pp 1731. Anthony Flaherty OFM pp 1748. Anthony O'Hanly OFM 1748. Redmund Gaffry 1765, listed 1786. Anthony Garrahan OFM cc 1803. Roger O'Connor (will dated 1809). Mordecai Fahy 1810, 1812, 1818, 1835. Michael Egan cc, William Hughes cc 1835.

Fuerty: Hilary O'Conry preb 1661. Thomas O'Murry per v 1668 (with Killmean). Richard Batagh pa 1683. Edmund Kelly (canon 1683, no parish) pp 1704, 1711, a friar, died before 1715. Francis Hurly friar 1712. Bartholomew Croghan 1715, Hugh Nereny pa 1739. Richard Lynch 1748, pp 1756 (d 1778). Edmund French pa 1779. Patrick Brennan pp 1789-1795. Bartholomew Keelty OP pp 1805, 1810, 1812, 1818 (d 1830). Owen Kennedy pp 1835. Cornelius Kielty cc 1835.

Kilbegnet: William O'Hirily preb 1661. Cormac Igoe preb 1668, pp 1683. Roger Noone pp 1704 (with Donamon). Roger Moore friar 1712. Bernard Hopkins pa 1739. Ambrose McDermott OP 1756 (d 1760). John Kelly pa 1779. John Tighe OP 1779. Patrick Reiny 1786, 1790, 1810, 1812, 1818. Michael Dwyer pp 1835 (will dated 1841).

Kilbride: Edmond Conry pp 1704 (with Killgefin), 1711. John Conry pp 1731, 1748 (with Kilgefin). James Hurly pp 1779-1802 (d 1802). John Kelly 1810, 1812.

Kilbryan: Bernard Beirne 1668 (with Tumna and Ardcarne). Donatus Callaghane pa 1683. Fergus Diginane pp 1704.

Kilcooley: Feargatius Conreus pa 1683. Cormac Cahane (Keane) pp 1704 (with Killukin and Ogulla), 1711 (given as Killiroly). Bernard Croghan pp 1788-1830 (with Killukin and Ogulla). Michael Lennon pp, Thomas Gilleran cc 1835.

Kilcorkey: Edmund O'Flannigan v 1661, 1668, per v 1683. Darby Keirne pp 1704.

Patrick Morvurnagh 1748. Patrick Gordon 1748. Thomas Teige 1786. Michael Gorman 1790. Anthony Garrahan OFM 1805, 1810 1812 (d 1835). Michael Harrington cc 1835.

Kilcroan: Owen Reily pp 1704. Luke Reiny 1786 (d c.1800) (with Ballinakill). Patrick Burke 1810 (with Ballinakill, Galway). Patrick Grehan pp, Andrew Egan cc, Patrick McDermott cc 1835 (with Ballinakill, Galway).

Kilgefin: Edmund O'Hanly preb 1668 (given as Kilgoglin). Cormacus Cahane (Keane) pa 1683 (with Cloontuskert). Edmond Conry pp 1704 (with Kilbride). Farrell Higgins pp 1704. John Conry 1748 (with Kilbride). John Hanley pp, Bartly Kieher cc, John Brenan cc 1835.

Kilglass: Terrence Neary pa 1683, pp 1704, died before 1715. Terence Rory 1711. ...Gebolan 1715. Charles Conry 1748, 1749, listed 1756. Hugh Kelly pa 1779, 1786. James Magee 1782. Patrick Hanly 1810, 1812. Denis Kelly v 1812. Maurice Gately adm 1818. Brian McDermott pp, Michael Quin cc 1835.

Kilkeevan: Thady O'Mulrenin (procurator of the dean) 1661, per v 1668 (with Baslick). James Renyn (Mulruine) per v 1683. Teige McDonogh pp 1704, 1731. Dominic Mulrenen 1748, 1749. John O'Connor 1762. Dermot Gorman pa 1779, 1786. Charles O'Conor 1789-1799. Patrick Brennan adm 1790. Henry McDermott 1810, pa 1812, pp 1835. Gerard O'Gara v 1812. John Boyde cc, Patrick McDermott cc 1835.

Killadoon: Thadeus McDonnogh OP pro v 1668 (with Aghanagh, Kilmacallan and Tawnagh). Peter Feighny pp 1704, 1712. Dominic O'Connor OP prior 1748.

Killaspugbrone: Bernard O'Comalane (aged 80) pp 1668 (with Kilmacowen). John Dugan pp 1704 (with Kilmacowen). David O'Flyn 1743 (with Kilmacowen), pp 1748 (with Kilmacowen). Malachy Keelty 1786 (with Kilmacowen).

Killcola: Fergal Berne pp 1704 (with Eastersnow). Miles Brennan pp 1731 (with Eastersnow). John Morris pa 1784 (with Eastersnow), 1786.

Killeroran: Dermot Gately per v 1668 (with Killian). Denis Bryan pp 1704. Patrick McDermott pp, Patrick Brennan cc, Patrick M'Gaurn cc 1835 (with Killian).

Killian: John O'Tumulty v 1661. Dermot Gately per v 1668 (with Killeroran). Richard Betagh pp 1704 (with Ahascragh). Patrick McDermott pa 1810, 1812, pp 1818, 1835. Patrick Brennan cc, Patrick M'Gauran cc 1835 (with Killeroran).

Killinvoy: Donagh McLagha v 1661, per v 1668 (with St John's). Cornelius Farrell pa 1683. Lawrence Geraghty pp 1704 (with St John's). Martin Owen O'Connor OSA (d 1729, buried Killinvoy cemetery). Andrew Egan pa 1739, 1748. Charles McDermott pa 1779, 1810. John Fitzgerald pa 1818 (with St John's), pp 1835 (with Kilmean, St John's and Rahara). Peter Cunniffe cc, John Fitzgerald jnr cc 1835.

Killosolan: Edmund Mac Keige v 1661, per v 1668. John Mac Teigge pa 1683. Bryan Flyn pp 1704. Edward Flynn pp 1731. Daniel O'Kelly 1748, 1756, 1768 (year of his will). Patrick Bitagh O Carm, Patrick Prendergast O Carm 1779. Edmund Kelly pa 1779, 1786. Charles McDermottroe pa 1812. John Morris pp 1835.

Killucan: William Brady 1810, pa 1818. Peter O'Connor pp, John O'Brien cc, Michael M'Grath cc 1835 (also Croghan and Ballinameen).

Killukin: Thomas O'Mulvihill preb 1661. James Mac Egan preb 1668. Cormac Keane (Cahane) pp 1704 (with Kilcooley and Ogulla). Nicholas Berne pp 1704, 1731. Mathias Forester cc 1731, 1749, listed 1756 (d 1779). Charles McDermott OFM 1748. Bernard Croghan pp 1788-1830 (with Ogulla and Kilcooley).

Killummod: Dermot O'Lenaghan v 1661, per v 1668 (with Eastersnow). Nicholas Beirne pp 1731. Malachy Donnelen 1786.

Kilmacallan: Thadeus McDonnogh OP pro v 1668 (with Aghanagh Kiladoon and Tawnagh). Malachy Brehune pp 1704 (with Ballinakill). Morish Brahany pp 1731 (with Tawnagh and Aghanagh). J. Connoghan friar 1749. Darby Brennan pp 1755-1782 (with Drumcolumb), (d 1782). Bryan Kelly pp 1782-1803 (with Drumcolumb), (d 1803). James Hester pp 1803-1836 (d. 1836). Felix Connolly cc, Terence Kenny cc 1835.

Kilmacowen: Bernard O'Comalane (aged 80) pp 1668 (with Killaspugbrone). John Dugan pp 1704 (with Killaspugbrone). David O'Flyn 1743 (with Killaspugbrone), pp 1748 (with Killaspugbrone). Malachy Keelty 1786 (with Killaspugbrone).

Kilmactranny: Thadeus MacDermottroe v 1661, per v 1668 (with Shancough). Donatus Dermott pa 1683, pp 1704 (with Shancough), 1712 (with Shancough). Brian McDermottroe 1712. Garrett Cullican friar (at Geevagh) 1712. Peter O'Connor 1748, 1749. James Hart 1812. Bernard McManus pa 1818, pp 1835 (d 1842). Michael Spellman cc 1835.

Kilmacumsy: Hugh O'Cunigane per v 1668 (with Shankill). Roger Brennan pp 1704 (with Shankill).

Kilmean: Thomas O'Murry v 1661, per v 1668 (with Fuerty). Theadeus Naghten jnr pa 1683. Thady Cornelly (Kerelly) pp 1704 (with Rahara), 1731. Patrick Mulligan 1721 (erected plaque at Toberrogue well). Francis Naughten 1748. Andrew Egan 1756. John Berne (OP) pp 1805, 1810. John Fitzgerald snr pp, John Fitzgerald jnr cc, Peter Cunniff cc 1835 (with Killinvoy, St John's and Rahara).

Kilmore: Roger Glanchy pp 1668. John Hanly (ord 1668) pa 1683. Cornelius (Carbry) Kelly (canon vf 1683, no parish) pp 1704. Patrick Reynolds pp 1704 (with Clooncraf), 1731 (with Clooncraf). James Keyn 1748. Thomas Cloghor 1748, (d Sligo 1774). (James) Riley 1749 (d 1760, age 72). Richard Martin 1749 (d 1770). James O'Beirne 1810, 1812. Edward Keogh pp, Patrick Hanly cc 1835.

Kilnamannagh: Donagh Beirne per v 1668 (with Tibohine). Terrence M'Gragh pp 1704 (with Tibohine), 1731. Edmund Lavin 1731 (with Tibohine). Jerome Duignan OP prior (Cloonshanville) 1748.

Kilross: Cornelius O'Sumaghan (with Ballinakill, Drumcolumb and Ballysumaghan), acting pp 1668. Henry Haert pa 1683 (with Ballysumaghan). Bryan Higgins 1712 (with Ballysumaghan). James Banaghan 1743 (with Ballysumaghan). Patrick Duffy pp 1812 (d 1831). Luke Cullinan pp 1831-1850.

Kilrudane: Magonius Morishy (M'Morris) per v (with Clunarde) 1683. Owen Conner pp 1704. Francis Dillon pp 1704, died before 1715.

Kilteevan: Dermot Hanly pa 1668. Edmund Gormley (priest 1683, no parish) pp 1704 (with Cloontuskert), died before 1715. Michael Feely 1731. Bernard O'Connor 1748 (with Roscommon). Lawrence O'Connor 1812.

Kiltoom: John O'Tumulty pp 1668. Bernard Donnell per v 1683. Bryan Doyle pp 1704, died before 1715. Anthony O'Flynn pa 1739, 1748. John Kelly pp 1771-1783. John Glennon pp 1783-1810. Michael Garvey pp 1810-1834 (with Cam). Terence G. O'Neill pp 1834-1837 (d 1837).

Kiltrustan: James Mac Egan v 1661. Edmund Hanly pp 1683 (with Bumlin). Pat Digginnan 1704 (with Bumlin), 1711 (with Bumlin). Carby O'Beirne 1748 (with Bumlin). Hugh Flynn 1756. Richard Rorke OSA pp 1805.

Lissonuffy: Thadaeus Gneale pp 1683 (with Cloonfinlogh), pp 1704. Thady McGreah 1711. Patrick Duffy 1748, 1756 (with Cloonfinlogh), (d 1763). Bryan MacDermottroe pa 1779. William Dolan 1810, pa 1812. John Lighe pp, Michael Moran cc 1835.

Loughglynn: Edmund Timothy 1748. Redmond Tressy pp 1779. Henry Clifford pp 1786. John Fitzgerald 1810, 1812. William Brady pp, Thomas Kelly cc, Michael M'Garrahy cc 1835.

Ogulla: Cormac Keane (Cahane) pp 1704 (with Kilcooly and Killukin). Cormack Mc Donagh pp 1731. Bernard O'Connor 1748, listed 1756. William Kelly pa 1779, pp 1786. Bernard Croghan pp 1788-1830 (with Killukin and Kilcooley).

Oran: James O'Finaghty preb 1661. William Hanly 1684 (erected plaque at well). Chris Dillon pp 1704 (with Cloonigormican). Patrick Conry pa 1739, 1748 (with Cloonygormican), listed 1756. Michael McDermottroe 1762. Matthew Mahon pa 1779. Denis O'Brien, friar (will dated 1804). Matthew May 1810, 1812. Patrick Hanley pp 1835.

Rahara: Laurence O'Fallon v 1661. Theadeus Naghten jnr pp 1668 (with Dysart). Hugh Gaffy pa 1683. Thady Cornelly (Kerelly) pp 1704 (with Kilmean). John Naughton pa 1739, 1749, 1756. Martin Geraghty pa 1779.

Roscommon: Thomas O'Donnellan v 1661. Donatus Kelly pa 1683. William Keogh pp 1704, 1711 (d 1741). Peter Conry 1731. Bernard O'Connor 1748 (with Kilteevan). Michael ..., v 1748. Matthias O'Connor 1757, 1762 (d 1763). John O'Connor pa 1779, 1786 (d 1794). James Winster co 1779. Eugene Kelly pp 1790-1801. Patrick Brennan 1801 (d 1803). George Plunkett 1803-1815. James Crump v 1812. Lawrence O'Connor pp 1815, 1818 (d 1819). Michael Mc Dermott pp 1819-1821. John Madden pp 1822, 1835 (d 1853). Michael Smyth cc, Michael M'Gowan cc 1835.

Shancough: Cornelius O'Sumaghan v 1661. Thadeus MacDermottroe per v 1668 (with Kilmactranny). Donatus Dermott pp 1704 (with Kilmactranny), 1712 (with Kilmactranny).

Shankill: Hugh O'Cunigane pa 1661, per v 1668 (with Killmacumsey). Roger Brennan pp 1704 (with Killmacumsey).

Sligo: Charles O'Tully r 1661, r 1668. Eugene Mihane pp 1679, pa 1683. Denis Kerrigan cc 1698, pp 1704 (with Calry), 1712. Michael McDonnagh, 1731, 1743. William McDonnagh, Thomas Brennan friar 1731, 1743 (with Calry). James Feighney OP 1743. Ambrose Gilligan OP 1743. Michael Killhauley OP 1743. James Scanlon OP 1743. John Gildea OP 1743. Mathias O'Connor 1743, cc 1748. John Flynn pa 1779, pp to 1809. John Moore v 1812. James Dunlevy pp 1832, pp 1835 adm (d 1838). Owen Feeny cc, Barth Hester cc, Edward Henry cc, 1835.

St John's: Donagh McLagha 1668 (with Killinvoy). Eugenius Lagh pa 1683. Lawrence Geraghty pp 1704 (with Killinvoy), 1731. Dominick Doyle friar 1731. Andrew Egan 1731. John Naughton 1731. Dermot Keelty pa 1739, 1748. Hugh Gunn 1756. Patrick Tully pa 1779, (d 1796). John O'Flyn 1786. Stephen Fallon 1810, 1812. John Fitzgerald pa 1818 (with Killinvoy), pp 1835. John Fitzgerald jnr cc, Peter Cuniffe cc 1835 (with Kilmean, Killinvoy and Rahara).

St Peter's: Terrence M'Gragh pa 1683. Patrick Flyn pp 1704 (with Drum). Walter Kelly pp 1739. William Keogh pp c. 1741 (with Drum), (d 1741). Edmund O'Fallon 1756, pp 1762. Redmond Fallon pa 1779 (d 1784). Edmund French 1786. Walter Walsh 1810, pa 1812, adm 1818. John Fallon (OP) v 1812. Martin O'Reilly pp, Maurice Nolan cc, Joseph M'Tucker cc 1835.

Tarmonbarry: Hugh Colly procurator of the prebendary 1668. Bryan Kelly pp 1704. Hugh Cox pp 1731. Hugh Nerney 1748, 1749, listed 1756 (d 1763). Thaddaeus Mullin 1810 (will dated 1811). Maurice Gately v 1812. James McNally pp 1835.

Taughboy: James McLea v 1661, per v 1668. Nicholas McLea (possibly ord 1668) pa 1683, pp 1704 (with Dysart). Bryan O'Fallon friar (will dated 1801).

Tawnagh: Thady McDonagh OP pro v 1668 (with Aghanagh, Kilmacallan, and Kiladoon). Morish Brehune pp 1704, 1731 (with Kilmacallan and Aghanagh). James Hester 1810, 1812. Nicholas Leonard 1812.

Tibohine: Donagh O'Beirne r 1661, per v 1668 (with Kilnamannagh), per v 1683. Manus M'Morris pp 1704. Anthony Ternan friar 1731. Terrence M'Gragh pp 1704 (part of, with Kilnamannagh), 1731 (with Kilnamannagh). Edmund Lavin 1731 (with Kilnamannagh), 1748, listed 1756. Edmund Timothy 1731, 1749. A. Duffy friar (OP) 1749, Bartholomew Kelly pp Frenchpark 1774. Patrick Flynn v 1812. William Costello pa 1818. Michael McDonagh pp, Owen Madden cc 1835.

Tisrara: Ambrose Fallon pp 1704 (pp of St Brigid's (not identified) in 1739). Francis Hanly 1739, 1748, 1749, 1756 (d 1761). John Madden pp 1761-1767. Thomas McDonnell pp 1767-1786. Thomas Kelly pp 1786-1828. Peter Kirwan pp 1828-1842.

Tumna: Eugene O'Dunneaghair v 1661. Bernard Beirne 1668 (with Ardcarne and Kilbryan). Donatus Bryne pa 1683. Thady Murry pp 1704. R. Dolan 1749.

Priests listed without a parish:
Charles Horan no parish 1668; Felix McDonagh ord 1668, pa Killmelane 1683; Thomas Higgins vg 1661 to 1688; Florence Donellene archdeacon 1683; John Hanly Killtridenis 1683; Hugh Kilmurry priest 1683; Gerordus Fearell priest 1683; Dominick McDermottroe pp Killordow 1704; Fr Burke friar 1712 county Roscommon; Phelim Knofin friar 1743; Bernard Lyne vg in 1650 (Mcalleghany), listed 1712 friar in county Galway; Teig Burke friar in county Galway 1712; Bryan Comn friar in county Galway 1712; James McKillcumy friar in county Galway 1712; Terence Gannon priest since 1704, listed 1715, no parish.

Dominican Friars of Roscommon and Cloonshanville 1683-1711
Roscommon: Michael O'Connor 1684-89; John Brukan 1684-1702; John Berne 1684-6; John Fiiny 1684-96; John Keogh 1684-88; Dominic O'Connor 1684-86, 1695-1702; Dominic Horan 1684; Peter Flynn 1684-89; James Flanagan 1684-96; Patrick Branan 1684-96; Ambrose Fitzgerald 1684-86; Patrick Hart 1684; Peter Hanly 1684; Pater Gavaghan 1684-89; Patrick Dur 1684; Michael Walsh 1684-1702; Dominic Rory 1684; Felix McDowell 1686, 1689; Hugh Flaherty 1686-1702; James Filane 1686; Patrick Plunkett 1686; Patrick McDermott 1686; Dominic Dillon 1686; Antoninus O Teige 1686; Ambrose O'Connor 1688, 1695-6; Philip McDowell 1688; Francis Dillon 1688-9; Patrick Flynn 1688-9; Dominic Kelly 1688-9; John McDowell 1688-9; Thomas DeBurgo 1688-1702; Augustine DeBurgo 1695; Dominic Hanin 1695-1702; William DeBurgo 1704; Dominic McGuior 1704.
Cloonshanville: Bernard McDermott 1683-96; Dominic McDermottroe 1683-1703; Charles McDermott 1683-96; Cormac Corkran 1683-85; Edmond McMorishroe 1683; Peter Costello 1686; Patrick Hartt 1686; Bernard McDermott 1689; Peter McDermottroe 1689-94, 1711; Antoninus McDermottroe 1689; Michael Sharcott 1689.

Obituary List of Priests for the Twentieth Century
Beati mortui qui in Domino moriuntur

Note: Clergy lists from 1836 until 1900 can be found in the Irish Catholic Directory, published annually since 1836.

Aghanagh Parish

1905	Apr 13	Very Rev T. Gordan PP
1957	Apr 20	Very Rev Joseph Lennon Adm
1958	Aug 22	Rev Patrick Crehan CC
1969	Jan 26	Very Rev James Neary PP
1969	May 1	Very Rev Richard Gallagher PP
1985	July 7	Very Rev Thomas Canon Kilroy PP
1987	Jan 13	Rev Patrick Flynn CC

Ahamlish Parish

1907	Apr 4	Very Rev William Crofton PP
1914	Jun 12	Rev James Connaughton CC
1917	Nov 8	Very Rev M. Shannon PP
1947	Aug 17	Very Rev John Keane PP
1969	Sep 22	Rev Austin Conway CC
1969	Nov 11	Rev Peter D. Lannon CC
1973	Dec 25	Very Rev Michael Casey PP
1988	Jun 21	Rev Michael Quinn CC

Ahascragh Parish

1923	Apr 15	Very Rev Patrick Shanagher PP
1930	Jan 9	Very Rev Michael Creighton PP
1937	Mar 23	Rev Joseph O'Beirne CC
1967	Mar 28	Mgr Malachy Brennan PP
1983	Apr 25	Very Rev John Canon McManus PP
1990	Sep 8	Very Rev Joseph Smith PP

Ardcarne Parish

1903	Jan 13	Very Rev R. H. Canon Kelly PP
1903	Sep 2	Rev Martin Davis CC
1927	Jan 25	Very Rev Thomas Flanagan PP
1930	Aug 25	Very Rev Richard Morris PP
1936	Aug 22	Very Rev T. Gallagher PP

1967	Nov 23	Very Rev J. J. Canon Glynn STL PP
1975	Jan 2	Mgr Charles Kelleher PP
1975	Jun 23	Very Rev John P. Kelly PP
1993	Jan 5	Rev Thomas Fannon
1996	Jul 9	Very Rev Henry Harte PP
1998	Oct 19	Rev Francis McManamon CC

Athleague Parish

1909	Feb 20	Very Rev James Canon Casey PP
1933	Feb 16	Very Rev Michael Canon Conry PP
1937	Mar 16	Very Rev Peter Donnellan PP
1969	Jun 16	Very Rev Bernard Canon Keane PP
1975	Feb	Rev Thomas Lavin CC
1985	Jul 8	Rev Niall Molloy CC
1986	Apr 13	Very Rev Joseph Giblin PP
1995	Jan 14	Very Rev Edward Jones PP

Athlone Parish

1904	Dec 20	Rev Patrick A. Kelly CC
1917	Jun 17	Mgr James Kelly PP DD VG
1921	Apr 29	Ven Archdeacon Francis Keane PP
1936	Dec 26	Rev William J. Cox CC
1955	Mar 30	Rev John Cunniffe CC
1955	May 24	Mgr John Crowe PP VG
1955	Nov 18	Rev Michael F. Kelly CC
1967	Oct 2	Rev Michael Beirne CC
1983	Mar 21	Mgr John McCarthy PP VG
1988	Apr 13	Rev John Feeney (St Aloysius College)
1994	Jan 31	Rev Thomas Moran (St Aloysius College)
1994	Aug 30	Rev James Morrison SMA

Aughrim Parish

1924	Dec 26	Ven Archdeacon Patrick Flanagan PP
1925	Oct 20	Very Rev Thomas J. Carney PP
1935	Mar 6	Rev P. J. Mattimoe CC (Montana)
1942	Jul 1	Very Rev Patrick J. O'Flynn PP
1955	Apr 22	Very Rev Christopher Donovan PP
1967	Apr 7	Ven Archdeacon Michael J. Connellan PP
1979	Aug 23	Very Rev James Brannelly PP
1980	May 28	Rev Christopher Donlon (SPS) CC

Ballinameen Parish

1906	Jan 29	Rev John Cummins CC
1922	Apr 22	Very Rev John Canon Foley PP
1954	Dec 19	Very Rev Patrick A. Sharkey PP
1966	Apr 21	Very Rev James Duignan PP
1968	Jul 28	Very Rev John P. Kerrigan PP
1982	Oct 14	Very Rev Michael Brennan PP

Ballintubber Parish

1900	Dec 3	Very Rev Michael Hanly PP
1906	Feb 10	Rev Patrick J. Lynch CC
1917	Mar 2	Very Rev James Martin PP
1931	Aug 31	Very Rev Bartholomew Canon Donnellan PP
1951	Jan 29	Very Rev Patrick Canon Cline PP
1972	Nov 3	Very Rev Patrick Canon O'Leary PP
1981	May 21	Very Rev Joseph Gallagher PP

Ballyforan Parish

1914	Oct 21	Rev Martin McDermott CC
1921	Nov 7	Rev Francis Lannon CC
1955	Oct 23	Very Rev Patrick Canon Neary PP
1983	Mar 6	Very Rev Peter Canon Gillooly PP

Ballygar Parish

1932	Jan 23	Very Rev Martin Canon Kielty DD PP
1962	Feb 15	Rev Michael Rhattigan CC
1972	Dec 4	Very Rev John Canon Feeley PP
1982	Jul 25	Very Rev John Scally PP

Boyle Parish

1911	Jun 11	Rev Patrick McDonagh CC
1934	Nov 10	Very Rev Timothy Canon Sharkey PP
1941	Jul 7	Very Rev P. J. Canon O'Beirne PP VF
1950	Jul 29	Very Rev James B. Canon Mulligan PP
1955	Feb 13	Very Rev Patrick Canon Casey PP VF
1960	Dec 22	Rev Seamus McLoughlin, Ph D CC
1977	Jun 29	Very Rev Thomas Canon Mahon PP
1988	Jun 28	Very Rev Kevin Canon Dodd PP
1989	Jan 14	Rev Michael Gethins CC

Castlerea Parish

1900	May 30	Rev Patrick O'Beirne CC
1906	Dec 31	Mgr Patrick Hanly PP
1916	Nov 5	Rev Peter Filan CC
1924	Dec 11	Rev Thomas F. Hanley CC
1928	Jan 9	Rev Patrick Mannion CC
1937	Mar 17	Mgr Michael Harte PP VG
1945	Jun 21	Very Rev Timothy Canon Hurley DD PP
1965	Jan 2	Rev Charles Kelly CC
1970	Feb 8	Mgr Patrick Duignan PP VG
1991	Feb 1	Mgr Patrick Collins PP VG
1991	Apr 20	Rev Padraig Skeffington CC
1997	Sept 19	Very Rev Sean Canon Kelly PP

Croghan Parish

1906	Jan 10	Very Rev Charles O'Brien PP
1925	Jul 26	Rev Bernard Fahy CC
1929	May 13	Very Rev John Canon McDermott PP
1933	Jan 23	Very Rev Matthew J. O'Reilly PP
1942	Sep 1	Very Rev M. Galvin PP
1972	Oct 8	Very Rev James Canon Donnellan PP
1984	Aug 31	Very Rev James Canon Gannon PP

Drumcliff Parish

1906	Mar 7	Rev James Fallon CC
1915	Nov 20	Rev John Canon Sloane PP
1941	Dec 1	Very Rev Thomas O'Beirne PP
1959	May 28	Very Rev Patrick Canon Kelly PP
1975	Nov 2	Very Rev John J. Fleming PP
1982	Oct 20	Very Rev Toby Butler PP

Elphin Parish

1907	Jul 7	Very Patrick Canon Mannion PP
1932	May 8	Rev Daniel Carney CC
1940	Mar 28	Rev John Mannion CC
1940	June 9	Very Rev Peter Canon Butler PP
1978	Feb 3	Mgr Peter J. O'Leary PP VG
1979	Jul 10	Very Rev Charles Carr PP
1987	Feb 6	Very Rev Patrick Gearty PP

Fairymount Parish

1930	Jan 23	Very Rev John Monaghan PP
1961	May 13	Very Rev Richard Mullaney PP
1973	Mar 24	Very Rev James O'Grady PP
1999	Jan 14	Very Rev Martin Keane PP

Frenchpark Parish

1915	July 10	Very Rev James Neary PP
1922	Jan 12	Very Rev Michael Feeley PP
1932	Dec 23	Very Rev Cornelius McHugh PP
1933	Aug 31	Very Rev Nicholas Dolan PP
1947	Aug 8	Very Rev P. J. Keaney PP
1964	Jul 17	Very Rev John Donnellan PP
1980	Mar 23	Very Rev Micheal P. Canon Flynn PP
1994	Jan 25	Rev Alphonsus C. Rushe CC

Geevagh Parish

1927	Oct 26	Very Rev George Canon Coyle PP
1936	Mar 8	Rev James Kelly CC
1941	Oct 6	Rev Patrick Lavin CC
1951	Jan 19	Very Rev Michael F. Devine PP
1971	May 11	Very Rev Edmund Mee PP
1976	Oct 21	Very Rev William Regan PP
1982	Sep 16	Very Rev Edward Curran PP
1994	Nov 12	Very Rev Thomas Sharkey PP

Kilbegnet Parish

1927	Dec 29	Very Rev John Grogan PP
1938	Oct 5	Rev P. J. Murray DD CC
1956	Jul 1	Very Rev Bernard Canon Crehan PP
1975	May 19	Very Rev Michael Tarpey PP
1977	Jan 11	Very Rev Martin Lohan PP

Kilbride Parish

1921	Jan 27	Very Rev Patrick O'Hara PP
1921	July 24	Very Rev Michael J. Brennan PP
1925	Jan 5	Very Rev John J. O'Kelly PP
1937	Oct 10	Rev Michael Joseph McGloin CC
1945	Sep 24	Rev Patrick J. O'Dowd CC
1957	Sep 14	Very Rev Michael Canon O'Beirne PP
1975	Nov 6	Very Rev Timothy Quigley PP

1975	Oct 10	Rev Luke Croghan CC
1986	April 19	Very Rev Thomas Moran PP
1988	Jul 29	Rev Timothy Casey CC

Kilgefin Parish

1955	Feb 15	Very Rev Thomas Canon Hurley CC
1973	Mar 23	Very Rev Matthew Canon O'Reilly PP
1983	Feb 11	Very Rev John Egan PP
1996	Sep 12	Very Rev Thomas Martin PP

Kilglass Parish

1905	Oct 22	Rev Martin Monaghan CC
1926	April 29	Very Rev P. J. Lynch PP
1933	May 11	Rev Bernard Neilan CC
1939	April 21	Very Rev John Finan PP
1942	Jan 22	Rev James Casey CC
1976	Nov 29	Rev Thomas Conry CC
1977	Jan 12	Very Rev Patrick Canon McKeon PP
1982	Jan 1	Rev Bernard Hughes (SPS) CC
1990	Jan 15	Very Rev Matthew Owens PP

Kiltoom & Cam Parish

1904	Jan 7	Very Rev Martin O'Beirne PP
1929	Nov 8	Very Rev Peter Canon Hughes PP
1944	Jul 9	Very Rev Michael Hargadon PP
1967	Mar 3	Very Rev Mark Kilbride PP
1974	Mar 17	Rev Brendan Fitzmaurice CC
1978	Sep 1	Very Rev William McGauran DD PP
1989	Jan 19	Very Rev Edward Higgins PP
1996	Jul 10	Very Rev John Greene PP

Knockcroghery Parish

1919	July 19	Very Rev Michael Kelly PP
1947	Jan 23	Very Rev Bartholemew Canon Kelly PP
1958	Mar 15	Very Rev Michael Cunningham PP
1969	Dec 3	Rev Thomas Turley CC
1978	Sept 15	Very Rev Colm Feeney PP
1985	Sep 14	Very Rev James Tiernan PP
1993	Jan 25	Very Rev Denis Killian PP

Loughglynn Parish

1900	Nov 30	Very Rev John Canon McDermott PP
1909	Dec 15	Rev John Dolan CC
1917	Sep 1	Very Rev William Canon White PP
1932	Jan 3	Rev John Dignan CC
1932	Mar 16	Very Rev Bernard Canon Geraghty PP
1942	Mar 29	Very Rev Michael Henegan PP
1948	Jul 17	Rev Peter Thompson CC
1958	Jun 1	Rev William Fallon CC
1966	May 20	Very Rev John Gallagher PP
1967	Jun 14	Very Rev James Tully PP
1972	Oct 8	Very Rev John Smallhorne PP
1977	Nov 26	Very Rev William Larkin PP
1991	July 12	Rev Thomas Lucy SPS
1994	Apr 4	Very Rev Peter Feely PP

Maugherow Parish

1993	Nov 5	Very Rev Colm Ward PP
1999	Mar 4	Rev John Walsh
1999	Aug 8	Rev Joseph Currid CC

Oran Parish

1923	Sep 4	Very Rev John Canon Doheny PP
1935	Jan 29	Very Rev Michael Canon Keane PP
1943	May 31	Very Rev Thomas J. Waters PP
1971	May 5	Very Rev Michael Devine PP
1980	May 11	Very Rev James Gaffney PP

Riverstown Parish

1901	May 30	Very Rev Andrew Quinn PP
1921	Feb 8	Very Rev John Canon Maher PP
1935	Nov 29	Very Rev John Curley PP
1953	Jun 1	Very Rev James Canon Roddy PP
1983	Apr 17	Very Rev Michael Canon Brennan PP
2000	Jun 4	Very Rev Canon Matthew McLoughlin PP

Roscommon Parish

1910	Apr 2	Mgr Richard McLoughlin PP VG
1910	Dec 6	Rev Thomas Finan CC
1912	Aug 8	Rev John Brennan CC

1930	Aug 4	Rev James McGowan CC
1943	Sep 7	Mgr Thomas Cummins PP VG
1962	May 1	Mgr Michael O'Donnell PP
1982	Jul 7	Very Rev John Canon Duffy PP
1991	Aug 4	Very Rev Thomas Hanly PP

Sligo Parish (including Calry, Coolera & Rosses Point)

1902	Dec 2	Rev Thomas P. Neary CC
1910	Jun 5	Rev Denis Mulleady CC
1912	Oct 10	Most Rev John J. Clancy DD (Bishop)
1926	Jul 17	Most Rev Bernard Coyne DD (Bishop)
1930	Apr 21	Rev Edward Hannon CC
1938	Apr 10	Very Rev Michael O'Flaherty DD D Ph (V. Pres. Summerhill)
1938	Sep 18	Rev John McGoldrick CC
1942	Oct 28	Rev Francis Feeney STL (Maynooth)
1944	May 30	Rev Thomas McElhone CC
1944	Jun 11	Rev Peter Cryan MA BD (Summerhill College)
1945	Sep 24	Rev Patrick O'Dowd CC
1950	Apr 5	Most Rev Edward Doorly DD (Bishop)
1965	Aug 22	Rev Patrick Kelly CC
1969	Jan 18	Rev Gerard Fannon CC
1965	Nov 1	Rev Seamus Creighton (Summerhill College)
1970	Apr 27	Rev Michael O'Connor CC
1970	Nov 9	Most Rev Vincent Hanly DD (Bishop)
1976	Aug 7	Rev Gerard Curley CC
1990	May 4	Rev John Crehan CC
1996	Aug 22	Most Rev Dominic Conway (Retired Bishop)

Strokestown Parish

1907	Mar 7	Very Rev Hugh Canon Gately PP
1907	Jun 12	Rev John Murray CC
1924	Oct 19	Rev John J. Hanly CC
1926	Mar 11	Mgr Roderick Gearty PP VG
1931	Aug 21	Ven Archdeacon John McDermott PP
1950	Dec 8	Very Rev Bartholomew Canon Currid PP
1963	Jan 3	Rev Andrew Doocey CC
1974	Dec 15	Very Rev Patrick Canon Hannon PP
1986	Feb 7	Rev Noel Mattimoe CC
1988	Jun 2	Very Rev Desmond McLoughlin PP
1989	Nov 5	Very Rev Patrick Brady PP

1991	Feb 15	Very Rev Bernard Canon Tiernan PP

Tarmonbarry Parish

1907	Mar 7	Rev John O'Keefe CC
1917	Oct 23	Very Rev Patrick Martin PP
1940	Mar 22	Very Rev Peter Canon Coleman PP
1970	Apr 19	Very Rev Martin J. O'Beirne PP
1977	Aug 31	Very Rev Joseph Conway PP
1986	Feb 4	Very Rev Brendan Rainey PP
1993	Feb 6	Rev Anthony Meehan CC

Tulsk Parish

1908	Mar 28	Very Rev John O'Brien PP
1939	Nov 4	Very Rev Thomas Lavin PP
1945	Sep 25	Rev Daniel J. Gilmartin CC
1959	Jan 27	Very Rev Patrick F. McGowan PP
1980	Dec 17	Very Rev Joseph Canon Kilmartin PP
1990	Oct 7	Very Rev Enda Farrell PP
1992	Apr 7	Rev Gerard Neary CC

Clergy List for the Jubilee Year 2000

Sligo Cathedral	Bishop Christopher Jones
	Very Rev Niall Ahern Adm VF
	Rev Ray Browne CC
	Rev Ian Kennedy CC
Sligo: St Joseph's & Calry	Very Rev Liam Devine PP
	Rev Leonard Taylor CC
	Rev Patrick Lombard CC
Sligo: St Anne's & Carraroe	Very Rev Dominic Gillooly PP
	Rev Stephen Walshe CC
	Rev James Murray CC
Aghanagh	Very Rev Brian Hanley PP
Ahamlish	Very Rev Cyrill Haran PP
	Rev James O'Kane (SMA) CC
	Rev Michael Glynn CC
Ahascragh	Very Rev Francis Glennon PP
	Rev Laurence Cullen CC
Ardcarne	Very Rev Canon Henry Tonra PP
	Rev Patrick McGovern (SMA)
Athleague	Very Rev Eugene McLoughlin PP
	Rev John Leogue CC
Athlone: St Peter's	Very Rev Canon Patrick Murray PP VF
	Rev Noel Rooney CC
	Rev John Middleton CC
	Rev Ray Milton CC

Aughrim	Very Rev Noel Durr PP Mgr Michael McGuinness CC
Ballinameen	Very Rev Francis McGauran PP
Ballintubber	Very Rev Seamus Cox PP Rev Alan Conway CC
Ballyforan	Very Rev Francis Beirne PP Very Rev Canon Joseph McElhone PE
Ballygar	Very Rev Canon Gerald Donnelly PP Rev Sean Beirne CC
Boyle	Very Rev Canon Gerard Hanly PP VF Rev Brian Conlon CC Rev John Deignan CC
Castlerea	Very Rev Canon Joseph Fitzgerald PP VF Rev Kevin Fallon CC
Coolera (Strandhill and Ransboro)	Very Rev Sean Creaton PP
Croghan	Very Rev Roger Leonard PP Rev Eamon Conaty (SSC)
Drumcliff	Very Rev Michael Donnelly PP
Elphin	Very Rev James Tighe PP Rev Martin Mulvaney CC
Fairymount	Very Rev Joseph Gilmartin PP
Frenchpark	Very Rev Canon Earley PP Rev Brendan Sherry CC
Geevagh	Very Rev Thomas O'Connor PP Rev Liam Sharkey CC

Kilbegnet	Very Rev Hugo McClure (SVD) PP
	Rev Peter Thompson (SMA) CC
	Very Rev Canon John J. Kelly PE
Kilbride	Very Rev Raymond Browne PP
Kilgefin	Very Rev Michael Breslin PP
	Rev Eamon O'Connor CC
Kilglass	Very Rev Patrick McHugh PP
	Rev Edmund Prendergast (MHM) CC
Kiltoom & Cam	Very Rev Colm Hayes PP
	Rev Hugh Lee (MHM) CC
Knockcroghery	Very Rev Thomas Beirne PP
	Rev Sean Kelly (SMA) CC
Loughglynn	Very Rev John O'Rourke PP
	Rev Michael McManus CC
Maugherow	Very Rev Canon Peadar Lavin PP
Oran	Very Rev James Casey PP
	Rev Seamus O'Neill (SSC) CC
Riverstown	Very Rev Anthony B. O'Shea PP
Roscommon	Rt Rev Mgr Charles Travers PP VF VG
	Rev John Cullen CC
	Rev Christopher McHugh CC
	Rev Francis Coltsman (SMA) CC
Rosses Point	Mgr Gerard Dolan PP
Strokestown	Very Rev Canon Ciaran Whitney PP VF
	Rev Mícheál Donnelly CC

Tarmonbarry	Rev William Ghent (SMA) ADM
Tulsk	Very Rev Austin McKeon PP
	Rev Donald McDonagh (SPS) CC

Priests Elsewhere

Fr John J. Gannon	Summerhill College, Sligo
Fr Edward Moore	Summerhill College, Sligo
Fr Gerard Cryan	Summerhill College, Sligo
Fr Declan Brady	Chaplain to Institute of Technology, Sligo
Fr Tom Hever	Sligo Social Services
Fr John Carroll	Chaplain to Sligo General Hospital
Fr Bernard Conway	Chaplain to Sligo General Hospital
Fr Hugh McGonagle	Chaplain to the Forces, Costume Barracks, Athlone
Fr Donal Morris	Chaplain to Castlerea Prison
Fr Michael Drumm	Mater Dei Institute of Education, Dublin
Fr Michael Duignan	Irish College, Rome
Fr Pádraig Greene	St Augustine's Church, Pleasanton, California
Fr Anthony Conry	Brazil

Retired Priests

Very Rev Thomas Foy	Nazareth House, Sligo
Very Rev Kevin McDermott	Sligo
Rev Thomas Garvey	New Inn, Galway
Very Rev Patrick Healy	Sligo
Very Rev Michael Dunning	Roscommon
Rev Gerard Horan	Boyle
Very Rev Michael Martin	Athlone

Orders of Religious in Elphin
A brief history

MEN RELIGIOUS

CLUNIACS

This order started at the Abbey of Cluny in 910 as a reform of the Benedictines. Their only house in Ireland was the Priory of SS Peter and Paul in Athlone. Tradition says the monastery was founded by Turlough O'Conor in 1150. Throughout the medieval period this was one of the most important and wealthiest monasteries in the diocese. In time, monks from this monastery took charge of many of the surrounding parishes. The monastery was suppressed c. 1542 but the monks may have continued in the area for some years. It is believed that all the monks were dead by 1570. The seal of the priory is preserved in the National Museum. The school opened by the Sisters of Mercy on the site of the monastery in 1934 was named 'An Scoil Cluineach ar choimirce NN Peadar agus Pól', thus preserving the name of this order in Athlone.

AUGUSTINIANS

The Canons Regular of St Augustine were introduced to Ireland in the early twelfth century (1127), as part of the reform movement in the Irish church. They established nine houses in the Elphin diocese, some of which were dependent on the larger foundations. These all faded away in the sixteenth century. Roscommon, (1140-1578), Cloontuskert (1140-1563), Inishmacnerin (1140/70-1596), Elphin (1140/42 – very short lived), Ardcarn (1140-1593), Derrane (1156-1578), Kilmore (1232-1580), Athleague (1256-1466) and Lissonuffy (? – 1592).

The Augustinian Friars (OSA) came to Ireland in the mid thirteenth century. While they had no foundation in Elphin, a member of the Banada community, Bernard O'Higgins, was Bishop of Elphin from 1542-1561. Bishop Beotius Egan, in his report to Rome in 1637, only mentions Augustinian friars at Roscommon, Derrane, Aughrim and on Church Island in Loch Cé. The friars from Dunmore, county Galway, had moved to Mayfield in Elphin diocese by 1645, and were in different locations in that area throughout the eighteenth century. In 1750 they considered moving to Derrymore, but were still in Mayfield in 1781. In the opening years of the nineteenth century, three members of this community, Frs Hussey, Kelly, and Triston, resided fifteen miles from Athlone, and acted as chaplains to the Catholic gentry of the area. Subsequently, in 1809, two of the aforementioned friars were given permission by Dr French, the ailing Bishop of Elphin, to establish 'a chapel and chapel-house' on the western side of the Shannon in Athlone. In the course of time, and contrary to the wishes of Bishop George T. Plunkett, the successor to Edmund French, they built a church and friary at College Lane, off Connacht Street. In the 1840s members of the community, notably Fr Michael Page, were leading advocates of the Temperance Movement, and also to the forefront in the organisation of various relief works during the Famine.

By the mid-nineteenth century there appears to have been only two friars attached to this church, and following the death of Edward Jennings, prior, in 1875, the Augustinian connection with St Peter's parish came to an end.

DOMINICANS

The Order of Friars Preachers, also known as 'Black Friars', was founded by St Dominic at Toulouse in 1215. They spread quickly and within a half a century had established houses in almost every European country including Ireland. Their earliest foundation in Connacht was at Athenry in 1241.

Sligo

A decade later, in 1252, Maurice Fitzgerald, Norman baron and outgoing Lord Justice of Ireland, who had already built a castle at Sligo, founded the Abbey of the Holy Cross for the Dominicans on the banks of the Garavogue and in close proximity to his stronghold. In 1414 Holy Cross was accidentally burned to the ground but was quickly restored by the prior, Bryan Mac Donagh. Most of the impressive ruin standing today, in particular the magnificent east window and distinctive central tower, supported by a high arch, dates from this period.

A century later further additions and improvements were carried out, including the provision of a longer nave and an additional transept. Also added was the beautiful cloister garth, of which three sides remain in perfect condition. The elaborate O'Crean tomb, and the impressive mural monument commemorating Donough O'Connor-Sligo and his wife, Eleanor, Countess of Desmond, date from the sixteenth and seventeenth centuries respectively.

For the greater part of the reign of Elizabeth I, the friars were left in relative peace, mainly through the intercession of the aforementioned Sir Donough. However, they were forced out, at least temporarily, when Sir Richard Bingham took up quarters in the abbey while besieging the nearby castle. After a few years the friars re-established themselves but many of them were burned to death when Sir Freder-ick Hamilton sacked both the town and the abbey in 1642. Following the enactment of the Edict of Banishment in 1698, the friars were finally compelled to leave the abbey after four hundred years.

After vacating Holy Cross, the friars moved to a new location at the rear of Pound Street (now Connolly Street), where they established a chapel and living quarters, the remains of which are still standing. After Emancipation the Dominicans acquired a site for a new church and priory in High Street, which was consecrated on the Feast of the Ephipany in 1848. Half a century later the church was length-ened by fifty feet, and a new sanctuary and high altar added. After structural defects were discovered in the body of the church in 1970, it was decided to demolish it and build a new place of worship on the site to a modern design. This was opened and blessed in May 1973 by Bishop Dominic Conway. The high altar and chancel window of the original building were retained in a private chapel now used by the friars themselves.

Today, after a span of 750 years, the Dominicans still maintain a community in Sligo, and over that period have provided three bishops from the Sligo house, namely Andrew O'Crean, and John Brett, (Elphin), and Eugene O'Hart (Achonry).

Ballindoon

The Abbey of Ballindoon, seven miles north of Boyle, in the ancient parish of Kil-ladoon, was founded in 1507 under the patronage of the MacDonaghs, Lords of Tirerrill. The founder's name was Thomas O'Ferghail, who became its first prior. The building, of unusual Gothic style and quite impressive, even in ruins, stands close to the north western shore of Lough Arrow and is 84ft in length and 23ft wide. The most remarkable feature of the church is the central tower and belfry which also acted as a rood-screen, with a narrow passage and two rooms on the ground floor and an arrangement of three arches on the first floor.

An inquisition in 1585 described the foundation as consisting of a church, a cemetery and a half quarter of land which, in 1603, was granted to one Francis Crofton. Two decades later it passed to Andrew Crean of Sligo and at the Restor-ation, to the King family of Boyle. According to Coleman, in his supplement to O'Heyne's *Irish Dominicans,* there were two friars attached to Ballindoon in 1756 and five in 1767, one of whom functioned as a parish priest. This, no doubt, was Fr Michael Reynolds, who was PP of Aghanagh c. 1760-1785. According to local tradi-tion, the friars, having been dislodged from the friary, settled in a mud cabin about two miles distant at a place subsequently known as Friarstown. Three of the penal day friars have been identified as Daniel Hart (prior), Con O'Rourke and Peter (O) Connor.

Cloonshanville

The Abbey of Cloonshanville, the location of an earlier Christian foundation, situated 'on the edge of an extensive bog' a mile east of Frenchpark, was founded in 1385 by Mac Dermot Roe of Artagh and was liberally endowed by him. In 1577 the abbey was leased to Hugh Boy O'Donnell and the lands the following year to the mayor of Galway. Three years later the priory, with its appurtenances, was leased to Bryan Mac Dermot, probably a descendant of the founder. Thereafter, the property changed hands by way of lease to William Taaffe who sold it to Lord Dillon, who in turn rented it to a family named Davis. By the end of the eighteenth century the building was 'very much in ruins', but the eastern window was intact. The sixty-feet high tower was still standing upon an arch but there was no trace of the cloisters. Near the belfry stands the vault of the Frenchs of Frenchpark, complete with coat of arms and inscription and incorporating a seventeenth-century crucifixion plaque.

Roscommon

The abbey at Roscommon was founded in 1253 by Phelim O'Conor, King of Connacht and, according to the *Annals of Loch Cé,* was consecrated by Thomas O'Connor, Bishop of Elphin, in 1257 for the Friar Preachers. The founder died in 1265 and was interred there, and over his tomb stands a memorial depicting a recumbent figure holding a sceptre and surrounded by figures of gallowglasses.

The friars at Roscommon were involved in the collection of money to finance the crusades in 1266. The buildings were burned in 1270 and repaired, only to be struck by lightning in 1308. In 1445 Pope Eugene IV granted an indulgence to all those who subscribed towards the cost of repair after it had been damaged 'by the calamities of war'. It was dissolved in the reign of Elizabeth I, apparently before 1569, when it was referred to in a survey as 'the late house'. In 1573 the property was leased to Thomas le Strange and four years later passed to Sir Nicholas Malby. The site was abandoned by the friars, until at least 1636 when a chalice was made for the use of the abbey. After the Restoration a large community grew up and provincial chapters were held in the countryside around Roscommon in 1678 and 1682. It was at this time that one member of the Roscommon community, Fr Thady Keogh OP, became Bishop of Clonfert from 1671 to 1687. After 1698 the friars were dispersed, but remained in the area, and there were six friars in the community in 1702. Throughout the eighteenth and early nineteenth centuries the friars lived in various locations to the west of Roscommon town. They moved residence many times, from Athleague to Mount Mary, where they had a novitiate for a time after 1770, to Gortnadeeve, and to Castlecoote. By then the old abbey had been partially demolished and the tower of the church collapsed in 1794. The last of the Roscommon Dominicans was Fr Bartholomew Keeher OP, who was parish priest of Athleague until his death in 1872.

Tulsk

Tulsk Abbey was founded in 1448 by Phelim MacDowell on a site donated by Phelim O'Conor and was consecrated 'to the glory of God and the honour of St Dominick'. It belonged to the era of the smaller rural foundations that sprang up in the fifteenth century. In 1595 Sir Richard Bingham, Governor of Connacht, 'repaired' Tulsk abbey by turning whatever conventual buildings remained into a fortification, and the following year, together with Cloonshanville, it was leased to William Taaffe. Extant documents reveal that in 1608 William Brounkar esq received a grant of 34 acres, arable and bog, belonging to 'Tulske friary'.

The Dominicans do not appear to have made any attempt to reside in Tulsk after the suppression of the monasteries, although a general chapter in Rome in 1694 enjoined the provincial to institute a prior for the convent. A century later nothing but the walls of the abbey remained, together with a strong pillar of masonry which supported the ends of two arches which opened to a chapel. Today the ruins consist of the outline of the church and the base of the tower.

Eight Dominicans occupied the See of Elphin between 1266-1765, namely: Mauritius O'Conor, Marianus O'Donnachair, Nicholas O'Flannagan, Richard MacBrien, Andrew O'Crean, Dominic Burke, Ambrose Mac Dermott, and John Brett.

CARMELITES (O CARM)

The Brothers of the Blessed Virgin Mary of Mount Carmel, better known as Carmelites, originated on Mount Carmel in the Holy Land. In 1226 Pope Honorius III approved of their Rule, but after the fall of Acre in 1291 they abandoned their original home and migrated to western Europe. By the early fourteenth century they had established houses in Ireland, and in 1336 founded a monastery at Caltra in the parish of Killosolan (Ahascragh), under the patronage of the Birminghams of Athenry.

After the Dissolution, the friars continued to minister in the area, before moving to Tohergar in the neighbouring parish of Killian (Newbridge) in 1775. Meanwhile, the order had established another monastery at Eglish in the parish of Ahascragh, which was dedicated to the Holy Cross. This arose from the finding there c. 1376 of a venerable cross and the subsequent building of an oratory on the site. Arising from this the Bishop of Elphin, William O'Hetigan, invited the Carmelites to establish a foundation there, and in 1436 Pope Eugene IV granted them certain facilities and privileges, namely, 'to build a monastery and church with a bell tower, bell, dormitory, refectory, cloister, cemetery, orchards and other necessary offices'. The local chieftain, Donal O'Kelly, on whose land stood the oratory, assigned a site and adjacent lands to the order.

The church, which was known locally as Teampall Mór, lay from east to west, and measured 81 feet long by 21 feet broad. The doorway was in the west gable, while, 'a fine spacious window of four lights' overlooked the altar at the opposite end. The cloisters were to the north of the church, together with an oratory and cells. To the south of the ruins is a graveyard, and adjacent to it stands a long narrow windowless building known as Teampall Maol.

The monastery at Eglish was abandoned in the mid-seventeenth century, and it is probable that the friars joined their brothers at nearby Caltra before moving to Tohergar c. 1775, where they remained until 1870. In that year the Provincial Chapter decided to close the friary but one friar, Fr John Hopkins, refused to leave and remained with his people until his death in 1873. He was buried within the church grounds alongside another Carmelite. A carving of the Madonna and Child, taken from the friary, can be seen on the wall at the entrance to St Brendan's Church, Tohergar.

There is some evidence to suggest that there was a Carmelite foundation at Tisrara in medieval times, while in the mid-nineteenth century, the Third Order of the Carmelites was established there. A gravestone in the local cemetery carries the following inscription: 'Master Décor Carmeli, In your Charity you will pray for the members of the Third Order of Our Blessed Lady of Mount Carmel, who are interred in this grave. May their souls rest in Peace. Mother of Mount Carmel pray for them.'

A tombstone inscription in Cam old cemetery records the death of Rev John Glennon, 'Order BVM de Mont Carmelo', who died in January 1773.

CISTERCIANS

The Cistercian Order, based on the Rule of St Benedict, originated at Citeaux in Burgundy at the close of the eleventh century, and fifty years later, in 1142, a foundation was made in Ireland at Mellifont, county Louth. In 1161 a 'daughter house' was established at Ath-dá-Learg on the banks of the Boyle river, and became widely known as 'Mainistir na Búile', the Monastery of Boyle.

The first abbot was Muirgheas Ua Dubhthaigh who supervised the building of the new monastery to a uniform plan common to all Cistercian foundations. Archdall, in his *Monasticon Hibernicum* (1796), described the abbey of Boyle as 'one of the finest buildings in the kingdom', and the remains, though fragmentary in places, are described as 'the best preserved in Ireland'. They comprise a gate-house, cloister, kitchen, cellars and a church. The latter is of various dates and is a most interesting example of the transition from Romanesque to Gothic in Ireland. Both the barrel-vaulted chancel and the transepts date from the twelfth century.

In the late twelfth century the monastery of Boyle became the 'mother-house' of two flourishing foundations, the Abbey of Assaroe in Ballyshannon and Knockmoy in county Galway. In 1227 the abbot of Boyle was among the five Irish Cistercian abbots who were deposed by the General Chapter of the Order in an effort to exclude non-continental influences. The following year the affiliation of Boyle with Mellifont was severed and it was joined instead with Clairvaux. This resulted in some of the monks at Boyle moving to Trinity Island and taking with them the manuscripts which in time became known as the 'Annals of Boyle'.

At the time of the Norman incursion into north Connacht, Boyle Abbey was occupied and partially burned. It came under attack again in 1235 when chalices and other valuables were looted by soldiers in the service of Richard De Burgo. Between 1161 and 1449 the Boyle foundation produced eight bishops, including four of Elphin – Florence Ua Maelruanaidh in 1175, Tomás Mac Fearghail MacDiarmada 1262, Maelseachlainn MacBriann 1295, and Donnchadha Ua Flannagain in 1303. The abbey was the favourite burial place of the Mac Dermots, Kings of Moylurg, the members of whose families continued to be buried there down to the end of the sixteenth century.

The Cistercians of Boyle had extensive possessions at the time of the Dissolution. These included out-farms known as 'Granges', where the monks of Boyle Abbey grew, harvested and stored their grain, and from which originated The Granges in Killaspugbrone parish, and the placenames, Grange, in the parishes of Ahamlish, Cam and Kilbride.

In 1569 Queen Elizabeth granted the abbey and its possessions at Boyle to Patrick Cusack of county Meath, 'containing one acre of land on which there were the walls of a church and belfry; a cloister, hall and dormitory; six gardens and orchards and some ruined buildings together with six acres of arable land and 160 acres of mountainy pasture'. In 1592 the Four Masters record that 'a large garrison of the English were stationed in a monastery on the banks of the river Boyle'. Four years later Tyrone and an army of 2,300 men besieged the abbey, then a 'fortress'. In 1603 Sir John King received a grant from the crown of the abbey and this was confirmed by another of January 1618.

According to the report of the vicar general, James Fallon, to Rome in January 1631, the monastery was in ruins with the exception of one chapel, which the Protestants used as a parish church, and according to another source, the cloisters had been adapted for use as a barrack. As far as can be ascertained Thomas Kiernan, living in 1650, was the last of the Irish Cistercians to bear the title of 'Abbot of Boyle'.

PREMONSTRATENSIAN CANONS

The Premonstratensian Order, or White Canons, sometimes called Norbertines, was founded in northern France in 1120 by St Norbert, one of the most noted promoters of the reform movement of Gregory VII. The order came to Ireland in the mid-twelfth century and established a monastery at Tuam. Half a century later, c. 1215, they established a foundation on Trinity Island, Loch Cé on the invitation of Clarus Mac Mailin O'Mulconry, son of the erenach of the nearby Inishmacnerin Island. He subsequently became abbot and archdeacon of Elphin. Generally acclaimed as one of the great churchmen of his time, he founded several religious houses and acquired substantial grants of land from noble patrons in both Roscommon and Sligo.

It was due to his influence that the sanctuary of Trinity Island was respected by the Anglo-Normans after they had overrun Moylurg in 1235. The Premonstratensian abbey was endowed by Murtagh McDermot, Prince of Moylurg, who was buried on the island, as was Clarus Mac Mailin and thirteen other abbots. Two of his successors as abbots were appointed bishops of Elphin – Giolla Íosa Ó Conchúir, in 1284, and Cathal Ó Conchúir in 1310. Two centuries later, in 1525, John Maxey, an English Premonstratensian was appointed to the See. In 1466 the abbey was accidentally burned by a lighted candle but was quickly rebuilt.

A notable feature of Trinity Church, recorded in the *Annals of Boyle,* was its shrine, described as 'a remarkable sculpture of a pyramidal figure', two and a half feet high by one and a half feet broad, depicting the Blessed Virgin seated on a chair with the infant Jesus resting on her right arm. On the Virgin's head was a crown surmounted by a scroll. Trinity Island survived into Tudor times with substantial properties on the mainland. Rory McDermot, King of Moylurg, was abbot from 1545 until his death in 1568. The abbey is said to have survived long after Dissolution, possibly into the seventeeth century. In 1580 Eugene O'Maoilchiarain, the last abbot of Trinity Island, and Gelasius O Cullenan, a Cistercian of Boyle Abbey, were both arrested and subsequently executed. The abbot's remains were interred in front of the altar in the church on his beloved Trinity Island. After the Dissolution Trinity Island was granted to Sir John King.

FRATRES CRUCIFERI

This Orders has its origins in the Holy Land and was often known as the Order of St John of Jerusalem. The brethren originally cared for pilgrims to Jerusalem. From the twelfth century there were several different congregations under the names Canons OSA of the Holy Cross, Fratres Cruciferi, Crosier Canons, Cross Bearers, and in England, Crutched or Crouched Friars.

Their houses in Ireland were of Augustinian Hospitallers from the beginning, and the name 'Cruciferi' may not have come into general use until after 1245. Though the Cruciferi in Ireland were not Military Hospitallers, they were not unlike the Brother Infirmarians of the Knight Hospitallers, and there are indications that the two orders had close connections. Fratres Cruciferi were in the Diocese of Elphin at a place called Rinn Dúin in the parish of Knockcroghery. There is reference to the Priory of Augustinian Hospitallers from 1232 onwards. This priory was located two hundred yards north of Rinn Dúin castle and seems to have been part of a medieval town. The priory and its lands were confiscated during the religious upheavals of the Elizabethan period, and were granted to Christopher Deavers in 1569. A ruined medieval church is all that survives to indicate where this religious house once stood.

FRANCISCANS

The Franciscans arrived in Ireland about 1233 and founded a friary at Roscommon in 1268. This was destroyed by fire the following year and never re-established. It was not until 1453 that the Franciscans returned to the diocese and founded a friary in Elphin town during the episcopate of Cornelius O'Mullally OFM (1449-1468). Franciscans were given charge of the church of St Patrick in the town, replacing the Canons Regular of St Augustine. The Elphin friars were Conventual Franciscans and were among the last of the Irish friars to accept the Observant Reform of the order, which they did in 1632. The friars lost possession of the friary in 1563 and it was leased by the crown to various individuals afterwards. The friary was demolished by 1629 and the stones were used to build a residence for the Protestant bishop. The friars were forced into hiding but continued to minister to the people of the area from their place of refuge at Drinane, near Elphin.

Bishop Boetius Egan OFM (1625-1650) had a chalice made for the use of the Elphin Franciscans in 1634. The friars again took up residence in Elphin for a few years around 1649. A chapter of the Irish Franciscans was held in Elphin in 1672. Throughout the eighteenth century the friars continued in the area as evidenced by the *Report on the State of Popery* in 1731. During this period the Guardians of the Elphin friary were nearly always members of the local landed families. In 1731 there were fifteen friars living at Drinane, about three miles from Elphin. This was a large number for the time and may have included Franciscans from other houses. It was also in that year that a former Guardian of Elphin Friary, Patrick French OFM, became Bishop of Elphin. In 1766 there were nine friars living in the Elphin community. In 1773 the friars were allowed to accept novices at their Elphin residence. However, by 1787 there was only one friar in Elphin and one novice studying in Rome. The latter, Fr Anthony Garrahan OFM, a native of Ballinagare in county Roscommon, returned in 1803 and held various appointments to parishes in Elphin diocese. In 1819 as parish priest of Kilcorkey, he had a chapel built at Ballinagare. He died in 1835 and his passing marked the end of a 400-year link of the Franciscans with Elphin.

During this period six Franciscans served as bishops of Elphin. They were: Robert Fosten 1418-30, an English Franciscan, Cornelius O'Mullally 1449-68, Bernard O'Donnell 1541, (already Bishop of Ferns, he died before reaching Elphin); Dermot O'Healy c. 1597, (he was martyred for the faith); Boetius Egan 1626-50, and Patrick French 1731-48, who was the last Franciscan to be Bishop of Elphin.

Franciscans (Third Order Regular)
Friaries of the Third Order Regular first begin to appear in Ireland in the early fifteenth century. There was a Franciscan Friary of the Third Order at Caldragh, in the ancient parish of Kilmacumsy, now part of Elphin parish. The date for the foundation of this house is uncertain but may have been some time before 1487. The friary was suppressed c. 1582 and its lands leased by the crown. The site of the friary is now marked by Caldragh old cemetery. There is some evidence to suggest that there were two further houses of this order at Knockvicar and Clonrahan (not definitely located) in county Roscommon.

Franciscan Brothers
At the beginning of the nineteenth century, the friars at Merchant's Quay Dublin, were approached by the parish priest of Milltown, county Dublin, for help in establishing a school in his parish. The *Catholic Directory* of 1821 tells us that the Franciscan Monastery at Mount Alverno, near Milltown, was directed by Micheal Dillon and had eight members. They ran a day school, an evening school and a Sunday school for the poor male children of Milltown and surrounding villages. In 1820, on the invitation of Christopher Dillon Bellew, Brothers Michael Dillon and Bonaventure Lee came to Mountbellew, county Galway. The Brothers continued under the juristiction of the Friars Minor until 1829, and in that year transferred their obedience to the Archbishop of Tuam, Dr Oliver Kelly.

The monastery at Farragher, in the parish of Oran, was built on lands bequeathed to Brother Benedict (Hugh) Farmer by his brother Daniel. Daniel and Hugh were the sons of Matthew Farmer. Mr Farmer came to the area from Fermanagh after his home there was burned. Hugh was professed as a Franciscan Brother at Mountbellew in 1839, taking the name of Benedict. Daniel died in 1854, leaving no children, and according to the terms of his father's will the Farmer lands at Farragher, Highlake, and Ballymacurley passed to his brother Hugh for the founding of a monastery. He in turn assigned them to the Franciscan Brothers. In 1855 Br Jerome Bennett commenced a free school in the area. Dr Browne, Bishop of Elphin, laid the foundation stone on 20 June 1857. By 1866, seven brothers lived there and in 1884 the school came under the National Board of Education. It had 114 pupils on the roll at the time. In 1907 a new school was built. The work of the brothers in Farragher was in primary education and agriculture. Until 1918 the monastery existed as a semi-independent entity, but in that year, along with the monastery at Clara, it amalgamated with the Franciscan Monasteries in the Archdiocese of Tuam under a common provincial superior. The school continued to exist until 1971, when the brothers withdrew from the monastery and school.

Today, many brothers work in Ireland, the United States and Kenya.

REDEMPTORISTS

 The Redemptorist Congregation was founded in the kingdom of Naples by Alphonsus Ligouri (1696-1787). He gave up a career in law to become a priest. He began his priestly ministry working for the poor in the city of Naples. Due to failing health he was invited to go for a period of relaxation to Scala, a small village in the hills above the Bay of Amalfi. However, this vacation turned into a mission. He became very conscious of the large percentage of those living in the hills around Scala who lived in complete forgetfulness of God. This experience led him to the decision to found the Redemptorist Missionary Congregation in 1732, which was finally approved by the Holy See in 1849.

After many initial difficulties and setbacks, the congregation grew and expanded in the southern part of Italy. After the death of Alphonsus it spread across the Alps into Northern Europe. This was due to the untiring efforts of St Clement Mary Hofbauer. The first Redemptorist mission in Ireland was given in 1851 in St John's Cathedral, Limerick, and two years later the first Irish foundation was established there.

The Redemptorists opened their first house in the west of Ireland at Killucan House in the parish of Croghan on 29 January 1899. Bishop Clancy was very anxious to introduce them to the Diocese of Elphin. However, Killucan was in close proximity to Carrick-on-Shannon and the neighbouring Diocese of Ardagh, and this seems to have caused problems.

There were a number of representations made to Rome requesting a relocation of the house. In June 1900, Rome requested the Redemptorists to move their house nearer the church of Drumlion. Bishop Clancy offered Rosses Point as an alternative location but the Redemptorists had already begun to negotiate the purchase of the former Clonfert Diocesan Seminary at Esker. In 1901 the Killucan community was dissolved and transferred to Esker.

The parish hall at Cortober, close to the former site of the Redemptorist House, now serves as a weekly Mass centre.

MARIST BROTHERS

 The Marist Order of Brothers was founded in France in 1817 by Fr Marcellin Champagnat who was beatified in 1955 and canonised in 1999. Within fifty years of foundation, schools were established in Europe, Australia, New Zealand and the islands of Oceania. Their first Irish foundation was in Sligo. Dr Gillooly, Bishop of Elphin, had heard of their work while a student in Paris. Anxious for the mental and moral well being of youth, he invited the Marist Order to his diocese and his second invitation was accepted in 1862. On 26 May of that year five Marist Brothers arrived in Sligo and two schools were opened in the town, a primary school in Quay St and a paying school in Chapel St.

Emerging from the nightmare of the Famine, most of the people had limited educational opportunities. The task confronting the brothers called for the exercise of high qualities of heart and soul and they gave the youth an excellent educational start. The brothers left Sligo in 1880, but were invited back by Bishop Clancy in 1898. Some years later, in 1903, at the request of Monsignor Hanley, they opened a primary school in Castlerea, and in 1928 at the request of Archdeacon McDermott, they took charge of a primary school in Stokestown. Generations of former pupils in these three towns have memories of a school that gave them more than the three Rs, and recall with pride the football teams, the plays and the choirs in which they took part. Sadly, through lack of vocations, the brothers departed from Strokestown in 1974, and from Castlerea in 1993, but St John's Sligo continues the proud record of service to the Elphin diocese, under the principalship of Br Finian.

Today, over 5000 Marist brothers work in fifty different countries in all five continents.

DE LA SALLE BROTHERS

In the spring of 1880 the Brothers of the Christian Schools, usually known as the De la Salle Brothers, were invited by Bishop Gillooly to take charge of an industrial school for boys at Summerhill, Athlone. The bishop was familiar with the work of the brothers from his student days in Paris. The brothers arrived in Summerhill on 19 July 1880 and set about establishing the school. Almost from the start there were difficulties, firstly with the government on the condition of the buildings, and secondly with the bishop on the debts incurred in remedying the former. The brothers withdrew from the school on 20 January 1882. This was the first foundation of the De La Salle Order in Ireland. The brothers also opened a novitiate in Summerhill, which was a source of conflict with the government inspector. When the brothers left Athlone a new novitiate was opened at Castletown, county Laois.

In the summer of 1930 the De La Salle Brothers were invited by Bishop Doorly to come to Roscommon town. They first took charge of the Boys National School, where the principal of the school, Mr Larkin, retired in 1930. This school (now demolished, and partly incorporated into the county Roscommon Famine Memorial) was located behind the Post Office. The De La Salle Brothers opened a secondary school to Intermediate Level in a new building in Abbey St, now the presbytery of Roscommon parish. However, due to circumstances outside their control, the Brothers were obliged to leave Roscommon in 1937. The community of brothers who served in Roscommon went to Skibbereen, county Cork, where they established St Fachtna's Secondary School. Their contribution to education in Roscommon is still remembered in the town and surrounding area.

The departure of the brothers in 1937 ended the links of the De La Salle Brothers with the Diocese of Elphin.

PRESENTATION BROTHERS

The Presentation Brothers owe their origin to Blessed Edmund Rice, who founded them in Waterford in the early years of the nineteenth century. Edmund Rice had been a wealthy businessman in the town, whose life was changed by the death of his wife and the handicap of his young child. Eventually, in 1802, he decided to devote his life and his wealth to the education of the poor children of Waterford. He left his comfortable house and went to live in a stable that became his dwelling and a school for the children. His life inspired other men with similar enthusiasm who joined him, not only as teachers but as a Christian community. They began to live a religious life and they used the rule of the Presentation Sisters, (founded in 1775), as a guide for their way of life. This group was known as the Society of the Presentation.

This society was later to divide into two congregations, the Christian Brothers and the Presentation Brothers. This division happened in Cork when one of the brothers, Br Micheal Augustine Riordan, decided to remain under the jurisdiction of Bishop John Murphy of Cork. On 1 July 1827 Br Riordan moved out of the North Monastery, the first foundation of the brothers in Cork, and founded the South Monastery. This became the centre of an expanding congregation of brothers who were called the Presentation Brothers. As the century moved on foundations were established in the United States, India, England and all over Ireland.

The brothers' involvement with the Diocese of Elphin dates from August 1897, when Canon Coyne, the parish priest of Boyle, with the consent of Bishop Clancy, invited the brothers to assume the running of the National Schools in the town. Canon Coyne was later to become Bishop of Elphin. The brothers were well received by the people of Boyle and lived in a dwelling near the schools. A new house was eventually purchased adjacent to the Cistercian Abbey. The old National Schools were replaced in 1904, due to the fact that the buildings were too small for the increased numbers attending. With the aid of a grant and funds raised locally, the new schools were completed and opened on 1 June 1904. They were situated some distance from the town, and were well ventilated and suited for education purposes. The brothers continued to teach in Boyle until 1918.

CHRISTIAN BROTHERS

The Christian Brothers were founded in 1802 by Blessed Edmund Ignatius Rice (1762-1844). Bishop Gillooly began negotiation with the Christian Brothers to establish a school in Sligo in late 1859, continuing the following year, but no foundation was established at that time. In 1860 Mrs Julia Ann Conmee left a portion of her estate to the then superiors of the Christian Brothers for the establishment of a school in or near Roscommon. Mrs Conmee (nee Farrell) was a native of county Roscommon who died in Dublin on 16 February 1860. The first attempt to use the Conmee bequest was made in 1872 but the fund was not sufficient to proceed at that time. The matter was considered by the brothers five or six times between 1872 and 1929. In the early 1930s a group of people formed a Roscommon School Committee which petitioned the brothers to open a school in Roscommon town. Their petition came to fruition when the Christian Brothers arrived in Roscommon in 1937.

A community of six brothers came to Roscommon under the guidance of Br T. C. Maloney, superior. They first lived in a house opposite the Courthouse in Abbey St and established their secondary school in the old De La Salle school. They immediately set about building new schools and a monastery using the Conmee bequest as their main source of funding. The secondary school was ready in August 1939, followed by the primary school in April 1940. For the first time second level education to Leaving Certificate level was available to the people of Roscommon town and the surrounding districts. The schools grew from strength to strength and in 1948 the then superior, Br Creed, introduced what was the first school bus transport system in the country. Following the introduction of free second level education, additional accommodation was built at the secondary school in 1967 and again in 1974. In 1987, due to declining vocations, the brothers left primary education and the primary school building became part of the secondary school. A further extension was added to the school in 1994. The school has been under lay principalship since then.

At present there are four brothers in the Roscommon Christian Brothers community. As well as teaching, the brothers are involved in all aspects of the pastoral life of Roscommon parish.

SOCIETY OF THE DIVINE WORD MISSIONARIES

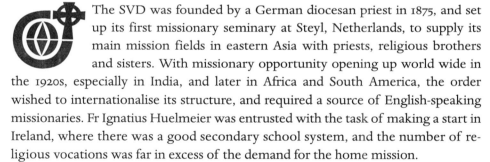

The SVD was founded by a German diocesan priest in 1875, and set up its first missionary seminary at Steyl, Netherlands, to supply its main mission fields in eastern Asia with priests, religious brothers and sisters. With missionary opportunity opening up world wide in the 1920s, especially in India, and later in Africa and South America, the order wished to internationalise its structure, and required a source of English-speaking missionaries. Fr Ignatius Huelmeier was entrusted with the task of making a start in Ireland, where there was a good secondary school system, and the number of religious vocations was far in excess of the demand for the home mission.

Final approval for the foundation was received from Bishop Doorly of Elphin in November 1938. In 1939 Donamon Castle, county Roscommon, which was domicile to the Caufield family for centuries, was purchased with some land from The Irish Land Commisson for £1,300. A novitiate was established as World War II broke out. The foundation was forced to rely on its own resources, as it was cut off from its Dutch headquarters. Thus began the story of the mutual goodwill and co-operation that has always existed between the SVD community at Donamon, and the clergy and laity of the neighbourhood and diocese.

A new church and a building block to accommodate over seventy students was completed in 1963. This event, however, coincided with a general fall off in religious vocations. Over the years the Donamon House has been used as a juniorate, seminary and provincialate for the Irish Province of the SVD, and had many ordinations for the order. The seminary of the Society of the Divine Word was transferred to St Patrick's College, Maynooth, in the late 1960s. By 1982 the students' residence at Donamon was made available to the Diocese of Elphin as a Pastoral Centre. It became a centre for religious and education courses, parish vigils, and retreats. Later the same building was leased to the Irish Wheelchair Association as a holiday and respite centre for people with physical disability.

The SVD celebrated fifty years at Donamon in 1989. Among the many activities at Donamon Castle at present is the editing and circulation of *The Word* magazine, and the printing and dispatch of Christmas cards. Currently over six million greeting cards are printed annually as a means of subsidising their missionary activities overseas, mostly in Third World countries.

WOMEN RELIGIOUS
AUGUSTINIAN SISTERS

The Augustinian canonesses were introduced to Ireland in the twelfth century (1144). They soon came to Elphin diocese, and had five convents all dependant on the mother-house at Kilcreevanty in the Tuam diocese. The houses were at Roscommon (1144-c. 1223), Derrane (1144-c. 1223), Ardcarne (1144-1590), Ballynagalliagh, near Drumcliff (?1223-1562), Termonkeelin (Kilkeevan parish) (1223-16th century). All of these convents were dispersed by the late sixteenth century.

On the invitation of Dr Brett, Bishop of Elphin, the Augustinian Sisters came to Athlone in 1748, and established an academy that lasted for two decades or so. There was at least one sister, and another sister probably accompanied her. In the Religious Census of Elphin of 1749 she is recorded as a boarding school mistress with eight children over fourteen in her household. The school seems to have continued for a number of years though she died a year after her arrival. There was no trace of this, the first foundation by a religious order of nuns in the Diocese of Elphin, by 1770.

PRESENTATION SISTERS

 A Presentation Sister arrived in the parish of Kiltoom & Cam in 1836 and was joined sometime later by another sister. They took charge of the recently built National School at Ballybay. It is said that there were 300 pupils attending the school from the start. Sr Mary Clare Xavier Grace 'took ill from the damp situation' and died just one year after her arrival but there is no record of when Sr Mary Angela Lynch left Ballybay.

URSULINE SISTERS

The Ursuline order was founded by St Angela Merici in Italy in 1535. Originally known as The Little Company, it was introduced to Ireland by Nano Nagle in 1750. Their principle apostolate was the education of the young. Bishop Browne invited the sisters to establish a boarding school for girls in Athlone in 1844. The school and novitiate at Summerhill flourished but the sisters transferred to Sligo in 1850 where they continued their work of education. In 1893 the secondary school adopted the Intermediate system of education and the well-known boarding school remained open until 1982. St Vincent's National School opened under the title of Nazareth School in 1851, and came under the Board of Education in 1902. The adjoining St Anne's Junior School amalgamated with St Vincent's in 1966, and continues today as Scoil Ursula, on a new site on the Strandhill Road.

In 1950, at the request of the Department of Education, the sisters started St Angela's College of Education for Home Economics at Lough Gill. It became a Constituent College of University College, Galway, in 1978. In 1957 four Ursuline sisters from Sligo started what is now the Kenyan Region of the Irish Ursuline Union. In 1980, at the request of Bishop Conway, some Ursuline sisters moved into the newly established parish of St Joseph's, at Ballytivnan in Sligo. The community at Finisklin, which numbered over seventy sisters in the 1950s, has now fourteen members and plans are being made to move to a smaller house.

In 1973 the Sligo Ursulines became part of an Irish Federation of Ursulines. Until that time all Irish Ursuline communities were autonomous. This Federation of Ursulines voted to form a centralised Irish Ursuline Union in 1978, which became an Associate Province of the Ursulines of the Roman Union in 1987.

Although not founded specifically to provide education, the Ursulines became involved in this apostolate from the mid sixteenth century. However, Angela Merici's counsel, to change with the changing times, was more clearly understood after the Second Vatican Council. Since then the Sligo Ursulines have responded to the needs for public health nursing, parish work, assisting the homeless and to the need for spiritual direction.

SISTERS OF MERCY

Founded by Catherine McAuley in Dublin in 1831, the Sisters of Mercy have been assisting the poor, providing education and caring for the sick, in the main towns throughout the Diocese of Elphin, since 1846.

After the First Vatican Council in 1870, Dr Gillooly, Bishop of Elphin with the approval of the Holy See, amalgamated the Sligo, Roscommon, Athlone and Elphin convents under a central government. A Reverend Mother was elected and arrangements were made for all present and future Mercy convents in the diocese to be governed by a local superior appointed by her. St Patrick's Convent in Sligo became the mother-house for the Sisters of Mercy in the diocese. Each year the Reverend Mother visited the convents and there was an annual Council Meeting of all the local superiors. The Reverend Mother was re-elected every third year.

The bishop also visited the convents every three years and his administrator audited the convent accounts until the 1970s. The central novitiate for the formation of Mercy Sisters for the diocese was in Sligo. A letter from Rome in 1926 pronouncing the Congregation of the Sisters of Mercy to be of Pontifical Rite lay unheeded for many years but eventually the Superior General and her Council took responsibility for all the congregational affairs of the Sisters of Mercy of the diocese.

An Extraordinary General Chapter of the Sisters of Mercy of the Diocese of Elphin took place in Sligo in 1969 during which a new Constitution and Statutes were adopted. The following year Mother Bonaventure Kelly was elected Superior General of all the Sisters of Mercy of the Diocese of Elphin in Ireland, the USA and Kenya, for a period of six years. A National Constitution for all the Sisters of Mercy in Ireland was adopted in 1985. At the General Assembly of 1991, the overwhelming majority of the sisters of the diocese voted in favour of the Union of the Sisters of Mercy in Ireland and the first Mercy Congregational Chapter took place in 1994. In 1995 the Mercy Sisters in the seven dioceses of Achonry, Ardagh and Clonmacnoise, Clonfert, Elphin, Galway, Killala and Tuam joined together to form the Sisters of Mercy of the Western Province.

Sligo

The first foundation of the Sisters of Mercy in the diocese was in Sligo in 1846 with the arrival of a group of sisters from Westport. From 1846-48 their principal work was instructing children and adults for the sacraments, visiting and caring for the sick, distributing alms to famine stricken sufferers and training orphan girls for domestic service. Later they attended patients in the Fever Hospital. When a new convent was completed, the sisters opened a public school in 1849 to which some 100 pupils came. In a parliamentary debate in 1858 St Patrick's Convent School in Sligo, as well as others, were referred to as 'models of conventional management in competent hands'. By 1890 there were 600 girls and 200 boys enrolled in the school. The sisters had a small boarding school, which later became an orphanage. Intermediate classes to qualify candidates as pupil teachers, and scholarships classes, were provided by the sisters. Though anxious to keep their schools abreast in academic subjects, the religious and moral training of the students was always their main aim.

From the beginning, a House of Mercy formed part of the work of the sisters. Here many young girls were trained in domestic duties and in 1860 a new laundry was opened to give training and employment to girls. Sisters took charge of the running of the workhouse in Sligo in 1899 and a convent was built for them beside the workhouse. The sisters continued to care for the residents after the abolition of the workhouse system in 1922.

In order to be closer to the people they served, three sisters moved to live in Cranmore housing estate in Sligo in 1982. That same year McAuley House was purchased for women in need of short-term care and later sisters began to care for homeless men at Maryville. When St Patrick's Convent was vacated in the late 1980s the sisters moved to a smaller purpose-built residence and to a number of smaller houses in town. The sisters from Sligo were responsible for starting the Mercy foundations in Ballina in 1851 and in Enniskillen in 1856.

Roscommon

A group of Sisters of Mercy arrived in Roscommon from Limerick in 1853, travelling by boat to Athlone, and then overland to Roscommon. Here they built a convent, an orphanage, a public laundry, and a bakery, and developed a farmyard. In 1902 they built a magnificent three-story school. Secondary education has been provided for girls in and around Roscommon town since 1929. In 1921 the new Irish government united all the workhouses in county Roscommon and established the Sacred Heart Home in Roscommon. Some sisters who were placed in charge had served in the workhouse in Castlerea. The existing building was upgraded and a new wing and day centre were opened in the 1960s.

The headquarters of the Mercy Order in Elphin was in Roscommon from 1976-1982 and the novitiate was transferred from Sligo to Roscommon in 1978. A new building called St Catherine's, named after Catherine McAuley, founder of the Sisters of Mercy, served as the novitiate for the Sisters of Mercy of the diocese until 1987 when it reverted to Sligo. Sisters involved in parish work and in family ministry now live in St Catherine's. In 1999 the original convent in Roscommon was vacated, and the sisters moved to a new and smaller convent nearby.

Athlone

A group of sisters from Roscommon started a Mercy foundation in Athlone in 1857. Initially their work involved visitation of the poor but soon a disused distillery was adapted as a House of Mercy and a laundry was developed in order to provide employment. The sisters ran night classes and soon a flourishing hosiery centre was established. After acquiring a farm, as in Roscommon, the sisters became self-sufficient.

During the period 1923-27 boarders and day-pupils attended the intermediate school which prepared girls for teaching, nursing, and the civil service. In 1929 the intermediate school became a full secondary school. The boarding school was transferred to Summerhill in 1965, and St Peter's day school was finally closed in 1974. St Joseph's, Summerhill, continues today as a flourishing school, albeit without boarders.

The sisters have also operated two fine primary schools in Athlone for many years and they assist in the parish of Ss Peter and Paul in a variety of ways. In 1986 a group of sisters moved to live in the Battery Heights area of the town in order to be closer to the people whom they serve.

Elphin

The Mercy Convent in Elphin was erected on a plot of ground obtained by Bishop French in 1812 as a site for a dispensary. The widowed Mary Archbold (nee Grace from Mantua House), who was professed as a Sister of Mercy in Roscommon in 1858, was instrumental in the establishment of the convent in Elphin in 1868. Sisters from both Sligo and Roscommon helped to form the new community.

The sisters became involved in instructing the young, caring for the sick and in running the local primary school. A secondary top which was added to the primary school in 1950 became a full secondary school for girls in 1967. Later it amalgamated with the grammar school in the town. The primary school continued under the care of the sisters until 1989, when the convent was sold. Some sisters continued to live in a house provided by the people of Elphin and to minister to the people of the parish until 1998.

Boyle

The first Mercy Convent to be established in the Diocese of Elphin, after the amalgamation of the convents in Sligo, Roscommon, Athlone and Elphin in 1870, was in Boyle in 1875. The new school which was built there in 1902 replaced the one which had served the area so well for a quarter of a century. The old building was used for a Hosiery School from 1903 to 1915 where dressmaking, knitting, embroidery, lace making and crochet were taught. Many men and women found employment in St Vincent's Laundry, which served the area for some sixty years. A new infant school was opened in 1965. The secondary top, which was started in 1952, became a full secondary school with common enrolment with St Mary's Boys' College and the Vocational School in 1967. The new secondary school building was opened in 1970. There are now plans for a new community college to be built in Boyle.

Castlerea

St Anne's Convent in Castlerea was founded in 1888. The schools which had been erected in the town were given over to the sisters fully furnished, and free of debt. Some 400 children were attending the schools at that time. The convent secondary school was begun in 1967. In the late 1980s the sisters joined with the other education providers in the town to build the new Castlerea Community School, which opened in 1993. Some sisters also lived at the Convent of Our Lady of Providence beside the workhouse which the sisters took charge of from 1908 to 1921. A Sister of Mercy became the first matron of Áras Phóil, a nursing home for the elderly which was called after a Sister of Mercy, and sisters have also been involved in the provision and running of services for handicapped children in the Castlerea area for a number of years.

Summerhill, Athlone

After the diocesan college was moved from Summerhill, Athlone, to Sligo in 1880, the Sisters of Mercy assumed responsibility for the orphanage which started there in 1882. At any one time some 150 girls found a home and were educated there for over eighty years. With the passing of the Adoption Bill in 1950 numbers declined and the orphanage was eventually closed in 1965. That year the boarding school was transferred from Athlone town to Summerhill and by 1974 all the secondary school pupils were attending St Joseph's College, Summerhill. A new primary school was built at Summerhill in 1963. The college was renovated in the 1980s and it has been run by a Board of Management since 1992. Some 600 students now attend the college.

Strokestown

Five sisters from Sligo started the Mercy community in Strokestown in 1891. They lived in a house in Church Street until their new convent, which was built on a site provided by Pakenham-Mahon of the Demesne, was ready in 1897. On their arrival in Strokestown the sisters were appointed to take charge of the primary school. In 1954 the old school was demolished and a new one was built. In order to make second level education available for the girls in the area, the sisters started a secondary top in 1955. In 1967 the local co-educational lay school, Scoil Mhuire, and the convent school were amalgamated. Some 350 students now attend this co-educational secondary school. Though the sisters vacated the convent building in the early 1990s, the four sisters who now live in a house nearby continue their educational work in the school. They are also involved in pastoral work.

Mullaghmore

The sisters purchased a site in Mullaghmore in 1929 for a convalescent home and holiday home. A new convent was built, providing accommodation for thirty-two visitors as well as a chapel for the people of the area. In recent years the building is used for retreats and renewal courses as well as for holidays. A primary school for some 50 pupils was opened in Mullaghmore in 1930. The school building is now used as a community centre.

Missions in USA and Kenya

Since 1956 many Sisters of Mercy from the Diocese of Elphin have been involved in the running of schools and in teaching in some six parishes in the Diocese of San Diego in the USA. Some sisters have served as Directors of Religious Education and have worked with the underprivileged and with ethnic groups. In 1991 twenty-six sisters from the Diocese of Elphin were still working in the American Region. Four nursing sisters undertook a mission in Mutomo in Kenya in 1962, providing community-based health care and have been involved in running a 150 bed hospital in the area for many years. A number of sisters have also been involved in education in Mutomo and in other parts of Kenya. In 1991 there were nine Sisters of Mercy from the Diocese of Elphin still working in Kenya.

FRANCISCAN MISSIONARIES OF MARY

On the invitation of Bishop Clancy, twelve Franciscan Missionaries of Mary came to Loughglynn in 1903 in order to help the poor of the area. They set up a Domestic Economy school and started cheese-making and butter-making in order to provide employment. This work continued until 1970.

Within a few years of their arrival, native Irish sisters were teaching in the local national school. From the 1940s there was a novitiate in Loughglynn for girls wishing to join the Franciscan Missionaries of Mary and the building was extended in the 1960s. The original building was converted into a nursing home in 1970 and twenty sisters now reside in the new part of the building. The Franciscan Missionaries of Mary model their lives on St Francis' love for the poor, on Our Lady as the model for all women, and find wholeness in contemplation before the Blessed Sacrament.

POOR SISTERS OF NAZARETH

The Sisters of Nazareth came to Sligo in 1910 in order to care for children who were forced to live in the workhouse. Initially the sisters took care of boys from four years of age but many remained under their care and attended the school they provided until they were teenagers. Several of these young people found work on farms in counties Galway and Roscommon. The sisters provided a home and education for between 100 and 150 children at any one time and it is estimated that from the time of their arrival in Sligo until 1990 they had cared for some 1,800 children. The sisters also provided a nursery for babies from the 1950s.

In 1954 the Nazareth House was extended in order to provide additional accommodation for elderly people and the interior of the main house was reconstructed in the 1960s. From then on, the sisters looked after entire families of children, some of whom had been orphaned. Group homes were provided for the children in the grounds of the Nazareth House from the 1980s until 1994.

The Nazareth House was registered as a nursing home in 1980, and began to develop its services for the elderly. Currently, eleven sisters and some 140 staff look after the many elderly people who are in need of residential care and support.

DAUGHTERS OF WISDOM (LA SAGESSE)

The Daughters of Wisdom came to Sligo from England in 1955 in order to provide a residential home and a school for the mentally handicapped throughout Ireland. After the necessary preparations had been made, Cregg House was opened in January 1956. The foundation stone for accommodation for over 200 residents was laid in 1961.

The setting up of a School for Mental Handicap Nursing was approved in 1966. St Cecilia's Special National School was opened in 1974 and the campus became known as 'The Sisters of La Sagesse Services, Cregg House'. In order to provide for a more independent and homelike environment, a chalet complex for up to 110 adults was opened in 1979 and in 1981 the first hostel was opened in Sligo town. As the new millennium dawns ten special houses for the handicapped are to be found in or near Sligo. A Hydrotherapy and Recreation Complex was also built at Cregg House in the early 1990s. The sisters and staff at Cregg House recognise the individuality of each person and help them to develop their full potential. They now provide day and residential services, schooling and houses for 215 children and adults with moderate, severe and profound learning disabilities.

SISTERS OF THE DIVINE MASTER

The Sisters of the Divine Master came to Athlone in 1969 and shortly after their arrival they opened a Liturgical Centre in the town. Their main purpose is perpetual adoration as well as catering for liturgical needs. They seek to develop a greater appreciation of good religious art in the homes. Eight members of this international community moved into a new building consisting of a convent, an oratory and a shop in 1983. The Chapel of Adoration is a haven of peace and tranquillity for all and a programme of perpetual adoration was begun in 1990. Three sisters established a new community of Sisters of the Divine Master in Dublin in 1992 and since 1998 the sisters have become more involved in the liturgical life of the parish of Ss Peter and Paul in Athlone.

SISTERS OF THE PRESENTATION OF MARY

The Sisters of the Presentation of Mary came to Castleblakeney, in Ahascragh parish, in 1963 to assume the management of St Cuan's Secondary School for girls. Over the next six years they expanded the school by building three extensions, one in 1965, another in 1967 and the main building in 1969. The sisters left Castleblakeney in 1987, and the school is now under diocesan trusteeship.

In 1982, the year that Anne Marie Rivier, the foundress of the Sisters of the Presentation of Mary, was beatified, the sisters went to Sligo to establish Perpetual Adoration at the Cathedral. Since then many of the laity have joined the sisters in perpetual adoration of the Blessed Sacrament in Sligo Cathedral.

SISTERS OF ST JOSEPH OF THE APPARITION

In March 1957 four Sisters of St Joseph of the Apparition left Manchester to take on the administration of Garden Hill Nursing Home and Maternity Unit in Sligo, following the example of their foundress St Emilie de Vialar who loved the sick, the poor and the needy. Towards the end of the 1960s the sisters built a new 30-bed hospital as well as an X-ray department at Garden Hill. Later they added a specially designed out-patient clinic and many other modern ancillary facilities. Three sisters and a large medical and administration staff now care for the sick at Garden Hill, and they are proud of the nursing and spiritual care that they provide. The Sisters of St Joseph of the Apparition also continue to serve the people of Sligo through various forms of pastoral work.

MISSIONARIES OF CHARITY

Bishop Jones and Mother Theresa
during her visit to Sligo in 1996

The Missionaries of Charity, founded by Mother Theresa of Calcutta (1910-1997) opened a house in Sligo in December 2000, in fulfillment of a promise she made on her visit to Sligo in 1996. This is a contempletive order and is the first such order of nuns in the history of the diocese. The community of sisters devote their lives entirely to prayer, apart from an hour of daily visitation in the Sligo parishes.

PART IV

The Parishes

The twelfth-century reforms of the Irish church, enacted during the synods of Rath Breasail and Kells, replaced the monastic structure with a hierarchical and territorial church. This resulted in the establishment of diocesan boundaries and subsequently parish structures. The Diocese of Elphin as we know it today was formed in 1152 and parish boundaries came soon afterwards.

There are thirty-eight parishes in the diocese at present, which is less than half the original number. Eighty-eight priests serve a Catholic population of over 68,000. While several of the parish boundaries are of comparatively recent origin, the Christian faith can be traced back to Patrician times. Every parish has at least one or two medieval church ruins, as well as holy wells and other relics that link us back to the early centuries of Christianity. The parish communities of the diocese have a unique Christian heritage that has characterised people, places and traditions.

The history of the diocese could never be fully chronicled without the story of its parishes. The parish histories contained in this book are a brief summarised version of centuries of people living the Christian faith. Every parish warrants its own publication, and we were fortunate to have had access to a number of locally published parish histories. The histories included here are strictly ecclesiastical and do not take into account the many commendable community activities which are daily undertaken by various dedicated groups working for the betterment of their parishes.

The parishes are listed in alphabetical order under the title by which they are now known, e.g. Ballyforan. The names of church areas and the places of worship are also given, e.g. Ballyforan, Dysart and Four Roads, as are the names of the ancient parishes which are now wholly or partially incorporated within the modern parishes, e.g. Taughboy, Dysart and Tisrara.

Contents

Abbreviations:
ED: Electoral District
By: Barony
Scales given for the parish maps are approximate.

Parish of Aghanagh
(Aghanagh) Counties Sligo & Roscommon
Churches: Ballinafad, Ballyrush & Corrigeenroe

THE PARISH of Ballinafad, also known by its ancient title of Aghanagh, lies in southeast county Sligo, along the shores of Lough Arrow. It stretches lengthwise from the parish of Riverstown to the summit of the Curlews, and thence around them to include the county Roscommon area of Corrigeenroe. It is bounded on the west by the Bricklieve Mountains with their 5,000-year-old megalithic tombs, and on the south by the Curlews and the parish of Boyle. The parish contains seventy townlands, fifteen of which are in county Roscommon. At the foot of the Curlews stands Ballinafad village, with the remains of the castle built by Captain John St Barbe in 1590.

The original church of Aghanagh was a Patrician foundation. According to local tradition it was built on a little mound to the north of the present graveyard, and overlooked Lough Arrow. Its patron was St Maine, who was the first and only abbot-bishop of the diminutive diocese of Aghanagh, and on his death it must have been absorbed by one of its neighbours.

Romanesque doorway in the north wall of Aghanagh church 1879.

Subsequently, a small monastic settlement was established there by the Arroasian branch of the Augustinians. Portions of this foundation have survived the ravages of time, but the eastern gable has disappeared. The walls are constructed of great blocks of stone, the masonry being coarse and rough. The doorway and windows are semi-circular headed, the stones of the windows being carved. The Romanesque doorway, which resembles that at Shancough, is in the northern side-wall, and looks out onto an ancient rath that adjoins the graveyard. Within the ivy-clad ruins stands the beehive-shaped tomb of John St Barbe, Constable of Ballinafad Castle, who died in May 1628. During the Famine years, in the mistaken belief that this was the final resting-place of an ecclesiastic, the remains of Fr Francis Egan PP, Aghanagh, were deposited within it, after a newly opened grave at the old thatched chapel had become waterlogged. Also in the early Christian period, a nunnery was located on the slopes of the Briclieves, on the border of Carricknahorna and Corradooey townlands.

Ruins of Aghanagh
church
(W.F. Wakeman 1879)

Between 1660 and 1760 there is no evidence of a fixed place of worship apart from the Mass Rock at St Maine's well, and the 'Stirring Rock' in the valley at Carricknahorna. In the 1930s Tobar Mháine was indicated as being on the west side of the Sligo-Boyle road, less than a 100 yards from the medieval church. A stone, believed to show the knee-marks of St Maine, is located on the lakeshore. Pilgrimage to the site had been discontinued by that date. Other holy wells are marked on the 1914 OS map at Castlebaldwin village, namely Tobar Bhríde, Tober Murray and Tobar Phádraig; another well, called Tobermahon, is to be found in the townland of Drumdoney on the main Dublin road.

Following the death of Fr Owen Conmy PP in 1704 the area was amalgamated with the parish of Boyle, and remained so until 1828 when Fr Terence Sweeney was appointed parish priest of Aghanagh.

The first church in Ballinafad village was built in 1760, by Michael Reynolds, Prior of the Dominican Abbey of Ballindoon, who was also PP of Aghanagh. In the course of the Ordnance Survey (1835) it was described as 'a poor building', and on the altar the following inscription was engraved: 'This house was built in 1760 by Fr Michael Reynolds of Ballindoon, at his own expense, for his own abode, and shelter for the faithful.' The site of this primitive structure was at the mouth of the stream running down by the castle from Ballaghboy. On Sundays it served as a place of worship, and for the remainder of the week as a schoolhouse and priests' residence. It subsequently served as a National School, and more recently as a Parochial Hall. The present church of Ballinafad was completed in 1860, and dedicated to the Immaculate Conception. It underwent extensive repairs in 1929, with the addition of a tower or belfry, surmounted by a Celtic cross. The presbytery alongside was built between the years 1876 and 1892.

Ballinafad was the birthplace on 14 November 1841 of John Healy who subsequently became Professor of Theology at St Patrick's College, Maynooth. He became

John Healy,
Archbishop of
Tuam, born in
Ballinafad in 1841

co-adjutor Bishop of Clonfert in 1884 and subsequently bishop of that diocese in 1898. He was appointed Archbishop of Tuam in 1903, died on 17 March 1918, and is buried in the cathedral of Tuam. For a time he edited the *Irish Ecclesiastical Record,* and was the author of a number of published works, notably *Ireland's Ancient Schools and Scholars, Life of St Patrick, Centenary History of Maynooth,* and *Papers and Addresses.*

Ballyrush, which originally belonged to the ancient parish of Tawnagh and subsequently to Riverstown, was annexed to Aghanagh in 1876. A decade earlier, in 1868, the old church, known locally as Greyfort, was replaced by the present church of St Patrick, which was extensively renovated and refurbished in 1931.

The church at Corrigeenroe, in county Roscommon, which was originally part of Boyle parish, was erected in 1829, on the site of a smaller thatched building that had been built around 1780. In 1857 it was remodelled and extended by Captain John Woulfe-Flanagan of Drumdoe for the benefit of his tenants, and in the church grounds are memorials to members of the Woulfe-Flanagan family. It was further restored in 1927, and solemnly dedicated to St Thérèse by Timothy Canon Hurley PP of Aghanagh.

Aghanagh parish church at Hollybrook serves the Church of Ireland community in the area. The construction of the church was commenced just before the Famine, but was not completed until some years later. It was built on a site donated by the Ffolliott family of Hollybrook House, who were also the principal patrons.

Key to the map

The townlands marked with an (R), are in Co Roscommon. The remainder are in Co Sligo.

01. Aghacarra (R)	10. Ardloy	18. Brickeen
02. Aghagowla (R)	11. Ballaghboy	19. Bricklieve
03. Aghanagh	12. Ballinafad	20. Bunnadober
04. Aghnasurn (R)	13. Ballyhealy or	21. Cams
05. Annagh	Hollybrook Demesne	22. Carricknahorna East
06. Annagh or Druminilra	14. Ballymullany	23. Carricknahorna West
(R)	15. Bellanagarrigeeny or	24. Carrowkeel
07. Annaghcor	Castlebaldwin	25. Cartron
08. Annaghgowla Island	16. Bellarush	26. Cartronroe
09. Ardlee	17. Bodorragha (R)	_. Castlebaldwin (see 15)

27. Cleavry
28. Cloghoge Lower
29. Cloghoge Upper
30. Cloongad
31. Cloonymeenaghan
32. Coolboy
33. Coolskeagh
34. Corlisheen
35. Cornacarta (R)
36. Corradoo East
37. Corradoo West
38. Cuilsheeghary Beg
39. Cuilsheeghary More
40. Derreenaghan (R)
41. Derreentunny (R)
42. Derryvunny (R)
43. Derrywanna (R)
44. Doonaveeragh

45. Doongeelagh (part of)
46. Doonsheheen
47. Drumderry
48. Drumdoe (R)
49. Drumdoney
_. Druminilra or Annagh (see 60)
50. Drumshinnagh
51. Gortalough
52. Heapstown
_. Hollybrook Demesne or Ballyhealy (see 13)
53. Illaunaprechaun Island (Crannóg)
54. Knockroe
55. Largan (R)
56. Lecarrow (CP Aghanagh)
57. Lecarrow

(CP Drumcolumb)
58. Lillybrook
59. Limnagh
60. Lissycoyne
61. Mountgaffeny
62. Mullaghfarna
63. Parkmore
64. Shanvoley (R)
65. Sheerevagh
66. Smutternagh (R)
67. Tintagh (R)
68. Treanmacmurtagh
69. Treanscrabbagh
70. Whitehill

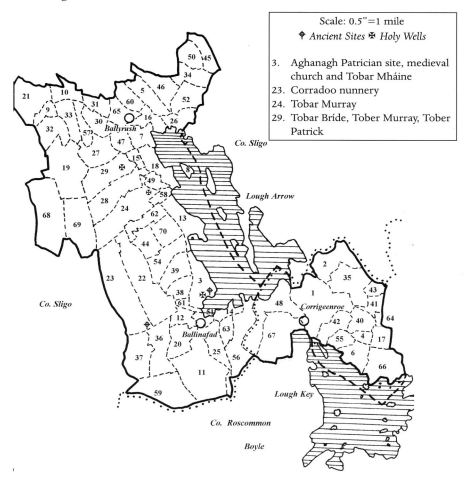

Scale: 0.5"=1 mile

✠ Ancient Sites ✠ Holy Wells

3. Aghanagh Patrician site, medieval church and Tobar Mháine
23. Corradoo nunnery
24. Tobar Murray
29. Tobar Bríde, Tober Murray, Tober Patrick

Co. Sligo

Lough Arrow

Co. Sligo

Co. Roscommon

Boyle

Lough Key

Corrigeenroe

Ballinafad

Ballyrush

Parish of Ahamlish
(Ahamlish) County Sligo
Churches: Cliffoney & Grange

AHAMLISH is the most northerly parish in the Diocese of Elphin. It is bounded on the east by the Dartry range, on the west by the Atlantic, on the south by Drumcliff and Maugherow, and on the north by county Leitrim. It includes within its boundaries the villages of Cliffoney, Grange and Mullaghmore, in addition to the monastic island of Inishmurray. This was originally O'Connor-Sligo territory, and that of their underlords, the O'Harts, one of whose strongholds was at Grange.

'Holed' stone near Teampall na mBan, Inishmurray

In the seventeenth century Ahamlish passed by grant to William, Earl of Strafford, and Thomas Radcliffe, and eventually to Sir John Temple, whose son, Henry, was created Viscount Palmerston in 1723. Henry John Temple, the 3rd Viscount Palmerston, when he succeeded to the Ahamlish estate, built a 'spacious chapel' at Cliffoney for his tenantry. This church of St Molaise, originally a rectangular thatched structure, was built between 1827 and 1830, and was reconstructed around 1865, being altered in shape from rectangular to cruciform. It replaced an earlier place of worship, which stood close to the junction on the road to Mullaghmore, as shown on an early nineteenth-century estate map. The parochial house and adjoining grounds were also donated by the aforementioned British statesman to Malachi Brennan PP, a gift graciously acknowledged by Bishop Burke in a letter to the *Champion*, or *Sligo News*, in May 1837. '... Lord Palmerston, by letter addressed to me, had remitted eight years' rent due on a holding occupied by the late parish priest of Ahamlish, and generously given, for the succeeding priests, upwards of twelve acres of prime land as a Glebe, subject only to the annual acknowledgment of one pound as rent ... His praises will be daily sounded, and echoed back, from the majestic mountains on his estate to the shores of the Atlantic.' It is currently held on a 999 year lease granted by Winifred W. Ashley to Bishop Coyne in 1927.

The church of Mary Immaculate, Grange, was built in the mid-nineteenth century and replaced an earlier place of worship on Grange hill, just north of the village. In 1842, Malachi Brennan PP advertised for architects and builders for the new church, and it is likely that it had been roofed before the onslaught of the Famine. The adjoining presbytery was built a quarter of a century later by John Healy CC, subsequently Archbishop of Tuam. A major reconstruction of this church, including a new roof, floor, seating, and windows, a number of which depicted the mysteries of the rosary, was carried out in 1956-58, at a cost of £15,000. The church was re-opened with a solemn blessing in February 1958.

Church of Mary Immaculate, Grange

The Mercy convent and chapel at Mullaghmore stands on the site of former bathing-lodges, which were destroyed during the troubles. The convent was opened in 1929, and the church, which can accommodate two hundred worshippers, was dedicated on Whit Monday in June 1930, by Edward Doorly, Bishop of Elphin.

In 1984, St Molaise's parish park was opened in Grange on a two-acre site, and contains a grotto, which resembles Teach Molaise on Inishmurray, and a replica of the medieval wooden statue of the saint.

The monastic island of Inishmurray, which lies about five miles off the mainland, consists of 209 statute acres and, in the words of John O'Donovan, contains the 'most perfect Cyclopean ruins in the world'. In the centre of the island stands a fine example of an early Celtic monastery, which was founded in the sixth century by St Molaise, who is referred to in early documents as 'Muirdeach', and whose name is retained in the Irish name of the island – Inis Muireadhaigh. There is a strong oral tradition of an association between the Inishmurray settlement and Colmcille.

The monastic remains lie principally within the enclosure known as the 'cashel', which encloses an area of approximately a third of an acre, and is sub-divided into three parts by low partition walls. This area contains a number of buildings including Teampall na bhFear (church of the men), Teach

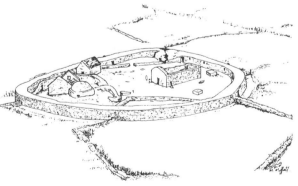

Inishmurray monastic settlement

Molaise (Molaise's House), and Teampall na Tine (church or house of fire). Teampall na bhFear, also known as Teampall Molaise and Teampall Mór, appears to have been the principal church of the monastery. Also within the cashel are beehive cells,

173

a number of small chambers and holy wells. Overall, the settlement is reputed to be one of the best examples of a primitive Irish foundation

In 798 the island was raided by the Vikings, and the Annals relate that 'Inishmurray was burned by the foreigners' in 807. Local tradition suggests that the monks left the island at the end of the twelfth century, when the O'Connors ousted the O'Dowds from the lordship of the nearby mainland. The island had a population of one hundred in 1836, but this decreased steadily over the following century, until the island was finally abandoned by its people in 1948.

The only other monastic foundation in Ahamlish was Staide Abbey, in the townland of Agharrow. According to tradition it was founded by St Molaise, and may have acted as a type of mainland 'stopping house' for the Inishmurray monks. It is said that it was from here that St Colmcille, stricken with remorse after the battle of Cooldrumman, crossed over to Inishmurray where he confessed his sins to St Molaise. By the second half of the sixteenth century Staide was deserted and in ruins. In 1588, twelve Spaniards, who had come ashore from the wrecked vessels of the Spanish Armada, were hanged within its walls.

Cross inscribed stone at St Brigid's Well, Cliffony

There are a number of holy wells in the parish, notably St Molaise's at Moneygold, St Brigid's at Cliffoney, and Tober Patrick on Dernish Island. At St Brigid's Well there is a block of reddish sandstone, on one side of which is inscribed or punched the figure of a cross, the design of which presents the appearance of an early Christian Cross, and on the head of which is a remarkable symbol known as a *Croix Gammeé,* or swastika. This site was a popular place for patterns in pre-Famine times.

Ahamlish (Ahamplish) Church of Ireland, in the ancient graveyard in the townland of Moneygold north of Grange, was erected between 1811 and 1813 on the site of an earlier Christian foundation. It had accommodation for one hundred worshippers before it closed in the mid twentieth century.

Key to the Map

01. Agharrow
02. Ardnaglass Lower
03. Ardnaglass Upper
04. Ballincastle
05. Ballinphull
06. Balynabrock
07. Ballyscannel
08. Breaghwy
09. Bunduff
10. Carrownamaddoo
11. Cartronkillerdoo
12. Cartron plank
13. Catlegal
14. Castlegowan
15. Cloonercoo
16. Cloontyprocklis
17. Cloyragh
18. Cloyspara
19. Conor's Island

20. Creevykeel
21. Creevymore
22. Dernish Island
23. Derry
24. Derrylehan
25. Doonshaskin
26. Drangan or Mountedward
27. Drumfad
28. Edenreagh
29. Gortaderry
30. Gortnaleck
31. Grange
32. Grellagh
33. Groagh
34. Illaunatir Island
35. Inishmurray
36. Inishacor
37. Kilcat
38. Kilkilloge

39. Kiltykere
40. Lislary
41. Lyle
42. Moneygold
–. Mountedward or Drangan
     (see 26)
43. Mount Temple
44. Mullaghmore
45. Mullaghmore West
46. Newtown
47. Newtowncliffoney
48. Rathfrask
49. Rathhugh
50. Silverhill
51. Srarevagh
52. Streedagh

Scale: 0.4"=1 mile
✠ *Ancient Sites* ✠ *Holy Wells*

1. Staid Abbey
5. St Brigid's Well, Cliffoney
22. Tober Patrick, Dernish Island
35. Monastic site, Inishmurray
42. St Molaise's Well, Moneygold

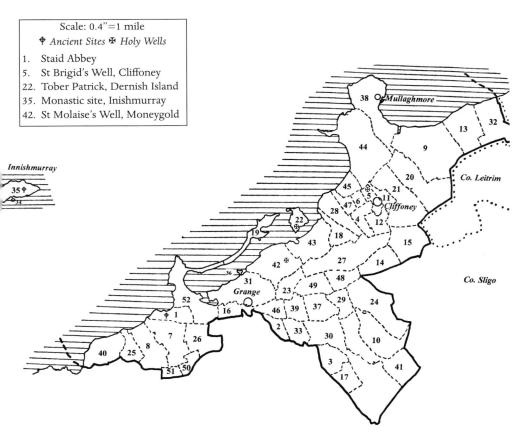

Parish of Ahascragh
(Ahascragh & Killosolan) County Galway
Churches: Ahascragh & Caltra

AHASCRAGH lies in the southwest part of the diocese, and is one of only two Elphin parishes located entirely in county Galway. It is bounded on the east, south and west by Clonfert Diocese, and adjoins Ballygar and Ballyforan parishes to the north. It is a union of the two medieval parishes of Ahascragh itself, and Killosolan, which related approximately to the present area of Caltra. The parishes were amalgamated under one parish priest following the Famine. Ahascragh is referred to by the Four Masters as Áth Eascrath Cuain, the ford of Cuan's Sandridge.

There are a number of holy wells of importance in the parish. The first of these is in Castlegar East known as St Cuan's Well, or sometimes referred to locally as St Cavan's Well, an anglicised version of Caomhán. St Cuan died in 788 according to the *Annals,* and pilgrims visit the well on 15 October in his honour. The pattern was discouraged in the early nineteenth century. There is a seventeenth century cruci-

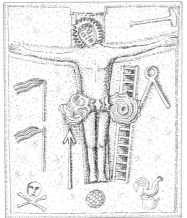

The crucifixion plaque at St Cuan's Well, Ahascragh

fixion plaque at St Cuan's well. This is one of the finest examples of such plaques in the west of Ireland. A plaster-cast copy can be seen in St Cuan's Church, Ahascragh. Other holy wells include one located near the present church in Caltra village, and dedicated to St Solan, and one called Tobar Mhuire in Ahascragh village. There is also a holy well adjacent to Chapel-Finnerty graveyard. The Crozier of St Grellan (Bachall Ghriolláin) was a famous relic preserved in the village of Ahascragh, but lost about 1837. It had been the battle standard of the O'Kellys of Uí Máine down the centuries.

In the *Papal Taxation List* of 1306, churches are listed for both Ahascragh and Killosolan, which identify the early Christian and medieval sites in this locality. There were two Carmelite friaries of the ancient Observant or White Friars in the parish. The earliest foundation was established before 1336 near the present church at Caltra, also known as Caltra na Pallice (Cealtrach na Pailise). It was founded by the Berminghams, barons of Athenry. This friary was leased to John Rawson in 1589 during the religious suppression but the friars continued to live in the surrounding area. Caltra is listed as one of the friaries which had been restored c. 1737. Bishop James O'Fallon of Elphin granted permission for a Carmelite novitiate at Caltra in 1774. However, shortly afterwards the friars moved to Tohergar in the neighbouring parish of Killian and Killeroran.

The Carmelite Friary at Eaglais, anglicised as Eglish, near Castlegar, was dedicated to the Holy Cross. The earliest reference to this foundation appears in 1437. It was a very extensive monastic settlement as the church was called Teampall Mór, which would indicate several other subordinate buildings including cloister, chapels and monastic cells. This friary also suffered during the suppression, having been confiscated and leased to Francis Sammes. It would seem the friars moved at that time to Caltra to join their fellow friars there. The extensive remains of the ruined friary stand today in Eglish cemetery, bearing testimony to the White Friars, whose lives were dedicated to Our Lady of Mount Carmel.

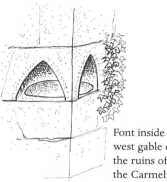

Font inside the west gable of the ruins of the Carmelite friary at Eglish

About three miles northwest of Ahascragh is Chapel-Finnerty cemetery. This site is associated with Fr James O'Finnerty who was born c. 1614, and erected a penal chapel in Chapel-Finnerty, as an existing inscribed plaque testifies. After his death he was interred in this cemetery. A vicar general of the diocese, he was said to have had special healing powers.

The parish suffered the same fate as others during the penal era. Evidence of where the people attended Mass can be traced to the Mass Rock at Greenville. The 1731 *Report on the State of Popery* shows that both Ahascragh and Killosolan had Mass Houses. The priest in Killosolan (Caltra) at that time was Fr Edward Flynn. According to Lewis' *Topographical Dictionary of Ireland* in 1837, the first church in Ahascragh was a 'large building with a burial ground annexed'. The present church was erected in the 1840s. It was redesigned and enlarged by William H. Byrne in the early 1930s. It was reconstructed by Owen Larkin of Ballinasloe during the pastorate of Rev Dean Malachy Brennan (1930-1967). It was rededicated by Bishop Edward Doorly on 20 August 1933, in honour of St Cuan, the patron saint of the parish. A plaque erected in the church recalls An Gorta Mór, and commemorates Fr Richard McLoughlin PP (1840-1849), who died of fever in 1849, like a number of other priests in the diocese.

The first church in the village of Caltra was thatched and local tradition tells us that it was accidentally burned and subsequently repaired. In 1837 Samuel Lewis records that 'a new church is about to be built'. The foundation stone for the present building was ceremonially laid on 25 July 1843, by Christopher D. Bellew, a Catholic landlord in the area. The church was re-designed by William H. Byrne in the 1930s, which entailed extensive reconstruction and enlargement of the building. It was rededicated in honour of Our Lady of Lourdes on 25 June 1939 by Bishop Edward Doorly.

The Church of
Our Lady of
Lourdes, Caltra

A number of national schools were opened in the parish from 1836 to 1898 at Ahascragh, Castlefrench, Killosolan, Caltra, Eglish, Castleblakney and Kilglass. All seven still continue to serve the educational needs of the parish today. In 1949 a secondary school was established at Ahascragh by Mrs Maureen Melody. It was transferred to Castleblakney in 1959 and in 1963 the Sisters of the Presentation of Mary came to the parish. The school was under their care from 1963 to 1987, but now operates under the stewardship of diocesan trustees.

Since the end of the seventeenth century there has been a Church of Ireland community in the parish. Two churches were built in the early nineteenth century. Castleblakney church was erected in 1812, and St Catherine's Ahascragh was built in 1814. The latter church still holds occasional services, while Castleblakney is currently being developed as a cultural centre. John Wesley, the founder of Methodism, preached on a number of occasions in Ahascragh during the period 1762 to 1784.

Key to the map

01. Acre East	23. Caltra Pallas (part of)	44. Course
02. Acre West	24. Cartron	45. Crannagh
03. Addergoole North	25. Castleblakney	46. Creggaun
04. Addergoole South	26. Castleffrench	47. Creggaun
05. Addergoole West	27. Castleffrench East	(Clonmacnowen By)
06. Ahascragh East	28. Castleffrench West	48. Creggaun (Dillon)
07. Ahascragh West	29. Castlegar East	49. Creggaun (Mac Hugh)
08. Annaghbeg	30. Castlegar West	50. Creggaunnagroagh
09. Ballintleva	31. Clonbrock	51. Currafarry
10. Ballybaun	32. Clonbrock Demense	52. Curry
11. Ballyboggan	(part of)	53. Dalysgrove
12. Ballyeighter (Dowdall)	33. Cloonbanniv	54. Derrymore
13. Ballyeigher (Mahon)	34. Clooncannon (Dillon)	55. Eglish
14. Ballyglass	35. Clooncannon (Kelly)	56. Ervallagheighter
15. Ballyglass (Mahon)	36. Cloonpee	57. Ervallaghoughter
16. Ballynahattina	37. Cloonshee	58. Eskerballycahill
17. Ballyvoneen	38. Cloonshee (Dillon)	59. Eskermore
18. Baunoges (part of)	39. Cloonshee (Kelly)	60. Ffrenchpark
19. Bredagh	40. Cloonshee (Rochford)	61. Gallagh
20. Bunavaun	41. Cloonshee (Trench)	62. Garryduff
21. Caltra	42. Cool	63. Glebe
22. Caltra Pallas	43. Cornamucklagh	64. Gortavally

65. Gortbrackmoor	78. Killuppaun (Mahon)	91. Loughaunboy
66. Gowla	79. Kinclare	92. Lughanagh
67. Graigueenavaddoge	80. Knockaunroe	93. Lurcan
68. Geenville	81. Lattoon	94. Meelick
69. Hundred Acres (part of)	82. Lecarrow	95. Mountain
70. Islands	83. Lehanagh	96. Rathbaun
71. Keave	84. Lislea	97. Shanboley
72. Keeloges	85. Lisnaclassagh	98. Srahloughra
73. Kilcrine	86. Lisnagree	99. Sruhaunfusta
74. Kilglass	87. Lissyegan (Hudson)	100. Ticooly (Carr)
75. Killeen	88. Lissyegan (Mahon)	101. Ticooly (O'Kelly)
76. Killosolan	89. Loonaghtan (Kelly)	102. Tummerillaun
77. Killuppaun (Clonbrock)	90. Loonaghtan (Mahon)	103. Weston

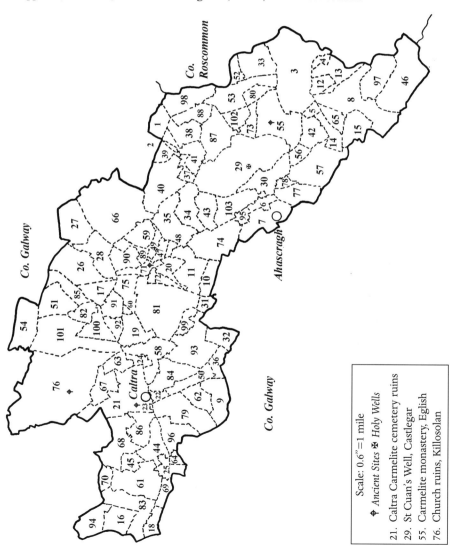

Scale: 0.6" = 1 mile

✛ *Ancient Sites* ✠ *Holy Wells*

21. Caltra Carmelite cemetery ruins
29. St Cuan's Well, Castlegar
55. Carmelite monastery, Eglish
76. Church ruins, Killosolan

Parish of Ardcarne

(Ardcarne & Tumna) County Roscommon
Churches: Crossna, Cootehall, & Drumboylan

T HE PARISH OF Ardcarne in north county Roscommon is bounded on the east by the Shannon, and by Aghanagh parish, Boyle parish, and Loch Cé on the west. It straddles the meandering course of the Boyle River, which widens to form Oakport Lough and Drumharlow Lake, before connecting with the Shannon near the ancient church site of Tumna. It stretches from Ardglass in the south, to Lough Skean in the parish of Kilronan in the north, thus making it one of the largest parishes in Elphin, comprising over 29,000 acres.

Ard Cárna was an important name in the ecclesiastical history of Ireland when it came to prominence at the Synod of Rathbreasail in 1111, to become the name of a diocese covering the territorial region of Moylurg and Tír Tuathail. However, by the Synod of Kells in 1152, the western portion of the Diocese of Ardcarna was amalgamated with the See of Roscommon, and Drumcliff in north county Sligo, to form the present Diocese of Elphin, whilst the eastern portion became part of the Diocese of Ardagh and Clonmacnoise. This resulted in the suppression of Ardcarna, although it still retains its titular as a diocese. Following the loss of the bishopric, Ardcarna continued as head of a rural deanery, and remained so until the vicar-foranship was transferred to Boyle. While the diocese of Ardcarna was shortlived, nevertheless it holds a distinguished place in the history of the Irish church.

Mac Firbis, in a tract called *De quibusdam episcopis*, gives Beo-aodh as the first abbot-bishop of Ardcarna who died in 523. His feastday is celebrated on 8 March.

Ruins of the ancient church and cromleac-like altar in the cemetery of Tumna

The Martyrologies of Donegal and Aongus speak of Beo-aodh as patron of Ardcarna. There is nothing left now of the ancient church except for a large earthen mound which is reputed to be his burial place. St Beaidh's Church of Ireland, built in 1860, on the site of an earlier church, is near the site of the seat of the

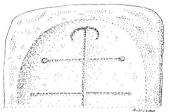

An early Christian slab at Ardcarne, reputed to be the burial memorial for St Beo-aodh

Ardcarna bishopric. The adjoining old and new cemeteries once formed part of a medieval village and ecclesiastical centre often referred to by the annalists. Here also, in the townland of Farranagalliagh, was a Benedictine nunnery, a cell to the Abbey of Kilcreevanty in county Galway.

The present parish of Ardcarne consists of the ancient parish of Ardcarna together with the ancient parish of Tumna. Territorially Tumna lies partially in Moylurg and partly in Tír Tuathail. Tumna was under the patronage of St Éadoin who is believed to be buried in the old graveyard there. This ancient church site of Tumna lies south of the Drumharlow Lake, and is now in the neighbouring parish of Croghan. Drumsillagh school was named Scoil Naomh Éadoine in honour of the patron saint.

There are other ancient places of ecclesiastical interest associated with the parish, including Knockvicar (Cnoc a' Bhiocaire), where there was a friary of the Third Order of Franciscans. Kilteasheen (Cill tSeisin), the church of St Seisan, was thought to mean the church of the little seat, so it was called locally the 'place of the Bishop's Seat'. Kilteasheen is mentioned as a church in the *Papal Taxation List* of 1306, as well as Kileelan (Cill Fhaoláin). Baile na gCeall is referred to by Mac Firbis as being a residence of the Mac Dermots. In Killeen, the foundations of a small church are traceable, which served as a chapel of ease to Ardcarne.

We have very little record of where Catholic worship was conducted during the penal days of the seventeenth and eighteenth centuries. There is at least one Mass Rock preserved in the townland of Rusheen. In the *Report on the State of Popery* of 1731, Ardcarne is recorded as having one Mass House, with Conor Rogers as priest.

There are three churches in the parish today, namely St Michael's Cootehall, St Patrick's Crossna, and St Patrick's Drumboylan. St Michael's Church in Cootehall was erected in 1845 during the pastorate of Fr Bartley Hester, who came to the parish from Riverstown in 1843. This church, which survives to this day, replaced an older church, originally

Church of St Michael, Cootehall

thatched, which had been erected at the close of the eighteenth century, and which served as a place of worship until 1845. In the early 1960s the church underwent major renovations and redesign. It was re-dedicated in January 1964 by Bishop Vincent Hanly. It is adorned with a number of beautiful stained glass windows by Catherine O'Brien (1881-1963).

Crossna old church which was demolished in 1905

St Patrick's Church Crossna, built at the commencement of the twentieth century, replaced an older church which is described by Dalton in his *History of Ireland* (1845), as 'a spacious Roman Catholic chapel to which a fine new steeple has been recently attached'. The present Romanesque-style church was erected on the site of the old church during the pastorate of Fr Thomas Flanagan, and was dedicated by Dr John Clancy, Bishop of Elphin on 7 May 1906. It stands on an elevated site overlooking Loch Cé, and was designed by W. H. Byrne of Dublin.

St Patrick's church at Drumboylan was built in 1930. The site on which this church stands is a truly historic one. It overlooks the location of the ancient ford on the Shannon by which St Patrick crossed into Connacht. The foundation stone was laid in May 1930 and the church was solemnly blessed and dedicated on 19 October 1930. Rev Richard Morris, who was instrumental in its erection, died in August, three months before its dedication. At the entrance to this church is a mural in mosaic, which depicts St Patrick baptising the Princesses Eithne and Fidelma at Ogulla, in the parish of Tulsk, and another scene of an Irish priest baptising an African. This mural, which was presented by St Patrick's Missionary Society in 1962, commemorates Mgr Patrick J. Whitney (1894-1942), the founder of the Society in 1932. He was born at Derreenargon, Drumboylan, was the first Superior General of the Society he founded, and for a period was Prefect Apostolic of Ogoja, in eastern

Nigeria. He died on 17 July 1942 and is buried at St Patrick's Missionary House, Kiltegan, county Wicklow.

Mgr Patrick J. Whitney (1894-1942)

The Church of Ireland community, as we have noted, is served by the Church of St Beaidh's which was built in 1860, replacing the older structure which had been destroyed by fire. The church possesses some remarkable stained glass windows by Evie Hone, (1894-1955) and Alfred E. Child (1875-1939). In 1997, a new Famine memorial was erected at the adjoining graveyard, to commemorate over nine hundred people who succumbed to disease and starvation during An Gorta Mór.

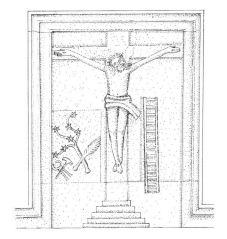

Ardcarne crucifixion plaque, dated 1668

Key to the map

01. Aghoo
02. Aghrafinigan
03. Annaghbeg
04. Annaghmagurthan
05. Annaghmona
06. Ardcarn
07. Ardconra
08. Ardeash
09. Ardglass
10. Ballyardan
11. Ballyformoyle
12. Barcullin
13. Behy
14. Blackfallow
15. Brackloon
16. Breanletter
17. Bridgecartron or Derrycashel
18. Bullock Island
19. Carrigeen
20. Carrowmore
21. Carrownagashel
22. Cartron
23. Castle Island
24. Church Hill
25. Cleaheen
26. Cleen
27. Clegna
28. Clerragh
29. Cloonacarrow
30. Cloonaghbaun
31. Clooncoose
32. Clooncruffer
33. Cloonfad
34. Cloongreaghan
35. Cloonkeen
36. Cloonybrien
37. Cooladye
38. Cootehall
39. Corderry
40. Cornagrea
41. Cornamucklagh
42. Corratrench
43. Cortrasna
44. Crooderry
45. Crossna
46. Cuilmore
47. Cuiltaboolia
48. Davis' Island
49. Dergraw
50. Derreen
51. Derreenacoosan
52. Derreenadouglas
53. Derreenahinch
54. Derreenanarry
55. Derreenannagh
56. Derreenargan
57. Derreenasalt
58. Derreenaseer
59. Derreenasoo
60. Derreenatawy
61. Derreendooey
62. Derreenine
63. Derrycashel
_. Derrycashel or Bridgecartron (see 17)
64. Derrygirraun
65. Derryherk
66. Derrynaskineen
67. Doogary
68. Dromore
69. Drumanilra or Mounteagle
70. Drumatybonniff
71. Drumboylan
72. Drumbrick
73. Drumbrisny
74. Drumcormick
75. Drumharlow
76. Drumlahard
77. Drumsillagh (ED Oakpark)
78. Drumsillagh (ED Tumna South)
79. Emlagh
80. Errironagh
81. Farranagalliagh East
82. Farranagalliagh West
83. Fostragh
84. Foxhill
85. Garrowloughter
86. Glebe
87. Glooria
88. Gortleck
89. Green Island
90. Grevisk
_. Hollymount (see 96)
91. Hughestown
92. Inishatirra Island
93. Kilfaughna
94. Kilmacarril
95. Kilteasheen
96. Knocknaculleen or Hollymount
97. Knockadaff
98. Knockadrehid
99. Knocknabeast
100. Knocknacarrow
101. Knockroe
102. Knockvicar
103. Lahans Island or Garravinch
104. Laughil
105. Leiterra
106. Lisfarrellboy
107. Lisgreaghan
108. Lismulkeare
109. Lurga
110. Lustia
111. Lyonstown
112. Moigh
_. Mounteagle (see 69)
113. Mountprospect
114. Moyoran
115. Oakport Demense
116. Orchard Island
117. Paddock
118. Powellshill
119. Rathdiveen (part of)
120. Reycroftspark
121. Rinn
122. Rockingham Demesne (part of)
123. Rusheen
124. Sally Island
125. Shanballybaun
126. Toberataravan
127. Tullyval
128. Turlagh
129. Usna
130. Woodfield

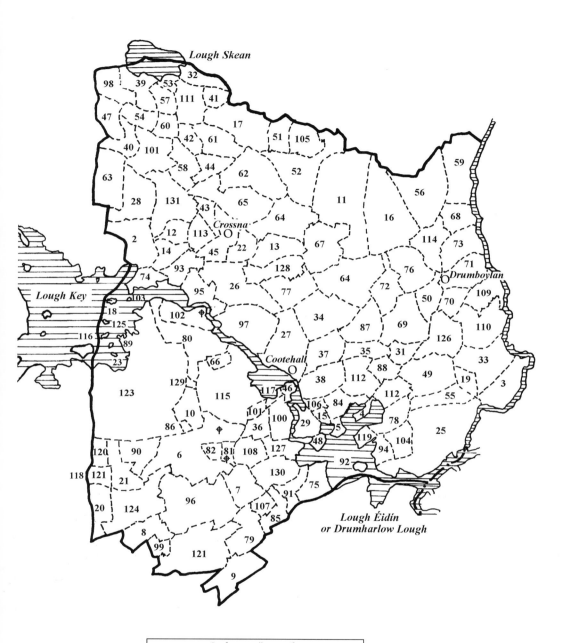

Scale: 0.65"=1 mile

☩ *Ancient Sites* ✠ *Holy Wells*

6. Ardcarne diocesan site
81. Benedictine nunnery, Farranagalliagh
95. Old church site, Kilteasheen
102. Franciscan friary, Knockvicar

Parish of Athleague

(Athleague & Fuerty) Counties Roscommon & Galway
Churches: Athleague & Fuerty

THE PRESENT PARISH of Athleague is an amalgamation of the medieval parishes of Athleague and Fuerty. These two parishes were united on the 8 May 1881. For some time prior to that date, Fuerty was united with Cams (Cloverhill or Oran). Located in the south-central part of the diocese, it straddles the county boundary between Roscommon and Galway. The River Suck meanders its way slowly through the parish from north to south, forming the county boundary in places.

Up to the fifteenth century, Athleague was known as Áth Liag Maenagain after the local saint, Maenagain. The exact place of abode of the saint is unknown, but it may have been close to the holy well known as Glúin Phádraig in the townland of Kilmore. Here St Patrick is reputed to have left an imprint of his knee on a stone. The site was bought for the parish by Fr Michael Conry PP in 1927, and renovated in 1995. A pilgrimage is still held to this sacred place. In the south western end of the parish is the townland of Abbeygrey or Mainistir na Liagh, which took its name from an ancient religious site. While references to this site are scanty, it is believed to have been occupied by a religious house in the twelfth-thirteenth century period. It may have been a small community of Augustinian Canons Regular associated with the Augustinian Priory at Roscommon. The death of Maolíosa Ó hAnainn, abbot of Roscommon and Athleague, is recorded in 1266. Care of this church was given to the monks of Rindoon in St John's parish in 1466. Ruins of a medieval church are to be seen at Churchpark, in the townland of Tromaun, at the eastern end of the parish. There are also the remains of an ancient church and some gravestones at Clooneen. This site was used as a killeen, or burial place for children, until

A tenth-century grave slab from Fuerty

the middle of the twentieth century. Ruins of an old church, of uncertain age, can also be seen at Chapeltown, in the townland of Keenagh.

The ancient parish of Fuerty has close links with St Ciarán who founded the famous monastery at Clonmacnoise. Local tradition says that Ciarán was born in the parish. In the cemetery at Fuerty there are two fine examples of tenth-century grave slabs, similar to those at Clonmacnoise. One of the slabs bears an early Christian fish symbol, which makes it unique in Ireland

The *Report on the State of Popery* in 1731 tells us that

there were two priests in the parish, both with assistants. The Mass House in Athleague was in ruins, but in the process of being rebuilt, and also one in Fuerty. The parish and its priests suffered greatly during the penal times due to the presence of a very anti-Catholic landlord in the district. A Mass Rock used during this period can be seen at Carnlough in Fuerty parish. Tradition says that a local lake, Black's Lough, also known as Loch an tSagairt, marks the place where a young priest drowned while fleeing the soldiers during these troubled times.

Church of Our Lady Assumed into Heaven, Fuerty

Athleague had close associations with the Dominican friars of Roscommon after their community was dispersed in the seventeenth century; in fact many of the parish priests of both Athleague and Fuerty in the seventeenth and eighteenth centuries were Dominican friars. The last of these was Fr Bartholomew Keher OP, who was parish priest of Athleague from 1865 to 1872. He was succeeded as parish priest by Fr James K. Casey (1873-1905), who was one of the most popular temperance poets of his day, and his writings did much 'to promote the great cause of temperance of which during his life, he had been, both by word and example, the zealous apostle'. His publications included, *Our Thirst for Drink, its Cause and Cure; Intemperance, an Ethical Poem,* and *Verses on Doctrinal and Devotional Subjects.*

The present church in Athleague, dedicated to St Patrick, was built by Fr Keher in 1842. It was renovated a century later, during the pastorate of Fr Bernard Keane. The renovations included a new sacristy on the east-

St Patrick's Church, Athleague

ern end of the church, and additions to the nave as well as many interior improvements. The masonry from the demolished mansion at Rookwood was used in the new extensions. The refurbished church was rededicated by Bishop Edward Doorly on 21 May 1944. The church in Fuerty, dedicated to the Assumption, was built in 1957. It replaced an earlier church, St Kieran's, which was built in 1812-14 by the then PP, Fr B. Keelty OP, an uncle of the priest who built Athleague Church.

There has been a Church of Ireland community in the parish since the early seventeenth century. The parishes of Athleague and Fuerty were united into one union in 1809. There was a church in Fuerty old cemetery, and another was built in Athleague in the 1840s on an earlier Christian site. This replaced one which was described in 1837 as being dilapidated. As the size of the community decreased, these buildings fell into disuse, but the Athleague church has recently been restored as an Angling Centre.

The south aspect of the church ruin at Churchpark, Tromaun

Key to the map

Townlands marked (G) are in county Galway. The rest are in county Roscommon.

_. Abbeygray or Monaster-
    lea (G) (see 63)
01. Aghagad
_. Aghagad Beg &
    Creemully (see 31)
02. Aghagower
03. Aghrane or Castlekellly
    (G)
04. Araghty
05. Athleague
06. Attifarry (G)
07. Ballaghdacker (G)
08. Ballinlig
09. Ballinturley
_. Bellagad or Rockwood
    (G) (see 67)
10. Bellanacarrow
11. Brackloon
12. Carrowkeel
13. Carrowreagh
14. Carrowstellan
15. Castlecoote
_. Castlekelly or Aghrane
    (G) (see 3)
16. Castlestrange
17. Clooncannon (G)
18. Clooneen
19. Cloonruff
20. Cloonykelly
21. Cloonyourish
22. Cloonyquin
23. Coalpits (G)

24. Coolaspaddaun (G)
25. Coollusty
26. Coolmeen
27. Cooly
28. Corderryhugh
_. Cornacask or Easterfield
    (see 34) (G)
29. Corra Beg
_. Corramore or Gorteen-
    cloogh
30. Correal
31. Creemully & Aghagad
    Beg
32. Curraghbagla (G)
33. Derrineel
34. Easterfield or Cornacask
    (G)
35. Emlaghkeadew
36. Farranykelly
37. Fuerty
38. Garrer (G)
39. Glebe (Athleaghe West
    ED)
40. Glebe (Fuerty ED)
41. Glennanammer
42. Gorteenbrack
43. Gorteenclogh or Corra
    More
44. Gorteenruckaun (G)
45. Gortmore
46. Holygrove (G)
47. Keenagh (Clanrickard)

48. Keenagh (Donnellan
    East)
49. Keenagh (Donnellan
    West)
50. Kilmore
51. Knockadangan
52. Knockaunrainy (G)
53. Liscoffy (Kelly)
54. Liscoffy (Madden)
55. Lisnagirra
56. Lisnagroagh
57. Lisnalannow
58. Lisnasillagh
59. Lisnatea
60. Lissacarrow
61. Lissaneaville
62. Mallyree (G)
63. Monasterlea or Abbey-
    grey (G)
64. Moyliss
65. Muff
66. Quiltinan
67. Rockwood or Bellaghad
    (G)
68. Scardaun
69. Srahaunnagort or
    Thornfield (G)
_. Thornfield or
    Srahaunnagort (G)
70. Toberavaddy
71. Toberkeagh
72. Tromaun

188

Co. Roscommon

Co. Roscommon

Fuerty

Athleague

Co. Galway

Co. Roscommon

Scale: 0.6"=1 mile
⚕ *Ancient Sites* ✠ *Holy Wells*

5. Old cemetery
18. Old church ruins and cillín
37. Medieval church and cemetery
50. Glúin Phádraig Well
63. Abbeygrey ancient site

La Tene stone,
Castlestrange

189

Parish of Athlone

(St Peter's & Drum) Counties Roscommon & Westmeath
Churches: Athlone, Drum & Clonown

THE PARISH OF Athlone, anciently referred to as St Peter's and Drum, covers the Connacht side of Athlone town as well as the areas of Drum (Drum Drestan) which lie in the rural hinterland to the west, and Clonown, which lies on the flood plain of the Shannon river to the south. This area, which was christianised in the sixth century, was also strongly influenced by the church reform movement of the twelfth century.

Athlone was probably greatly influenced by the sixth-century monastery at Clonmacnoise, a few miles to the south, and several early Christian settlements on Lough Ree to the north. There were two early monastic settlements in the parish. The monastery at Drum, which extended over five acres, was founded by Diradius in the fifth century, while the monastery at Clonown, which took its name from St Eamhain, was a sixth-century foundation. Among the early abbots of Clonown were St Ailitid and St Colman. This monastery was raided as late as 1089 by Mun-

Fragment of an early grave slab at Clonown

ster men. A fragment from an early Christian cross-slab with an outline ring-cross can be seen in the present church at Clonown. The remains of a church with a well-preserved Romanesque style window at Cloonakilia suggests that there was an early Christian settlement there also.

The Cluniac monastery of Ss Peter and Paul was founded by Turlough O'Conor, King of Connacht, in Athlone in 1150. This monastery was located near the present St Peter's convent. The Cluniac monasteries arose from the first attempt to reform the Benedictine order. They were to be subject directly to the Holy See and to observe the strict form of the Benedictine life. This was the only Cluniac monastery in Ireland and its title was also significant. The mother abbey at Cluny itself was dedicated to SS Peter and Paul and St Malachy's monastery in Armagh also had the same title. There are many references to the priory and its priors from the thirteenth to the fifteenth century. The papal authorities seem to have had great confidence in the Athlone monks and the records show that from the late fourteenth century many mandates authorised the prior of this Cluniac monastery to act on behalf of the Holy See in various disputes.

The influence of the Cluniac Monastery in Athlone extended over a wide area of the south of the diocese. At one stage there were fifteen rectories assigned to the priory and at least three of these, Cam, Kiltoom and Drum, were served by members of the community. One of these, Kiltoom, was under Cluniac control from 1431 onwards.

The old church of Ss Peter and Paul, Athlone (1790-1937)

The monks celebrated Mass in these parishes or paid a priest to do so and in return the monks received the tithes from the parishes. In time the monastery of Ss Peter and Paul became one of the richest monasteries in Connacht. It was suppressed in the middle of the sixteenth century, after which its property was joined to that of Athlone castle, which had been built on land belonging to the monastery. The church of the monastery, by then a grain store, was destroyed by fire following an attack by the Irish on the town in 1572. From 1587 the castle became the residence of successive Presidents of Connacht and in 1759 it passed to the Incorporated Society for the Promotion of Protestant Schools in Ireland.

The late seventeenth century was very turbulent in Athlone but the names of two parish priests survive from just after this period. They were Fr Hugh Gaffey, who died in 1703, and Fr Patrick Flyn, registered priest of the parish in 1704. A Mass House existed in Pearse St in 1784. This was replaced by St Peter's parish church,

which was built in Chapel St about 1790. This church was enlarged in 1809 and a belfry was added to it in 1856. It served as the parish church until the opening and dedication of the new church of Ss Peter and Paul in 1937. Work commenced on this very imposing building in August 1930. Often mistaken for a cathedral, it was built on a site acquired from the military barracks in Athlone. The church, in Roman Renaissance style, measures 220 feet by 100 feet and the

Ss Peter and Paul, Athlone

outside walls are sixty feet high. The twin towers are symbolic of Ss Peter and Paul, and are 126 feet high.

There are many interesting features in this church, including the marble sanctuary

Drum
medieval
monastic
settlement

and a number of stained glass windows from the Harry Clarke studios. One of these in the St Patrick side chapel is of particular interest. The main theme is the life of St Patrick and his links with the Diocese of Elphin. The old church was converted to a parish hall and officially opened on 7 January 1959. It is now known as the Dean Crowe Theatre, dedicated to the memory of Rt Rev John Crowe VG and Dean of Elphin, 1883-1955.

A church was built in Clonown (Cluain Eamhain) five miles south of Athlone about 1825. It was dedicated to St Brigid, as it is adjacent to St Brigid's Well. This church was replaced by a new building in a post-conciliar style, which contains some traditional and conventional features. It is located near the old church, on the opposite side of the road, and was dedicated to Our Lady of the Wayside by Bishop Vincent Hanly on 27 May 1965. The old church was converted into a parish hall.

Close to the ancient monastic site at Drum (Drum Drestan) there is a well dedicated to St Brigid, which probably predated it. The ruins of a post-Reformation church, probably late eighteenth century, are to be found in the cemetery surrounding the ancient monastic site. It was in this church that the people of Drum worshipped until a site was acquired for a new church in 1862. The new nineteenth

St Brigid's Well,
Drum

century church of St Brigid was built shortly afterwards and opened for divine worship about 1873. It was reconstructed in 1964 and re-dedicated by Bishop Hanly on 23 May 1965.

St Joseph's Convent, Summerhill

The Augustinian Sisters came to the parish of St Peter's in 1748 and had a school for girls there. The venture lasted about twenty years. These were the only nuns in the diocese at that time. The Augustinian Friars first came to Athlone during the eighteenth century and were authorised to move their Dunmore (county Galway) priory to Athlone in 1809. The friars remained in the town until 1875.

Bishop George Browne introduced the Ursuline Sisters to Summerhill, Athlone in 1844, where they operated a boarding school until 1849. Bishop Brown moved his residence to Athlone in 1851 and established the Diocesan College at Summerhill in 1857. The college moved to Sligo in 1880 but retained the name Summerhill. The De La Salle Brothers operated an Industrial School for boys at Summerhill from 1880 to 1882

The Sisters of Mercy started their work of caring for the needy and educating the young in Athlone in 1857. In 1882 a further group of Mercy Sisters went to Summerhill to care for orphans, a work they continued there for eighty years. They began to provide secondary education for boarding and day pupils in Athlone in 1925, and they opened a new primary school on the site of the Cluniac monastery in 1934. St Aloysius College for boys, under diocesan trusteeship, was opened in Athlone in 1960.

The last religious order to come to St Peter's parish was the Sister Disciples of the Divine Master, who opened a convent near the parish church in 1983 where they have had a liturgical centre since 1969.

A Church of Ireland was built within the site of the Cluniac monastery in 1804. This church was replaced by a new church built off Pearse St in 1842. The building served the parishioners well until St Peter's parish was united with the parish of St Mary's on the east side of town.

Key to the map

Townlands marked (W) are within the Athlone UDC area, and therefore part of county Westmeath. Those marked (R & W) lie partly within the UDC area, and partly without, and so are in county Roscommon. The parts within the UDC boundary are administered by Westmeath County Council.

01. Ardagawna	20. Cornafulla	38. Inchinalee Island
02. Ardkeenan	21. Crancam	39. Johnstown Demesne
03. Ardnanure	22. Crannagh	40. Keeloges
04. Bellanamullia	23. Crannagh Beg	41. Keelty
05. Bellaugh (R & W)	24. Crannagh More	42. Kilmocolmock
06. Belrea	25. Creagh	43. Kilnamanagh
07. Bogganfin (part of) (W)	26. Creggan	44. Lisdillure
08. Bunnaribba	27. Cregganabeaka	45. Long Island
09. Callowbeg	28. Cuilleen	46. Long Island (Little)
10. Carrickynaghtan	29. Cuilglass	47. Mihanboy
11. Carrickynaghtan &	30. Curraghaleen	48. Monksland (R & W)
Garrynagawna Bog	31. Curraghnaboll	49. Moynure
12. Cartron	32. Curryroe	50. Newtown
13. Cloonakille	33. Dooghan	51. Rooskagh
14. Cloonark	34. Doovoge (R & W)	52. Taduff East
15. Cloonboley	35. Drum	53. Taduff West
16. Cloongowna	36. Drumlosh	54. Taylorstown
17. Cloonillan	37. Garrynagawna	55. Thomastown Demesne
18. Cloonown	_. Garrynagawna Bog or	
19. Cloonrollagh	Carrickynaghtan (see 11)	

A window in Cloonakilla Church

Athlone UDC

SS. Peter's
& Paul's

Drum

Cloonown

R. Shannon

Scale: 0.6"=1 mile
☥ *Ancient Sites* ✠ *Holy Wells*
5.   Cluniac monastery
13. Cloonakilla monastic site
18. St Brigid's Well, Drum
32. Drum church and cemetery

Seal of the priory of Ss Peter
and Paul, Athlone. Probably
fourteenth-century, it shows a
madonna and child over a triple
arch, below which is a monk.
The inscription reads: 'S' prioris
sci Petri de Athlyon. Now in the
National Museum of Ireland.

Parish of Aughrim

(Aughrim, Kilmore & Clooncraff) County Roscommon
Churches: Aughrim, Kilmore & Half-Parish

THE PARISH OF Aughrim (Each Druim) is situated in the extreme northeast of county Roscommon, in a heavily glaciated lowland region, with a myriad of lakes and low hills. It is bounded on the north and east by the Shannon and by the offshoots of Kilglass Lake and Lough Boderg on the south. The historic village of Jamestown guards the bridge over the Shannon, linking Leitrim and Roscommon. In pre-Christian times the area formed part of the territory of Tír Uí Bhruin or Tirebrine, a name which had been retained by the diocese under the title of 'Prebendary of Tirebrine'. In 1872, the ancient parishes of Aughrim, Kilmore and Clooncraff were united to form the present parish of Aughrim. Clooncraff is more commonly known as Half-Parish.

Fragment from a ninth-century grave slab at Aughrim old cemetery

The first Christian church stood within the site of the present old Aughrim cemetery and the recently restored ancient church ruin marks the actual spot. The restoration of this historic site also led to the discovery of a fragment of a ninth-century grave slab with an inscribed Celtic Cross which clearly indicates the existence of an early Christian foundation. The Canons Regular of St Augustine are reputed to have had a monastic foundation on this site in the early twelfth century. Aughrim church is listed in the *Papal Taxation List* of 1306. The existence of a Mass Rock in the townland of Carricklom, not far from the present church, commemorates another place of worship where people gathered during the penal times to celebrate Mass.

Aughrim parish church is situated in the townland of Rodeen and this site dates back to 1790 when the first church was erected there. This old church building, often referred to as 'Rodeen Chapel', was almost completely replaced at the beginning of the twentieth century by the present building. Part of the original is still preserved in the transepts of today's church. When the present structure was completed in 1907, it was solemnly dedicated in honour of Our Lady of Perpetual Help by Bishop John Clancy, on 13 October 1907. The church was again extensively renovated in recent years, and Bishop Dominic Conway performed the re-dedication ceremony on the same date in 1985. The Church of Ireland, in the townland of Carricklom, was built in 1744, and described in 1837 as a 'neat plain building with a spire … lately repaired'. It is now demolished.

The parish of Kilmore is referred to in Irish as 'Cill Mór in Tír Uí Bhruin na Sionna', in order to distinguish it from the many other places called Kilmore throughout Ireland. It is intimately associated with Patrician times. According to the *Tripartite Life,* St Patrick came here and went to a place called Maige Glais (Moyglass), where he laid the foundations of Kilmore (Cill Mór) or 'the great church'. In 1232 the church of Cill Mór was consecrated, Con Ó Flannagáin then being prior, and he established the Canons Regular of St Augustine there. It belonged for three centuries to the Augustinians and is mentioned several times in the *Annals of Loch Cé.* It was suppressed by Elizabeth I in 1590 and the abbey and lands were granted to Tyrell O'Farrell, later to Sir Patrick Barnwell, and some twenty years later leased by him to Dr Edward King, Protestant Bishop of Elphin (1611-1639).

Church of Our Lady of Perpetual Help, Aughrim

It is likely that the abbey church was used for Protestant worship for a number of centuries. Through time it was allowed to fall into decay and sometime in the late eighteenth or early nineteenth century it was demolished. With no record of the size of the abbey church, one can only conjecture that the present entrance to Kilmore Church of Ireland and graveyard is part of the old building. This graveyard has many beautiful tombs and carved headstones. The present building was erected in 1828, and has a small spire.

St Brigid's Church Dangan serves the Kilmore area of Aughrim parish. The original church, a plain barn-type structure, was built in the late 1820s, and in 1842 it was re-constructed as a cruciform church. A plaque above the door reads: 'This church was erected through the exertions of the Rev Edward Keogh PP of Kilmore, aided by his parishioners. AD 1842.'

In the townland of Kilbride there is the trace of a nunnery said to have been founded by St Caoca (Cocha) who came to the area with St Brigid. The type of St Brigid's Cross traditional in this area is an interlaced pattern unlike the usual design, and St Brigid's Well was a place of pilgrimage for many years. A church existed also in the townland of Cloonfad during the nineteenth century and apparently closed when Aughrim's new church was opened in 1907. It was situated beside Cloonfad House where Dr George Joseph Plunkett Browne, Bishop of Elphin (1844-1858) was born.

Cross on a boulder at Cloonglasney Beg, Clooncraff

Clooncraff (Cluain Creamha) in modern times called the Half-Parish, stretches along the southern boundary of the modern union, embracing the many scattered lakes of the area. Almost half of the ancient parish of Clooncraff lies within the modern parish of Elphin. In

1837 Lewis records that there were two chapels in the parish: one in Clooncraff townland, and one in Drumamullan, near Creeve, and now part of Elphin. Clooncraff graveyard contains traces of an ancient monastic settlement and has strong associations with St Finnian of Clonard. The recently discovered Tullylough eighth-century cross, which was found in a Crannóg near Clooncraff, is another important antiquity associated with the Christian faith in these parts. There is also an inscribed cross on a boulder at Cloonglassney Beg, which would indicate another Christian site related to the penal or post-penal period.

Half-Parish church was built in 1844, during the pastorate of Rev Edward Keogh PP (1825-1872), and serves the Clooncraff area of Aughrim parish. It was extensively renovated in the 1970s and dedicated in 1975 in honour of St Oliver Plunkett, in the year of his canonisation. It was re-dedicated following further improvements by Bishop Christopher Jones on 11 December 1994, on the occasion of the 150th anniversary of its erection. It is the only church in the diocese dedicated to St Oliver Plunkett.

The Church of Ireland church at Kilmore

Key to the map

01. Aghamore
02. Aghawaracahill
03. Annagh
04. Ardanaffrin
05. Ardgallagher
06. Ardleckna
07. Ardlougher
08. Ardmacroan
09. Aughrim
10. Ballagh
11. Ballycummin
12. Bealragh

13. Boyanagh
14. Bryan Beg
15. Bryan More
16. Carrickilla
17. Carricklom
18. Carrigeenduff
19. Carrowcuill
20. Carrowmore
21. Carrownaglearagh
22. Carrowreagh
23. Cartron (Hartland)
24. Cartron (King)
25. Charlestown

26. Clogher
27. Cloonavery
28. Clooncommon Beg
29. Clooncommon More
30. Clooncoose
31. Clooncosker
32. Clooncraff
33. Cloonfad Beg
34. Cloonfad More
35. Cloongarvan
36. Cloonglasny Beg
37. Cloonglasny More

38. Cloonmeane	62. Drumcleavry	86. Lissavilla
39. Cloonshannagh	63. Drummod	87. Lowfield
40. Cloonshee	64. Fearagh (Caddell)	88. Lugateane
41. Cloonsillagh	65. Fearagh (Mahon)	89. Meelick
42. Cloonteem	66. Garrymona Island	90. Milltown
43. Corbaun	67. Glebe	91. Moneyduff
44. Corgullion	68. Gragullagh	92. Moyglass
45. Corkeenagh	69. Grange	93. North Island
46. Corlis	70. Kilbride	94. Pollnamoghil
47. Cornasleehan	71. Kilcanoran	95. Rat Island
48. Corralara	72. Kilcock	96. Rathevin
49. Corry (Ballintubber North By)	73. Kilcroy	96. Rathnarovanagh
	74. Killinaddan	98. Rockville
50. Corry (Roscommon By)	75. Kilmore	99. Rodeen
51. Creaghnakirka	76. Knockavreaneen	100. Roo
52. Cuilmore	77. Knocknagawna	101. Rushport
53. Cuiltyconway	78. Lackagh	102. Scrabbagh
54. Cuiltyshinnoge	79. Lackan	103. Skeagh
55. Cullenrevagh	80. Lahagboy	104. Tawnagh More
56. Curry	81. Lecarrow	105. Tooloscan
57. Dangan (Nugent)	82. Liscolvan	106. Toomore
59. Derreen Island	83. Lishugh	107. Tully
60. Dooneen	84. Lisnanuran	108. Tullynahearka
61. Drumamoodan	85. Lissadorn	

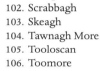

Scale: 0.5"=1 mile

⚘ *Ancient Sites* ✠ *Holy Wells*

9. Medieval church and cemetery, Aughrim
32. Medieval church and cemetery, Clooncraff
70. Ancient nunnery ruins, Kilbride
75. Medieval church and cemetery, Kilmore

Parish of Ballinameen

(Kilnamanagh, Estersnow & Kilcolgagh) County Roscommon
Churches: Ballinameen & Breedogue

THE PARISH OF Ballinameen is located in northwest Roscommon, between Lough Gara and the main Boyle-Roscommon road, a few miles to the south of Boyle. In 1839, Ballinameen was in union with the present parish of Croghan, under the title Croghan, Killucan and Ballinameen. Breedogue was attached to Frenchpark, which at that time was part of the union of Tibohine, a large area extending as far west as Loughglynn and Lisacul. Within the present boundaries of Ballinameen are included the greater parts of the ancient parishes of Kilnamanagh, Kilcolgagh and the western part of Estersnow or Easternsnow.

The parish appears to have been christianised by St Patrick, St Brigid and St Attracta in the fifth century. St Dabonna, a disciple of St Patrick, has been mentioned as the patron of the old parish of Kilnamanagh. Both the *Book of Armagh* and the *Tripartite Life* record that he founded two churches in the relatively small area of Greagraide or Coolavin, to the north of Ballinameen parish. One of these was at Drumne, now called Machare, and the other at Cill Attracta or Killaraght (in the Diocese of Achonry). St Patrick left a paten and a chalice with St Attracta who was a native of the area. Hospitality and charity towards all was one of the primary rules prescribed by Patrick for Attracta and her nuns. Attracta erected a hospice for the reception of pilgrims and travelling merchants, one of the first in this area.

Kilnamanagh

St Brigid, though born in Leinster, was the daughter of a Connacht woman. The baby was taken by her mother to the kingdom of the O'Conors, near the slopes of Cruachan. It was here she spent her early years. The area where she is reputed to have lived is now called Breedogue. There is hardly a spot in Ireland more frequently mentioned in the lives of St Patrick than the territory where Brigid spent her youth. Her fame became so great that her father demanded that she return to Leinster, but on her request she was permitted to return to Connacht.

Little else is known about the parish of Ballinameen until there is mention of finding the Cross of St Attracta (a Celtic cross) in the early part of the fifteenth century. The *Calendar of Papal Letters* notes that the cross and cup of St Attracta were venerated in the church in Killaraght in 1413.

St Attracta, after a design by Henry King

The Four Masters refer to the townland of Derrycough in the north of Ballinameen parish for the year 1487. This suggests that it must have been a place of some importance at that time. Red Hugh O'Donnell, Prince of Tír Chonaill, raided the McDermott territory of Moylurg and committed great depredations in Derrycough. In the townland is the site of an ancient church, which stood on fairly high ground. The field in which the church stood is known as Cluain na cille or meadow of the church. The 1731 *Report of the State of Popery in Ireland* indicates that there was one Mass House and one named priest, Miles Branan, who at that time was serving Kilcolgagh/Easternsnow.

Breedogue was known as Kilnamanagh (Cill na Mánach), or the church of the monks. The holy well in that area is called St Patrick's Well. There are ruins of a medieval church and cemetery to the south of it. The 1731 *Report* also indicates that 'Killnemanach' had one Mass House and two named priests – Terence McGrah and Edmund Lavin.

There are two churches in the parish; St Brigid's at Breedogue, and St Attracta's at Ballinameen, the names reflecting the history of the early Christians in the area.

St Brigid's church, Breedogue, replaced an earlier penal chapel, which was located near Breedogue Bridge. It was a thatched building and in 1863 was reported as being in very poor structural condition. In 1859, on the appointment of Fr Matthew Barrett as PP, the process of acquiring a site for a new church began. This imposing new structure, built in the 1860s, after great efforts by the people and the parish priest, was designed by W. Goldie, who also designed Sligo Cathedral and other churches in the diocese. It was constructed by William Hunt and Son, Sligo, and was consecrated on 14 February 1869, with the bishops of both Elphin and Achonry in attendance. Fr Fortescue SJ preached the opening sermon. This present church, St Brigid's, was extensively renovated in 1963, and rededicated by Bishop Hanly on 8 June 1964.

Church of
St Attracta,
Ballinameen

There was an old church in Ballinameen village, which was constructed in the early 1800s. By 1824, this building was also being used as a hedge school. The foundation stone for the present church was laid in 1900 and dedicated in honour of St Attracta on 27 June 1903. John Whelan of Strokestown built the church, and William H. Byrne was the architect. It was built in the gothic style, comprising a nave, sanctuary, transepts and gallery. It was extensively renovated in 1972, and re-dedicated on 25 August of that year.

The first national school in Ballinameen parish was sanctioned in 1844. At that time there were approximately 2,784 inhabitants in the old parish of Ballinameen, and close on 200 children were attending school. By 1862 there were 538 Catholic children and two children of the Established Church attending the three schools in the old Ballinameen parish. A new national school was opened at Kingsland in 1848, serving the Breedogue church area.

Key to the map

01. Acres
02. Annagh (part of)
03. Ardagh
04. Ardcolagh
05. Ardmore
06. Ardmoyle
07. Ballinvoher (Frenchpark By)
08. Ballinvoher (Boyle By)
09. Barnaboy
10. Bawn Island
11. Bella
12. Callow or Runnawillin
13. Camlin
14. Carkfree
15. Carrigeen
16. Carrigeencarragh
17. Carrowkeel (ED Breedoge)
18. Carrowkeel
19. Carrowmoneen
20. Carrownagappul
21. Carrownurlar
22. Carrowreagh
23. Cloonacarrow
24. Clooneen
25. Cloonmacmullan
26. Cloonmagunnaun
27. Cloonshagan (part of)
28. Cornaveagh
29. Corroy
_. Creen or Tonroe (see 55)
30. Derrycoagh
31. Dooneen
32. Dower
33. Drishaghaun
34. Emlagh
_. Feenagh or Tonroe (see 56)
35. Finisclin
36. Granny
37. Kilnamanagh
38. Kingsland
39. Knockglass
40. Knockroe (part of)
41. Lackan
42. Lurgan
43. Mantuar
44. Oldtown
45. Portnacrinnaght
46. Ratallen (part of)
47. Runnabehy
48. Runnaboll (part of)
49. Runnameelta
50. Runnaroddan
_. Runnawillan or Callow (See 12)
51. Sheerevagh
52. Slieveroe
53. Sracocka
54. Tartan
55. Tonroe or Creen
56. Tonroe or Feenagh
57. Tournagee
58. Treanagry (part of)
59. Treanamarly
60. Tullaghan

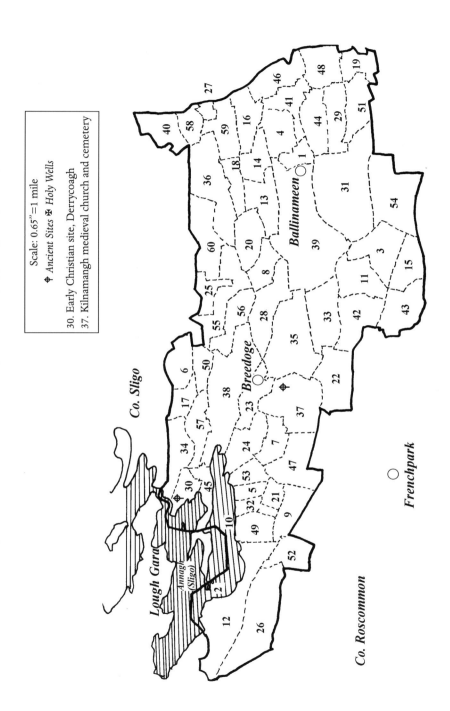

Scale: 0.65" = 1 mile
✠ Ancient Sites ⊕ Holy Wells

30. Early Christian site, Derrycoagh
37. Kilnamangh medieval church and cemetery

Ballinameen

Breedoge

Frenchpark

Co. Sligo

Co. Roscommon

Lough Gara

Annagh
(Sligo)

Parish of Ballintubber

(Ballintubber, Kilcroan, Drumatemple) Counties Roscommon & Galway
Churches: Ballintubber & Ballymoe

T HE PARISH OF Ballintubber is located on the north-east Galway-west Roscommon county boundary. The half parish of Ballymoe, is situated mainly in county Galway, and is served by the church at Ballymoe which is dedicated to St Croan. The half parish of Ballintubber lies entirely in county Roscommon, and is served by the church of St Bride in Ballintubber. This historic village became the principal seat of the O'Conors, the Royal Family of Connacht, after the Anglo-Norman invasion of Ireland at the end of the twelfth century. Their castle, erected in the early fourteenth century, served as a bastion of the Catholic revival through the centuries until it was finally destroyed in the eighteenth century. The ruined castle today dominates the skyline of this former royal seat, and is a reminder of turbulent times and bygone years. The current extent of the parish has evolved over time and encompasses the old parishes of Ballintubber, Drumatemple, Kilcroan, and two townlands of the parish of Ballinakill.

Ballintubber
Castle

Kilcroan, the 'church of St Croan', is named after an early holy virgin who, according to tradition, ministered in the area and whose feast day is 27 January. Kilcroan was an independent parish in pre-Reformation times but the name is now given to an ancient Christian site which surrounds the ruins of an early stone church.

Within the walls of this ruin is a vault in which lie the remains of Bishop Burke, a native of the parish, who was consecrated Bishop of Elphin in 1827 and died in 1843. There is a tradition of Mass Rocks in the area, and in 1731 we find record of a priest, with a 'Mass House, lately erected', suggesting some religious observances during the penal period. The 'Mass House' may be the chapel later recorded in 1837 as a ruin in the townland of Curries.

Post-penal reorganisation saw Kilcroan being joined with Ballinakill or Glinsk, as a new parish unit. A new church was built in the village of Ballymoe in 1821 and was extended in 1857. By 1869, Glinsk was detached and joined with the neighbouring parish, Kilbegnet. In the late nineteenth century the jurisdiction of Ballymoe church was extended to its present limits in county Roscommon, and was joined with Ballintubber as a single parish. The church in Ballymoe was demolished in 1954 and the present church erected on the same site. It was blessed and opened for divine worship on 12 June 1955, and dedicated to St Croan, patroness of the ancient parish.

Fr Flanagan of Boystown

The townland of Drumatemple derives its name from a church of the pre-Reformation parish. This church was already in ruins by the middle of the seventeenth century. The parish was later served by the church at Ballintubber until a rationalisation in the 1870s ceded five townlands of county Roscommon to the jurisdiction of Ballymoe church. From the townland of Leabeg, Edward Joseph Flanagan emigrated to the USA in 1904 and as the Fr Flanagan (1886-1948), founder of Boystown, Nebraska, was renowned for exemplary pastoral care of youth.

Ballintubber parish is dedicated to St Bride, the area being variously called 'Toberbride' and 'Baile Tobair Bríde' in ancient references. A local well was the focal point of 'Bride' worship since prehistory, diluting to a 'pattern' which died towards the middle of the twentieth century. A pre-Reformation church ruin stands in the old cemetery close to the well. A later church was dedicated in 1827 in the present cemetery. This church had an adjacent ash tree to serve as a belfry to call the congregation to church and prayer. In 1898 that church was replaced by the present parish church of St Bride, which was renovated in its centenary year.

Ballintubber, for the most part, was an independent parish, though in 1413 it is recorded jointly with that of Baslick. Its prominent status emanated from its location in the chief stronghold of the O'Conors for centuries, and the close connections fostered with that family. This was expressed in the support and patronage of the O'Conors for the church in Ballintubber, and especially by the right of presentation on the appointment of a parish priest ceded to the O'Conor head for cent-

Ballintubber church

uries – one of the rare examples country-wide, only lapsing in recent times. Ancient ecclesiastical sites in the area are indicated by name at Killerr, Tobermakee, and Timanagh, the 'house of the monks'.

In Church of Ireland arrangements, Kilcroan was part of the union of Donamon. At Ballymoe stands the disused church, dated 1832, of the parish of Drumatemple which was part of the benefice of Oran. Ballintubber parish, with that of Kilkeevan and Baslick, formed the benefice of Ballintubber with the parish church at Castlerea.

St Brigid's Well, Ballintubber

Key to the map

01. Ardnamullagh	11. Ballyglass West (G)	21. Cleaboy
02. Ashpark	12. Bellacagher	22. Cloondarragh (G)
03. Ballaghaugeag East (G)	13. Bohagh	23. Cloondarragh East
04. Ballaghaugeag West (G)	14. Bookalagh (G)	24. Cloonagrassan
05. Ballaghymurry (G)	15. Bracklagh (G)	25. Cloonee (G)
06. Ballintober	16. Brackloon	26. Cloonruff (G)
07. Ballyfinegan	17. Caran	27. Cloonykerny
08. Ballyglass Middle (G)	18. Carrowbaun	28. Corlackan (G)
09. Ballyglass North (G)	19. Carrowreagh	29. Corliskea (G)
10. Ballyglass South (G)	20. Cartron	30. Cornamucklagh (G)

31. Corrastoona Beg
32. Corrastoona More
33. Curries (G)
34. Drumatemple
35. Dundermot
37. Durrow (G)
37. Emlaghglasny
38. Enfield
39. Foghanagh Beg
40. Foghanagh More
41. Frenchlawn
42. Gilkagh East (G)
43. Gilkagh West (G)
44. Gortboy

45. Keelty
46. Kennyborough
47. Kilcooley (G)
48. Killerr
49. Kilsallagh (G)
50. Knockalaghta (Wills)
52. Knockagonnell (G)
53. Laragh and Ross
54. Leabeg
55. Leamore
56. Lecarrow
57. Lisnageeragh (G)
58. Marnellsgrove (G)
59. Rathcarran

60. Rathnalulleagh
61. Raveege
62. Rosmeen
63. Shankoagh
64. Timanagh
65. Toberkeagh
66. Tobermakee
67. Tobinstown (G)
68. Treanboy (G)
69. Turlagh
70. Willsgrove

Scale: 0.6"=1 mile
⚓ Ancient Sites ✠ Holy Wells

6. St Brigid's Well, medieval church and cemetery
9. Kilcroan medieval church and cemetery
26. Mass Rock

Parish of Ballyforan

(Dysart, Tisrara & Taughboy) Counties Roscommon & Galway
Churches: Ballyforan, Four Roads & Dysart

THE PARISH OF Ballyforan lies in the south west of county Roscommon, and includes nine townlands of east county Galway. The River Suck partly borders the parish on the western end, and meanders its way through the southern end. The parishes of Ahascragh, Ballygar, Athleague, Knockcroghery, and Kiltoom and Cam in Elphin, and Taughmaconnell in the Diocese of Clonfert, all adjoin the parish.

Ballyforan is a comparatively modern name in ecclesiastical terms, and is now the official title of this parish. It comprises three ancient parishes, namely Dysart, Taughboy and Tisrara. These parishes were amalgamated in 1872, and both Dysart and Tisrara lost their parochial status. However, they still retain their independence as three vibrant parish communities.

Fifteenth-century east chancel window in Tisrara medieval church at Carrowntemple

Tisrara forms the northern part of the parish and includes the villages of Four Roads and Mount Talbot. Tisrara, comprising two Irish words Tígh Srathra, meaning 'Straddle House', derives its name from a medieval religious hostel strategically located along the ancient western pilgrim route to Clonmacnoise. It was here that people stopped to rest, reflect and nourish body and soul before continuing on their pilgrim way. Today, this site is marked by an ancient cemetery with a multi-period church ruin and vaulted chamber dating from the thirteenth to the seventeenth centuries. It is reputed to have housed a Carmelite community who provided hospice care for the ongoing throngs of pilgrims who travelled to and from Clonmacnoise. Archaeological excavations were carried out on the site in 1994, which revealed a Patrician site and evidence of an extensive settlement. The remains of the medieval edifice, partially restored in 1994, helps one to visualise how this building might have looked during its former days of glory. The restoration work was awarded a National Heritage Award in 1997 in recognition of the best example of a modern restoration of an ancient building.

Tisrara church suffered under the suppression, and it wasn't until 1731 that we have a Mass House recorded there. In the late eighteenth century we see the emergence of a place of worship at Four Roads, in the town-

Church of the Good Shepherd, Tisrara

land of Carrowntemple (the quarter of the church), near where the first church stood. This eighteenth-century penal chapel was replaced in 1843 by a cruciform church dedicated to Christ the King, which provided a place of worship for the people of Tisrara until 1972. It was demolished at that time to be replaced by the completely new post-conciliar Church of the Good Shepherd, which facilitated the implementation of the new liturgical norms. The new edifice was dedicated by Dr Dominic Conway on 1 July 1973, the feast of St Oliver Plunkett. While the church design lacks traditional gothic features, nevertheless it incorporates the stone, marble and some of Harry Clarke's (1889-1931) best examples of Irish stained glass artistry from the old church.

Dysart forms the south-easterly end of the parish, and derives its name from the Irish word Díseart, meaning hermitage or hermit's church. It reflects the contemplative nature of the early church, where people sought isolation to communicate with their God. Dysart ancient cemetery, with its twelfth to seventeenth century church ruins, marks the site of the first Christian church in

St Patrick's Church, Dysart, built in 1825 and renovated in 1901

Dysart, which was a place of worship for the greater part of twelve hundred years. This old church was partially restored in 1992, and is well worth a visit to view its re-instated romanesque doorway. A penal chapel was built at Carrownadurly in the late eighteenth century near where the present church of St Patrick was erected in 1825. This church underwent major renovations in 1901, and was re-dedicated on 17 March 1958, following further major improvements.

Bishop James Fallon (1709-1786) was parish priest of Dysart prior to his appointment as Bishop of Elphin 1756. He administered the diocese from Cloonagh House in Dysart and is buried in an uncommemorated grave in Dysart old cemetery. Fr Patrick Costello (1905-1988) was a native of Dysart, Superior General of St Patrick's Missionary Society from 1938-1950, and rector of the Society's seminary from 1950 to 1956.

Taughboy, an ancient parish encompassing the village of Ballyforan, is in the south-western end of the parish. The anglicised word Taughboy, derives its name from the Irish words Teach Buidhe, meaning 'house of piety', and owes its origin to the medieval church in Taughboy ancient cemetery. This site has been a place of worship from Patrician times, as confirmed in a recent archaeological excavation. The multi-period church ruin of the twelfth to seventeenth centuries, bears testimony to the centuries of Catholics that worshipped there.

Church of
St Joseph at
Ballyforan

Ballyforan became the centre of worship following the erection of a church in the village at the commencement of the nineteenth century. However in 1857, the present church of St Joseph was built and continues to serve the spiritual needs of the people in that area. It has a massive grey west tower and buttressed nave, and has undergone renovations in 1900 and again in 1956. The parish is unique in that its parish boundaries have remained unaltered right through history, except for the period 1860 to 1872 when Rahara in the parish of Knockcroghery was amalgamated with Tisrara.

There are no local saints or pattern days associated with the parish, neither are there any holy wells, except for pilgrimages to Glúin Phádraig, Brideswell, and St Cuan's Well in the adjoining parishes of Athleague, Kiltoom & Cam, and Ahascragh. The name Boughill is recorded in the *Papal Taxation List* of 1306, but as no other reference appears elsewhere, it is difficult to ascertain whether or not it refers to Boughill in the parish of Ballyforan. Lisín na bpaistí, the children's graveyard, in the townland of Muckloon, is also a place of historical interest in the parish.

The Anglican community worshipped at Mount Talbot church, which was erected in 1766 to replace an earlier church. It ceased to be a place of worship in 1965

The names of Dysart, Taughboy and Tisrara are worth recalling because they denote contemplation, piety, and hospitality which are all so relevant to the life of a Christian in every age.

The parish is almost equal distance from Athlone, Ballinasloe and Roscommon, and benefits from the economic progress occurring in these centres of trade and commerce. The gradual rise in population is indicative of a parish with future challenges for its pastoral carers.

Late twelfth-century romanesque doorway at Cummeen, Dysart

Key to the map

Townlands marked (G) are in county Galway. The remainder are in county Roscommon.

01. Ardecolman	30. Cloondarah	63. Gortaphuill
02. Attiknockan	31. Cloonlaughnan	64. Jamestown
03. Ballina	32. Commeen	65. Kiladerry (G)
04. Ballyforan	33. Commons	66. Kilnagralta
05. Ballyglass	34. Coolatober	67. Lenanamalla
06. Ballyglass (Dodwell)	35. Coolderry	68. Lisduff
07. Ballyminton	36. Coolderragh	69. Lisgillalea
–. Ballyrevagh & Porteen (See 81)	37. Cornapallis	70. Lismaha
	38. Cornacollia (G)	71. Lisnagavragh
–. Ballyvreagh West & Porteen (see 82)	39. Correal	72. Lisnamucklagh (Athlone North By)
	40. Creehermore	
08. Boughil (G)	41. Cronin	73. Lisnamucklagh (Athlone South By)
09. Bredagh	42. Cuillawinnia	
10. Breeole	43. Cuilleenirwan	74. Lissaphuca
11. Breelole West	44. Cuilleenoolagh	75. Lisseenamanragh
12. Caltraghduff (G)	45. Cuilnakeava	76. Liswilliam
13. Carrickbeg	46. Curraghadoon	77. Milltown
14. Carricknagat	47. Derrinlurg	78. Mount Talbot
15. Carroward	48. Derrycahill	79. Muckloon (G)
16. Carrowkeel	49. Derryfadda (G)	80. Mullaghardagh
17. Carrowmore	50. Derreen (G)	81. Porteen & Ballyrevagh
18. Carrownadurly	51. Errick Beg	82. Porteen & Ballyrevagh West
19. Carrowntarriff	52. Errick More	
20. Carrowntemple	53. Feevagh	83. Shanballylosky
21. Carrowntlieve	54. Feevagh Beg	84. Srahgrave (G)
22. Carrownurlar	55. Feevagh More	85. Taghboy
23. Cartron	56. Funshinagh	86. Tibarney
24. Cartronkilly	57. Funshinagh (Madden)	87. Tirconnellbeg
25. Cloghan	58. Funshinagh (Trench)	88. Torpan Beg
26. Cloghnashade	59. Garrynagran	89. Torpan More
27. Cloonagh	60. Garrynphort	90. Tullyneeny
28. Cloonakilleg	61. Glenrevagh	91. Turrock
29. Cloonca	62. Gortananny (G)	

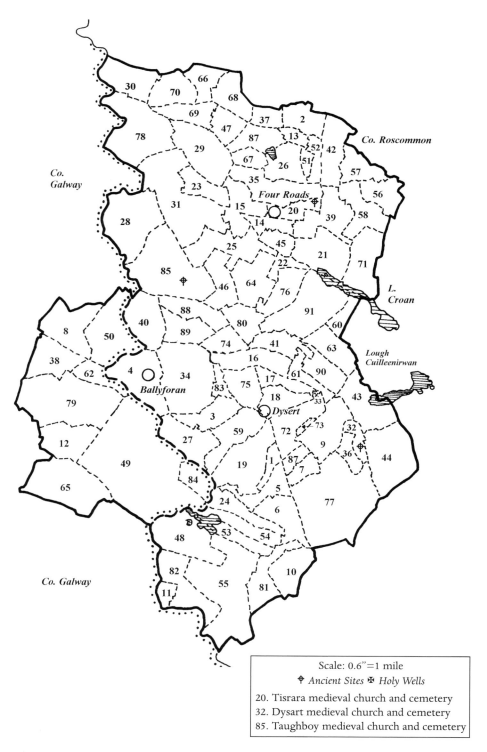

Co. Roscommon

Co.
Galway

Four Roads

L.
Croan

Ballyforan

Dysert

Lough
Cuilleenirwan

Co. Galway

Scale: 0.6"=1 mile
✟ Ancient Sites ✠ Holy Wells
20. Tisrara medieval church and cemetery
32. Dysart medieval church and cemetery
85. Taughboy medieval church and cemetery

Parish of Ballygar
(Killeroran & Killian) County Galway
Churches: Ballygar, Newbridge & Tohergar

The parish of Ballygar is situated in east county Galway and is one of five parishes of the diocese located in that county. The parish is traditionally known as Killeroran and Killyan (Killian), and incorporates three parish areas, namely Ballygar, Newbridge (formerly known as Gort an Iomaire) and Tohergar. The River Suck borders the parish to the east, and the River Shiven is an important waterway which runs through part of the parish on the western end.

The derivations of the ancient names of the parish denote an area steeped in Christianity from earliest times. The names Ballygar and Newbridge are relatively new to the annals of the parish. It is in the ancient cemeteries of Killeroran and Killian that the origins of the faith of this parish are firmly embedded. While no in-depth study or investigation of these sites has been documented, a cursory glance points to the early beginnings of the faith in this locality. *The Papal Taxation List* of 1306 records churches for both Killeroran and Killian. The centre of worship revolved around these two sites from Patrician times. The sites today are ancient burial grounds with the ruins of two medieval parish churches, which date from the thirteenth to the seventeenth centuries.

West gable of the ruin at Killian

St Brendan's Well in Doranstown is also an indication of an early Christian settlement. The site has traces of early buildings, as well as an inscribed limestone plaque of the crucifixion, a pilgrims' route, together with a burial ground. St Brendan has been venerated at this site for centuries, and the curing of facial ailments, especially the eyes, has been attributed to water from the well. The annual pilgrimage to the site took place each year on 16 May, which was the local Pattern day. St Brendan is still honoured as the patron saint of Tohergar church and a number of local parish organisations still bear his name.

Abbeygrey or Mainistir na Leithe, bordering the parish, had a significant influence in the general area. It was commonly known as the Ring, and had a moat which is reputed to have been the site of a monastic settlement. At the beginning of the nineteenth century the stones from the site were taken to provide a new wing to Aughrane Castle. A holy water font is all that remains of the monastery, and people use water from this font for curing eye and foot problems. Ballygar suffered from the penal laws and suppression of Catholic worship like all other parishes. There is local evidence of Mass being celebrated in townlands such as Muckinagh, Ballaghlea, Lissavruggy, Cappagh, Boherhannagh, Tommard and Kentstown. In the *Report on the State of Popery,* 1731, Mass Houses are listed for both Killeroran and Killian.

The arrival of the Carmelites in Tohergar in 1770 from Caltra, seeking a place of refuge during the penal laws, was a great source of consolation and support to the Catholic community in the area. There was widespread enthusiasm amongst the people for the wearing of the brown scapular of Our Lady of Mount Carmel and the dead were buried in the brown habit of the Carmelites. The friars chose a very secluded place for their convent and church and even to this day only people with local knowledge are able to find it. They also established a school attached to the convent and provided valued education to the young especially during the hedge school era. The friary was part of the parish until 1870 when the Provincial Chapter decided to close it. Fr John Hopkins, the last Carmelite to reside at Toghergar, refused to close the friary and continued to look after the spiritual needs of the people until his death in 1873. He is buried in a marked grave alongside a fellow Carmelite within the church precincts. The four walls of the church still stand and over the main entrance the Carmelite coat of arms. An early stone carving of the Our Lady and Child, from the friary, is enshrined in a niche at the entrance to Toghergar church.

Madonna and Child taken from the Carmelite Friary, Tohergar, and now inserted at the entrance to St Brendan's Church.

The first evidence of a parish church to emerge, as the penal laws became less stringent, was at Ballaghlea. The church was known as Teach an Aifrinn and was central to both Killeroran and Killian. It ceased to be a place of worship when St Patrick's church, Newbridge, was opened in 1866. Newbridge church is unusual in that it has a small chapel annexed to it which locals call the old chapel. This was originally a market house and is now converted into a side chapel. The present building has served the people as a place of worship for over 130 years. It underwent major renovations in the 1970s and was rededicated by Bishop Dominic Conway on 26 October 1980.

St Mary's Church, Ballygar

A church was erected about 1760 to serve the people of Killeroran on the outskirts of Ballygar on a site which is now the Town Hall. This church remained in use until the present church of St Mary in Ballygar was built in 1857. It was dedicated on 5 September 1858, and was extended by 40 feet in 1957 to accomodate its growing worshipping population. It was rededicated on 8 December 1957 by Bishop Vincent Hanly. St Brendan's Church at Tohergar was erected in 1860 and, following the closure of the Carmelite friary in 1870, this became the sole place of worship to serve this part of the parish.

A number of noteworthy people were natives of the parish, including Most Rev Augustine Cheevers, who was born at Killyan House, Newbridge in 1686, appointed Bishop of Ardagh and Clonmacnoise in 1751, and subsequently became Bishop of Meath in 1756 until his death in 1778. Most Rev Patrick Delaney, (1853-1926), a native of Newbridge, was Archbishop of Hobart, Tasmania. Rev John Dignan (1880-1953) was born in Ballygar and appointed Bishop of Clonfert in 1924, where he remained until his death on 12 April 1953. Monsignor John Hynes (1875-1949), a native of Lisquell, Newbridge, was a distinguished priest of the Diocese of Elphin and became President of UCG. He died 8 January 1949, four years after retiring from the presidency. The parish was fortunate to have the presence of two Catholic landlords within its confines, namely the Cheevers and the French families. The Cheevers had a private oratory in their residence and Mass was celebrated there a number of times during the year.

Three priests ministered in the parish up to recent times but this is now reduced to two, residing respectively in Ballygar and Newbridge. The parish has a very significant number of native priests who serve in many parts of the world, especially the USA.

The educational needs of the parish are well catered for with four primary schools. St Mary's College in the town of Ballygar has been providing second-level education since 1948. It is now a well-equipped modern college, surpassing all the expectations of its founders.

In the early nineteenth century, a church on the outskirts of Ballygar village served a small Church of Ireland community. A new church was erected in the town of Ballygar in 1850 by local landlord Denis Kelly, and it continued to be a place of worship until 1926. However, when the church closed it was demolished and rebuilt as the Catholic church of Gortanumera in the parish of Portumna, county Galway, in the Diocese of Clonfert.

Key to the map

01. Aghrane or Castlekelly (part of)	11. Barnacurra	22. Charlestown or Pollinamucka
02. Ballinglass	12. Blean na Gloos	_. Castlekelly or Aghrane (see 01.)
03. Ballinvoher North	13. Boggauns	
04. Ballinvoher South	14. Boherbannagh	23. Cloghbrack
05. Ballybaun	15. Buncam	24. Cloonascarberry (Cheevers)
06. Ballygar	16. Cappagh	
07. Ballynacorra (Davies)	17. Carrowmore (Cheevers)	25. Cloonascarberry (North)
08. Ballynacorra (Ffrench)	18. Carrowmore (Kelly)	
09. Ballynacorra (Netterville)	19. Carrownafreevy	26. Cloonascarberry (South)
10. Ballynalahy	20. Cartron	27. Cloonavihony
	21. Cartron Earl	

28. Cloonfinnoge
29. Cloonkeen (Davies)
30. Cloonkeen (Ffrench)
31. Cloonkeen (Kelly)
32. Cloonkeen (Netterville)
33. Cloonlyon
34. Cloonabricka
35. Cloonshivna
36. Cloonshivna (Kelly)
37. Cornadrum
38. Cornananta Beg
39. Cornananta More
40. Corrabaun
41. Creeveroe (Davies)
42. Creevroe (Ffrench)
_. Creggangrogy (see 72)
43. Curraghboy
44. Drinaun
45. Eskermurry
46. Ffrench's Acres
47. Gortacoosaun

48. Gunnode
49. Hermitage
50. Islands
51. Kentstown
52. Kilclogh
53. Kilcoosh
54. Killeroran
55. Killian
56. Kilmore
57. Lahacrogher
58. Liscuill
59. Lisheenteige
60. Lissavruggy
61. Muckanagh (North)
62. Muckanagh (South)
63. Newbridge
64. Newgrove
65. Newtown
66. Newvillage
_. Pollnamucka or
 Charlestown (see 22)

67. Riversdale
68. Rushestown
69. Shanbally Beg
70. Shanbally More
71. Slievemurry
72. St Brendan's or
 Cregganagrogy
73. Summerhill
74. Tirur
75. Tohergar
76. Tonnacurra
77. Toomard
78. Trihill East
79. Trihill West
80. Tully (ED Ballynakill)
81. Tully (ED Killeroran)
82. Tullyroe
83. Windfield
84. Woodbrook

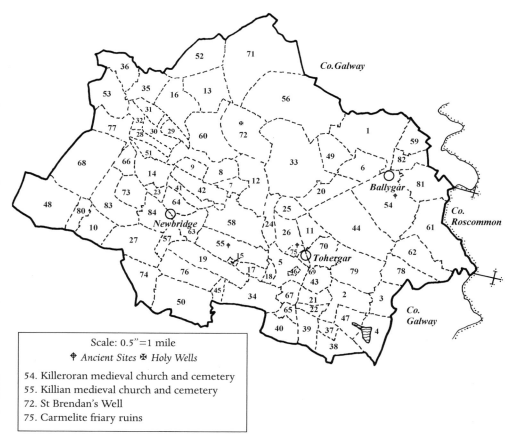

Scale: 0.5"=1 mile
✟ *Ancient Sites* ✠ *Holy Wells*

54. Killeroran medieval church and cemetery
55. Killian medieval church and cemetery
72. St Brendan's Well
75. Carmelite friary ruins

Parish of Boyle
(Boyle & Kilbryan) County Roscommon
Church: Boyle

T HE PARISH OF Boyle nestles at the foot of the Curlews and embraces the ancient territory of Moylurg, the original homeland of the warlike Mac Dermots. According to local tradition, St Patrick appointed Comgell, or Connell, Bishop of Ath dá Lairg, a place subsequently the site of the Cistercian abbey. There is evidence of a foundation on Trinity Island centuries before Clarus Mac Mailin founded the monastery of the Premonstratensians there in 1215. Mac Mailin, abbot of Trinity Island and archdeacon of Elphin, was one of the great churchmen of his time and founded several religious establishments.

The abbey on Trinity Island was endowed by Murtagh Mac Dermot, Prince of Moylurg, and so began an association with that family that lasted until it was dissolved and the Mac Dermots lost their ancient patrimony. After his death, Murtagh was buried on the island as was Donagh O Moore, Bishop of Elphin, who died in 1231, and the celebrated Clarus Mac Mailin. Sir Conyers Clifford, President of Connacht, who was killed in the Battle of the Curlews in 1599, was also buried there. It was there, circa 1585, that the famous *Annals of Loch Cé* were compiled at the behest of Brian Mac Dermot of Moylurg. The abbey survived long after Henry VIII's dissolution order. Local tradition suggests that the Canons continued their labours in the area until 1690.

Boyle Cistercian Abbey

Of the modern foundations, pride of place must go to the monastery of Boyle, founded by the Cistercians in 1161, although not completed until 1220. It was built according to a uniform plan, being so arranged as to form a quadrangle surrounding an open space. The church formed the north side, with the kitchen and refectory forming the south side; the chapter-house and other rooms, with the monks' dormitories overhead, lay on the east, and the building set aside for the lay brethren formed the western side. Architecturally, it has been described as 'the finest of the Cistercian churches to survive in Ireland', and is a good example of the transition from Romanesque to Gothic architecture in Ireland.

The Mac Dermots were the principal patrons, endowing it with a great deal of land, which included the site of the present town of Boyle. Between the twelfth and the sixteenth centuries it was the principal burial place of the Mac Dermots, Kings of Moylurg.

The abbey escaped confiscation under Henry VIII, but it came in for notice in Elizabeth's reign. In 1631, James Fallon, the vicar general of Elphin, reported that the Cistercian monastery at Boyle 'is now in ruins; it has been turned into a mansion with the exception of one chapel, which the Protestants use as a parish church'. Brian Ó Cuilleanáin was the last abbot of Boyle. He died in London on his way to Ireland in 1639. After his death, another Cistercian, Thomas Kiernan, living in 1650, succeeded him as titular abbot of Boyle. As far as can be ascertained he was the last of the Irish Cistercians to bear the title of 'abbot of Boyle'. There were three different assignments of the abbey lands, the third and final one in the reign of James I, to Sir John King.

Boyle was amalgamated with the neighbouring Sligo parish of Aghanagh in 1704, a situation which continued until 1828. Dr James Brannally was the last to hold the position of parish priest of both Boyle and Aghanagh, and after his death the parish was again divided, with Corigeenroe, in county Roscommon, becoming attached to Aghanagh, under the pastorship of Fr Terence Sweeney.

The earliest parish church of which there is knowledge was at Assylinn, which also gave its name to the parish at an early period. The Ordnance Surveyors of the 1830s noted that the ruins of the ancient foundations were 'of considerable extent', and there were also indications of the existence of a round tower on the site. At one time it was the site of a small village and a marketplace. All that remains today is a portion of what appears to have been the original side-wall. Local tradition tells us that in post-Reformation times a small Mass House, or chapel, was opened in Chapel St, next door to the old St Patrick's, the first of the modern churches. Built in 1823, the latter was a substantial two-bay rectangular building, with pollarded gables and Gothic windows. It was simple, spacious by comparison with

St Patrick's pre-emancipation church, Chapel St, Boyle

penal chapels, and presumably quite adequate for the period. In September 1840, Fr Theobald Mathew preached a charity sermon in Boyle to raise funds for repairs to the chapel and parochial schools.

This building was replaced in 1882 by St Joseph's Church on the Carrick Road,

The old Church of St Joseph, Boyle

the foundation stone of which was laid in June 1876 by Bishop Gillooly on a site known as the Nuns' Field. The design, which was described as 'a perfect example of nineteenth century Gothic revival', was by George Goldie, who also designed the Cathedral in Sligo. The church cost over £8,000 to build, much of which was collected locally from 1869 onwards. It was originally to be dedicated to St Mary, as evidenced by the inscription on the silver trowel presented to Bishop Gillooly on the day of the laying of the foundation stone. What occasioned the change to St Joseph is not known.

Goldie's *Magnum Opus* served the people of Boyle for close on a century until tragically, on the afternoon of 26 April 1977, the magnificent Gothic structure was burned to the ground. The origin of the fire still remains a mystery. It started in a confessional on the west side and quickly spread to the roof which became an inferno within minutes. The sacristy was the only portion of Goldie's classic design to survive. Three years later, the new St Joseph's, designed by Patrick Rooney and Associates, rose phoenix-like from the ashes. The foundation stone for the new church was blessed by Pope John Paul II at Knock on 30 September 1979 during the papal visit to Ireland. It was ceremonially laid by Bishop Dominic Conway on 4 May 1980, and the new church was dedicated on 14 December 1980. Standing on the site of the original church, the design, in a basic circular form, surmounted by a dome, gives a total unified appearance and reflects the close association between priest and community. The unsupported wood-beamed roof is one of the most striking in Ireland, and lends a warm halo to the many ceremonies which take place in this beautiful post-conciliar church.

St Joseph's Church, Boyle

The Sisters of Mercy, in response to numerous requests from Fr Joseph McTucker PP, established a convent in Boyle in 1875, and became involved in education and ministry to the sick and poor of the parish. In 1929, a new convent chapel – 'a beautiful example of church architecture' – was dedicated to Christ the King by Bishop Edward Doorly.

Between 1897 and 1918 the Presentation Brothers conducted the national school in the parish. In 1955, on the initiative of Bishop Vincent Hanly, St Mary's College, a secondary school for boys, was opened in temporary accommodation, with Fr Kevin Dodd as its first principal. A year later the present college of St Mary's was opened, and it continues to provide second level education for the town and the surrounding area.

The Boyle Family Life Centre was established in 1987 following a decision to regionalise pastoral care centres in the diocese. A permanent residence was acquired in 1991, which today serves the pastoral needs of the region.

There has been a Church of Ireland community in the Boyle area since the sixteenth century. In June 1765, the Select Vestry accepted the offer of a site from Lord Kingston, on one acre of ground on the Green, north of the main street, and transferred their church there from Assylinn. Built by Oliver Grace, the new church was completed by 1777, and was enlarged several times after that. A substantial restoration of the church was undertaken in the mid-1980s, and it continues to serve the Anglican community of Boyle. The Presbyterian Church on the Carrick Road was built in 1858. Since the 1960s it is known as the Federal Church and serves both the Presbyterian and Methodist congregations.

Boyle Mass Rock

Key to the map

01. Aghnagrange
02. Ardcorcoran
03. Ardmore
04. Ardsallagh
05. Ash Islands
06. Ballinphuill
07. Ballybaun
08. Ballykeevican
09. Ballylugnagon
10. Ballymore East or Corbally
11. Ballymore West
12. Ballynanultagh
13. Ballytrasna
14. Behy
15. Bellspark
16. Breandrum
17. Brislagh
18. Carrickmore
19. Carrigeenagowna
20. Carrowmore (part of)
21. Carrownageeragh
22. Cashelfinoge or Lugnamuddagh
23. Church Island
24. Coolnagranshy
25. Copse
_. Corbally or Ballymore East (see 10)
26. Cornaglia

27. Cornameelta
28. Deerpark
29. Derrymaquirk
30. Doon
_. Drum or Warren (see 77)
31. Drumanone
32. Drummans' Island
33. Drumshannagh
34. Erris
35. Evikeens
36. Fawnanierin
37. Garrow
38. Glebe
39. Grallagh Beg
40. Grallagh More
41. Grange Beg
42. Grange More
43. Greatmeadow
44. Harepark
45. Hermit Island
46. Hogs Island
47. Keeloges
48. Kilbryan
49. Killerdoo
50. Kiltybrannock
51. Kiltycreaghtan
52. Knockadoo
53. Knockadoobrusna
54. Knockarush

55. Knockavroe
56. Knocknacloy
57. Knocknashee
58. Leam
59. Lecarrow
60. Letfords Park
61. Lisserdrea
62. Lowparks
_. Lugnamuddagh or Cashelfinoge (see 22)
63. Mocmoyne
64. Pollower
65. Rathdiveen (part of)
66. Rockingham Demense (Boyle Rural ED)
67. Rockingham Demense (part of) (Rockingham ED)
68. Stag Island
69. Sheegorey
70. Spa
71. Tawnyeden
72. Tawnytaskin
73. Termon
74. Tinacarra
75. Tivannagh
76. Trinity Island
77. Warren or Drum

A window on Trinity Island, Loch Cé

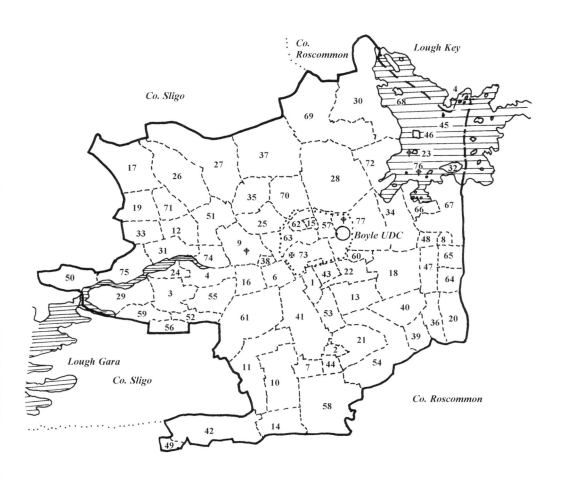

Co.
Roscommon

Lough Key

Co. Sligo

30

4

68

45

69

46

23

17

27

37

72

76

32

26

28

35

70

19

71

51

25

34

66

67

62 15 57

77

33

12

9

63

73

60

48

8

31

74

38

65

50

75

24

4

6

43 22

18

47

64

29

3

55

16

1

13

40

59

52

61

41

53

36

20

56

21

39

2

11

7 44

54

Lough Gara

Co. Sligo

10

58

42

14

49

Boyle UDC

Co. Roscommon

Scale: 0.6"=1 mile
⚜ Ancient Sites ✠ Holy Wells

9. Assylinn church and cemetery
23. Monastic ruins
76. Monastic ruins
77. Cistercian abbey ruins

Parish of Castlerea

(Kilkeevan) County Roscommon
Churches: Castlerea, Cloonbonniffe & Trien

Kilkeevin
medieval church

THE PARISH OF Castlerea, or Kilkeevan, to give it its ancient title, lies in the far west of county Roscommon, bounded on the north by Loughglynn and on the south by Ballintubber parish. Castlerea town, on the River Suck, is the economic centre of the area. It claims notoriety from being the birthplace in 1815 of Sir William Wilde, noted antiquarian and oculist, and father of the playwright Oscar Wilde. It was in this town also that Dr Douglas Hyde, later first President of Ireland, was born in 1860. To the west of the town is Clonalis House, the nineteenth-century ancestral home of the O'Conor Don. This house contains priceless records of the Gaelic tradition, as well as archival material which traces sixty generations of the O'Conor lineage since 75 AD, and of their sustained support for the Catholic population over the centuries.

The first church in the parish was founded by St Patrick around 433 AD, according to the *Book of Armagh*. 'Then Patrick came to the territory of Cer, the eldest son of Queen Maeve, and there he founded three churches. He also founded a church in Ardlice, called Sean-Domhnadh, and he placed over it Caomhán, a holy deacon and monk, a youth who was very dear to Christ and St Patrick.' This church, Cill Chaomháin, or Kilkeevan, was situated at Arm, west of the present town of Castlerea. A church was also founded by St Patrick at Emlagh. In 1015, St Brochaid was recorded as the leader of the community, and it was there that the Cross of Emlagh, or Brochaid's Cross, was made. The church was destroyed by fire in 1236. All that remains today are fragments of High Crosses.

St Caolainn is one of the patrons of the parish and there are many sites bearing her name. According to legend she is venerated as the 'Patroness of the Blind'. She is first mentioned between 434 and 440 AD when the Nunnery of Moor was founded. Caolainn, the first abbess of this community, was a member of the O'Flynn clan, which provided endowments for both the nunnery and a church in Tarmon Mór (Tarmon Caolainne). St Caolainn's holy well at Moor was known for generations as a place to seek a cure and a popular pattern was held there on 19 June until recent times. An ancient church also existed at Cloonbonniffe, and is now marked by an unused cillín graveyard not far from the modern church. A Patrician church named Kilcoose was founded in the townland of Clooncoose, and a later church was founded in the townland of Cloonkeen.

During the turbulent years of the Reformation, the churches and religious communities were closed down and their lands confiscated. The ancient church of Kilkeevan was destroyed in 1537, but was replaced in the early 1600s by a chapel at Oldtown, in the townland of Arm. Only the ruins of Kilkeevan now remain, and within the precincts stands the ancestral tomb of the royal O'-Conors.

The modest chapel at Oldtown served the faithful until the construction of the old St Joseph's Church in Castlerea in 1798. The parish priest of Castlerea, Fr Charles O'Conor, was instrumental in purchasing the site for this new chapel, a mile from town on the Ballinlough road, from Lord Mount Sandford. It was a small cruciform building, with three balconies to accommodate the often large congregation. Local tradition has it that the bell in St Joseph's was the first to be rung in Connacht when Catholic Emancipation was announced in 1829. This chapel was the focus of worship throughout the dark days of the Great Hunger, but by the end of the nineteenth century it had become too small for the bustling market town of Castlerea. The decision was taken to construct a new, larger church in the centre of Castlerea.

The last Mass in the old church of St Joseph was celebrated in 1898, the centenary of its erection, having served the people of Kilkeevan well during a difficult time. Some of the stones from the church were used to build the walls around the present Fairgreen, and the altar was given to the chapel of the Sacred Heart Home in Roscommon.

St Patrick's Church, Castlerea

In 1893, Fr Hanly and John Clarence of Ballisodare signed an agreement to construct a new church, 160ft in length, 60ft in width at the transepts, and 65ft to the roof-ridge, with a seating capacity of 1,500. The cost would be £8,650, and the foundation stone was laid in June of 1893 by Bishop Gillooly. Local parishioners contributed what they could,, and often helped with physical labour. Fr Hanly, unwilling to lay the whole burden of the cost on his parishioners, went to America on a fund raising mission, and collected a substantial sum at the World Fair in Chicago. The O'Conor Don family donated the Stations of the Cross, which were brought specially from Jerusalem. The High Altar is constructed in Caen Stone and marble. The interior furnishing pushed the eventual cost to £13,000.

Reconstruction, from remaining fragments, of one face of the tenth-century cross at Emlagh

The old St Joseph's Church in Castlerea, built in 1798

The church was dedicated to St Patrick, and the opening ceremony was performed on Sunday 16 August 1896, by Bishop John Clancy of Elphin, with three other bishops assisting. The church today stands as an architectural gem of Norman-revival style and is a tribute to both the faith and generosity of the people who ensured its erection.

Trien church, about three miles south of Castlerea, dedicated to St Caolainn, was built in 1871; before this date the local people had to walk to the old St Joseph's on the far side of the town. The site at Trien was bought from William Kelly for £5, whereupon he donated £1 towards the cost of the chapel. Many local stonemasons and labourers worked on the construction of this small, ashlar faced chapel, which has recently been redecorated and refurbished.

The church of Cloonbonniffe lies to the west of Castlerea, and was built in the 1870s. The site was donated by the O'Conor Don. The church was dedicated to St Brigid, and a stained glass window bearing her image is to be seen in the sanctuary. The church was originally of cut-stone, similar to Trien, but was plastered during renovation in the mid-1940s. The bell, which until then was housed in the tower over the front door, was re-located to a specially built bell-tower to the side of the chapel, dedicated to the memory of Capt John Vaughan. In 1984, the church was entirely renovated, with the walls being dry-lined, and a new limestone altar and ambo installed. New seating and a new tabernacle were also installed.

Fr Michael O'Flanagan (1876-1942), better known as the 'Patriotic Priest', who was to the fore in advancing Irish independence, was a native of Cloonflower, Castlerea. His was the first voice heard in the inaugural Dáil session in 1919, when he said the opening prayers.

The Church of Ireland community was served by Holy Trinity Church, which was supported by the benefice of Ballintubber, comprising the parishes of Ballintubber, Kilteevan and Baslick. The church was located in the present Church of Ireland cemetery at Castlerea. This was replaced by a more modern building in 1819, also dedicated to the Holy Trinity, which closed in 1997.

Key to the map

01. Adragool
02. Annagh
03. Annaghmaghera
04. Ardrass
05. Arm
06. Ballindrumlea
07. Ballinphuill
08. Ballymulrennan
09. Beagh
10. Breanabeg
11. Caher
12. Carradooan
13. Carrowgarve
14. Carrowkeel
15. Carrowmore
16. Castlereagh
17. Cloonaff
18. Cloonalis
19. Cloonavindin
20. Cloonbonniffe
21. Clooncah
22. Cloonchambers
23. Clonnconra
24. Clooncoose North

25. Clooncoose South
26. Clooncraffield
27. Clooncran
28. Cloondacarra
29. Cloondacarra Beg
30. Cloonelt
31. Cloonfad
32. Cloonfelliv
33. Cloonfower
34. Cloonkeen
35. Cloonlatieve
36. Cloonree
37. Cloonroughan
38. Cloonsuck
39. Cloontarsna
40. Cloontrask
41. Creggameen
42. Creggancor
43. Creggaslin
44. Creglahan
45. Demesne
46. Derreen
47. Drumalough
48. Emlagh

49. Foughil
50. Harristown
51. Kilmore
52. Knockmurry
53. Knockroe
54. Liveelick
55. Lisboy
56. Lisliddy
57. Listhomasroe
58. Longford
59. Meelickaduff
60. Mewlaghmore
61. Moor
62. Rampark
63. Rathbarna
64. Rathleg
65. Southpark Demesne
66. Taghnarra
67. Taghnoose
68. Termon Beg
69. Termon More
70. Tonrevagh
71. Trien
72. Willsbrook

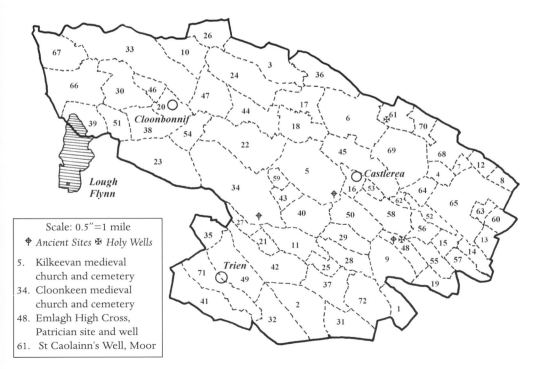

Scale: 0.5"=1 mile

⚲ *Ancient Sites* ✠ *Holy Wells*

5. Kilkeevan medieval church and cemetery
34. Cloonkeen medieval church and cemetery
48. Emlagh High Cross, Patrician site and well
61. St Caolainn's Well, Moor

Parish of Coolera [Strandhill and Ransboro]
(Kilmacowen & Killaspugbrone) County Sligo
Churches: Strandhill & Ransboro

The district of Coolera, which includes the ancient parishes of Killaspug-brone and Kilmacowen, was part of the ecclesiastical union of Sligo until it was created a parish in its own right in 1998. The peninsula, which is surrounded on three sides by the tidal waters of the Atlantic, is dominated by the bold and majestic cairn-topped Knocknarea and embraces the pre-historic cemetery at Carrowmore, and the off-shore island of Coney which boasts of strong Patrician associations.

Killaspugbrone
early monastic site

Killaspugbrone, one of the most ancient sites in Elphin, lies about a mile from the modern village of Strandhill, on a site overlooking the tidal flats of Cummeen Strand. Cill Easpaig Brón, or the Church of Bishop Bronus, is said to have been founded by Patrick himself. The saint, accompanied by his disciple, Bronus, crossed from Tireragh, in west Sligo, to Cúil Irra, the home of Bronus. Patrick marked out a site, Cashel Irra, inside which Bronus built his primitive church. The existing church remains, in terms of style and plan, present indications of considerable antiquity – for example, the location of the original doorway in an elevated position in the centre of the western gable. In time, this was replaced by a door on the south-side wall, which gave some protection from the prevailing westerly winds. The eastern window is extremely elegant in style, with its mouldings and inclined sides, while the masonry surmounting the slopes of the western gable was probably built as a screen for the roof of the church to shield it from the prevailing winds blowing in from the Atlantic. It is most likely that the present ruin dates from the eleventh or twelfth centuries rather than the fifth. Part of the fabric is thought to date from as late as the fifteenth century. In recent years the Atlantic storms have inflicted considerable damage on the structure and particularly the graveyard walls.

Following the Reformation, Killaspugbrone was used for Anglican services until it fell into disuse around 1680. In 1811 the ruins were repaired by the Select Vestry of St John's who also built the wall around the graveyard in 1814. When St Anne's Church of Ireland, at nearby Tully, was consecrated in October 1855, the baptismal font from Killaspugbrone was placed inside the church door, where it is still in use. St Anne's forms part of the union of St John's.

The offshore islands of Coney and Oyster were traditionally part of the parish of Killaspugbrone, but are currently served from Rosses Point. The former, the only inhabited island in the diocese, has many Patrician associations – St Patrick's Well, St Patrick's Wishing Chair, a huge chair-shaped boulder on the west side of the Island, and Dúnán Phádraig, a small island on Cummeen Strand which, irrespective of variations in the tide, is never covered by the water.

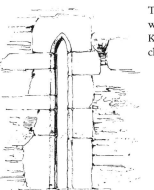

The east window of Kilmacowen church

The other early Christian site in Coolera, is Kilmacowen, 'the Church of the Sons of Eoin', a Munster chieftain who founded the church in the sixth century. He had six sons, all of whom entered the religious life. In time this structure fell into disuse, and the existing building seems to date from the thirteenth century. The only portions now surviving are the eastern gable and a section of the side walls. Adjacent to the churchyard, on the north side, is a holy well called Tobar Phádraig, with a stone, said to bear the imprint of the saint's knee. The surrounding burial ground, the final resting-place of both Catholic and Protestant families of the neighbourhood, contains many fine memorials, including a number of well-preserved box-tombs dating for the early nineteenth century. The late James Canon Roddy PP, Riverstown, who died in June 1953, is interred in the Roddy family plot.

At Templenabree, in the south-western corner of Kilmacowen parish, near the northern shore of Ballisodare Bay, stands the eastern gable of an ancient church, which derives its name from Teampall na Brúighe, meaning, 'the church of the sea-marsh'. Local tradition says it was a nunnery, and on old maps it is marked as Temple na Galliagh Doo (Teampall na gCailleach Dubh), the 'church of the black-robed nuns'. It's possible that Templenabree was originally built as a church and passed into the hands of a community of nuns in the thirteenth century, after Kilmacowen had replaced it as a parish church. Other ecclesiastical remains are to be found in the townlands of the Granges, on the southern side of Knocknarea, where four quarters of land belonged to the Cistercian Abbey of Boyle, and were known as 'Grange na Mánach', the 'Grange-lands of the monks', as late as the seventeenth century.

Amongst the penal day priests who ministered as fugitives in the parishes of Killaspugbrone and Kilmacowen, were Owen Mihan (Meehan), 1698; John Dugan

1704, and John McDonagh. About the same period there are references to a young priest, named Mac Dermott, who said Mass 'in the fields at Drynahan'. At an inquiry held in Sligo in 1743-44 it was stated that David Flynn was parish priest of the parishes of Kilmacowen and Killaspugbrone. He subsequently became pastor of St John's parish, and on his death in 1778 was buried in Sligo Abbey.

The first church built in Coolera in relatively modern times, was that in the townland of Drinaghan, on a site where Mass was celebrated during penal times. This small thatched chapel of Ransboro, or Wrensborough, situated on the eastern brow of Knocknarea, was probably built in the late 1790s. The structure was so primitive that the ribs of a whale are said to have been used as a support for the roof. Around 1820 it was replaced by a plain chapel that ran from east to west, and over the succeeding decades further additions and extensions were carried out, including the building of a belfry. This church is still to be seen today, although it has been converted into a modern residence. In 1959 a decision was made to abandon the old church and to build a new place of worship at the more central location of 'The Redgate'. Work began on the new church in 1962, and the foundation stone was laid the following year. It was opened and blessed by Bishop Hanly in June 1967. Good fortune came the way of the parishioners a few years later when success in a prize-bond draw cleared off the outstanding debt. The name of the old church, Ransboro, was transferred to the new site, and Our Lady Star of the Sea Church was solemnly consecrated by Bishop Conway on 8 September 1974.

In olden times there were three holy wells at Scardan in the parish of Killaspugbrone, called Lady Well, Patrick's Well, and Brigid's Well, where pilgrims gathered annually on 15 August. The devotional scenes witnessed there inspired a local balladeer to pen the following lines:

St Patrick's church, Strandhill

It's on the lands of Scardan
That Blessed Holy Place
Where miracles are performed
All by the Queen of Saints;
The deaf to hear, the dumb to speak,
The lame and blind they say –
Are all restored to their perfect health
On Our Great Lady Day.

Over a century ago the pattern ceased, and recent land reclamation operations have reduced the wells to a trickle.

The growth of Strandhill as a popular seaside resort led to the erection of a church at the western extremity of the peninsula. The foundation stone was laid in March 1920, and it was opened and dedicated to St Patrick in August 1921, fifteen hundred years after the first church in Coolera was founded by the apostle himself at nearby Killaspugbrone.

Key to the map

01. Ballybeg
02. Barnasraghy
03. Beanfield
04. Breeoge
05. Carrowbunnaun
06. Carrowcrin
07. Carrowdough
08. Carrowkeel (part of)
09. Carrowmore
10. Cartron Honoria Duff
11. Cartronabree
12. Cloverhill or
    Knocknashammer
13. Coney Island
14. Culleenamore
15. Culleenduff
16. Cummeen (part of)
17. Doonan Patrick Island
18. Drinaghan

19. Glen
20. Graigue
21. Grange East
22. Grange North
23. Grange West
24. Killaspugbrone
25. Kilmacowen
26. Knocknahur North
27. Knocknahur South
28. Knocknarea North
29. Knocknarea South
_. Knocknashammer or
    Cloverhill (see 12)
30. Larass or Strandhill
31. Lecarrow
32. Lisheenagooravan
33. Lisawully
34. Luffertan
35. Maguins Island

36. Oakfield or Derry-
    darragh (part of)
37. Primrose Grange
38. Rathcarrick
39. Rathonoragh
40. Rinn
41. Scardan Beg
42. Scardan More
43. Seafield
44. Siberia or Slieveroe
_. Slieveroe or Siberia
    (see 44)
_. Strandhill or Larass
    (see 30)
45. Templenabree
46. Tobernaveen
47. Tully
48. Woodpark

Scale: 0.6"=1 mile

✠ *Ancient Sites* ✠ *Holy Wells*

24. Patrician site and medieval
    church
25. Medieval church and St
    Patrick's Well
37. The Granges
45. Medieval church, nunnery
    and Tobar Phádraig

The Parish of Croghan

(Killucan, Killumod, & part of Kilcolgagh) County Roscommon
Churches: Croghan & Drumlion

The modern parish of Croghan is situated in the triangle between the towns of Boyle, Elphin and Carrick-on-Shannon, in north county Roscommon, bounded by the Shannon on the east, and Ballinameen parish to the west. The parish of Croghan is of late nineteenth century origin, and is an amalgamation of parts of several ancient parishes.

The present entity of Croghan was established in the late 1850s, when Killucan in the north and Killumod in the south were joined, and the eastern parts of Eastersnow and Kilcolgagh were attached to it, along with a small portion of the ancient parish of Tumna, lying south of the Boyle River. However, the area administered by Croghan in the 1850s extended the whole way from Carrick-on-Shannon to Ballinameen village. Only in 1861 did Croghan and Ballinameen become two separate parishes.

The names of the ancient parishes are derived from the those early Christian saints, namely Luken, and Lumad; Tumna, the 'grave of the women', on the shores of the Boyle river at the point where it meets the Shannon, was in fact the grave of St Éadoin, from which comes Lough Éidín, the original name of Drumharlow Lake. There were many monastic settlements in the area. Eastersnow or Estersnow, the most renowned, is derived from the ancient name 'Díseart Nuadhain', the hermitage of the holy man, St Nuadh.

St Michael the Archangel, Drumlion church

In penal times, Myles Brennan, then priest in the area, resided in the townland of Gloria, and tradition has it that he and other religious hid on an island in Clogher Lake for safety from the crown forces. Fr George T. Plunkett (1756-1827), who was born at Bothar, became parish priest of Croghan in the latter half of the 1700s, and subsequently in 1810 became Bishop of Elphin. The population of the parish, as defined by its modern boundaries, stood at about 7,500 in the 1840s, but a report by Fr Matthew Barrett PP during the Famine period tells us that between October 1846 and October 1847, six hundred people died. Emigration further reduced the numbers in the parish in the 1850s.

It was around this time that Arthur Fulton and his wife emigrated from Croghan to the United States, and in the mid

1900s their grandson Peter Sheen (1895-1979), became Bishop Fulton-Sheen, auxiliary Bishop of New York (1951-1966), and subsequently Bishop of Rochester (1966-69). He returned to consecrate the church in Croghan in 1952.

Today there are two churches in the parish, one in Croghan village and the other in Drumlion. Both are dedicated to St Michael the Archangel. The first Catholic church in Croghan was a penal chapel erected in 1790 in the townland of Kilcola, but it was replaced by a new church in the village of Croghan in 1816. Additional land had to be acquired from Guy Lloyd of Croghan House in 1856, so that the building could be considerably enlarged and renovated. This work was completed in 1857. Over ninety years later in 1949 a further extension was made to the front of the church. On 20 April 1952, the church as we know it today was re-dedicated in honour of St Michael the Archangel by Bishop Fulton-Sheen. Fr Nicholas Green and Fr Peter O'Connor, who were responsible for building the first church in Croghan, are interred in uncommemorated graves within the confines of the present church.

The old Croghan Catholic church

The building of the present church of St Michael at Drumlion commenced in 1854 under the guidance of Fr Matt Barrett, a native of the parish. The foundation stone was laid by Dr John Kilduff (1820-1867), Bishop of Ardagh, on Easter Monday of that year. Two years later, on 27 July 1856, the church was solemnly dedicated, and the sermon was preached by Dr D. W. Cahill of Dublin, a 'noted patriot and preacher'. A modern wood carving of the archangel graces the inside of the church today.

The Redemptorist congregation opened a mission house at Killucan in 1899, at

St Michael's
Church,
Drumlion

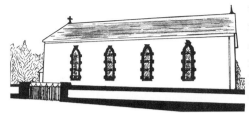

the request of Bishop Clancy, but their tenure was brief. In 1901 the Killucan community was dissolved and transferred to Esker, county Galway. Cortober Parish Hall, which stands near the site of the former Redemptorist house, is today used as a Mass centre.

The traces of ancient monastic settlements dot the parish at the cemeteries of Killucan, Killumod, Tumna and Eastersnow. The old Church of Ireland at Estersnow was erected in 1707, and replaced by a new building which was erected near the village of Croghan in 1862, and continues to serve the community to this day.

As we enter the twenty-first century, Mary McAleese, whose father left the Croghan townland of Carroward in 1939, has become President of Ireland (1997), and with the rise in economic prosperity and confidence, Croghan, with a proud past, looks forward to a promising future.

Key to the map

01. Ardchamoyle
02. Ardkeenagh
03. Ardlavagh
04. Ardmore
05. Ballindrehid
06. Ballinvilla
07. Ballyculleen
_. Ballynahoogh or
    Cavestown (see 14)
08. Bunreagh
09. Canbo
10. Carroward
11. Carrowmore
12. Carrowreagh
13. Cartron
14. Cavetown or
    Ballynahoogh
15. Clogher
16. Clooneigh
17. Cloongownagh
18. Cloonmaan
19. Cloonshaghan (part of)
20. Cloonskeeveen
21. Cordrehid
22. Cortober
23. Croghan
24. Cuiltyconeen
25. Culleenatreen or

Flagford
26. Dacklin
27. Danesfort
28. Deerpark
29. Derraun
30. Derrylow
31. Dorrary
32. Drishoge
33. Drumercool
34. Drumerr
35. Drumlion
36. Enagh
37. Estersnow
38. Farranagalliagh
39. Faus
40. Finnor
_. Flagford (see 25)
_. Gardenstown (see 53)
41. Glebe
42. Glooria
43. Kilcolagh
44. Killappoge
45. Killukin
46. Killummod
47. Knockacorha
48. Knockadalteen
49. Knockananima
50. Knocknafushoga

51. Knockroe
    (ED Kilumod))
52. Knockroe (part of)
    (ED Rushfield)
53. Legvoy or Gardenstown
54. Lisdaly
55. Lodge
56. Lugnashammer
57. Macnadille
58. Meera
59. Mullaghmore
60. Rathallen (part of)
61. Rock
62. Runnaboll (part of)
63. Scregg
64. Sroankeeragh
65. Tawlaght
66. Toormore
67. Toorymartin
68. Treanagry (part of)
69. Tullyboy
70. Tullyleague
71. Tullyvohaun
72. Tumna
73. Woodbrook

R. Shannon

Carrick-on-Shannon

16
17
72
24
18
20
73 31
58 70
66 10 1 64 65 48 59 22
67 21
57 47 49 45 27
3 53 63
30 Drumlion
35 41
36 34 61
8 33 55 128
56 34 13
4 23 6 29 7 5 25
50 54 9
Croghan
Lisdaly
44 12 46
60 51 40
43 26
11 Canbo L.
62 L.Corbally

69
71
2 15 37
42 14 38
52 68 19
Cavetown
39
5
18
22

Scale: 0.65"=1 mile
⊕ Ancient Sites ✠ Holy Wells

37. Estersnow medieval church and cemetery
45. Killulin medieval church and cemetery
46. Killummod medieval church and cemetery
72. Tumna old church

Parish of Drumcliff

(Drumcliffe) County Sligo
Church: Rathcormac

'Beloved of my heart, also in the west,
Drumcliff at Culcinne's Strand' (St Columba)

To the north of St. John's and Calry parishes lies the once extensive parish of Drumcliff, which in former times included both Rosses Point and Maugherow (q.v.). At Cooldrumman, in 553, took place the famous 'Battle of the Books' which was fought over the first recorded case of copyright. St Finian of Moville brought back from Rome a copy of the Psalms which he valued highly, and which he did not want copied. However, Colmcille secretly made a copy of it, and when Finian found out, he claimed the copy. Colmcille refused, and the dispute was referred to the High King at Tara. He ruled in favour of Finian, saying that

according to law, 'To every book its son-book, as to every cow its calf'. Colmcille refused to accept the judgement, and the High King marched against him. The battle had political overtones, as an army of Ulstermen and Connachtmen, settling old scores, fought with Colmcille against the High King, Diarmaid. Over 3,000 men are reputed to have died in battle. The High King himself was killed, and Colmcille, repenting, went to St Molaise on Inishmurray who, as penance, sent him into exile in Iona, to where he sorrowfully departed, determined to 'win more souls for Christ, than had died in battle'.

In 575 or thereabouts, St Columba returned from Iona and founded the monastery of Drumcliff close to the site of the battle which had proved the turning point of his career. Entries in the various Annals indicate that the monastery was a place of note between the end of the ninth and the middle of the sixteenth centuries. We read of the death of seven comharbs, or successors of the founder, St Columba, four erenachs, three abbots, and one priest. Drumcliff attained its zenith as a monastic settlement in the thirteenth century. There is no mention of it in the Annals after 1503, when the last successor of Columba died. At a Chancery Inquisition in April 1606, there is reference to 'a church and a house belonging to the parson of Drumcliff, to the west end of the church'. It is probable that this was the reconstructed remains of part of the monastic buildings, and was presumably used by the Protestants until its incorporation in the new Church of Ireland building.

In ancient times this foundation of St Columba was widely known as Druim Chliabh na gCros, Drumcliff of the Crosses. While there is no longer any trace of the monastic foundation, the glories of former times are reflected in a 13ft-high sculptured cross of great beauty and antiquity, and the stump of a Round Tower, which rises to a height of forty feet.

The cross depicts scenes from both Old and New Testaments. On the east side are the figures of Adam and Eve, and above that a representation of David and Goliath. The carving on the centre of the head is quite worn but appears to be the last judgement. On the west side, above an interlaced ornament, is a group of three figures, supposedly representing the seizure of Christ in the garden, and, above that, in the centre of the cross, the crucifixion scene. Close by stands the shaft of another undecorated cross.

St Columba's Church of Ireland, built in 1808, with its distinctive tower which was completed two years later, now stands on the site of the ancient monastery which, according to tradition, went by the name of the Teampall Buidhe, (the Yellow Church). The discovery in 1999 of parts of a shaft of a high cross sunk in its walls would seem to substantiate the theory that sections of the medieval buildings were incorporated into the present church.

The graveyard surrounding the church is the burial place of W. B. Yeats (1865-1939), whose great-grandfather had been a rector of the parish. Yeats' remains were re-interred here after World War II, from France where he had died in 1938, and today hundreds of visitors come annually to see his last resting place, 'Under Bare Ben Bulben's Head' ... 'Cast a cold Eye on Life on Death – Horseman pass by.'

St Columba's Church, Rathcormack

Other early monastic remains lie at Keelty and at Ballynagalliagh (Baile na gCailleach), which was the site of a convent attached to the Benedictine nunnery at Kilcreevanty in Galway. There are holy wells at Tober Colmcille in Kintogher and Tober Patrick in Urlar.

Half a mile from Drumcliff stands the modern parish church of Rathcormac, which was built by Fr O'Callaghan in 1833, on the site on an earlier church. Dedicated appropriately to St Columba, the cost of construction was in the region of £500, of which £150 was contributed locally in amounts ranging from £1 to 2s.6d. A former unnamed parish priest had bequesthed £100 for the purpose and a number of local Protestant families also contributed to the fund. St Columba's was subsequently improved and enlarged and the entire ground floor seated. This work was commenced by Fr Patrick O'Gara PP, and completed by his successor Andrew Morahan when he became PP in 1861. St Columba's was rededicated on 1 September 1963, by Bishop Vincent Hanly, following extensive renovations, which included the building of the now distinctive belfry, entrance porch and a baptistry. The presbytery was built in the late 1930s by Tom O'Beirne PP.

Remains of a round tower at Drumcliff

In the nineteenth century the parish had one of the largest non-Catholic populations in the county. A substantial percentage of these were Non-Conformist, mainly from a farming background. There was also a Presbyterian church at Drum, which closed over fifty years ago.

Key to the map

01. Ballinvoher
02. Ballygilgan (part of)
03. Ballynagalliagh
04. Barnaderg
05. Barnarobin
06. Carney (Jones)
07. Carney (O'Beirne)
08. Cartronmore
09. Cartronwilliamoge
10. Cashelgarran (part of)
11. Castlegal
12. Cloonderry
13. Clooneen
14. Cloonmull
15. Collinsford
16. Coolbeg
17. Cooldrumman Lower
18. Cooldrumman Upper
19. Creaghadoo
20. Cullagh Beg
21. Cullagh More
22. Doonierin (part of)
23. Drum East
24. Drum West
25. Drumcliff Glebe
26. Drumcliff North
27. Drumcliff South
28. Drumcliff West
29. Drumkilsellagh
30. Finned
31. Glen Lower
32. Glen Upper
33. Glencarbury
34. Gortarowey
35. Gortnagrelly
36. Keelty
37. Kilsellagh
38. Kiltycooly
_. Kingsmountain or Slievemore (see 46)
39. Kintogher
40. Lislahelly
41. Lisnalurg
42. Lugatober
43. Lugnagall
44. Magheragillerneeve or Springfield
45. Rahaberna
46. Slievemore or Kingsmountain
_. Springfield (see 44)
47. Teesan
48. Tormore
49. Tully
50. Urlar

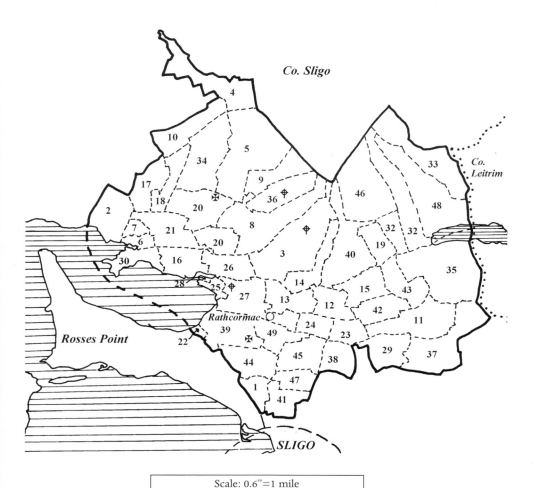

Co. Sligo

Co. Leitrim

Rosses Point

Rathcormac

SLIGO

Scale: 0.6"=1 mile
⚲ Ancient Sites ✠ Holy Wells

3. Ballynagalliagh nunnery site
20. Tobar Phádraig
27. Drumcliff monastic site, Round Tower and High Cross
36. Keelty old church and cillín
39. Tobar Colmcille, Kintogher

Parish of Elphin

(Elphin, Creeve, Shankill & Kilmacumsey) County Roscommon
Churches: Elphin, Creeve & Kilmaryal

THE PARISH OF Elphin is the most central parish in the diocese, almost of equal distance from its northern and southern extremities. It borders six parishes and was the location for the first Cathedral of Elphin. The town became the episcopal seat of the diocese in 1152 and the centre of administration for all diocesan affairs. It retained its diocesan status until the Reformation and ensuing penal laws. While Sligo is now the Cathedral town, the diocese still retains its medieval name, as do many other Irish dioceses.

The foundation of the diocese in its present form only dates from the twelfth century but the bishopric of Elphin is of much greater antiquity, dating from the mid-fifth century when St Patrick appointed St Asicus as the first Abbot-Bishop of Elphin.

The origins of the faith in the diocese are firmly embedded in the parish of Elphin and well documented in the *Tripartite Life of St Patrick,* the Patrician documents and the *Book of Armagh.* So from the very early writings we know there was a vibrant Christian community in Elphin under the spiritual care of Asicus whose artisanship inspired many early Christian works of art in silver, copper and brass.

There is little evidence of the ancient Christian church of Elphin today except for the island townland of Abbeycartron, which identifies the site of the early

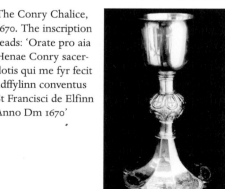

The Conry Chalice, 1670. The inscription reads: 'Orate pro aia Henae Conry sacerdotis qui me fyr fecit adffylinn conventus St Francisci de Elfinn Anno Dm 1670'

church. The ruined eighteenth-century Anglican Cathedral marks the site of the first Cathedral church at Elphin, and St Patrick's Well recalls the national apostle's influence in establishing the first church there. In the *Papal Taxation List* of 1306 two churches were recorded for Elphin, Teampall Mór and Teampall Phádraig. Teampeall Mór refers to St Mary's Cathedral, and Teampall Phádraig stood on the site where the first Patrician church was erected. This site was subsequently occupied by the Canons Regular of St Augustine in 1453, and then by the Fransicans.

The arrival of the Canons Regular of the Augustinian order in the twelfth century, and their replacement with the Franciscan order in the fifteenth century, ensured the continued spiritual care of the people of this region. Indeed the Franciscans remained attached to Elphin up to the nineteenth century despite the fact that they had to take refuge outside the town in Drinane during the

Reformation and subsequent penal laws. The last Franciscan superior of Elphin was Fr Anthony Garrahan who died as parish priest of Kilcorkey in 1835 and thus ended the Franciscan link with Elphin and the diocese. The Franciscan friary at Abbeycartron has totally disappeared but excavation in the 1950s revealed evidence of its foundations. The Third Order of the Franciscans had a religious house at Caldragh but nothing remains of this except that the site is marked by an ancient cemetery.

In the *Report on the State of Popery* of 1731 Mass Houses are listed for Creeve and Kilmacumsey, as well as one three miles from Elphin. But efforts failed to establish one in the town itself. The Franciscan friary at Drinane is recorded as having fifteen friars at the time. In 1824 churches are listed for Creeve, Ballyroddy, Flaskagh, Ryefield and Elphin.

The present parish of Elphin com-prises the greater parts of the ancient parishes of Elphin, Creeve, Shankill and Kilmacumsey. In fact, a large portion of the ancient parish of Elphin now forms the northern part of Tulsk. Several townlands, including Flaskagh, Fox-borough, Killina, Cloonyquinn and Laghtcausk, were transferred to Tulsk in 1868. Prior to the transfer, the present church of Killina was erected in 1860, as its date-stone indicates, and replaced an earlier church at Flaskagh.

Elphin Cathedral (Church of Ireland). Courtesy of *Cathedrals of Ireland* by Peter Galloway (Belfast 1993)

There is evidence of an early Christian site at Shankill, where St Patrick appointed St Mathona as abbess of a monastery there. The ruins of medieval parish churches and ancient cemeteries also exist at Creeve and Kilmacumsey. It was at Sgiath na bhFeart in the ancient parish of Kilmacumsey, that the Archbishop of Armagh, Edmund Maguaran (1587-1593) was killed on 23 June 1593, in a battle between his friend Hugh Maguire and Sir William Bingham's crown forces. It is reputed that the remains of the archbishop are interred in a sepulchral mound near the site.

There are a number of holy wells in the parish, the most revered being Tobar Mhuire near Elphin where pilgrims flocked up to recent times during the pilgrimage season from 15 August to the 8 September. The other holy wells include Tobar Grellan at Creeve, St Patrick's Well in Mantua and St Patrick's Well near the Cathedral site, which many historians claim is the derivation of the word 'Ail Finn', the fair rock.

Three churches serve the parish at present, namely Elphin, Creeve and Kilmaryal (Mantua). A chapel at Ryefield served the people in the northern end of the parish from c.1800 until 1896 when the church ceased to be a place of worship following the opening of the new church in Elphin.

St Patrick's
Church, Elphin

The present church of St Patrick at Elphin was built in 1894 and replaced an earlier church dating back to about 1800. St Brigid's church at Creeve was erected in 1858-59 on the site of an older church built in 1810. The Church of the Most Holy Trinity at Mantua in the townland of Kilmaryal was opened for worship on 1870. Prior to this, people in the Mantua area worshipped in Ballyroddy penal chapel and, for a period, in Mantua House, the ancestral home of the Grace family.

The vicar general of the diocese, Rev James Fallon, made two very detailed reports to Rome in 1631 and 1637 respectively, outlining the state of the diocese during that period. Of Elphin he says; 'The episcopal See that is the town of Elphin, is now occupied by the Anglican bishop and his people, and they are using the Cathedral as a place of worship.' (See Part II.)

The medieval Cathedral building was subsequently destroyed in 1641 but completely rebuilt in 1757-58, and the ruins of the present tower date from that time. The nave of the Cathedral was rebuilt in 1823, and an apse in semi-medieval style was added in 1872. The Cathedral continued to be the Anglican place of worship until 25 October 1961, when the episcopal seat was transferred to St John's church, Sligo. The ancient titular of St Mary the Virgin was added to that of St John, and this church then became known as the Cathedral of St Mary the Virgin and St John the Baptist, thus continuing to preserve the link with the original Cathedral.

St Brigid's Church,
Creeve

The old Cathedral building at Elphin was demolished in 1964, but partially restored in 1982. The parish of Elphin has experienced much ecclesiastical change over the centuries and little remains today to remind us of its former glory as a Cathedral town and centre of administration of the diocese. The annual diocesan pilgrimage to the old Cathedral site in recent years has revived the historical significance of Elphin and the prominent place it holds in the annals of the diocese.

Elphin has been an important seat of learning from the time of Asicus to modern times. The establishment of a Diocesan School by the Church of Ireland in the early eighteenth century played a significant role at a time when educational institutions were few. It was in this school that eminent people like Oliver Goldsmith, William Wilde and Percy French received their early education. The opening of the Bishop Hodson Grammar school in 1869 continued the great legacy of learning that has been part of this parish from earliest times. One of the principal seats of the Maolchonaire was at Cloonahee, Elphin. It was here that one of the Four Masters, Fearfeasa Ó Maolchonaire, was born, as well as Flaithrí Ó Maolchonaire (Florence Conry), who later became Archbishop of Tuam (1609-1629) and founder of the Irish Franciscan College at Louvain in 1607.

The Sisters of Mercy have been part of the parish since 1868 providing both primary and post-primary education to generations of children and young people. The convent was vacated in 1988, but some sisters remained in temporary residence until 1999, providing much valued pastoral care.

Church of the Holy Trinity, Kilmaryal

Elphin as a Cathedral town may be consigned to history, but it continues as a parish Christian community nurturing the seeds of faith first planted in this hallowed ground in the mid fifth century.

Interior of St Mary's Church of Ireland Cathedral, Elphin c. 1900

Key to the map

01. Abbeycartron
02. Ardnagowna
03. Assaun
04. Athroe
05. Attiaghgrania
06. Ballyholaghan
07. Ballymurray
08. Ballyroddy
09. Ballysundriven
10. Barrinagh
11. Boherroe
12. Brackloon
13. Caldragh
14. Caldrymoran
15. Caran
16. Caranlea
17. Carrigeen
18. Carrigeenacreeha
19. Carrigeengappul
20. Carrigeenynaghtan
21. Carrowcrin
22. Carrowkeel (ED Elphin)
23. Carrowkeel (ED Lisgrave)
24. Carrowkeel Upper
25. Carrownamaddy
26. Carrownamorheeny
27. Carrownacaran
28. Carrowncully
29. Carrowngarry
30. Carrowntogher
31. Carrownurlar
32. Cartron
33. Cartron (ED Rossmore)
34. Cartronagor
35. Cartroncaran
36. Cartroncarrowntogher
37. Castletown
38 Chanterland or Windmill Park
39. Cherryfield or Drishaghan
40. Cleenraugh
41. Clogher Beg
42. Clogher More
43. Cloonahee
44. Cloonboyoge
45. Clooncullaan
46. Cloonkerin
47. Cloonroughan
48. Cloonybrennan
49. Clooncattan
50. Cloonyeffer
51. Commeen
52. Coolmeen
53. Corbally East
54. Corbally Middle
55. Corbally West
56. Corgarve
57. Corry East
58. Corry West
59. Creeve (ED Creeve)
60. Creeve (ED Rossmore)
61. Creevolan
62. Deanery
63. Drinaun
–. Drishaghan or Cherryfield (see 39)
64. Drumlish
65. Drumman
66. Drummullin
67. Dunmurraghoe
68. Edenan
69. Edenan & Kinclare
70. Elphin
71. Emlagh
72. Erriblagh
73. Glenballythomas (part of)
74. Gortnacloy
75. Gortnacrannagh
76. Grallagh
77. Killeen East
78. Killeen West
79. Kilmacumsey
80. Kilnamryall
81. Kinard
82. Kinclare
_. Kinclare & Edenan (see 69)
83. Kye
84. Leecarrow
85. Lisboy
86. Lisgarve
87. Lismacool
88. Lismageevoge
89. Lisnaboll
90. Lisnagard
91. Lisphillip
92. Loughbally
93. Lugboy
94. Lurgan
95. Martry
96. Moheedian
97. Moneylea
98. Mulleenduff
99. Ovaun
100. Portobello
101. Raheen
102. Rathardeagher
103. Rathroe
104. Ross Beg
105. Ross More East
106. Ross More West
107. Runnacocka
108. Runnaroddaun
109. Runnaruag
110. Runnateggal or Ryefield
–. Ryefield or Runnateggal (see 110)
111. Scor Beg
112. Scor More
113. Shankill
114. Skeanavart
115. Stonepark
116. Tansyfield
117. Teermore
118. Toberrory
119. Tonaknick
120. Tullycartron
121. Tullyloyd
122. Turlagh
–. Windmill Park or Chanterland (see 38)

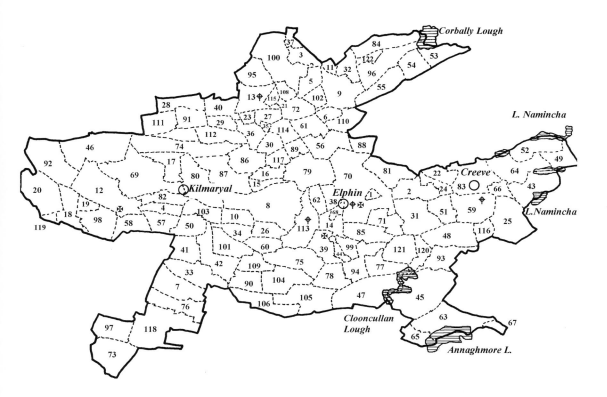

Parish of Fairymount
(Tibohine (part of)) County Roscommon
Churches: Fairymount & Tibohine

T HE PARISH OF Fairymount is located in northwest Roscommon, embracing the ridge and hill country between Castlerea and Frenchpark. Anciently known as Tibohine, the modern name derives from the high sandstone hill of Mullaghnashee, or Fairymount, which is capped by the Carn Cloch, or Giant's Grave. This structure was referred to in the *Tripartite Life* as Ard Senlis. The modern parish is served by two churches, the Church of the Sacred Heart in Fairymount and by St Baoithín's Church at Tibohine.

St Baoithín from a stained glass window by Ethel Rhind (1879-1952) in Tibohine church

The name Tibohine has its origins in the activities of St Baoithín, who took charge of the church founded here by St Patrick. In 640 AD, Baoithín is recorded as being the abbot-bishop of this community which he extended and made widely known. The settlement was originally known as Teach Baoithín Airtigh, or Tibohine Artagh, meaning the house of Baoithín of the territory of Airteach, and the saint is said to have been the son of the local chieftain, Cuanach. He was also grandson of Éanna of Airteach, who had offered 'a ridge in every nine' in his territory to St Patrick on which to build churches. Airteach encompassed all of northwest Roscommon, between Lough Gara and the Suck River. Although Baoithín's monastery is believed to have extended over a wide area, it probably centred on the old cemetery at Tibohine, where a small portion, covered with ivy, still stands in the old graveyard. It was occasionally known as Cruachán Airtigh. The foundation flourished from the sixth century, and was described in the *Book of Lecan* as: 'An áit ba mhó cliú in Airteach, ba é Tí Baethin é.'

The settlement was plundered in 1230, and again in 1233, and suffered final destruction in the Cromwellian period of the seventeenth century. The original parish or union of Tibohine, traditionally known as Airteach, which was co-extensive with the civil parish of the same name, was one of the largest in Connacht. It stretched from Lough Gara in the north to Cloonarragh townland in the south, and from east to west encompassed the present parishes of Loughglynn, Lisacul, Tibohine, Fairymount and part of Frenchpark. In 1837, there were three chapels in the union, at Loughglynn, Frenchpark and Tibohine. By 1839 the union had been split into three separate parishes, Tibohine, Loughglynn and Lisacul, and Frenchpark. Frenchpark was united with Ballinagare (Kilcorkey) in 1869.

The O'Conors, landlords in the locality, gave permission for a church to be built at Carrowgarrif, adjoining Tibohine townland. No trace of this church remains. This building was in use for almost a century until it was destroyed during penal times. In the *Report on the State of Popery* in 1731 there are three Mass Houses, with Frs Terence McGrah, Edmond Timoty and Edward Lavin recorded as serving the parish of Tibohine. In 1829, with the coming of Catholic Emancipation, the O'Conor Don granted a site for a new church in Teevnacreeva townland, just north of the present church. This stone chapel, which had a thatched roof, was often in poor condition and had no seats, with the faithful standing for Mass.

Tibohine old cemetery

In the 1850s, with the break-up of the old parish of Tibohine, Fr O'Reilly became PP, and Fairy-mount became the parish church, with Tibohine being the curacy. In the latter part of that decade it was decided to build a new church at Tibohine, and the De Freynes donated the site for the new struct-ure. On 9 June 1861 Bishop Laurence Gillooly dedicated the church to St Baoithín. The architects were Weightman, Hadfield and Goldie, and the church was con-structed by Patrick Hunt and Sons, Sligo. The old church at Teevnacreeva was con-verted into a girls' school, and subsequently became Conor's Parish Hall. Renovations were carried out on St Baoithín's in 1913, and again in the 1990s.

In 1881, Fr Bernard Coyne, later to become Bishop of Elphin, was appointed to the parish. He was very active in the local branch of the Land League, which was then at the height of its power, and was instrumental in securing land rights for the local tenantry.

The parish church is located at Fairymount, high on the southern slopes of Fairymount Hill, or Ard Senlis as it was anciently referred to. In 437 AD, St Patrick brought Lalloc, daughter of Dararca, to this hill. There they founded a church west of the hill, of which no ruins remain. In the townland of Cureentorpan in this local-ity, a children's burial ground known as Kilhooly is located. There is a tradition that a Patrician church was also built at Cloonfinglas, which was about a quarter of a mile from the present church.

A simple stone slated church was built around 1831 where the present parochial hall stands. Tradition has it that it was small and in bad repair and was often flooded. The present church of Fairymount is believed to have been built in 1867, with much voluntary labour. It was dedicated to the Sacred Heart and opened on Christmas Day. When first in use, conditions were primitive with an earthen floor and no seats. This situation was remedied in time, and by 1901 a new altar was installed. A growing confidence in the church was reflected in this locality by the installation of a remarkable set of eight windows executed by Michael Healy, (1873-1941), a member of the Dublin-based stained-glass studio, An Túr Gloinne. Renovations involving a new roof were carried out in the 1960s, and a new sandstone altar was installed in 1990.

The church at Portahard, in the neighbouring parish of Frenchpark serves the Church of Ireland community for the parish of Tibohine (Taughboyne) and surrounding parishes.

A Penal Chalice, dated 1611, in Fairymount church

Key to the map

01. Aghacurreen
02. Ballinphuill
03. Barnacawley
04. Buckhill
05. Carrowgarve
06. Cartron Beg
07. Cartron More
08. Clashcarragh
09. Clerragh
10. Cloggarnagh
11. Cloonarragh
12. Cloonfad
13. Cloonfinglas

14. Cloonsheever
15. Cornamucklagh & Falmore (part of)
16. Cureentorpan Eden
–. Falmore & Cornamucklagh (see 15)
17. Glebe East
18. Grallagh
19. Kilgarve
20. Leitrim
21. Lisdrumneil
22. Lisduff
23. Lissacurkia

24. Lissananny
25. Lissergool
26. Moyne
27. Mullaghnashee
28. Parkeel
29. Rathkeery
30. Ratra
31. Stonepark
32. Teevnacreeva
33. Tibohine
34. Turloughree

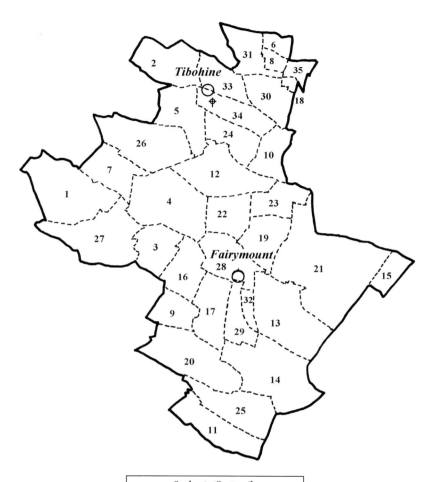

Scale: 0.6"=1 mile

✟ *Ancient Sites* ✠ *Holy Wells*

34. Tibohine medieval church and
cemetery

Parish of Frenchpark
(Tibohine (part of) and Kilcorkey) County Roscommon
Churches: Frenchpark & Ballinagare

Interior of
the old church at
Ballinagare
(Berna Chapman)

THE PARISH OF Frenchpark is situated in northwest county Roscommon, and about midway on the north-south axis of the diocese. It is bounded on the east by Elphin and on the west by Fairymount. The church of St Asicus at Frenchpark serves the northern portion of the union. This church has the distinction of being the only one in Elphin dedicated to the diocesan patron saint, and it is here that the parish priest resides. The half parish of Kilcorkey is served by a curate and the Church of the Sacred Heart in the village of Ballinagare. Frenchpark, named after the French family, was for a time the seat of Lord de Freyne, whose eighteenth-century ancestral home graced the locality. The village was originally known as Dún Gar and is renowned as the home of the Hyde family, where Dr Douglas Hyde, *An Craoibhín Aoibhinn* (1860-1949), spent his younger years.

In pre-Reformation times Kilcorkey was the name of an independent parish. Today the name is also given to a townland, where an ancient church site and cemetery are located. This foundation was said to have been originally a nunnery, but it was in a ruinous state, with most of its architectural features lost, together with its history, when John O'Donovan visited the area in 1837. It was to this locality, near Ballinagare village, that Denis O'Conor came to live in 1720, due to a restoration of part of the O'Conor ancestral lands. His door was always open to the co-religionists of the province who had suffered distress during the later penal law period. There was a welcome too for the last of the harper-composers, Turlough

Charles O'Conor
of Ballinagare

O'Carolan, who was patronisd by the O'Conors, and whose harp is now on display at Clonalis House, Castlerea. Denis was succeeded by his son, Charles O'Conor, who did much to preserve the cultural and literary heritage of Gaelic Ireland, and to improve the conditions of his fellow Catholics at that difficult time. He was co-founder of the Catholic Committee, a movement that led finally to Catholic emancipation in 1829.

Around 1750 the first building used for worship in the village of Ballinagare was built at the angle formed by the Castlerea and Elphin roads. It was a barn church, thatched, and of considerable size, with its gable to the Elphin road, and was also used as a school. This church served until the erection of a new church in 1819.

In 1804 Friar Anthony Garrahan, former Provincial OFM, came to Ballinagare from Elphin to the funeral of his brother, Fr Gilbert. At the behest of Owen O'Conor Don he remained on as parish priest and proceeded to organise the building of a new church. This was built by the voluntary labour of parishioners, and was roofed with sandstone flags that were to be found in the area. Fr Anthony was later to be interred within its walls. The church was in use until 1966, and still stands across the road from the present church.

Rev Thomas Judge was appointed parish priest of the union of Kilcorkey and Frenchpark in 1880. He was parish priest for seventeen years and moved to Frenchpark during his ministry. Since that time the parish priest has resided in Frenchpark. The foundation stone for the present Church of the Sacred Heart in Ballinagare was laid on 14 June 1965. It was opened and dedicated for divine worship on 5 June 1966 by Bishop Vincent Hanly, and has the unusual feature of all natural light being focused on the altar and coming from behind the congregation.

The townland of Tully holds the remains of Killmogue church and graveyard. It is also the site of St Patrick's Well where it was believed that ailments were cured. Lasair's Church is recorded in the townland of Killaster where a field is known as the 'Church Field' and a well is called Tobar Lastrach.

Early ecclesiastical interest at Frenchpark (Dún Gar) would have focused on the religious foundation at Cloonshanville. It is believed that Cloonshanville was an early Christian foundation established by Comedus, a disciple of St Patrick. A sandstone cross standing over three meters in height, about a quarter of a mile to the

The Dominican Abbey of Cloonshanville

southwest, may belong to that period. A Dominican friary dedicated to the Holy Cross was established at Cloonshanville in 1385, under the patronage of the McDermot Roes, and remained so until it passed into the possession of the Davis family in the seventeenth century.

The remains of the foundation consist of an imposing but much weathered belfry tower, standing on the pointed arches of a square building, and surrounded by the ruins of associated buildings. One of these contains a well-preserved seventeenth century crucifixion plaque, which stands over an inscription to the memory of Patrick French of Galway. He was born in 1538 and was the first of his family to settle in the area.

A Mass House is believed to have existed in the townland of Portahard, northeast of Frenchpark, near the Protestant church. A Catholic church was built of limestone in what was probably the village green of Frenchpark in the townland of Corskeagh in 1825. The French family contributed generously towards the cost. It was probably a very simple church, which was remodelled in 1882 as a cruciform building, and dedicated to St Asicus. A stone belfry was added to the front in 1889. An extensive refurbishment of the church involving a new roof, a new altar, Stations of the Cross, and removal of the gallery was completed in 1979. Until the mid-nineteenth century, Frenchpark church area was united with the present parishes of Loughglynn and Fairymount in the then extensive parish of Tibohine.

Dr Douglas Hyde

The Church of Ireland is situated in the townland of Portahard, and serves as the place of worship for the parish of Tibohine (Taughboyne) and surrounding parishes. The church was erected c. 1740 and was commonly used for worship by Dr Douglas Hyde (1860-1949), where his father, Arthur Hyde, was rector from 1867-1905. A section of the church has been developed as an Interpretative Centre commemorating Dr Hyde as first President of Ireland (1938-45). He was interred in the Hyde family burial plot in the adjoining graveyard after his death in 1949.

Ogham stone at Ballinagare. Tentative reading: '(The stone of) Cuvet'

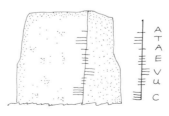

Key to the map

01. Arraghan
02. Balaghcullia
03. Ballincool
04. Ballyconboy
05. Ballynahowna
06. Ballinagare
07. Brackloon
08. Carrowbane
09. Carrowreagh
10. Cashel
11. Cashelnagole
12. Cloggarnagh (part of)
13. Cloonshanville
14. Coramucklagh &
Falmore (part of)

15. Corskeagh
16. Deerpark
17. Derreen
18. Drummin
19. Dungar
_. Falmore &
Cornamucklagh (see 14)
20. Frenchpark Demense
21. Garrynphort
22. Gortnagoyne
23. Kilcorkey
24. Killaster
25. Kilvoy
26. Knockroe
27. Leggatinty

28. Lugakeeran
29. Mountdruid
30. Mullen
31. Peak
32. Portahard
33. Raheely
34. Rathkineely
35. Rathnalog
36. Sheepwalk
37. Sheevannan
38. Tullaghan
39. Tully
40. Turlaghnamaddy

Scale: 0.6"=1 mile

✠ *Ancient Sites* ✠ *Holy Wells*

13. Cloonshanville Dominican Abbey ruins
23. Kilcorkey medieval church and cemetery
24. Killaster old church and Tobar Lastrach
39. Killmogue old church and graveyard, and St Patrick's Well

Parish of Geevagh
(Killadoon, Kilmactranny & Shancough) Counties Sligo and Roscommon
Churches: Geevagh, Highwood & Glenkillamey

T HE UNION OF Geevagh, situated in the east of county Sligo, consists of the three ancient parishes of Killadoon, Kilmactranny and Shancough. It embraces seventy-eight townlands, with one, Kilmacroy, being in county Roscommon and containing part of the village of Ballyfarnon. The parish spans a wide area stretching from the heathery slopes of Arigna to the limestone plateau of Highwood, which overlooks Lough Arrow. Within its confines is the site of the pre-historic battlefield of the Northern Moytura, and the remains of a stronghold of the MacDonaghs, the hereditary chieftains of Tirerrill, at Ballindoon. Memories of churches and shrines of former times are perpetuated in the local placenames, namely, Kilmactranny, Killadoon, and Kilmacroy. There are three churches in the modern union, at Geevagh, Highwood and Glenkillamey.

The old parish of Killadoon takes its name from the church of Cill Dhuibhdúin, the church of Doyne or Devine. This was replaced by a medieval church of the Premonstratensians or White Canons, whose motherhouse was on Trinity Island in Loch Cé. It was subsequently mentioned in a grant of James I to William Crofton, as 'the site, ambit and precinct of the cell, or chapel of Kilvegoone in the Barony of Tirerrill, with one half quarter of land and the tithes'. Some small remains of the church of Killadoon, which fell into disuse in the seventeenth century, are still visible. In the townland of Kilkere stood the church of St Kiar or Cill Ceire; and close by, to the north of the Black Lough at Highwood, a ruined church known locally as Killrogain, (St Grogan).

Ballindoon Dominican Abbey

The Dominican Abbey of St Mary at Ballindoon, on the shores of Lough Arrow and seven miles north of Boyle, was founded in 1507, under the patronage of the Mac Donaghs, Lords of Tirerrill, and became their principal burial place. This sixteenth-century abbey is unusual and unique in Irish architecture because of its central tower-screen, and identical east and west windows. In 1603, after the Reformation, the abbey and its lands were granted to Francis Crofton. In 1633, this grant passed to Andrew Crean of Sligo, and three decades later to the King family of Boyle. After vacating the abbey, the friars retired to a place known locally as Friarstown, where they managed to preserve a community until the mid 1700s. The ruins of the abbey are quite well preserved, even after the lapse of half a millennium, and the adjoining cemetery is the burial place of both Catholics and Protestants of the neighbourhood. Terence MacDonagh (1640-1713), known as the 'Great Counsellor', and spokesman for his fellow Catholic countrymen during the initial onslaught of the penal laws, lies at rest at the base of the tower. To the north of the abbey, close to the lake shore, was St Dominic's well, which was a place of pilgrimage on 4 August, the saint's feastday. There were also monastic settlements at Annaghloy and on Inishmore island in Lough Arrow.

The church at Kilmactranny was known locally as the Teampall Chill Mhic a Treanaigh. It seems to have been a very old church as mention of it is made in the *Annals of Lough Cé* as far back as 1236. In the *Taxation List* of 1306, it is recorded as 'Kilmactrena', but at that stage the 'church was waste'. The present Church of Ireland, built in 1811, stands on the original site. An inscribed marble plaque within recalls the memory of Rev Arthur Hyde, who was rector there 1852-67. He was the father of Douglas Hyde (1860-1949), Gaelic scholar and first President. A plain Latin cross, about 4ft high, can be seen to the north of the church, and had an inscription which is no longer legible. Not far distance at Foyoges are the remains of a church and also a graveyard beside which is a large flagstone, known locally as 'The Bishop's Grave', said to be the final resting place of St Clarus de Melia.

Shancough or Shancoe, the third ancient parish comprising the present union, is mentioned in the *Tripartite Life* as Senchua, 'the old cave'. The present ruin is that of a small medieval church, rectangular in shape, which stands on a small plateau and measures 60ft long by 20ft wide. However, a third of the length is taken up by a dark room connected internally with the church proper by a doorway. The outer doorway of the church is placed in the side-wall, facing the north. The site of the church appears to have been an oval rath. A very unusual feature is that there is no surrounding graveyard. Neither inside or outside are there any traces of burials, although it is stated that unbaptised children were sometimes interred there. Local tradition suggests that a cave, or souterrain, runs beneath the church, hence the origin of the name, 'Senchua'.

Across a deep valley, on the slope of

St Ailbhe's Well

Braulieve, is the lonely mountain shrine to St Ailbhe, whose death is recorded by the Four Masters under the year 545, 'Ailbe of Senchua Ua nOiliolla'. In addition to a holy well, Tober Eilive, there are the remains of the saint's cell, possibly a reconstruction, and a rough slab, seven feet by two, in a recumbent position, which tradition tells us is his final resting place. As recent as the opening decades of the twentieth century, stations were performed here between the 15 August and 8 September, and so great was the veneration in which the saint was held, that sick persons were carried up the mountainside and placed on a mattress on Ailbhe's gravestone overnight, in the expectation of a recovery. Early in the last century, Dr Bernard Coyne, Bishop of Elphin, had a stone cross erected on the site.

Two miles north of Shancough is the cemetery of Carraig a' Teampaill, also known as 'Corrig', which, as the name implies, was the site of an ancient church. Close by is St James's Well, a place of pilgrimage in olden times. The custom has been recently revived. There are many Mass Rocks and caves in this general area which, according to tradition, were used during penal times.

St Joseph's
Church,
Geevagh

The people of Geevagh, before the building of the modern church, attended Mass in a penal chapel in the townland of Cabragh. The present parish church, was built in 1828 on a site provided by the Keoghs, the local landlords, descendants of John Keogh of Mount Jerome, a great champion of the Catholic cause. It was reconstructed and altered in 1896, and dedicated by Archbishop John Healy of Tuam in 1903. Further improvements were made in 1995, and the church was re-dedicated on 22 October of that year.

The church of Our Lady of Lourdes at Glenkillamey, near the summit of Braulieve mountain, has the distinction of being both the smallest and the most elevated church in Elphin. Prior to 1914, the people of Glenkillamey came across the mountain to attend Mass in Geevagh, or went to Arigna in the neighbouring parish of Kilronan. Bad weather and distance frequently prevented the elderly and very young from getting to church, so it was decided to construct a new church. On 10 January 1910 the foundation stone of this church was laid, and it was blessed and opened on 14 January 1914. The present church replaced this chapel in 1955, and was dedicated to Our Lady of Lourdes on 18 June 1956 by Bishop Vincent Hanly.

St Brigid's church, Highwood (Coill Uachtair), replaced an earlier thatched building of the same name which, according to local tradition was built c. 1805 and was extensively renovated and extended in 1891. Sixty years later it was decided to demolish it and build a new church on the same site, incorporating portions of the original structure. The new church, which overlooks the ruins of Ballindoon Abbey and commands enchanting views of Lough Arrow, was dedicated by Bishop Vincent Hanly on 30 September 1957.

Key to the map

01. Andresna
02. Annaghgowan
03. Annaghloy
04. Ardline
05. Aughnacloy
06. Ballindoon
07. Ballinlig
08. Ballinphull
09. Ballyculleen
10. Ballynary
11. Ballynashee
12. Barroe Lower
13. Barroe North
14. Barroe South
15. Barroe Upper
16. Bullaun
17. Cabragh
18. Carrickard
19. Carricknaglass
20. Carricknagrip
21. Carrigeenblike
22. Carrigeenboy
23. Carrowcashel
24. Carrowmore
25. Carrownadargny
26. Carrownyclowan

27. Cartronavally
28. Cloghmine
29. Clooneenhugh
30. Cloystuckera
31. Coolemoneen
32. Coolmeen
33. Coolmurly
34. Cornamucklagh
35. Crannoge Island
36. Crawhill
37. Creevagh
38. Cuilnagleragh
39. Derry Beg
40. Derry More
41. Derrylea
42. Derrynaneane
43. Derrynaslieve
44. Derrysallagh
45. Dromore
46. Drumbeg North
47. Drumbeg South
48. Drumbeg West
49. Drumsoghla
50. Foyoges
51. Garoke
52. Glen

53. Highwood
54. Inishbeg Island
55. Inishmore
56. Kilkere
57. Killadoon
58. Kilmacroy (R)
59. Kingsborough
60. Knockacappul
61. Knockmore
62. Knockroe
63. Lahardan
64. Magheralackagh
65. Mount Town
66. Moytirra East
67. Moytirra West
68. Muck Island
69. Raunatruffaun East
70. Raunatruffaun West
71. Rover
72. Shancough
73. Straduff
74. Tap
75. Treanmore
76. Tully
77. Tullynure
78. Ummeryroe

Scale: 0.45"=1 mile
✠ *Ancient Sites* ✠ *Holy Wells*

6. Dominican Abbey ruins
10. Site of Annaghloy Abbey
18. Kilmactranny church and graveyard
24. St James' Well
41. Killrogain old church
44. St Ailbhe's Well and grave
50. Old church and cemetery
55. Old monastery
56. Old church
57. Killadoon
72. Shancough church ruins

Parish of Kilbegnet

(Kilbegnet, Ballinakill & Donamon) Counties Galway & Roscommon
Churches: Creggs & Glinsk

S TRADDLING THE Galway-Roscommon county boundary, between Ballymoe and Ballygar, with the greater part lying in county Galway, this parish has a long and proud history. It is a union of the two ancient parishes of Kilbegnet and Ballinakill. Ballinakill is now referred to as the half parish of Glinsk, and in recent years the venerable name of Kilbegnet has often been substituted by Creggs, the name of the village closest to the parish church. From 1821 to 1869 Glinsk was attached to Kilcroan (Ballymoe) parish, and was served from there, but since that time it has been united with Kilbegnet.

Kilbegnet (Cill Bheagnait, or the church of St Begnat) took its name from St Begnat, sister of St Cuan of Ahascragh, whose feastday is on the 4 February. Little else is known about her. Ballinakill, translated as 'place of the church', is identified

A medieval
Madonna and Child
from Ballinakill

by an earthen enclosure surrounding Ballinakill Abbey, of which little remains. The thirteenth-century gothic church, with its fourteenth-century extension, was the burial place of the MacDavid Burkes. Ballinakill Abbey has a south window with fine tracery in a flamboyant design. Set in the wall inside is the effigy of a Norman knight believed to be a likeness of William DeBurgo. A holy well at Kilcolumb is located near a ruined church of the same name. O'Donovan, in 1837, speculated that the church was 'probably a small chapel of ease dedicated to St Colmcille'. St Colm is the patron of Glinsk parish (feast day, 9 June). There are also holy wells to be found at Buncrower, Curraghbeg and Milford.

In pre-Norman times the parish belonged to the ancient territory of Clanconway under its local chieftain, O'Finaghty, who ruled from his fort at Donamon. The castle, which was built on a fort in 1154, is one of the oldest Irish castles still inhabited. With the arrival of the MacDavid Burkes in 1307, this parish came under Norman influence, and its story was intertwined with this family until the sale of Glinsk-Creggs estate in 1854. Glinsk Castle, built by the Burkes in the 1640s, continues to stand guard in the glen of Glinsk and is now a National Monument.

The parish is closely linked with the epic march of O'Sullivan Beare in 1602, when a number of his followers were given shelter in this parish, and some of their descendants still reside in the locality.

During the penal times, in the early years of the eighteenth century, Dr Carbery O'Kelly and other bishops of Elphin were given refuge by the Burkes 'under the roof of' Glinsk Castle. During that century the Dominican friars resided at a number of places in the parish. Most notable of these was a friary at Friaryland, known as Talamh na mBráthar. Mention is made of a Mass Rock at Carnaglouch. In 1748 Luke Richard Concannon OP was born in Creggs and baptised in Glinsk. He was later consecrated as first Bishop of New York in 1808. However, he never saw New York, having died of fever at Naples on the 13 June 1810 on the journey to his See.

The *Ballinakill Petition* was a famous plea for help signed by Fr Gillion (Glinsk) and Fr Mulrennan (Kilbegnet) which was presented to the House of Commons in London, on 25 March 1855. It was a call to the international community to witness the large-scale evictions and other happenings on the Glinsk-Creggs estate. The desire for land reform continued to be strong in this parish, and Charles Stewart Parnell (1846-1891) addressed a Land League Meeting in Creggs on 27 September 1891. It was his last public meeting.

The original church of Kilbegnet was located in what is now the old cemetery and is believed to date from Patrician times. In 1306 it is recorded in the *Papal Taxation List* and served as a place of worship until its destruction during the Cromwellian period. In 1731 there was a Mass House shared between Kilbegnet and Donamon, but by 1777 Kilbegnet had a church erected at the crossroads known as Crosswell. The date of the church is inscribed on an old holy water font now preserved in the present church. The present church of Kilbegnet was erected during the ten-year pastorate of Fr Andrew Egan (1839-1849) and is situated on an elevated site which commands a wonderful view over an extensive area. The church, dedicated to the Blessed Virgin Mary, was extensively renovated during the 1960s, and was rededicated by Bishop Hanly on 9 August 1965. Lewis's *Topographical Dictionary* tells us that in 1837 there were 4,677 people living in Kilbegnet, and that there was a public school at Crosswell, attended by 100 children. In the Glinsk district there were five hedge schools, with an attendance of 340 pupils.

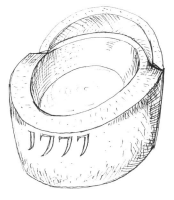

Font in St Mary's Church, Kilbegnet

The church at Glinsk, built in 1843, is dedicated to St Michael the Archangel, and takes its name from the nearby St Michael's holy well, which was a place of pilgrimage, with a pattern associated with the feast of Michaelmas. According to the *Report on the State of Popery* in 1731, a Mass House existed in Ballinakill and was ministered by Carbery O'Kelly, Bishop of Elphin (1718-1731), assisted by a young priest.

Some time later a church was erected in the townland of Glinsk, not far from the ruined castle. Fr Patrick Burke, later Bishop of Elphin (1827-43), served as priest for this church. It was subsequently replaced by the present building in 1843 in the townland of Keeloguesbeg, which has retained the title of 'Glinsk church'. It has remained unaltered apart from a few additions made in the mid-twentieth century.

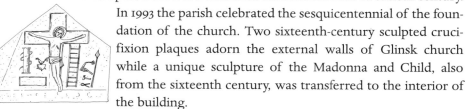

Crucifixion plaque on the gable of St Michael's Church, Glinsk

In 1993 the parish celebrated the sesquicentennial of the foundation of the church. Two sixteenth-century sculpted crucifixion plaques adorn the external walls of Glinsk church while a unique sculpture of the Madonna and Child, also from the sixteenth century, was transferred to the interior of the building.

In 1939 the Divine Word Missionaries purchased Donamon Castle and subsequently established a seminary there. A new extension, including a church, was built in 1963 by the Divine Word Missionaries, but the seminary was subsequently moved to St Patrick's College Maynooth. Part of the building was then leased to the Diocese of Elphin as a Pastoral Centre, which was opened in September 1982, providing many church-related, pastoral and spiritual enrichment courses for parishes and various groups. The Pastoral Centre closed in September 1995 following a diocesan decision to have more localised centres strategically placed throughout the diocese. The parish is now administered by the Divine Word Missionary Society, and Fr Hugh McClure SVD became its parish priest in August 2000.

The Church of Ireland community worshipped in Donamon church, which was built in 1854 by George Caulfield (1808-1896), and replaced an earlier church. In June 1978, the last regular Sunday Service was held there. A Presbyterian church was built in the village of Creggs in 1861, opened for worship in 1863, and continued in use until the mid 1920s.

Donamon Castle

Key to the map

Townlands marked with (RN) are in county Roscommon. The remainder are in county Galway.

01. Aghalateeve	06. Ballynakill	11. Camderry
02. Ardagh	07. Ballynahowna	12. Carrowkeel (RN)
03. Ballincurry	08. Boggauns	13. Carrownaglogh (RN)
04. Ballinlig	09. Boleythomas	14. Cartron (RN)
05. Ballyfinegan	10. Bracklin (RN)	15. Clooncah

16. Clooncullaun
17. Clooncunny
18. Cloonfaghna
19. Coolroghaun (RN)
20. Corgarve
21. Corlackan
22. Cornaveagh (RN)
23. Corrspark
24. Cregauns
25. Creggs
26. Cuilnacappy
27. Curraghbog
28. Curraghmulmurry
29. Curraghrevagh
30. Dereen
31. Derryhippoo (RN)
32. Donamon (RN)
33. Faartan
34. Fairfield
35. Funshin
36. Garraun More
37. Garraun North (RN)
38. Garraun South (RN)
39. Glinsk

40. Gorteenfadda
41. Gortmorris
42. Gortnadeeve East
43. Gortnadeeve West
44. Gortnalavey
45. Keeloges East
46. Keeloges West
47. Keelogesbeg
48. Kilbegnet (RN)
49. Kilcolumb
50. Kilmacrickard
51. Knockmascahill
52. Lahaghglass North
53. Lahaghglass South
54. Leaha
55. Leananmarla
56. Lenarevagh
57. Lisduff
58. Lisnageeragh
59. Milford
60. Milpark
61. Moat
62. Moneen
63. Moneenroe

64. Newtown
65. Oughtagh
66. Oughtagh (RN)
67. Park
68. Rabbit Park
69. Rosdaul
70. Rosmoylan (RN)
71. Shanballyeden (RN)
72. Skehaghard
73. Sonnagh
74. Tallavnamraher
75. Tobbermore East
76. Tobberroe West
77. Tonamaddy (RN)
78. Trean Park
79. Ussey

Scale: 0.5"=1 mile
✠ *Ancient Sites* ✠ *Holy Wells*
6. Medieval church and cemetery
48. Medieval church and cemetery
62. St Michael's Well
74. Dominican friary site

Co. Galway

Co. Roscommon

Co. Galway

Parish of Kilbride

(Kilbride & Derrane) County Roscommon
Churches; Four-Mile-House & Derrane

THE PARISH OF Kilbride is situated in the centre of county Roscommon, just north of Roscommon town. It comprises of 19,287 acres. It was very badly affected during the Famine, with almost fifty percent of the population dying. The earliest map showing the parish dates from the seventeenth century. The names Kilbride and Derrane are clearly inscribed on it. The modern parish also comprises these two areas. From the penal times until 1860 the parish constituted the united parishes of Kilbride, Kilgefin and Cloontuskert, these other parishes lying to the east. In 1860 Cloontuskert was established as a separate parish, and in 1875 Kilgefin was detached from Kilbride and united with Cloontuskert, while Kilbride itself was united with Oran. This arrangement continued until 1888, when Kilbride became a separate parish once more.

The parish has a number of early Christian sites. There were four churches in the parish during the Middle Ages, dating from perhaps the twelfth century or earlier. In the townland of Ballinderry is the ancient church of Cill Bhríde, which gave the parish its name. Fr Canice Mooney, in *Dictionnaire d'Histoire et de Géographie Ecclésiastiques,* mentions that there was a *paruchia* of churches loyal to Colmcille in the northern part of Elphin diocese, and that 'on the other hand it is beyond doubt that several churches in the southern half belonged the *paruchia* of St Brigid, and owed their allegiance to her house in Kildare'. Kilbride is one of the churches he lists, and this would indicate an early date for Cill Bhríde. He also mentions a holy well dedicated to her in Kilbride, which is no longer a place of pilgrimage.

St Brigid

In Derrane stands the abbey or priory of St Mary's Derrane. It was an Augustinian foundation, part of the Aroasian reform introduced by St Malachy, and supported by Turlough O'Conor, the High King. It was founded about 1150, and in the Aroasian tradition consisted of a double abbey, one for the canons and another for the canonesses, who had pastoral duties in the care of the sick and the poor. O'Conor was also the founder of the Augustinian abbey in Roscommon town. Fr Mooney, in his *Dictionnaire,* states that the eleventh, twelfth and thirteenth centuries saw the transfer of some ancient monastic foundations to the Canons Regular of St Augustine. He mentions Derrane as one of these foundations, and this would seem to indicate that it was the centre of worship from a much earlier date.

In the townland of Grange there are the remains of Grange Abbey. Little is left of it now, and the grounds surrounding it were used at one time as a place of burial, as was often the case with other sites. The seventeenth century *Books of Survey and Distribution* records that this was formerly a Cistercian house and land.

Ruins of
Grange Abbey

Finally there is Kinnity Abbey, as it is known locally, with a well nearby. Little is known of this abbey, but it is mentioned in the Patent Letters of James I where reference is made to a grant from the King to George Sexton of Dublin of the 'Tithes, great and small, of Monaster-Eneyan, otherwise Kennety, 2 quarters'.

The building of the present church of St Brigid at Four-Mile-House commenced in 1834 on a site provided by Robert Geoff, and was still under construction in 1837. It replaced an earlier church, which was also in the same townland of Ballinderry. The *Roscommon Journal,* noting the occasion, writes: 'For some time past the wretched parishioners of Kilbride have been obliged to hear the word of God in the open air for the want of a chapel. In the

Four-Mile-
House Church

midst of winter would be seen a congregation of hundreds of poor persons surrounding a miserable hovel, near the Four-Mile-House, exposed to the pitiless pelting of a winter's day, and up to their knees in sludge and filth, attending Mass which was celebrated in a hut scarcely big enough to contain the clergyman and the owner's family.' Four-Mile-House church was extended in 1959 by fifteen feet, providing extra seating accommodation and including the erection of a gallery and bell tower.

Local tradition tells us there was a small chapel or Mass House in Derrane prior to the building of the present church in 1857. Plans were put in place to build a church in 1845, when at a meeting of the parishioners of Derrane, convened on 28 September of that year, a resolution was passed to the effect that a new church be built on a site donated by Basil and William Sandys, who also donated £10 to the building fund. However, the failure of the potato crop had begun, and the years of famine were at hand. The building of the church had to be postponed, but was finally commenced in 1857. Bishop George Browne, assisted by his co-adjutor bishop, Laurence Gillooly, laid the foundation stone for the new church in April 1858. Some of the stones used in the construction of the building were from the ruins of the adjacent Abbey of St Mary's. The church was opened for divine worship in 1860, and dedicated in honour of the Blessed Virgin Mary. A century later, it was extensively renovated and re-dedicated on 6 May 1959 to Our Lady of Lourdes by Bishop Vincent Hanly.

A hypothetical reconstruction of the east gable of Ballinderry church

Key to the map

01. Ballinderry	19. Cloonerk	35. Grange
02. Cappagh	20. Cloonerra	36. Kinitty
03. Carroward	21. Coggalbeg	37. Leitrim
04. Carrowbaun	22. Coolteige	38. Lisgobban
05. Carrowboy	23. Corbo	39. Lisheenanierin
06. Carowcrin	24. Cornashinnagh	40. Lisheenloughtin
07. Carrowkeel	25. Corradrehid	_. Midgefield (see 34)
08. Carrownalassan	26. Cory (part of)	41. Mountpleasant
09. Carrowntornan	27. Curry (ED	42. Mullymucks
10. Cartron	Cloonfinlough)	43. Rathconor
11. Cashelmeehan	28. Derrane	44. Rathmore
12. Casheltauna	29. Derrycanan	45. Roxborough
13. Clare	30. Derryconny	46. Smaghraan
14. Cloonarragh	31. Dooherty	47. Tonlegee
15. Cloonbony	32. Drumdaff	48. Tully
16. Cloonconny	33. Fearmore	
17. Clooneigh	34. Glennameeltoge or	
18. Cloonelly	Midgefield	

35

16
18
41
13
27
9
39
20
34
10
3
5
7
48
21
12
37
25
31
24
8
40
15
36
Four Mile House
29
44
1
11
43
46
26
47
22
32
28
14
19
23
Derrane
42
33
38
30
4
6
45
17

Scale: 0.48"=1 mile

⊕ *Ancient Sites* ✠ *Holy Wells*

1. Ballinderry medieval church and cemetery
28. Derrane Augustinian priory ruins
35. Grange Abbey ruins
36. Kinitty Abbey ruins

Parish of Kilgefin
(Kilgefin, Cloontuskert & Lissonuffy) County Roscommon
Churches: Ballagh, Curraghroe & Ballyleague

THE PARISH OF Kilgefin lies nestled between the slopes of the Sliabh Bán hills and the northern arm of Lough Ree, in eastern county Roscommon. There are three churches in the modern union, at Ballagh, Ballyleague and Curraghroe. Within the parish boundaries lie three ancient parishes, and a small portion of a fourth: Kilgefin in the west, Cloontuskert along Lough Ree, Lissonuffy in the north, and two mountain townlands from the old parish of Cloonfinlough.

Prior to 1860 the parishes of Kilgefin and Cloontuskert were united with Kilbride. In 1860, Cloontuskert was established as a separate parish, and in 1875 Kilgefin was detached from Kilbride and united with Cloontuskert. The united parish of Lissonuffy and Cloonfinlough was a parish in its own right until the mid-nineteenth century. It straddled the Sliabh Bán hills, with a chapel at Curraghroe serving the east end, and the western portion coming under Carniska. In 1845 there was a population of 4,000 in Lissonuffy, which suffered severely in the Great Famine. Fr John Boyd was PP at this time and was succeeded by Fr Andrew Quinn, who was to be the last parish priest of Lissonuffy. In November 1849 Fr Quinn was transferred to Oran, and Lissonuffy was divided between the new parish of Strokestown and Kilgefin, with the new more natural boundary running along the summit of Sliabh Bán. However, in 1880 the Curraghroe area was attached to Tarmonbarry parish until it transferred to Kilgefin in 1937.

St Patrick came to the parish in the fifth century, and after founding churches in Kilmore and Kiltrustan, founded a third church in the townland of Kilmacoo in the parish of Kilgefin. In the year 520 St Brendan and his brother St Faithleach travelled north by way of the Shannon, and came to shore about a mile west of the village of Ballyleague. About fifty yards from the landing place there is a well, still known as St Faithleach's Well, which according to tradition has curative powers.

Grave slab from Cloontuskert

Cloontuskert Abbey (Cluain Tuaiscirt na Sionna), founded by St Faithleach, was dedicated to St Anne and inhabited by the Canons Regular of St Augustine. There are a number of late ninth and early tenth century inscribed grave slabs, set into the wall of the ruined abbey. Ambrose Mc Dermott OP, Bishop of Elphin 1707-1717, is laid to rest in this ancient cemetery. Restoration work has taken place on the abbey in recent years.

Cloontuskert
Augustinian
Abbey

As part of their preparations for the Marian Year in 1987, the residents of Cloontuskert erected a grotto of Our Lady at the edge of the village.

In former times and up to about 1870 public devotions known as 'Stations' were performed around St James's Well in the townland of Kilmacuagh. Some distance from the well there is a site called 'Caltra', which means a church or an old grave-yard, on the site of a former church. Here stood St Mochua's Church founded in 600, from which the townland derived its name, Kilmacuagh.

The ancient parish church of Kilgefin became disused about 1620. According to Canon Thomas Hurley (d. 1955), there was no trace of any church building in use in Kilgefin between 1620 and 1710. However, in Aughaverna, Pollinaffrinn, and Ballinwolly, Masses were celebrated in the open air. About 1710 a small Mass House was constructed at Ballaghadarna, and in 1760 it was replaced by a more substantial church, situated on Noone's Hill. It served its purpose down to 1803. At this time Rev Patrick Hanly PP (1801-1826), a native of Kilmacuagh, erected in the townland of Ballagh a slated church consisting of a nave, two transepts and a sacristy. It was dedicated to St Mary. In 1875 the nave of this church was taken down by the Rev Eugene White (Administrator 1875-78) and replaced by a new nave, while the old transepts were retained. In 1898 the presbytery, to which nine acres of land were attached, was erected under the guidance of the Rev B. J. Donnellan PP. In 1928, the bell and belfry were erected in the church grounds.

However, in 1956 this church was demolished and replaced by a modern church with the same titular. The new church is a pre-concilliar building, similar in design to St Anne's in Sligo and St Croan's in Ballymoe. It has beautiful checker-board ceiling, wooden panelling and three carved wooden altars. Modern construction techniques allowed the ceiling to be unsupported by pillars,

St Mary's Church, Ballagh, parish of Kilgefin

thus adding to the feeling of space and brightness. From the outside, the distinctive bell tower incorporates the main entrance door, and access to the large gallery.

The building of a church at Curraghroe commenced in 1815, but was not completed until 1831, and served the needs of the people for a hundred and fifty years. In 1961 the church underwent a major re-construction, and the old building was almost completely replaced with a new one, except for the four walls of the original church. It was solemnly blessed and re-dedicated under the patronage of St Cecilia in March 1967, the only church in the diocese with the titular of the patroness of sacred music.

The village of Ballyleague lies near the Shannon, and across the bridge is its sister-village of Lanesboro in county Longford. The earliest place of worship in Ballyleague was a penal chapel, but there is no evidence of when it was erected. In 1844 work began on building a new church, but because of the Great Famine it was not completed until 1869. There was an urgent appeal for funds launched in 1860 to finance the completion of the church, and the replacement of the roof which was blown off by a storm during the intervening years. The church served the people for the better part of a century, and in 1966 it was decided to build a completely new place of worship on the same site. This church was dedicated on 11 May 1969, to Our Lady of the Holy Rosary, and is in the post-conciliar style.

A new diocesan secondary school for boys was opened in September 1957, and provided second level education until 1968, when it was amalgamated with Lanesboro Vocational School. A parochial hall adjoining the church now occupies the premises. Modern Ballyleague is a picturesque tourist village on the banks of the river Shannon.

In the Church of Ireland, the area was part of the union of Cloonfinlough, and was served by nearby Kilgefin church, which was erected in 1824 by the Board of First Fruits, and is now demolished.

Key to the map

01. Aghamuck	12. Bogwood or	20. Cartron or Old Glebe
02. Aghawerriny	Carrowntogher	21. Cloonaddra
03. Anrittabeg	13. Bunnageddy (part of)	22. Cloonagerragh
04. Ballagh	14. Caltragh	23. Clooncashel Beg
05. Ballincurry	15. Cappagh	24. Clooncashel More
06. Ballinwolly	16. Carroward	25. Cloonmustra
07. Ballyclare	17. Carrowmoneen	26. Cloonshee (Connor)
08. Ballyclare Island	_. Carrowntogher (see 12)	27. Cloonshee (Hartland)
09. Ballyclare Island North	18. Carrowreagh or	28. Cloontuskert
10. Ballyglass	Keelcurragh	29. Cooltacker
11. Ballyleague	19. Cartron (ED Drumdaff)	30. Coolshagtena

31. Corry (part of)
32. Culleenanory
33. Culliaghy
34. Curraghroe
35. Doonahaha
36. Doughil
37. Drinagh (part of)
38. Erenagh
39. Erra
40. Fairymount
41. Ferrinch Is.
42. Gallagh
43. Garden Town
44. Gortgallan
45. Gortyleane

46. Granaghan (Dillon)
47. Granaghan (Martin)
_. Keelcurragh (see 18)
48. Killattimoriarty
49. Killavackan
50. Kilmacananneny
51. Kilmacuagh
52. Kilnacloghy
53. Kilnalosset
54. Kilnasillagh
55. Kilroosky
56. Knockavurrea
57. Lisnanarriagh
58. Moher
59. Moneen

60. Mongagh (part of)
61. Mountdillion
_. Old Glebe (see 20)
62. New Glebe
63. Portnahinch
64. Shanballymore
65. Sheehaun (Hughes)
66. Sheehaun (Martin)
67. Trila (Dillon)
68. Trila (Martin)
69. Trilacroghan
70. Tuam
71. Tullyvarran

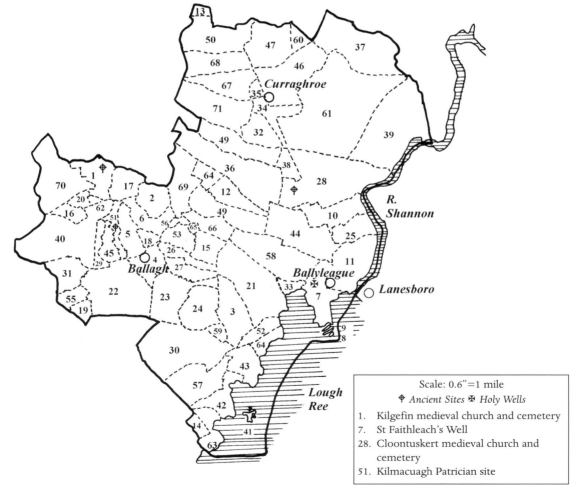

Scale: 0.6"=1 mile

☩ *Ancient Sites* ✠ *Holy Wells*

1. Kilgefin medieval church and cemetery
7. St Faithleach's Well
28. Cloontuskert medieval church and cemetery
51. Kilmacuagh Patrician site

Parish of Kilglass

(Kilglass) County Roscommon
Churches: Kilglass, Rooskey & Slatta

THE PARISH OF Kilglass is situated in the north of county Roscommon, skirted by the River Shannon on the east, and to the north is bounded by the beautiful expanse of lakes nestling at the foot of the Legan, Knockhall and Mullaghmacormack hills. Its waterways are a haven for anglers and attract an abundance of visitors during the tourist season. This parish, with its undulating hills and valleys, is primarily a rural area steeped in the traditions of Celtic Ireland. The ancient name for the region was Tír hAinlighe or Cinél Dubhthaigh, but its best-known name was Déantacht na dTuath, the 'Deanery of the Tuaths'. According to O'Donovan, this locality was an Irish-speaking district in 1837.

The parish has three church areas served by Kilglass, Rooskey and Slatta. The Rooskey area was once part of the parish of Tarmonbarry, but in 1879 became part of Kilglass parish, during the re-organisation of parish boundaries. At the same time, on the western edge of the parish, several townlands (Moyglass, Rathinagh and Clooneen) were transferred to the parish of Strokestown, and on the southern edge Ballyfeeney and Kilgraffy townlands, part of the ancient parish of Bumlin, were added to Kilglass.

While the lakes, with their Crannóga, point to pre-Christian times, a cursory glance at the terrain of the parish will unearth evidence of Christianity which can be traced back to Patrician times. The national apostle St Patrick is commemorated at Tobar Phádraig, while Tobar Bearaigh honours St Barry who has long associations with this parish as well as being patron of the adjoining parish of Tarmonbarry. Cill Ghlas is anglicised in modern times as Kilglass, meaning green or grey church. So the origins of Christianity are enshrined even in the placename. Indeed many of the townland names begin with Kil, indicating the ancient presence of a church. Local examples include Kilbeg, Kilgarve, Killegan, Ballykilcline. Kilverdon in the neighbouring parish of Strokestown, was formerly part of Kilglass parish.

The earliest church stood in Kilglass graveyard, which is a part of Aughamore, a sub-denomination of Ballykilcline. According to Archdeacon Michael Connellan (1883-1967), 'the original patron saint must

Church of the
Sacred Heart,
Kilglass

270

have been Glas, for Glas was a frequent name in centuries past'. In the *Papal Taxation List* of 1306, Kilglass is described as deserted, but reference is also made to a church in Kilverdon and in Kilbarry for the Rooskey and Tarmonbarry areas. In a papal letter of 16 November 1405, Kilglass church was referred to as St Mary's Church.

Scene at a Mass Rock during penal times

The Cromwellian Wars, and subsequent penal laws (1695), destroyed the places of worship and like other parishes, the people had to take to the hills and secluded places to celebrate the Eucharist. One of the best preserved Mass Rocks is to be found in Kilglass parish, situated on the eastern side of the 600 foot-high Legan Hill, and unlike other Mass Rocks is recorded on the OS Maps. This would imply that this particular Mass Rock must have been used as a place of worship for a considerable length of time. On 26 August 1979 Bishop Dominic Conway led the people on pilgrimage back to this penal site and celebrated Mass after a lapse of over two centuries.

According to the *Report on the State of Popery* in 1731 one Mass House existed in Kilglass. The first church built in post-penal times was erected between 1760 and 1770 on the top of the hill of Mullaghmacormack, on the border of the townland of Kilgarve. This church was in use in 1824 and simultaneously used as a schoolhouse. The priest at that time resided in Ballykilcline and a room of his residence served as a schoolhouse. In the 1790s a church was built on the site of the present Kilglass church. This church was extended in the early nineteenth century. In 1837 there was a church in both Kilglass and Mullaghmacormack. However, in the re-organisation of the parish boundaries in 1879, Bishop Gillooly closed Mullaghmacormack church amidst much opposition. The present church of Kilglass was erected by William Nally of Edgeworthstown, Longford, in the 1890s, replacing a century-old church on the same site. It was dedicated to the Sacred Heart on 29 June 1896, by Bishop John Clancy, assisted by Bishop John Lyster of Achonry and Bishop Joseph Hoare of Ardagh and Clonmacnoise. It was extensively renovated in 1958, and rededicated by Bishop Dominic Conway on 30 August 1992, after further renovations.

Church of Our Lady of Mount Carmel, Rooskey

In the Rooskey end of the parish a Mass House was shared between Rooskey and Tarmonbarry. However, by 1824 Rooskey had its own church, which was also used as a school. In 1844 a new church was erected by Rev James McNally PP, Tarmonbarry, as the inscription on the tower indicates: 'Mount Carmel Church erected by the Rev James McNally PP Tarmonbarry AD 1844.' The site for Rooskey church was donated by the local landlord, J. A. Tredennick, who also gave a liberal donation of £40 towards its construction. The church underwent major renovations in 1899 and again in the 1950s, when it was considerably enlarged, and changed from being cruciform in shape to rectangular. It was dedicated by Bishop Vincent Hanly on 23 November 1954. in honour of Our Lady of Mount Carmel. The sanctuary was remodelled in the 1970s to comply with the liturgical revisions of the Second Vatican Council.

In the Slatta church area Mass was celebrated for some time in a private dwelling in Dooslatta. The date of the present church of St Anne at Slatta is unknown but local tradition tells us that the building was originally used as a corn store in Famine times prior to its conversion into a church. It is situated in the townland of Moher and was probably used as a place of worship following the closure of Mullaghmacormack church. St Anne's was renovated in 1958 and re-dedicated on 23 March 1958 by Bishop Vincent Hanly.

Kilverdon (Cill Bhearnáin) was once part of Kilglass parish, and the medieval church situated in Clooneen (Cluainín Bhearnáin) townland served the western end of the parish. This area, as mentioned above, has been part of Strokestown parish since 1879. However, many people from Kilglass are interred in Kilverdon cemetery, which is reputed to be one of the oldest in the region.

Ballykilcline was one of the most densely populated areas in the parish because it was not subject to the local landlords, but came under the direct control of the British Crown. However, in the mid-nineteenth century there was mass emigration from this townland because of huge rental arrears. The remnants of the famine village have been the subject of much research in recent times, and a book entitled *The End of the Hidden Ireland*, by Robert J. Scally (Oxford, 1995) has been published detailing the plight of the people during those years. The parish also suffered a record population decrease of 58.2% during An Gorta Mór (1845-49). This undoubtedly was one of the worst affected areas in the entire country. Today, Kilglass has happily recovered from the scars of that horrendous period of history and continues to flourish as a closely-knit parish community.

The Anglican community of Kilglass worshipped in the church which was originally in Kilglass cemetery, but a new building was erected in 1825 in the townland of Ruane, which is now in ruins. In Rooskey village an Anglican church was erected in 1813, but ceased to be a place of worship at the end of the nineteenth century and is now demolished.

Key to the map

01. Aghamannan	20. Derryonogh	38. Killastalliff
02. Ballyfeeny	21. Dockery's Island	39. Killegan
03. Ballykilcline	22. Dooan	40. Knockhall
04. Ballymartin	23. Doonslattagh	41. Lavagh
05. Ballymoylin	24. Drumagissaun	42. Lecarrow
06. Barravally	25. Drumman Beg	43. Legan
07. Carrigeen	26. Drumman More	44. Meelick
08. Carrownskeheen	27. Gillstown	45. Moher
09. Caul	28. Glebe (E.D. Rooskey)	46. Moneenbog
10. Cloonaufill	29. Glebe (E.D. Kilglass	47. Muckanagh
11. Clooneen (Blakeny)	North)	48. Mullaghmacormack
12. Cloonfad	30. Glen	49. Pigeon Island
13. Coarse Island	31. Illanamoe Island	50. Rabbitt Island
14. Corgowan	32. Illangarve Island	51. Rooaun
15. Crunkill	33. Inishmoylin Island	52. Roosky
16. Culleenaghamore	34. Kerlagh	53. Roosky New
17. Derryfecle	35. Kilbeg	54. Slattagh Beg
18. Derrymacstur	36. Kilgarve	55. Slattagh More
19. Derrymoylin	37. Kilgaffy	56. Tully

Scale: 0.6"=1 mile
✠ Ancient Sites ✠ Holy Wells
29. Kilglass medieval church
43. Legan Mass Rock

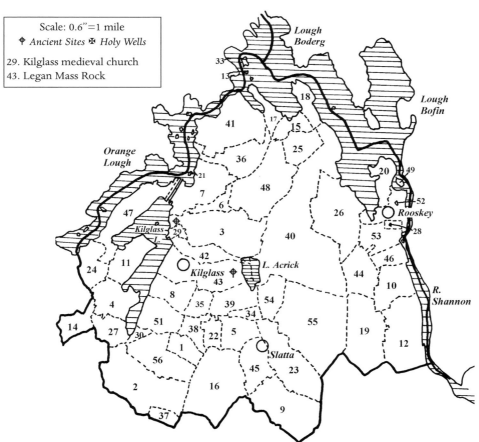

Parish of Kiltoom & Cam
(Kiltoom & Cam) County Roscommon
Churches: Kiltoom & Curraghboy

THE PARISH OF Kiltoom & Cam is located in south county Roscommon. Lough Ree forms the eastern boundary and the parish extends westwards for about ten miles. It is bounded on the north by Knockcroghery parish, on the west by Ballyforan, and on the south by St Peter's Athlone. The Clonfert parish of Taughmaconnell lies to the southwest. The land rises from the lakeshore to its highest point, 491ft, on a range of Eskers running northeast to southwest through the parish. The parish has three turloughs, the largest of which is Lough Funshinnagh (600 acres). A small tributary of the Shannon, called the Cross River, rises and flows through the western part of the parish.

The present parish is a union of the medieval parishes of Kiltoom and Cam, as represented today by the civil parishes of the same names. A succession of parish priests for the union exists from 1771. The parish has a number of early Christian sites. Little remains of Kiltoom old church, except part of the southern wall. The window in this wall suggests a twelfth-century date. The circular site suggests an early Christian settlement, and it was used as a cemetery until recently. Early references, while scanty, indicate a link with Clonmacnoise, which is quite close over the water. By the fifteenth century Kiltoom had come under the control of the Cluniac monks of Athlone. A report by the Church of Ireland bishop in 1622 sug-

The chancel window in the ruins of Cam old church

gests that the church was still standing, but it may have fallen into disrepair soon after that. St Patrick's Well is located near the old cemetery in Kiltoom townland, but there is no tradition of any organised pilgrimage there. The name Kiltoom derives from Cill Tuama, the church of the tomb, or the church of St Tumna.

Cam ruined church and cemetery, in Cam townland, probably dates from the twelfth or early thirteenth century. The window in the gable is very similar to the one in Melaghlin's church in Clonmacnoise from that period. The church is built in what was obviously a circular enclosure, indicating an earlier date for its foundation. The name Cam derives from the Irish

Cam Maigh Bríde, the crooked plain of St Brigid. The church was dedicated to St Brigid, and may have been a convent at first. The *Book of Hy-Many* says that Cam was one of the principal churches of the *tuath,* and had the right to a baptismal penny for all baptised in Hy-Many, which it shared with Drum and Clonown, also dedicated to St Brigid. Cam also came under the control of the Cluniac monks in Athlone. The lands of Cam were leased in 1583 to the new Protestant landowners, and while the church may have been in use by 1622, like Kiltoom, it was not in Catholic hands. The cemetery had its first recorded burial in 1622, and was used for Catholic and Protestant burials

St Brigid's Well (Tobar Bríde) in Brideswell townland, is the oldest Christian site in the parish. St Brigid, the patroness of Cam parish, has been continuously honoured at this site on the last Sunday in July since the earliest days of Christianity in the area. A bathing enclosure was erected beside the well in 1625 by Randal Mac Donell, 1st Earl of Antrim, and remains unchanged to the present. The church granted a plenary indulgence in 1661 to pilgrims going there, and a similar indulgence was granted to Croagh Patrick at the same time. The 1731 *Report on the State of Popery in Ireland* records that large crowds assembled there at certain times. While the pattern was suppressed by the local clergy in the nineteenth century, the traditional stations were continued by the people. In 1957, the Rev B. Fitzmorris CC (1912-1974) revived the pattern, celebrating Mass at the well and holding the evening stations, which continue to the present.

After the Reformation the Catholic community were left without churches in which to offer Mass. Near Cam old church is an area called Log na bPéist, where Mass was said in those dark days. In Kiltoom the Mass Rock can be seen from the old cemetery. By

St Brigid's Church, Curraghboy

1731 a Mass House had been built at Feamore and a second at Curraghboy. There is also some evidence to suggest that a Mass House was located at Lissygreaghan. After Catholic Emancipation, the then parish priest, Rev Terence G. O'Neill, built the present church in Curraghboy, dedicated to St Brigid in 1830, and in the following years he built the church at Ballybay. He also set about the building of national schools in the parish in 1832. The churches built in the 1830s serve the people today, having undergone many renovations over the years. The Church of St Brigid, Curraghboy, was solemnly blessed and re-opened by Bishop Vincent Hanly on 9 March 1969, following renovations to accommodate the new liturgy. The parish church at Ballybay, Kiltoom, was renovated and dedicated as the Church of the Risen Christ by Bishop Dominic Conway on 28 July 1974. This was the first time in its 140-year history that it had a special patron. One of the chalices in use in this church bears the date 1683, and the inscription '... for the use of the chapel of St Brigid, Athlone.'

Bishop John Reddington on his ordination as bishop in St Peter and Paul's Church, Athlone, 1954

Most Rev John Reddington was born in Rackans in the parish in 1910. He joined the Society of African Missions (SMA) and was ordained in 1934. He was consecrated Bishop of Joss, Nigeria, in 1954 at the church of Ss Peter and Paul, Athlone, and retired as bishop in 1974. He died in Dublin in 1994.

From the time of the Reformation there has been a small Protestant community in Kiltoom parish, never more than about two percent of the total population. At first they used the old churches of Kiltoom and Cam, but for how long is not certain. A single church in a central location was proposed in 1704, but it was not until 1785 that a Church of Ireland was built in Moyvannan townland as an extension to a castle there. It continued in use until a new church was built in Cornaseer townland in 1836. As the numbers declined, this church was closed in the 1940s.

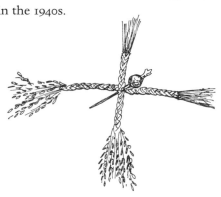

A St Brigid's Cross made from oats and a potato by Thomas Dolan, Cornalee, Curraghboy, around 1960. Now in the National Museum

Key to the map

01. Ardmullan	15. Carrick (ED Rockhill)	29. Cornalee
02. Atteagh	16. Carrick (ED Kiltoom)	30. Cornaseer
03. Ballycreggan	17. Carrickbeg	31. Corraclogh
04. Ballylion	18. Carrowkeeny	32. Corralea
05. Ballymullavill	19. Carrrowmurragh	33. Corramore
06. Barry Beg	20. Carrowncloghan	34. Corrantotan
07. Barry More	21. Carrownderry	35. Crib Island
08. Bogganfin (part of)	22. Carrownolan	36. Curraghboy
09. Bog Island	23. Carrownure	37. Curry
10. Bredagh	24. Cartron	38. Derryglad
11. Brideswell	25. Cloghans Glebe	39. Derrynasee
12. Caltraghbeg	26. Coolagarry	40. Eskerbaun
13. Cam	27. Coolnageer	41. Feamore
14. Cappalisheen	28. Cornageeha	42. Flegans

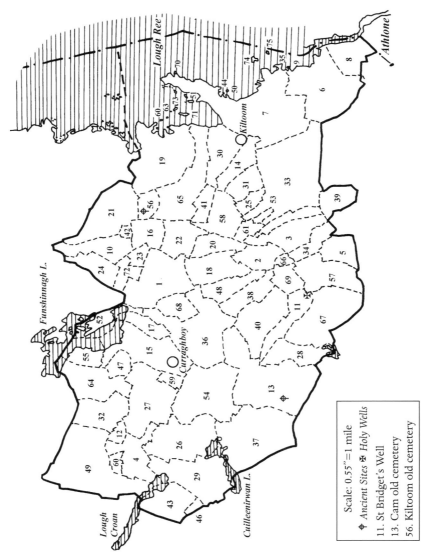

Scale: 0.55"=1 mile
⊕ Ancient Sites ✠ Holy Wells
11. St Bridget's Well
13. Cam old cemetery
56. Kiltoom old cemetery

Parish of Knockcroghery

(Kilmeane, Killinvoy, St John's, & Rahara) County Roscommon
Churches: Knockcroghery, St John's & Rahara

T HE PARISH OF Knockcroghery lies in southern county Roscommon, along the western shores of Lough Ree. It is bounded on the north by Roscommon and Kilteevan, and on the south by Kiltoom and Cam, extending westwards for more than eight miles to Athleague and Tisrara. Knockcroghery is a modern union of several medieval parishes, namely St John's, Rahara, Kilmeane and Killinvoy, and the tiny ancient parish of Portrun. This union dates from the 1840s.

Knockcroghery is a parish with a rich Christian heritage stretching back to the early centuries of the first millennium, as evidenced by the seventh- or eighth-century crucifixion plaque and sheet iron bell found in St John's circa 1861, and now in the National Museum. There are a number of holy wells, such as St Catherine's at Toberreeoge, Tober Liagan in Carrowkeel townland, dedicated to St Brigid, and St John's Well. The latter gave its name to the parish, and a pattern is held there on 24 June each year, St John's Day. However, some sources suggest the original dedication may not have been to St John the Baptist, but to a native Irish saint.

Each of the medieval parishes had its own church, traces of which can still be

Early Christian grave slab from St John's

seen today. According to the *Book of Hy-Many*, Kilmeane was one of the seven principal comharbs of that *tuath*. Ruins of the medieval parish church are all that remain in the cemetery of that name. In the small cemetery at Portrunny evidence of a church structure has been found. This church was dedicated to St Dermot, who was associated with the nearby island of Inis Cleraun (later known as Quaker Island), in Lough Ree. Teampall Dhiarmaida on the island dates from the early sixth century. Ruins of the medieval parish church of Killinvoy are still in existence in the old cemetery at Killinvoy. In the cemetery at Rahara are the ruins of a medieval church and many tombstones dating from the early eighteenth century. The name of the townland of Scrine (Scrín) suggests a church site containing a reliquary or shrine of a saint. There was a sizeable Quaker community (Society of Friends), particularly in the Ballymurray area, as evidenced from the 1749 *Synge's Elphin Diocesan Census*. Ruins of a Quaker Meeting-House and cemetery can still be seen there.

St John's parish has a great wealth of ecclesiastical buildings dating from the medieval period. On a peninsula jutting into Lough Ree, in the townland of Warren, is the abandoned medieval town of Rindoon (Rinn Dúin). Construction of this town began in 1227, and soon two churches were built there. The first of these was the Priory of St John the Baptist for the Fratres Cruciferi, founded in the reign of King John of England. There are references to this priory and its clerics throughout the fourteenth and fifteenth centuries, even though Rindoon was deserted by the mid-to-late thirteenth century. The priory and its lands were confiscated in the religious upheavals of the Elizabethan period and leased to new Planters in 1569. The second church built in Rindoon was founded for the Premonstratensian Canons, and was dedicated to the Holy Trinity. The founder of this church was Clarus Mac Mailin, archdeacon of Elphin, who died in 1251. It seems that this foundation did not survive the death of the town itself. A lack of sources makes it difficult to be certain which church was located inside the town. The ruins of a church near the castle of Rindoon are probably those of the Premonstratensian church, while the priory, the ruins of which still exist, was located half a mile away outside the town walls. In the townland of Ballybrogan are the ruins of the medieval church of Kilcommon with its circular enclosure, which was used until recent times as a local cemetery. This church is also recorded in the *Papal Taxation List* of 1306

An eighteenth-century font from Killinvoy

There are a number of sites in the parish which bear testimony to the faith of the people during the centuries of persecution. One of these is the village of Ballinasagart (Baile na Sagart) in Lisphelim townland, where priests were sheltered during those dark days. Between this village and Lough Funshinnagh there is the site of a Mass Rock. Two other penal sites exist at Lios an Aifrinn and the Chapeleen, both in Rahara parish. Tradition says that Fr John Fitzgerald Snr, who was from the locality, built the old church in Rahara itself about 1800, and this building was extended in 1840. Three other churches emerged during the eighteenth century: at Glanduff for St John's parish, Culleen for Killinvoy parish (now a parish hall), and at Ballymurray for Kilmeane parish. National schools now occupy the sites at Glanduff and Ballymurray. In the 1840s, due to the clerical shortages, these parishes were all served by one or two priests, and were formally organised into the union of Knockcroghery after the Great Famine. For a short period between 1860 and 1872, Rahara was joined with Tisrara (Four Roads), but reverted to Knockcroghery after that date.

The present Church of St John the Baptist, in the townland of Killiaghan, which serves the Lecarrow area, was built in the early 1840s, replacing an earlier chapel at Glanduff. It was redesigned by Bernard Rhattigan, Sligo, in the 1950s and reconstructed by J. Killian of Knockcroghery. The church was rededicated by Bishop Hanly on Sunday 17 June 1957.

St Patrick's
Church,
Knockcroghery

The contruction of a new church at Knock-croghery began in 1879 and was completed in 1885. It was dedicated to St Patrick by Bishop Laurence Gillooly on 18 October 1885, and replaced the chapels at Culleen and Ballymurray, where people had worshipped in the post-penal period. A tower and spire were planned in 1914 and eventually built in 1950. Today St Patrick's serves as the parish church.

The old church at Rahara was erected at the beginning of the nineteenth century and extended in 1840. A new modern-style church, also designed by Bernard Rhattigan of Sligo, was erected in the 1960s and blessed and dedicated by Bishop Hanly in honour of Mary Immaculate on 8 December 1967.

Most Rev Bernard Coyne (1854-1926) was born at Sandfield in this parish. He was Bishop of Elphin from 1913-1926.

The Church of Ireland community first used the medieval parish churches, but these soon fell into disrepair. A new church was built in Knockcroghery village in 1822, and this continued in use until the 1950s. The building was demolished a decade later.

Font at Tobar
Largan, Rahara.
Originally from
Rahara medieval
church

Key to the map

01. Ballagh	18. Carrowmoney	35. Cribby Islands
02. Ballinlig	19. Carrownamaddy	36. Crowsgap
03. Ballybrogan	20. Carrowndrisha	37. Cruit
04. Ballyglass	21. Carrownure Lower	38. Curraghalaher
05. Ballymurry	22. Carrownure Upper	39. Curraghnaveen
06. Barnacullen	23. Carrowphadeen	40. Curry
07. Binmuck	24. Cartron	41. Dogs Island
08. Black Island	25. Cartronperagh	42. Farbreagues
09. Bogganfin	26. Clooneen	43. Fearagh
10. Bolinree	27. Coolaphubble	44. Galey
11. Caltragh	28. Cooltona	45. Galey Beg
12. Carnagh East	29. Corboley	46. Ganaveens
13. Carnagh West	30. Corgarve	47. Glebe
14. Carrigan Beg	31. Cornamaddy	48. Glenfin
15. Carrigan More	32. Cornamart	49. Glenrevagh
16. Carrigeens	33. Corroy	50. Gortacarnan
17. Carrowkeel	34. Creggan	51. Gortaganny

Scale: 0.5"=1 mile
☩ Ancient Sites ✠ Holy Wells

3. Kilcommon medieval church and cemetery
62. Killinvoy medieval church and cemetery
66. St John's Well
83. Kilmaine medieval church and cemetery
87. Rahara medieval church and cemetery
88. St John's church and cemetery
100. Rindoon Abbey and village ruins

Parish of Loughglynn

(Tibohine (part of)) County Roscommon
Churches: Loughglynn, Lisacul & Gortaganny

THE PARISH OF Loughglynn is situated midway on the north-south axis of the Diocese of Elphin, and at its most westerly extreme, at the Roscommon-Mayo county boundary. It adjoins the Elphin parishes of Kilkeevan and Fairymount. Ballyhaunis lies to the south of the parish, with Ballaghaderreen, the Diocesan See of Achonry, lying just to the north. The parish is rural in character, and is characterised by rolling lowlands studded by lakes, Lough O'Flynn and Lough Glynn being the largest.

Loughglynn's early ecclesiastical history is closely bound up with the story of Airteach and Tibohine. Airteach encompassed all of northwest Roscommon, between Lough Gara and the Suck River, and was a territory of ancient origin. Teach Baoithín Airtigh, or Tibohine Artagh, meaning the House of Baoithín of the territory of Airteach, is located in the neighbouring parish of Fairymount, and the saint is said to have been the son of the local chieftain, Cuanach.

In pre-Reformation times Loughglynn, together with Frenchpark, was included in the extensive civil parish of Tibohine. This situation continued up to the mid-nineteenth century, and Tibohine was one of the largest parishes in Connacht. It comprised over 20,606 acres, with a pre-Famine population of almost 6,500 people. It stretched from Lough Gara in the north to Cloonarragh townland in the south, and from east to west encompassed the present parishes of Loughglynn, Lisacul, Tibohine, Fairymount, and the Frenchpark area. In 1837, there were three chapels in the union, at Loughglynn, Frenchpark and Tibohine. By 1839 this Union had been split into three separate parishes, Loughglynn/Lisacul, Tibohine, and Frenchpark, with Breedoge joining Frenchpark temporarily. Both of the churches at Loughglynn and Lisacul had separate parish priests until 1865.

The Franciscan Missionary of Mary Convent, Loughglynn

Through the nineteenth century the process of division and amalgamation continued, and what emerged were the present parishes of Loughglynn and Fairymount, while Frenchpark formed a new unit with the old parish of Kilcorkey. Three churches now serve the parish of Loughglynn: the parish Church of Our Lady of Good Counsel at Loughglynn, the

Church of St Mary, Gortaganny, and the Church of Christ the King served by a curate at Lisacul. There is also a chapel in the Franciscan Missionary of Mary Convent at Loughglynn.

An ancient church ruin and cemetery at Kilroddan (Cill Rodáin or Rodan's church) marks the location of an early Christian site in the Loughglynn area. This was possibly the site of an early monastery. A small Protestant church described as a chapel of ease was later built nearby in 1815. A glebe house was added in 1828. An ancient cemetery and the remains of an ancient Christian church survive near the river at Cloonard. There are ruins of an old church, Teampall Maol, in Cloonmullin, later used as an infant's burial place. St Brigid's Well is situated in Loughglynn Demesne and is believed to have been a place of pilgrimage.

In 1798 a barn church was built in Loughglynn village near the priests' graveyard. This served the needs of the community until the building of the present church. The then bishop, Dr Clancy, laid the foundation stone in 1905, and the building was dedicated in October 1906 to Our Lady of Good Counsel. It is built in a Gothic style, featuring a striking octagonal bell turret with a spire, polished granite interior pillars, and richly moulded arches. The architect was William Byrne of Dublin.

Church of Our Lady of Good Counsel, Loughglynn

In 1903 Dr Clancy purchased the old mansion of the Dillon family on the north side of Loughglynn Lake and invited a community of the Franciscan Missionaries of Mary from Belgium to take up residence there.

In the Lisacul area there are the remains of an ancient church and cemetery at Kilrooan (the church of Rowne) which may have had a monastic origin. A part of a wall and a large stone holy water font are the only remains. On the road from Lisacul through Figh townland one passes Bóithrín na gCorp. Here, a mound of clay served as a resting-place for people carrying uncoffined dead to Kilrooan cemetery during the Great Famine. A thatched church existed from the seventeenth century off the Lisacul-Curasallagh road. Tradition has it that St Patrick passed here. The church became a school in the 1830s. It is believed that there was a Patrician church in Drummad, Lisacul. There is also a St Patrick's Well in Drummad. Silverfield is the site of a childrens' burial place where many families have immediate

The Church of Christ the King, Lisacul

relations buried. This site has become known as 'Calvary' and the burial site and a cross were blessed in 1955 to commemorate the dead.

The present church at Lisacul was built in 1850. It was originally a simple structure with plain glass windows and wooden altar. In the late 1800s a slab inscribed with the Ten Commandments was placed over the main entrance to the church. The church was re-designed in 1940 by W. H. Byrne of Dublin, and reconstructed by Messrs Dolan of Castlerea. It was re-dedicated by Dr Doorly, Bishop of Elphin, on 26 October 1942, in honour of Christ the King. The main altar was a gift from Dr Doorly who had served for nine years as curate in Lisacul. Most Rev Thomas O'Doherty (1877-1936), a native of Corracoggil in this parish, was Bishop of Clonfert from 1919-1923, and subsequently Bishop of Galway from 1923-1936. He was a fluent Irish speaker and for many years secretary to the Irish Hierarchy. He died on 15 December 1936.

Church of St Mary, Gortaganny

The original church at Gortaganny was built in the 1830s, and is preserved as the nave in the present church. A higher section with a belfry was added during a major reconstruction in 1880, and in 1930 the sacristy and choir loft were added. The whole building was re-roofed in 1995. The church is dedicated to the Blessed Virgin Mary, and is now served by the parish priest from Loughglynn. At one period Mass was celebrated in a private house in Carrowbehy. The townland of Clooncan, which is a short distance from the church, was in the parish of Kilkeevan until 1886. Killeen is the local name for the childrens' burial ground in Clooncan.

Loughglynn Church of Ireland parish was a perpetual curacy in the Diocese of Elphin, and in the patronage of the Rector of Taughboyne (Tibohine). The present Anglican church is at Portahard, near Frenchpark.

Key to the map

01. Aghaderry
02. Aghadrestan
03. Aghalour
04. Ballyglass East
05. Ballyglass West
06. Breanmore
07. Caher
08. Carrowbehy
09. Carrownaknockaun
10. Cloonacolly
11. Cloonagh
12. Cloonard
13. Cloonargid
14. Cloonbunny
15. Clooncah
16. Clooncan
17. Cloondart

18. Cloonmaul
19. Cloonmullin
20. Cloontowart
21. Coolagarry
22. Corracoggil North
23. Corracoggil South
24. Corracommeen
25. Creevy
26. Cuiltyboe
27. Curraghard
28. Curraghsallagh
29. Derreenamackaun
30. Derrinea
31. Derry
32. Derrylahan
33. Driney
34. Druminagh

35. Drummad
36. Errit
37. Figh
38. Glebe West
39. Gortaganny
40. Kilroddan
41. Kilrooan
42. Kiltybranks
43. Kiltymaine
44. Lecarrow
45. Lissydaly
46. Loughglinn
47. Loughglinn Demense
48. Meelick
49. Tawnyrover
50. Tully
51. Urrasaun

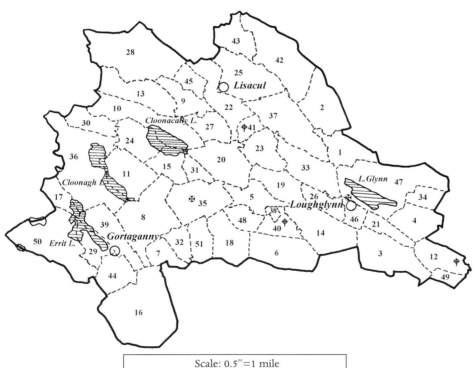

Scale: 0.5"=1 mile

✠ *Ancient Sites* ✠ *Holy Wells*

12. Cloonard old church and cemetery
35. St Patrick's Well, Drummad
40. Kilroddan medieval church and cemetery
41. Kilrooan old church and cemetery
47. St Brigid's Well, Drummad

Parish of Maugherow
(formerly part of Drumcliff) County Sligo
Church: Maugherow

MAUGHEROW, originally part of the parish of Drumcliff, is a small rural area in the Barony of Carbury, consisting of twenty-six townlands. It is bordered on the south by Sligo Bay, on the west by the Atlantic, on the north by Ahamlish parish, and on the east by Drumcliff. It includes the uninhabited offshore islands of Ardboline and Horse Island, the fishing villages of Ballyconnell and Raughly, the pointed hill of Knocklane, with its promontory fort, and Ardtarmon Castle, recently restored. Formerly, this was the ancient stronghold of the O'Harts, and subsequently the seat of the Gores, ancestors of the Gore-Booths, whose modern demesne at Lissadell lies within the parish boundary.

Ballintemple
cross-slab
*(Courtesy of
Stella Durand)*

Early Christian sites in the area included Kilmacannon which, with its cemetery, was wiped out in the early nineteenth century by the encroachment of blowing sands. Another medieval church and burial ground stood at Ballintemple, and was known as Ballintemplebeolan, after an ecclesiastical family by the name of Ó Beoláin, anglicised as Boylan or Boland. An ancient site marked on the 1837 OS Maps as Teampall na gCailleach Dubh, or church of the black-robed nuns, would seem to indicate the presence of a religious order. Another ruined church lies in the Lissadell estate, near to the seashore, and close by is the reputed site of the ancient church of Bunbreeoge.

The Church of St Patrick at Cloghboley is not the first to have stood on this site. Towards the close of the eighteenth century what was described as 'a nice chapel' was erected on an elevated site, fully exposed to the Atlantic breezes. It was renovated and greatly improved in 1845 by Patrick O'Gara PP of Drumcliff. On Christmas Day 1856, it was thronged to capacity and during Mass, as gale force winds increased in severity, a rumour circulated throughout the congregation that the building was about to collapse. Unfounded as it was, there was a mad rush for the door and in the resulting crush, worshippers suffered severe injuries. Following this incident a number of the faithful stayed away on Sundays and holy days, while most of those who did attend preferred to remain outside, exposed to the weather.

Shortly afterwards, the parishioners, headed by the then parish priest, Patrick O'Gara, decided to build a new church on the same site. In July 1859 an advertisement appeared in the *Sligo Champion* seeking tenders for the stonework, roofing, slating, etc. of the new building. By the following year sufficient funds, in the region of £800, had been collected to lay the foundation stone of a Gothic structure designed by Hadfield and Goldie. By December 1861, the walls were in place, but the funds were exhausted. At that stage Patrick Kelly, who had replaced Patrick. O'Gara as parish priest, made a public appeal for subscriptions to fund the roofing of the church. Due to prevailing economic conditions, which were particularly severe in that area, the church, described in contemporary records as 'a handsome stone edifice', was not finally completed and furnished until 1882. Five of the stained glass windows were the gift of Andrew Morahan PP, who had succeeded Fr Kelly in 1866.

During Mass on the morning of Sunday, 19 November 1882, a severe storm blew up and, as Owen O'Connor CC was reading the last gospel, a bolt of lightning hit the belfry sending a portion of it, together with a large iron cross, through the roof into the body of the church resulting in one fatality and numerous injuries to members of the congregation.

In 1949 the church was re-roofed, the interior studded and re-plastered, and the stonework raked out and re-pointed, at a cost of £23,000. A decade later a new wooden floor was laid at a cost of £1,000 10s. In January 1965, a plan for the alteration of the church in accordance with the new liturgical requirements was approved. The work started in October 1965, and was carried out by Kilcawley & Company, Sligo. The new stone altar was made by Diamonds of Sligo, and the first Mass was celebrated in the reconstructed building on Christmas Day 1965.

On 22 March 1989, as if in defiance of the adage that lightning never strikes twice, Maugherow church was struck by lightning for the second time in little over a century. Bolt lightning struck the pinnacle of the roof, and fire, fanned by a strong

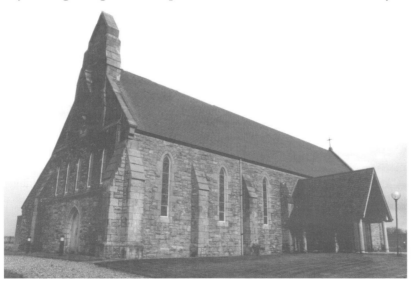

St Patrick's
Church,
Maugherow

breeze, quickly enveloped the church leaving it a smoldering ruin. This misfortune gave the parishioners an opportunity of re-designing the church to comply more fully with the post-conciliar liturgical requirements. Within the space of two years a refurbished church, embellished by a number of stained-glass windows by the Irish artist, George Walsh, rose from the ashes. The alterations to the interior of the church in the 1960s were limited due to the narrow design of the building, which was very dark, with the altar obscured from the congregation by supporting pillars. Today's modern interior is filled with light, and allows the altar to assume a central position, surrounded by seats for the faithful. The use of wood in the floor and roof-beams creates a warm communal atmosphere. The building combines the best of the traditional with the inclusiveness of the new liturgy.

The solemn opening and dedication of the reconstructed church was performed by Bishop Dominic Conway on 8 September 1991. Maugherow was created a parish in 1972, with Canon Colm Ward, who had been the CC since 1942, as its first parish priest. He retired in 1991, and died in 1993, after ministering to the district for almost 50 years, a unique record in the annals of the diocese.

The Church of Ireland, Lissadell, which was opened in 1856, replaced a smaller thatched church on the same site. The clock in the tower was installed in 1876, in memory of the local landlord, Sir Robert Gore-Booth. In 1896, St Kevin's Chapel of Ease at Munninane (Mullaghnaneane) was opened to cater for worshippers at the eastern end of Lissadell parish.

St Kevin's
Chapel of Ease

Key to the map

01. Aghagad	10. Ballygilgan (part of)	19. Doonowney
02. Ardboline Island	11. Ballymuldory	20. Horse Island
03. Ardtermon	12. Carrigeens	21. Kilmacannon
04. Ardtrasna	13. Cashelgarran (part of)	22. Lissadell
05. Attiduff	14. Cloghboley	23. Mullaghnaneane
06. Ballineden	15. Cloghcor	24. Raghly
07. Ballinphull	16. Cloonagh	25. Rahelly
08. Ballintemple	17. Cloonelly	26. Seal Rocks
09. Ballyconnell	18. Doonfore	

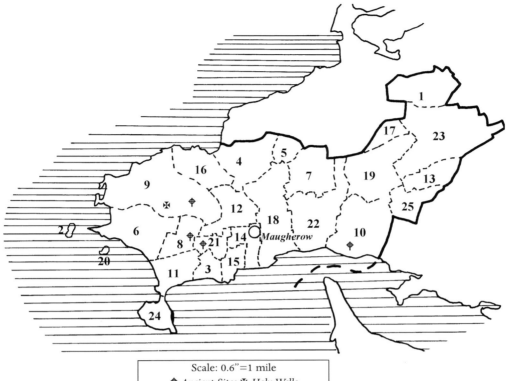

Scale: 0.6"=1 mile

✛ *Ancient Sites* ✠ *Holy Wells*

8. Old church and graveyard
9. Teampall na gCailleach Dubh and St Colmcille's Well.
10. Bunbreeoge old church site
21. Medieval church and graveyard

Parish of Oran

(Oran, Cloonygormican & Donamon) County Roscommon
Churches: Ballynaheglish, Cloverhill & Cloonycolgan

T HE MODERN PARISH OF Oran (Uaran), comprising the church areas of Cloverhill, Cloonycolgan, and Ballinaheglish, is an amalgamation of the medieval parishes of Oran, Cloonygormican, and Donamon. The parish derives its name from the Irish word, Fuarán, meaning a living spring of cold (fuar) water. In the *Tripartite Life* we are told: 'St Patrick elicited from the bowels of the earth a living and very clear fountain, which was afterwards very dear to himself, and which gave the name Uaran-Garad to the place and to the church built there.'

Dear Uaran, (cold spring)

O Cold Spring I loved, loved for my good,

Sad my lament, O dear God,

That my drink is not from the beloved cold spring.

Remains of a
Round Tower
at Oran

The holy well of Oran lies along the main road between Roscommon and Ballymoe. A statue of St Patrick erected in 1932 marks the spot. Across the road in Oran cemetery part of an ancient round tower and the side wall of the old church are still visible. More than 300 years ago a stone wall was built around the well, and a plain stone cross erected inside it. The then parish priest, Fr William Hanley, is credited with this development. The dedication on the stone has the engraving: 'Pray for the soule of Fr William Hanley who caused this monument to be made in ye honour of God and St Patrick of Ireland, Anno Domini, IHS 1684.' A pattern or little pilgrimage in honour of the patron, St Patrick, is held each year on Garland Sunday. The influence of St Patrick in the parish seems to be all-pervasive in that all three present churches at Cloverhill, Clooneycolgan and Ballinaheglish, have adopted him as patron.

The 1731 *Report on the State of Popery* shows that there was a Mass House in Cloonygormican parish, served by a Fr Patrick Kean, but there was no place of worship in Oran which was then united with Drumatemple. About a mile and a half from Cloverhill church is the cemetery of Ardkieran, where St Kieran, according to tradition, is said to have spent a short time before moving Clonmacnoise, where he established a monastic settlement, noted for its spirituality, scholarship and learning.

St Patrick's
Church,
Cams,
Cloverhill

The present church at Cloverhill is located in the townland of Cams. This church was originally small, and according to the *Roscommon Messenger* of 1857, efforts were made to 'put the chapel in some tolerable repair'. In 1860 a further appeal for funds was made to complete the renovation, which included the erection of a belfry. In 1870, it was decided to enlarge the church, and land for the extension was leased to Bishop Gillooly in 1871 and the church was completed by 1887. Cloverhill for ecclesiastical administration was united with Fuerty until 1881. The Burke family, of which Dr Patrick Burke, Bishop of Elphin 1827-1843, was a member, had close associations with this church. Tradition has it that Dr Burke took ill while returning from his *Ad limina* visit to Rome and that he died at his brother's house in Cloverhill parish. The western transept of the church is known as the 'Burke Memorial Chapel' which, incidentally, is the oldest part of the building. The stained glass windows in the building were inserted in 1906 by the White family, Rockfield. Fr Michael Dunning PP was instrumental in having the church renovated in the 1980s. It was re-dedicated by Bishop Conway on 20 November 1983.

Clooneycolgan church has a long history stretching back to the time of the Great Famine. The work commenced in 1848 but had to be discontinued because of lack of funds. An appeal was made to parishioners who had emigrated to the USA, and letters were written by the then parish priest, Fr Andrew Quinn. It would appear that the response was positive because the building was completed in 1867, and dedicated to St Patrick on 27 May 1888, Trinity Sunday. It should be noted that Clooneycolgan was linked to Kilbegnet parish for administrative church purposes at that time. In 1981, a decision was made to reconstruct and renovate the church. It too was re-dedicated by Bishop Conway on 13 February 1983.

St Patrick's Church,
Ballynaheglish

In the 1700s, a church was located in Ballynaheglish, near Briarfield in the north of the parish. This church was replaced in the early nineteenth century by one at Ballymacurley, the site of which also came to be known as Ballynaheglish, or Churchtown. The church was again replaced in 1930 with a new structure of similar design, and dedicated to St Patrick, like the other churches in the parish. Ballynaheglish enjoys the status of being the parish church. It was opened and dedicated in August 1932 by Edward Doorly, Bishop of Elphin. The building underwent considerable renovations in 1959, and has since been tastefully altered and adapted for the modern liturgy.

The Franciscan Brothers (OSF) founded a monastery and primary school at Farragher in the parish in 1855. Bishop Brown laid the foundation stone for the monastery in 1857. The school operated until the Brothers left the parish in 1972.

Mgr Thomas Finnegan, a native of Oran, was ordained in 1951 for the diocese of Elphin. He was President of Summerhill College Sligo (1967-1979), Director of the Regional Marriage Tribunal (1979-1982), and PP of Roscommon (1982-1987). He was appointed Bishop of Killala in 1987.

The Church of Ireland community worshipped at the church at Donamon and in the northern end of the parish at Aclare, in the townland of Clashaganny, which is now demolished.

Key to the map

01. Ardlagheen Beg	22. Carrowduff Upper	More (see 2)
02. Arlagheen More or Highlake	23. Carroweighter	43. Island Lower
	24. Carrowgarve	44. Island Upper
03. Ardmore	25. Carrownageeloge	45. Killinraghty Big
04. Arignagh	26. Carrowndangan	46. Killinraghty Little
05. Ballinturly	27. Cartron	47. Kiltultoge
06. Ballydooley	28. Clogher	48. Lisnalegan
07. Ballyglass Lower	29. Cloonamuinia	49. Lissagallan
08. Ballyglass Upper	30. Clooneenbaun	50. Lissanisky
09. Ballymacfarrane	31. Cloonmullenan	51. Newtown
10. Ballymacurley North	32. Cloonycolgan	52. Newtown Carrigans
11. Ballymacurley South	33. Creeve	53. Newtown Farragher
12. Ballymaglancy	34. Creevelea	54. Oran
13. Ballynaheglish	35. Dooneen	55. Peak
14. Brierfield	36. Emlagh Beg	56. Rabradagh
15. Bushfield	37. Emlagh More	57. Rathmew
16. Cams	38. Emlaghnagree	58. Runnabackan
17. Caran	39. Emlaghyroyin	59. Runnamoat
18. Caran Bog	40. Fearaghafin	60. Rushpark Farragher
19. Carrigans Park	41. Gortcloonagh	61. Slieve & Corbally
20. Carrowbaun	42. Gorticmeelra	62. Tonbaun
21. Carrowduff Lower	_. Highlake or Ardlagheen	63. Turksland

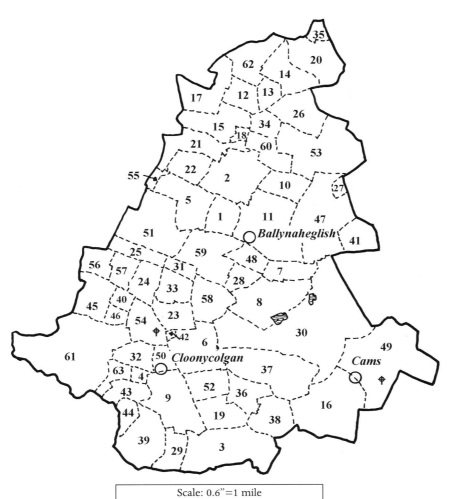

Scale: 0.6"=1 mile
☙ *Ancient Sites* ✠ *Holy Wells*

50. Ardkieran old cemetery
55. St Patrick's Well, Oran Round Tower
    and cemetery

Parish of Riverstown
*(Killmacallan, Ballinakill, Ballysumaghan, Drumcolumb, Tawnagh &
Kilross) County Sligo*
Churches: Riverstown, Sooey & Gleann

THE UNION OF Riverstown, which embraces one hundred and one townlands and comprises the ancient parishes of Kilmacallan, Ballinakill, Ballysumaghan, Drumcolumb, Kilross, and Tawnagh, seems to have been in existence since the mid eighteenth century, at which time it was under the care of Fr Darby Brennan. This present union dates from 1876 when Ballyrush was detached from the parish and annexed to Ballinafad.

Kilmacallan church, the ruins of which lie on a hillside in Ardagh townland, was originally a Patrician foundation. Today, it is more commonly known as

Old cross at
Drumcolumb

Templemore by local people, and has been a burial ground for a number of centuries. The rectory of Kilmacallan was appropriated to the Priory of Inchmacnerin in Loch Cé. Previous incumbents of the union of Riverstown were interred within the ruins, namely Darby Brennan PP who died in July 1782, his successors Bryan O'Kelly PP 1782-1803, and Canon James Hester PP 1803-1836. Close by the church remains are the foundations of an old building known locally as Teach na gCailleach Dubh, the house of the black-robed-nuns. Within a hundred yards of this graveyard is a holy well known as Tobar Muneen, or Monica's Well.

Ballinakill, lying at the heart of Riverstown union, is mentioned in an inquisition of 1585 as the 'Vicarage of Culea', and in another as the 'Rectory of Coolea'. A small mound in the centre of the graveyard marks the site of an ancient church. A century ago the eastern gable was standing and its lancet window resembled that of Kilmacowen. Within the graveyard is the enclosed plot of the Cogan family of Rockbrook and Killadoon. Close by is Lady's Well, where a pattern took place on 8 September. Ballysumaghan, which corresponds to the present area of Sooey, contains the remains of the old parish church of Kiltycloghan, and the family vault of the Neynoes of Castleneynoe. A weathered tombstone records the death of Fr Patrick Duffy of Sooey in October 1831, aged 85.

Kilross lies at the extreme northern edge of the union, and is overlooked by the mountains of Slieve Daéan and Slieve Dargan. The church of Kilross, 'church of the wood', was founded in 1233 by Clarus MacMailin, Prior of Trinity Abbey, Loch Cé. A small section of the ruin still stands, and it has been suggested that portion of the structure served as a residence for the clergy, while the remainder formed the church. The surrounding graveyard serves as a burial place for both Catholics and Protestants, including the family of Bishop John Clancy. The vault of the Ormsbys of Castledargan House stands close to the church. At Kilellin, in Ballygawley, are the ruins of an earlier church, and a pillar stone alongside, popularly known as Cloch an Easpaig. This is believed to mark the burial place of an early bishop. Close by is a holy well which was much frequented until a century ago.

Drumcolumb, a fragmented civil parish, is so called from its origin as the site of a Columban foundation. In the *Life of St Columba,* we are told that the saint 'after founding the churches of Emlaghfad, passed into the Barony of Tirerrill, and receiving from the inhabitants of that district a tract of land, called then Druimnamac, but later Drum Cholm Cille, built thereon a church, presented it, in token of his affection, with a bell called Glassan, and erected on the south side of it a tall cross; foretelling at the same time that all would go well with the church , so long as the bell and cross remained.' Today, there are some remains of a church, with a disused graveyard attached, in the townland of Drumcolumb. Close to the church is a ring-headed fragment of a high cross of uncertain date. Nearby, is a well known locally as Tobar Choilm, and a ravine where Mass was celebrated in penal times.

Tawnagh church is considered to be one of the oldest in the union. It was a Patrician foundation and finds mention in the *Tripartite Life.* The present ruin, according to a mural tablet in the eastern wall, was erected in 1733 for Protestant worship on the site of the original church. In 1768 a porch and vestry were added, and functioned as a place of worship until the present Church of Ireland was built in Riverstown. The unroofed structure stands on the round summit of a low hill, and is sur-

Church of the
Sacred Heart,
Riverstown

rounded by a well-tended graveyard, a peaceful place of burial for both Catholics and Protestants alike. Traditionally, St Patrick is the patron saint of Tawnagh, and a well, a little north of the church, is called St Patrick's Well and was the focus of a pattern-day on 17 March.

There are three modern churches in the union: Riverstown, Sooey and Gleann. The foundation stone of the Church of the Sacred Heart in Riverstown was laid in October 1940, to replace an earlier church erected in 1801 by Bryan Kelly PP. It was a slated chapel that was raised around an older thatched building on the same site. On Christmas Day 1841, the gallery of this chapel collapsed during Mass and several people were injured. The modern building is of classical design, and has accommodation for 700 worshipers. It is an impressive church, resembling the style of a Roman basilica, with a campanile in sandstone ashlar. Features include a Venetian west window, coffered barrel-vaulted ceiling, and transepts with side chapels separated from the nave by Corinthian colonnades.

The Church of the Assumption, Sooey, in the townland of Carrowkeel, built by Fr Luke Cullinan, was completed in 1837, and replaced an earlier thatched chapel on the old road to Sligo, in the townland of Sooey. Fr Cullinan, who died in 1850, is buried within the church. An inscribed plaque on the exterior wall records his memory, while another, bearing a Latin inscription, records the re-dedication of the church by Bishop Hanly, after major renovations, in August 1961.

St Colum's Church, Gleann

St Columba's Church, Gleann, known locally as St Colum's, is in the townland of Drumlaheen in the eastern end of the parish. It was built in the early Gothic style between 1903-1905, and dedicated in June 1907 by Bishop John Clancy.

The Church of Ireland community is served by Tawnagh parish church in Riverstown, which was built in 1817. Before that date, the old church at Tawnagh, about a mile distant, was used for Protestant worship. Ballysumaghan Church of Ireland, in the northern edge of the parish, was built in 1828 on the Neynoe Estate, and is the burial place for many of the local Protestant families.

Key to the map

01. Aghalenane	20. Carrigeenboy	38. Cooperhill
02. Aghoo	22. Carrowcrin	39. Cooperhill or
03. Annaghcarthy	23. Carrowkeel (CP.	Gobbadagh
04. Ardagh	Ballynakill)	40. Cuiltydangan
05. Ardcumber	24. Carrowkeel (CP	41. Cuiltylough
06. Ardkeeran	Tawnagh)	42. Doonally
07. Ardleebeg	25. Carrownagark	43. Doonamurray
08. Ardneeskan	26. Carrownagilty	44. Doongeelagh (part of)
09. Ardvarney	27. Carrowspurraun	45. Dowrea
10. Arnasbrack	28. Carrowreagh	46. Drumcolumb
11. Ballydawley	29. Cartronduffy	47. Drumdoney
12. Ballygrania	30. Cartrontonlena	48. Drumederalena
13. Ballynakill	31. Castledargan	49. Drumee
14. Ballysumaghan	32. Cloghfin	50. Drumacool
15. Behy	33. Cloonagh	51. Drumnasoohey
16. Bellanascarva	34. Clooneally	52. Drumraine
17. Boleymount	35. Clooneenroe	53. Emlagh
18. Carrickcoola	36. Cloonskirt	54. Emlagh (det. portion
19. Carricknagat	37. Coolbock	of)

55. Falnashammer	70. Knockaun	87. Rockbrook
56. Fidwog	71. Knockbreenagher	88. Rooghan
57. Gaddan	72. Knocknacross	89. Rosmore
58. Gaddan Beg	73. Knocknageeha	90. Rusheen (CP Ballynakill)
59. Glen	74. Knockrawer	91. Rusheen (CP Tawnagh)
–. Gobbadagh or Cooperhill (see 39)	75. Knockroe	92. Sooey
60. Killala	76. Lavally (part of)	93. Springfield
61. Killeenduff	77. Lavinscartron	94. Srananagh
62. Kilross	78. Lisbanagher	95. Tawnagh
63. Kiltycloghan	79. Lisconny	96. Tobernaglashy
64. Kiltylough	80. Lissaneeny	97. Tully Beg
65. Kingsbrook	81. Lissergloon	98. Tully More
66. Kinkillew	82. Lurgan	99. Tunnagh
67. Knockadoo	83. Mullaghmore	100. Turnalaydan
68. Knockanarrow	84. Murillyroe	101. Whitehill
69. Knockatober	85. Ogham	
	86. Rathmulpatrick	

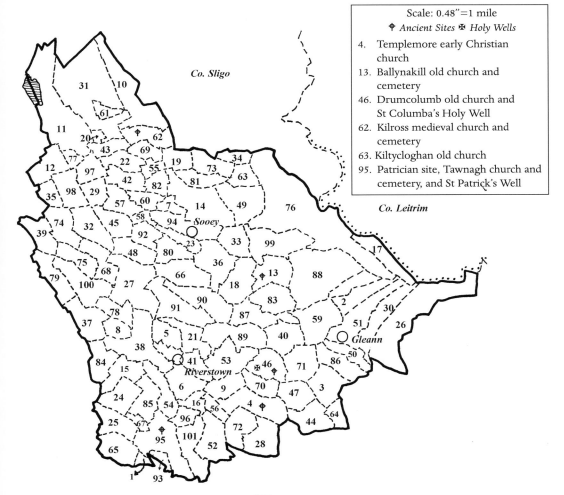

Scale: 0.48"=1 mile

✠ *Ancient Sites* ✠ *Holy Wells*

4. Templemore early Christian church
13. Ballynakill old church and cemetery
46. Drumcolumb old church and St Columba's Holy Well
62. Kilross medieval church and cemetery
63. Kiltycloghan old church
95. Patrician site, Tawnagh church and cemetery, and St Patrick's Well

Co. Sligo

Co. Leitrim

Sooey

Gleann

Riverstown

Parish of Roscommon

(Roscommon and Kilteevan) County Roscommon
Churches: Roscommon and Kilteevan

THE PARISH OF Roscommon, comprising fifty-seven townlands, is situated mid-county, lying between northern Lough Ree and the parish of Athleague. It includes Roscommon town and the ancient parish of Kilteevan, which lies to the east. Historically, Roscommon was an important town, strategically located as a gateway to the west, and a Royal Castle was built there in 1269. The parish takes its name from St Coman who evangelised the area in the sixth century. According to the *Annals of the Four Masters,* the first Abbey of Roscommon was founded in the year 742, the year in which St Coman, first Abbot-bishop of Roscommon and Abbot of Clonmacnoise, died.

Reputedly, this monastery was situated on the site of the present Church of Ireland and its adjoining cemetery, off Church Street in the town. This location is affirmed by the rediscovery in 1990 of the ninth-century stone plaque commemorating Joseph. The antiquarian Sir George Petrie had documented this plaque in 1863. The inscription on the plaque reads, 'Bendachad for anmain Ioseph' ('a blessing on the soul of Joseph.' See page 302). There are two Josephs recorded in the *Annals of the Four Masters* who are associated with the Abbey of Roscommon: 'AD 811. Joseph, scribe of Ros-Commain, died.' 'AD 828: Joseph, son of Nechtan, Abbot of Ros-Commain died.' A number of venerable and learned scribes resided at the abbey, and scholarship indicates that Joseph the Scribe is the Joseph commemorated in the plaque.

Roscommon
Dominican
Abbey

The abbey was subject to attack at various times during its long history – events which are documented in the *Annals*. It was pillaged by the Danes in 807 but more often than not suffered attack by the Irish. For example, in 1050 the bell-house (An Cloigtheach) was burned by the men of Breifne, and in 1135 both houses and churches were plundered by the Conmhaicaí of county Mayo. The *Annals* also tell us that, in 1170, the Abbot Connaienis of Roscommon Abbey exhumed the remains of St Coman and enshrined them in a silver reliquary, which was subsequently lost. A regular succession of abbots followed St Coman in the bishopric of Roscommon until the Synod of Kells in 1152, when the Sees of Roscommon, Elphin, Drumcliff and part of Ardcarne were amalgamated to form the Diocese of Elphin. Whilst the fortunes of the monastery ebbed and flowed against the background of internecine strife over the centuries, the Canons Regular of St Augustine occupied it in 1150, when it had been restored following a burning by a Munster cohort in 1134. A synod of all the Connacht clergy was held there in 1158.

In 1253, Felim O'Conor, King of Connacht, founded the Dominican Abbey in Roscommon. In 1578, Sir Nicholas Malby, Governor of Connacht, was given a grant of the property of both the canons and the friars of Roscommon. Religious practice was forced underground. The Dominican Abbey in Roscommon was in ruins. With the introduction of the penal laws the friars were banished. However, by 1756 there were sixteen friars in Roscommon, one of whom was a parish priest in 1767. Subsequently they managed to maintain a presence in the area until 1872 when Fr Bartley Kehir, the last Dominican prior of Roscommon, who was then parish priest of Athleague, died. He is buried in Fuerty.

Restored twelfth-century doorway at St Coman's Church, Roscommon

There are various sites in the parish which have religious links. In the townland of Ballypheason (Baile an Phearsúin), near the angle formed by the Circular Road with Lanesborough Street, and on the south side of the street, is a field locally known as 'The Hummawn Field'. The well of St Coman, or 'Dabhach Chomáin', is situated in this field. There is also an early Christian site at Ballinaboy, about three miles to the northeast of Roscommon town on the road to Lanesborough, which has an inscribed cross-slab and is the reputed site of St Ronan's oratory. There are two holy wells, Tobernagreaghta (the well of the wounds) and St Brigid's Well, situated close together, a few hundred metres to the southeast of the site.

The Cross of Cong, which was crafted at Clooncraff (Kilteevan) in 1123, is Roscommon's most famous ecclesiastical artifact. The original is housed in the National Museum, but the parish has an excellent replica, which was presented on the occasion of the dedication of the Sacred Heart Church in 1903. The cross is a reliquary which was believed to contain a fragment of the True Cross. It is so named, as it was found in Cong in the early part of the nineteenth century, having been missing for several generations.

Clooncraff was a dependency of the Augustinian house of Roscommon. Other minor sites include Cloonsellan Abbey, which dates back to the thirteenth century, though it is not clear with which of the Roscommon abbeys it was linked. Felim O'Conor, King of Connacht, may have built it as a country residence for the Dominicans of Roscommon. Crocan Cill Barra in Clooncraff is thought to have been the burial place of the monks of Cloonsellan Abbey, and a hermit's cell survived in Cealtra Field in Clooncraff until the early part of this century. Cloontogher church and graveyard date back to the late fifteenth and early sixteenth century, and Cloontogher Mass Rock, which is situated within a conjoined ring fort, was used during penal times.

Kilteevan (Cill Tighe Cháin/Cill Taobháin), on the eastern end of the parish, has provided a place of worship since 1782, as a date on a holy water font testifies. This first late-eighteenth-century church was thatched and was replaced by a larger church erected in 1819 near the village crossroads, which was further extended in 1842. The present church, built in 1962, stands on an elevated site overlooking its predecessor. It was dedicated in honour of St Joseph by Bishop Vincent Hanly on 25 August 1963.

The eighteenth-century courthouse which was used for Mass from 1836-1903, now the Bank of Ireland, Roscommon

The post-Reformation history of Catholic churches in Roscommon town dates back to 1757, when a church was built in Chapel Lane during the pastorate of Fr Matthew O'Connor (d. 1763). This church was in use until after the Emancipation Act of 1829. The old Court House in the Square, now the Bank of Ireland, was purchased for £20 by the then PP, Rev John Madden, in 1829 and converted into a chapel with galleries. There was a striking painting of the crucifixion over the altar. The whole conversion cost £2,000 and the first Mass was celebrated in the building in 1836. It served as the parish church for Roscommon until the opening of the Sacred Heart Church in 1903. The baptismal font in the Sacred Heart Church, which bears the date of 1717, is the original from the first church in Chapel Lane, so the link can be made back over the centuries. The site for the church was donated by the Sisters of Mercy, and funds were raised at home and abroad to assist towards building this

Gothic church which was to be a memorial to the late bishop, Dr Gillooly, a native of the parish. P. J. Kilgallen of Sligo was the architect, and the building was erected by Thomas Fee of Longford. The blue limestone used in the building was supplied from a quarry in nearby Tremane. The foundation stone was laid on 17 March 1897, and the dedication ceremony took place on 18 June, 1903. This magnificent architectural gem is one of Roscommon's remarkable landmarks and stands out as the most imposing church in the county. Its sixty metre tower, mounted spire and turret-clock forms an essential part of the skyline of the county town. This gothic church, fitted with forty-eight stained glass windows, abounds in symbolism and is adorned with exquisite mosaic works in Italianate style. The building is cruciform in

Church of the Sacred Heart, Roscommon

design, with nave arcade and stately rows of granite pillars. The sanctuary, with its imposing high altar, has an attractive rood screen surmounted with a crucifix. The church, erected in less prosperous times, remains a great source of pride and hope to worshippers in their religious quests.

The Sisters of Mercy came to Roscommon in 1853. They set about caring for the needs of the parish and surrounding districts. They opened an orphanage and schools in the parish and from 1929 they had a secondary school for girls in the town. In 1921 they took charge of the Sacred Heart Home, formerly the Roscommon Workhouse. Today, the sisters continue to administer to the nursing, educational and social needs of the parish. From 1930 to 1937 the De La Salle Brothers were in charge of a primary and intermediate school in the parish. In 1937 the Christian Brothers came to Roscommon and built new primary and secondary schools for boys in the area and they still continue their role in education and other pastoral activities in the parish.

At present there are about 1,500 families in the parish, which is fortunate to have a parish-based family life centre, Vita House, opened in 1993, which provides a variety of pastoral and community services.

The present St Coman's Church of Ireland was built in 1775 on the site of an earlier church. This site was formerly the location of the Augustinian foundation in Roscommon in the twelfth century, and had Patrician roots, being the site where St Coman founded his church. During reconstruction of the church in 1845, twelfth and fourteenth century doorways were incorporated into the tower, and also a fourteenth

The old church in Chapel Lane, Roscommon

century cut-stone window was placed in the east gable. The surrounding graveyard was the resting-place for both Protestants and Catholics of the town until the opening of St Coman's new cemetery in June 1912.

A Presbyterian church was built in Roscommon in 1863. This building now serves as the County Museum. A Methodist church was built in 1904, and now serves as the Church of Ireland Parish Hall.

Key to the map

01. Acres	22. Carrownabrickna	43. Emmoo
02. Aghmagree	23. Carrowroe	_. Gallowstown or Lisnacroghy
03. Annagh More	24. Cartron (Brett)	
04. Ardkeel	25. Cartron (Coote)	44. Killeenboy
05. Ardnanagh	26. Clonbrackna	45. Killarney
06. Ardsallagh Beg	27. Clooncah	46. Kilteevan
07. Ardsallagh More	28. Cloonconra	47. Lisbride
08. Ballinaboy	29. Clooncraff	48. Lisnacroghy or Gallowstown
09. Ballingard	30. Clooneskert	
10. Ballindall	31. Cloonlarge	49. Lisnamult
11. Ballyboughan	32. Cloonmore	50. Loughnaneane
12. Ballybride	33. Cloonmurly	51. Newtown
13. Ballygalda or Trust	34. Cloonsellan	52. Ranelagh
14. Ballymartin Beg	35. Cloontimullan	53. Rathbrennan
15. Ballymartin More	36. Cloontogher	54. Rinnany
16. Ballynacullia	37. Cloonybeirne	55. Slevinage
17. Ballypheasan	38. Creevyquin	56. Tonlegee
18. Barnhill	39. Derrinturk	_. Trust or Ballygalda (see 13)
19. Belderg	40. Derrycabry	
20. Bohergave	41. Derrydonnell	
21. Carrowmore	42. Doogarymore	

'Joseph' slab from the site of St Coman's monastery

Font in the Sacred Heart Church, Roscommon

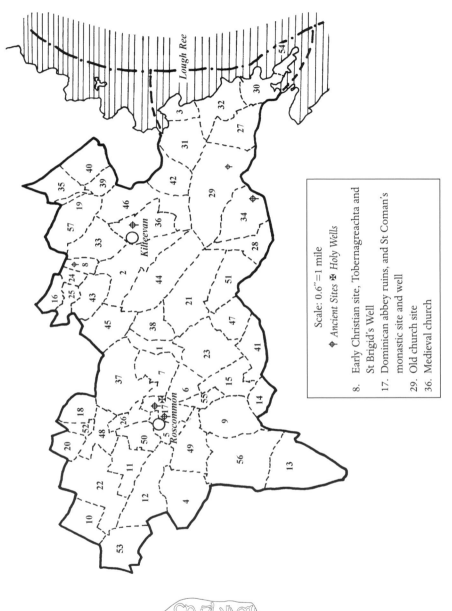

Scale: 0.6″ = 1 mile

✟ *Ancient Sites* ✠ *Holy Wells*

8. Early Christian site, Tobernagreachta and St Brigid's Well
17. Dominican abbey ruins, and St Coman's monastic site and well
29. Old church site
36. Medieval church

Lough Ree

Killeevan

Roscommon

Cross-inscribed
slab, Ballinaboy

303

Parish of Rosses Point
(formerly part of Drumcliff) County Sligo
Church: Rosses Point

THE PARISH OF Rosses Point lies to the northwest of Sligo town, and is one of the newly formed parishes in the diocese. Traditionally part of Drumcliff, it was attached to Sligo from 1898 to 1995, and served by a curate from the Cathedral parish. In 1995, due to a large influx of families and its position as a commuter town to Sligo, it was created a parish in its own right by Bishop Christopher Jones.

St Columba's Church, Rosses Point

The parish forms a peninsula, surrounded by the waters of Sligo Bay and Drumcliff Bay. To the west lie the open waters of the Atlantic and the lighthouse on the Black Rock. Its ecclesiastical history is overshadowed by the monastic settlement at Drumcliff, but we find frequent mention of the Rosses in the *Annals of the Four Masters.* Rosses Point was part of the ancient way, called the Fearsat, which ran from Tireragh, in west Sligo, across the Ballisodare estuary at low tide, to the Coolera peninsula, on to Cummeen Strand, from where it came ashore at Ballincar, near Rosses Point, and then by way of Lissadell Strand to Maugherow and north Sligo. Most of northern Sligo belonged to the diocese of Killala before the Synod of Kells in 1152, and this was probably due to the influence of this line of travel. In the *Tripartite Life,* St Patrick is reported to have visited the Rosses on his way from Connacht to Ulster, passing through Killaspugbrone on the far side of Sligo Bay, and continuing to Maugherow. There is no tradition of the national apostle having founded a church in the area, but there are remains of an ancient church at Lower Rosses, which was probably built at a later date. There is also a tradition of a cillín at this site, known locally as Lisín na bPáistí.

From earliest times, down to disestablishment in 1869, the Rosses was church lands, originally belonging to the religious of Drumcliff and later to the Bishop of Elphin. According to an Exchequer Inquisition held at Sligo on 7 July 1612, the

Upper Rosses was called Rossibeolain, after the Drumcliff ecclesiastical family named Ó Beoláin; and the Lower Rosses, Rosse McAnerleyne, believed to be the origin of the name Killerlean, which was common in the area a century ago. Over the course of the centuries these lands passed to the Cooper family of Markree Castle, and eventually in 1867 to William Middleton, great-uncle of W .B. Yeats. Both Jack and W. B. Yeats spent many of their summers at his home, Elsinore, and their poetry and paintings abound with images of the area. Under William Middleton's patronage Rosses Point developed into a popular touring spot with hotels and bathing lodges. The village always had a history of seafaring, and many young men of the area have spent time at sea, in both the merchant fleet and serving in both World Wars.

Two islands, Coney and Oyster, face the village across the narrow but deep stretch of water known as Sruth na Míle, or Channel of a Thousand Currents. Both islands are traditionally part of the parish of Coolera, on the opposite side of the Bay, but are currently served from Rosses Point

There was no place of worship in the village for most of the nineteenth century, with the people hearing Mass in local houses or travelling to Rathcormac, three miles away. However, this situation changed in October 1878, with the opening of the present Church of St Columba in the village, which had been built through the exertions of Fr Andrew Morahan of Rathcormac, who also added a local school. The church was erected on part of the Middleton estate, and was constructed by handymen of the locality, in concrete throughout. It initially served less than 100 local families and an enlarged congregation in the summer season. The presbytery, originally styled 'Stella Maris Hospice', is situated beside the church and was built by Bishop Clancy between 1902-04. In 1898 the Point became attached to the Cathedral parish until its elevation to parochial status in 1995.

The Sisters of La Sagesse came to the area in the 1950s, and commenced caring for girls with mental handicap and profound learning difficulties. In 1961 extensive residential accomodation for both boys and girls was provided at Cregg House, and a School of Nursing was established five years later. The sisters and the school have become bye-words for excellence in care throughout the northwest.

The Church of Ireland in the village, dating from 1854-55, was partially endowed by the Coopers of Markree, the then landlords, and subsequently by the Middletons. The architect was William Deane, and Henry Caldwell of Sligo was the contractor.

Key to the map

01. Ballincar
02. Ballyweelin
03. Cregg

04. Creggconnell
05. Doonierin (part of)
06. Rosses Lower

07. Rosses Upper

Scale: 0.6"=1 mile
✠ *Ancient Sites* ✠ *Holy Wells*
2. Cillín
6. Old church site

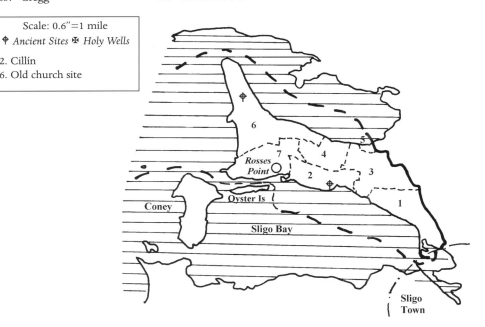

St Columba's
Church of Ireland,
Rosses Point

Sligo: Parish of St Anne's & Carraroe

(formerly part of St John's) County Sligo
Churches: St Anne's, Sligo & St John's, Carraroe

ST ANNE'S and Carraroe is a comparatively new parish, officially created in 1979, and carved out of the larger Cathedral parish, which encompassed Sligo town. Its modern boundaries, when combined with those of the present Cathedral parish, parallel almost exactly that of the ancient parish of St John's. The parish of St John the Baptist has been so called since the time of the Anglo-Normans, who had a special devotion to him. The present church of St John the Baptist is now the Church of Ireland Cathedral, and lies in the Cathedral parish.

The parish chapel, also dedicated to St John, which stood at the bottom of Chapel Hill, was the principal place of Catholic worship in Sligo until the erection of the Cathedral of the Immaculate Conception in 1874. This chapel was erected before 1711, and functioned as a Pro-Cathedral from the 1830s onwards. From an extant deed, dated 1776, we know that a Mass House was situated on the site, and that it was probably constructed of stone and slated. In the same year, the decision was taken by the then parish priest, Fr John O'Flynn, (subsequently Bishop of Achonry) to build a larger church to accommodate a growing population. Tradition has it that the new church was erected around the old building, and thus ensured the continuation of worship on the site. It was a large and commodious building, with balconies and galleries. The chapel was extended after the Famine, at substantial cost, and served the parish well until the opening of the new Cathedral in Temple Street in 1874.

This brought to a close over 150 years of worship in this eastern end of town, which now forms St Anne's parish. The old church of St John was converted into an Industrial School for girls, operated by the Sisters of Mercy, and towards the end of the 1960s was used as part of their secondary school. It was demolished in 1986 to make way for a Cheshire Home.

The modern church of St Anne's was constructed in direct response to the spiritual needs of this eastern side of Sligo, as in the 1940s and 50s several new housing estates had been built there.

St Anne's
Church,
Sligo

307

Even though the Dominican church catered for this area, it was a conventual church, and thus no baptisms, marriages or funerals were performed there.

On 26 July 1956, the Feast of St Anne, Bishop Vincent Hanly blessed and laid the foundation stone of the new church. The formal blessing and opening took place on 3 August 1958, restoring a place of worship to this part of Sligo after a gap of over eighty years. St Anne's is of a classical pre-conciliar design, which made use of the advantages of modern construction techniques to create a large spacious interior, full of light, without the need for supporting pillars. The altar is of Carrara marble, and contains a relic of St Anne. The Stations of the Cross and the Holy Family mural were hand carved in wood by artists in the South Tyrol in Italy. The distinctive bell tower is seventy-five feet high, and provides access to the large gallery. The building can accommodate over 1,000 people.

For several years the church remained within the Cathedral parish of Sligo but, following decades of urban growth, it became a separate parish in 1979. Today, St Anne's is a developing area with a considerable young population.

East window and high altar of Sligo Abbey

The Dominican Abbey, whose imposing ruins lie in St Anne's parish, is evidence of the Order's long association with Sligo. The friars built their first church there in 1252, and it formed the nucleus of the small town which grew up under its sheltering walls. The abbey was burned accidentally in 1414, but was quickly restored by Bryan Mc Donagh, the prior. It was finally destroyed by Sir Frederick Hamilton in July 1642, during the Cromwellian period, when he burned the town and killed almost 300 people. The abbey has remained in ruins ever since and until 1848 continued to be the chief burial place for the Catholics of the town. A new Dominican church was built in High St in 1845, the friars moving there from a small chapel at the rear of Pound Street. A modern building, Holy Cross, replaced this structure in 1973, thus ensuring that the Dominicans have had a continuous presence in Sligo for over 700 years.

The Sisters of Mercy operate primary and secondary schools in the parish. They came to Sligo in 1846, and their first mission was home visitations and caring for the sick and destitute. In 1849, a new convent, St Patrick's, and a public school were

opened. By the beginning of the twentieth century the sisters were operating a
laundry, Industrial School, an orphanage,
primary school, and a senior boarding
school, all on a site on Chapel Hill. A
new secondary school was built in 1976,
and extended twice since. The three

Mercy Convent,
Sligo c. 1875

primary schools under their care were amalgamated in 1995, and now have an
enrolment of over 500 children, the largest in the northwest. St Patrick's Convent
was sold in 1990, and the remaining sisters moved to a new, smaller residence. Their
commitment to the parish is strong, and there are several teaching sisters, three
working in the community, and a number of retired sisters who visit the house-
bound and undertake many other pastoral activities.

Carraroe church area is served by St John's Church which was built in 1893-96,
under the patronage of Bishop Gillooly, re-dedicated in 1962, and served as a curacy
from Sligo Cathedral. The church was originally designed to serve the large rural
area stretching from Carraroe to Ballisodare, and the countryside adjoining Lough
Gill. The need for this church had been long felt, as the people of the district had to
travel three or four miles into Sligo to attend Mass. The late Peter O'Connor JP, of
Cairnsfoot House, donated generously to its erection. The people of the area subscribed liberally to the funds, as did their co-parishioners in Sligo. The church was
built by John Clarence of Ballisodare, and blessed and dedicated on Sunday 2 August
1896, by Dr John Clancy. Built in the Gothic style, the church was given the titular
of St John, the only Catholic church in the
then parish to retain the name of its original
patron. The church was renovated in the mid
1990s after an electrical fire, and a striking
reredos was installed which incorporates a
new tabernacle. The expansion of Sligo town
has left Carraroe with over 700 families and a
combination of both urban and rural areas,
and in recent years Carraroe has had its own
resident curate. St Enda's NS, a short distance
from the church, meets the educational
needs of the area, and there is a fully
equipped community centre adjacent to the
presbytery.

St John's
Church,
Carraroe

The ancient pilgrimage site of Tobernalt, or the Holy Well, is situated in this
part of the parish. This tranquil place of visitation set in primeval woods is an ideal
setting for prayer and reflection. Originally a simple Mass Rock hidden in a wooded

glen beside a holy well, 'The Well', as it is popularly known, is an oasis of peace for the countless people who visit it each year.

Tobernalt. A place of refuge during penal times and today a renowned pilgrim site

Key to the map

01. Abbeyquarter North	17. Cottage Island
02. Abbeyquarter South	18. Cuilbeg
03. Aghamore Far	19. Drumaskibbole
04. Aghamore Near	20. Glynn Island
05. Ballyfree	21. Goat's Island
06. Caltragh	22. Green Island
07. Carns	23. Hawk Island
08. Carns (Duke)	24. Knocknaganny (part of)
09. Carrickhenry	25. Lahanagh
10. Carrowgobbadagh	26. Tonafortes
11. Carrowkeel (part of)	27. Tonaphubble
12. Carrownamaddow	28. Tullynagracken North
13. Carrowroe	29. Tullynagracken South
14. Cleveragh	
15. Commons	
16. Cornageeha	

Street & Estates within Sligo Borough Boundry

St Anne's Urban
Abbey St
Abbeyquarter
Abbeyville
Ashbrook
Back Avenue
Bank's Drive
Bridge St
Burton St
Cairns Drive
Carroll Drive
Castle St
Cemetery Road

Chapel Hill
Chapel St
Circular Road
Cleveragh Road
Cleveragh Drive
Colleary Drive
Connolly St
Cranmore Road
Cranmore Drive
Cranmore Place
Cairns View
Crozon Crescent
Crozon Downs
Crozon Park
Devins Drive
Doorly Park
Edenhill
Fatima Ave
Garavogue Villas
Geldof Drive

Heatherview
High St
Highfield Road
Jail Road
Joe Mc Donnell Drive
Langan Drive
Market St
Martin Savage Tce
Marymount
Mass Lane
Mc Neill Drive
Old Market St
Pearse Crescent
Pearse Tce
Pilkington Tce
Riverside
Rockwood Parade (part of)
Saddleworh, Tonaphubble
St Anne's Tce
St Asicus' Tce

St Brigid's Place
St Joachim's Ave
St Muiredeach's Tce
The Stirrups, Tonaphubble
Water Lane
Yeats Drive

Carraroe Urban
Ardcarn
Cairns Road
Caltragh Heights
Cornageeha
Fernadale
Green Road
Greenfort Est
Knocknaganny
Markievicz Heights
Rathanna
Upper Pearse Road
Woodtown Lodge

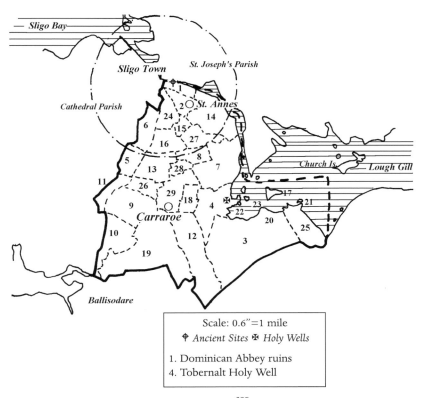

Scale: 0.6"=1 mile
✠ *Ancient Sites* ✠ *Holy Wells*

1. Dominican Abbey ruins
4. Tobernalt Holy Well

Sligo: The Cathedral Parish

(part of St John's) County Sligo
Church: Cathedral of the Immaculate Conception

THE CATHEDRAL PARISH of the Diocese of Elphin is located in Sligo, and is graced by the imposing nineteenth-century Cathedral of the Immaculate Conception. However, the parish is of greater antiquity, having been originally dedicated to John the Baptist by the Normans in the twelfth century. From the early nineteenth century to the 1980s, the Cathedral parish was much larger, stretching from Strandhill in the west to the Leitrim border at Calry. A major re-organisation of the urban parochial structure took place from the late 1980s due to the growth of Sligo town, and the Cathedral parish now occupies the urban area south of the river Garavogue and west of the Dominican Friary.

St John's
Church of Ireland
Cathedral, Sligo

The Church of Ireland Cathedral of St Mary the Virgin and St John the Baptist lies immediately to the rear of its Catholic neighbour, and it is there that we must turn for a historical perspective.

The local Norman lord, Maurice Fitzgerald, erected a castle in Sligo in 1245, and also a hospital or rest-house dedicated to the Holy Trinity, which was possibly the forerunner to St John's. Fitzgerald also built the Dominican Abbey of Holy Cross in 1252. By the mid-1300s, after a period of war, a new parish church was built, dedicated to John the Baptist to whom the Normans had great devotion. This church survives to the present day, although vastly altered, with the tower being the only original portion remaining. From the fourteenth to the sixteenth century St John's was central to a tithe-yielding area known as 'The Rectory between the two Bridges', or 'Inter Duos Pontes'.

With the coming of the Reformation, St John's was claimed for the crown by Owen O'Connor who later became the first Anglican Bishop of Killala. St John's was now to play an important role in the evolution of the Protestant faith in Sligo. It became the Anglican Cathedral for the united Dioceses of Elphin and Ardagh in 1961, following the closure of the old Cathedral in Elphin. The titular of 'St Mary the Virgin' was added to that of St John in order to provide the link between the old and new Cathedrals. Today, St John's stands as one of Sligo's architectural gems.

Following the Reformation, the Catholics of the town continued to worship in the partially-ruined Dominican abbey until the friars abandoned it in 1698. They later built a small thatched chapel in Pound St. It is uncertain when the first Mass House or parish chapel was erected in Sligo, but it was probably around the early 1700s. In 1712, Thomas Corkran, a local merchant, confessed to a local Court of Inquiry that he had heard Mass two weeks earlier at the 'chapel or Mass House in Sligo'. In 1776, the landlord, William Burton, leased the 'Mass House ... in Abbeyquarter' for thirty-one years at an annual rent of £1-10s. The chapel, dedicated to St John, was located on a lane subsequently called Mass Lane or Chapel Lane. The site is presently occupied by the Cheshire Home at the bottom of Chapel Hill, now in the parish of St Anne's.

Fr John O'Flynn was appointed parish priest of Sligo in 1775, and commenced a campaign to erect a larger church to accommodate a growing population. The new church was constructed around the old building, thus ensuring the continuation of worship on the site. The church was large and commodious, with balconies and galleries.

By the late 1820s, due to the absence of a Cathedral in the diocese, St John's parish chapel was functioning as a Pro-Cathedral, with the presiding bishop residing for a period in Sligo. In June 1845, Bishop Browne convened a meeting to organise the raising of funds for a new building, more fitting for the title of Cathedral, and 'both suitable to the wants of the area, and worthy of the diocese'. A committee was formed to collect funds and, by the end of that summer, a substantial fund had accumulated. However, the plans were abandoned when the potato crop failed and the Great Famine decimated the country.

Cathedral of the Immaculate Conception, Sligo

In the immediate aftermath of the Famine the chapel was extended, at substantial cost, but it was only in 1858, with the appointment of Dr Laurence Gillooly as bishop, that the plans for the new Cathedral were re-examined. A site, known as the 'Bowling Green', was purchased in Temple Street, and work on the new building commenced in earnest in 1869, with Joseph Clarence of Ballisodare as builder. The architect was George Goldie of London (1828-1887), designer of many of the churches in the diocese. The old parish chapel of St John, having served the faithful of the town for over 150 years, was closed and was eventually converted into an Industrial School for girls, run by the Sisters of Mercy, and towards the end of the 1960s was used as part of their secondary school. It was demolished in 1986 to make way for a Cheshire Home.

Cardinal Paul Cullen of Dublin solemnly opened the new Cathedral of the Immaculate Conception on 26 June 1874, although the tower was not yet complete. Peter O'Connor, a prominent local businessman, donated the famous chimes, familiar sounds to all Sligonians, in memory of his daughter. The Cathedral underwent extensive renovation in 1975, to celebrate the centenary of its erection. (For further details on the development of the Cathedral, see the chapter entitled 'The Cathedrals of Elphin'.)

St Mary's, Sligo, c. 1900. Diocesan Centre of Administration

St Mary's presbytery, often referred to locally as 'the Palace', was built by Clarence of Ballisodare between 1878 and 1880, and designed by Goldie. Constructed of cut limestone, it was badly burned during a fire in 1936, but was restored to its former glory shortly afterwards. The nearby Gillooly Memorial Hall, designed by local architect Patrick J. Kilgallin, was erected in 1904-1906 to provide a centre for the promotion of temperance and total abstinence, especially among the working people of the parish, through social outlets. The hall is situated on a plot described as the 'Malt-House'. The façade is of limestone ashlar, faintly Jacobean-classical in style, with a balcony on the front and includes a statue of Bishop Gillooly on the parapet.

In the nineteenth century, the Cathedral parish, or Sligo town parish as it was commonly known, covered a much larger area than it does today. It comprised the ancient parishes of St John's, Calry to the northeast, and Kilmacowen and Killaspugbrone on the Coolera peninsula to the west. Calry had been united with St Johns in 1704, and with the addition of the other parishes, the area was often

The Temperence Gillooly Memorial Hall, Sligo (Architect's drawing)

called the Union of Sligo. Rosses Point was detached from Drumcliff and attached to the Cathedral parish in 1899, and served by its own priest. Priests who lived in St Mary's presbytery also served Calry, Carraroe, Ransboro and Strandhill. Eventually there were resident priests in these areas. New churches were built at St Anne's in 1958, Ransboro in 1967, and Ballytivnan (St Joseph's) in 1983. Rapid population growth necessitated the re-organisation of the parochial structure, and the creation of parishes in St Anne's and Carraroe in 1979, and St Joseph's and Calry in 1988. Rosses Point remained part of the Cathedral parish until 1995 when it was elevated to the status of a parish.

Strandhill and Ransboro obtained parochial status in 1998. The much-reduced Cathedral parish is now a wholly urban area, with a large, growing population. Although the Borough of Sligo is divided into several parishes, the Cathedral remains the focal point of Catholic worship in the town.

The College of the Immaculate Conception (Summerhill), on an elevated site overlooking the Cathedral, was founded originally at Summerhill, Athlone in 1877 as a diocesan college by Bishop Browne. The school was transferred to a newly-built premises in Sligo in 1880. The large cut-limestone building was supplemented by

Summerhill College, Sligo

a new wing, which included dormitories and a chapel, in the late 1940s. Increased pupil numbers, due to the introduction of free secondary education, necessitated the addition of a new extension and hall on an adjoining site in late 1969. The hall was named in honour of Fr Edward J. Flanagan, founder of 'Boys Town', and fomer pupil of Summerhill. Today, it has an enrolment of over 1,000 boys and a staff of almost 60, making it one of the largest colleges in the country.

The Ursuline Sisters came to Elphin in 1844, when Bishop Browne invited them to set up school at Summerhill in Athlone. In 1850, nineteen sisters transferred to Sligo to set up a new school there. The convent in Finisklin was built in 1850 on a seven-acre site previously known as 'Seaville', and the nearby St Vincent's national school was founded in 1854. A secondary school was opened in 1893, and also a boarding school which was in operation until 1982. In 1966, a new national school, Scoil Ursula, was built

Ursuline Convent, Sligo

on the Strandhill Road, and the old building was closed. The continuing commitment of the Ursulines to education in Sligo was underscored in 1991 with the addition of a large extension to the secondary school.

The Sisters of Nazareth, based at Nazareth House, came to Sligo in 1910 to care for orphans who were living in the workhouse. They administered the orphanage from that date until the early 1990s. In the 1950s, the sisters also undertook to provide residential care for the elderly and, in 1980, Nazareth House became a registered nursing home. Today there are eleven sisters and 140 staff caring for a large number of elderly people in the pleasant surrounds of this former suburban villa.

The Sisters of St Joseph of the Apparition came to Sligo in 1957 from Manchester, and assumed the administration of Garden Hill Nursing Home, with its accompanying maternity unit. The sisters are involved in a variety of parish works, including bereavement counselling, visiting the housebound-elderly and other pastoral activities.

In 1982, Sisters of the Presentation of Mary were invited to Sligo to set up a chapel of Perpetual Adoration at the Cathedral. Since then, many Sligo people have participated in daily adoration of the Blessed Sacrament. In 1998, the Chapel of St Bernadette was built on Rockwood Parade in the town centre and provides a daily opportunity for reflection and silent prayer, an oasis in the midst of a busy commercial urban centre.

St John's national school, or 'The Brothers' as it is more popularly known, lies in the shadow of the Cathedral in Temple Street, and is run by the Marist Brothers. Sligo was their first foundation in Ireland when Dr Gillooly invited them to Elphin in 1862. They opened two primary schools in Sligo, and provided education for boys over the age of seven in the town until the opening of other parish schools in the 1980s. They moved from Quay Street to the present site in 1942. The brothers have a proud association with Sligo, and gave not just the basic education but introduced their pupils to the world of drama, choirs, music, and of course football. The brothers continue to be involved in teaching and other apostolic work in the parish.

In the 1960s Sligo, like many other Irish urban centres, experienced much housing and industrial development. This presented new and challenging issues for the pastoral carers of the parish. The Sligo Social Services Council was established in 1969, and operated from a premises in High Street. In 1973, Fr Christopher Jones (subsequently Bishop Jones) was appointed director, and two years later the former Retreat House in Charles Street was acquired as a centre from which the council continues to provide a wide range of personal and community services.

St Michael's Family Life Centre was opened in 1995 in the former residence of the Marist Brothers on Church Hill. This centre offers personal development and a wide range of pastoral orientated courses and much spiritual enrichment.

John Wesley, the founder of Methodism, visited Sligo on a number of occasions between 1758-1789. The present Methodist church in Wine Street opened in 1832 and was the third place of worship in the town since Wesley's time. In 1823 the Presbyterians in Sligo became a separate congregation, having previously been united with Ballymote. In 1828 the present church in Church Street was built through the exertions of the Rev James Heron.

Key to the map

01. Finisklin
02. Cumeen (part of)
03. Rathedmond
04. Ballydoogan
05. Oakfield or
    Derrydarragh (part of)
06. Knocknaganny (part of)
07. Maugheraboy
08. Knappagh Beg
09. Knappagh More
10. Caltragh (part of)

Streets & Estates within the Sligo
Urban Area
Adelaide St
Ardnaveigh
Ballydoogan
Beulla Tce
Cedar Drive
Charles St
Church Hill
Church St
College Road
Dominic St
Emmet Place

Far Finiskin
Fish Quay
Gallows Hill
Gibaraltar
Hanley Tce Temple St
Hanly Tce (Maugheraboy)
Harmony Hill
Jinks Ave
John St Upper
John St Lower
Kevinsfort (Barn Owl road
    ect)
Knappagh Road
Knocknarea Villas
Larkhill Road
Lord Edward St
Love Lane
Lyndale
Lynns Dock
Market Yard
Maugheraboy
Maugheraboy Estate
    (Willow Park ect)
Nazareth Home
New Houses on Sea Road

New St
O'Connell St
Oakfield Crescent
Oakfield Park
Oakfield Road
Orchard Lane
Quay St
Quay St Lower
Queens Store Road
Rockwood Parade (part of)
Rose Hill
Springhill Court
St Joseph's Tce
St Patrick's Tce
Sráid na Mara (Sea Road)
Summerhill Village
Temple St
The Park
The Park Ave
Thorn Hill
Tobergal Lane
Treacy Ave
WasteGarden
Wine St
Wolf Tone St

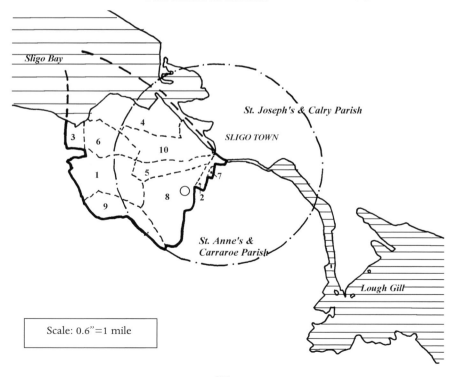

Scale: 0.6"=1 mile

Sligo: Parish of St Joseph's & Calry

(Calry) County Sligo
Churches: Ballytivnan & Calry

THE PARISH OF St Joseph's and Calry was created in 1988. Before this the ancient parish of Calry was a curacy within the Sligo Cathedral parish. Calry stretches along the north shore of Lough Gill and the north bank of the Garavogue river, which bisects Sligo town, thus the North Ward of Sligo lies wholly within Calry, and forms the urban St Joseph's section of the parish. The parish is one of great beauty, with the land falling gently from the slopes of Keelogyboy and Castlegal mountains to the island studded shores of Lough Gill. On the opposite shore lies the wooded highlands of Slieve Killery and Slieve Daéan, and the world-famous Isle of Inishfree. The former demesne of Hazelwood is located along the lakeshore. Previously known as Annagh, it formed part of the lands owned by the O'Connor-Sligo and subsequently by the Wynnes.

The name of Calry is derived from Calraidhe, the territory of the descendants of Cal. St Patrick is reported to have visited the area, as in the *Tripartite Life* it is mentioned that 'he went out to the districts of Callrigi Tremaige, and constructed a church at Drumlias, and baptised many, and erected and founded a church at the plain of Ailmaige, called Domnach Ailmaige'. Drumleane, a neighbouring parish in county Leitrim, formerly embraced most of the modern parish of Calry.

Inis Mór or Church Island

The two largest islands on Lough Gill, namely, Church Island or Inis Mór, and Cottage Island, each contain ecclesiastical remains. An early Christian ruin lies on Church Island and belonged to the O'Rourkes, chieftains of Breifne. In 1416, according to the Annals, 'the church of Inis Mór was burned, and Screaptra Ó Curnín and the Leabhar Gearr of the O'Curneens, as well as many other precious objects, were burned.' The church is said to have been founded by St Loman. The building is oblong, has loophole windows and a recess at one end. Near the door there is a cavity in a rock, known as 'Lady's Bed', which was a frequent place of pilgrimage for pregnant women. St Loman, whose feast day is on 4 February, is mentioned in the *Martyrology of*

Tallaght. The ruin on Cottage or Gallagher's Island belonged to the church of Kilross, in Riverstown parish, which in turn belonged to the Premonstratensians of Trinity Island on Loch Cé.

At Deerpark stand the remains of a court tomb, one of the best examples of its type in the country, dating from about 2000 BC. A religious site is reputed to have been sited on the same hill, a nunnery called Enach Ard, founded by the female saints, Osnat, Muadhnata and Talulla, all sisters of St Molaise of Inishmurray. In later years their successors moved the foundation downhill to Clogher, at a place called Teampall a' Chlochaire, on the shores of Lough Colga, in the modern burial ground of Cloghermore. St Connell's Well lies on the lakeshore in the townland of Clogher Beg.

An annual pilgrimage to a Mass Rock site, on the side of Edenbaun Mountain, has been revived in recent years. Among the names of Elphin diocesan priests listed during the penal days by Edmund Teige, vicar general of Clonmacnoise in 1668, were: Malachy Conry, Prebendary of Calry and Drumcliffe and Roger Harte, Perpetual Vicar of Ahamlish and Calry. By 1704 Calry parish was united with Sligo (St John's) parish, under Fr Denis Kerrigan as parish priest. He was ordained in 1685 by Bishop Dominic Burke of Elphin at Caltra in county Galway. In March 1744, at an enquiry at Sligo, Gilbert King, High Sheriff, recorded that 'Thomas Brennan, Frier at Cloghermore in the union of Sligoe did exercise Popish ecclesiastical jurisdiction in this county.' It is possible that this friar was attending the old church which stood at Churchfield or Chapelfield, to the right of the road leading down to Clogher cemetery. This church, possibly a Mass House, was probably in use up until the building of St Patrick's Church, Calry, in the very early nineteenth century. St Patrick's was renovated in the 1940s,

St Patrick's Church, Calry

and again in the 1990s. The sanctuary has been beautifully re-designed, with the installation of a reredos to incorporate the tabernacle, and which forms a fitting backdrop to the altar.

Owing to substantial population growth in the North Ward area of Sligo in the 1970s, the community felt the need for a new place of worship. People in the area had attended Sunday Mass in the chapel attached to St John's Hospital, but it was far too small to cater for an expanding population. In March 1983, Bishop Dominic Conway laid the foundation stone for a new church on a site donated by the Sisters of Mercy, adjacent to St John's Hospital. The stone was one of those which had been blessed by Pope John Paul II at Knock during the papal visit to Ireland in 1979.

The church was dedicated to St Joseph on 30 October 1983 by Bishop Conway.

St Joseph's Church,
Ballytivnan

The design used is very modern, consisting of a low pitched roof with strong buttress walls at each corner. The natural slope of the site allowed for the construction of a community centre under the church. The interior is plain, with wood and glass dominating, and the Stations of the Cross are depicted in stained-glass windows set into the side walls. The tabernacle stands in a curved reredos wall, which also incorporates stained glass representations of Pobal Dé. The entire wall behind the altar is glazed, offering panoramic views of Ben Bulben and Truskmore. In keeping with the relationship with the mountains, the altar is of roughly hewn limestone. In 1988, Ballytivnan became the parish church for the new parish of St Joseph's and Calry, thus restoring the ancient parish of Calry to parochial status.

Adjacent to the church is a burial ground, containing remains of countless numbers of victims who died in the nearby workhouse during the An Gorta Mór. A striking memorial was erected on this site on the occasion of the 150th anniversary of the Famine.

The Sisters of Mercy assumed the administration of the workhouse in 1899, on the invitation of the Board of Guardians, to care for the sick and elderly of Sligo. In the late 1960s, the old workhouse was demolished, and the Health Board built the modern hospital of St John's on the site. Today the sisters continue to work in the hospital, which now offers a range of rehabilitation and long-term care facilities for the elderly. In 1983, the Ursuline Sisters opened a house in Cartron, where they assumed the care of a Chapel of Adoration and assist in other pastoral works.

Calry Church of Ireland was built in 1823, to serve the substantial Anglican population on the north side of Sligo. The tall graceful spire has been a Sligo landmark for almost 180 years.

Key to the map

01. Annagh Island	11. Black Tom's Island	21. Cormorant Island
02. Ballure	12. Carncash	22. Corwillick
03. Ballyglass	13. Carrickoneilleen	_. Deerpark or Maghera-ghanrush (see 36)
04. Ballynamona	14. Carrowlustia	23. Doonally
05. Ballytivnan	15. Cartron	24. Edenbaun
06. Barroe	16. Church Island	25. Fairy Island
07. Bellanode	17. Clogherbeg	26. Farranacardy
08. Bellanurly	18. Cloghermore	27. Faughts
09. Bellawillin Beg	19. Clogherrevagh	28. Formoyle
10. Bernard's Island	20. Colgagh	

29. Glackbaun
30. Hazelwood Demense
31. Keelogyboy
32. Kiltycahill
33. Lisduff
34. Lisgorey
35. Loughanelteen
36. Magheraghanrush or
    Deerpark
37. Monk's Island
38. Mullaghgar
39. Rathbraughan
40. Rathquarter
41. Shannon Eighter
42. Shannon Oughter
43. St Connell's Island
44. Swan Island
45. Tiffin's Island
46. Tully
47. Willow Island
48. Willowbrook
49. Wolf Island

Streets & Estates in Urban Area

Ardaghowen
Ash Lane
Avondale
Ballinode
Barracks St
Bartons Smith's Promendae
Beechwood Court
Benbulben Tce
Cartron Bay
Cartron Heights
Cartron Point
Cartron Hill
Connaughton Rd
Dartry View
Duck St
Elm Park
Forthill
Fr Flannagan Tce
Glencarraig
Glendallan

Holborn Hill
Holborn St
Hyde Bridge
Lake Isle Rd
Markievicz Rd
Mulbury Park
Old Bundoran Rd
Rathbraughan Park
St Edward's Tce
St John's Tce
St Michael's Tce
Stephen St
The Mall
Yeats' Heights
Institute of Technology,
    Sligo

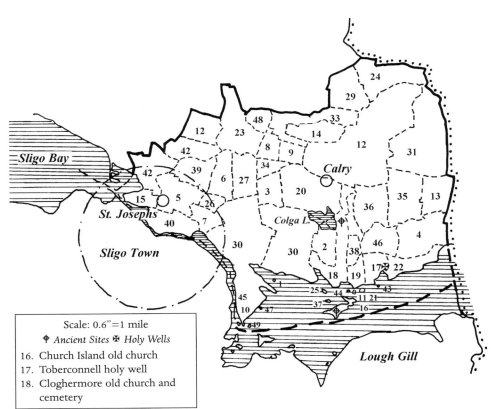

Scale: 0.6"=1 mile
✠ *Ancient Sites* ✠ *Holy Wells*
16. Church Island old church
17. Toberconnell holy well
18. Cloghermore old church and
    cemetery

Parish of Strokestown

(Kiltrustan, Lissonuffy, Bumlin & Cloonfinlough) County Roscommon
Churches: Strokestowm, Kiltrustan & Carniska

STROKESTOWN, or Béal Átha na mBúille, is the fifth largest town in county Roscommon situated in the easterly end of the diocese and adjoining the parishes of Kilglass, Tarmonbarry, Kilgefin, Kilbride, Tulsk, Elphin and Aughrim. It nestles at the foot of Sliabh Bán. Strokestown is an eighteenth-century planned town and one has to go to the hinterland to discover the antiquities of this modern heritage designated town. Derived from the Irish term for a fording place, Strokestown is today a fast developing residential town.

The parish is a combination of the ancient parishes of Kiltrustan, the greater part of Cloonfinlough, parts of Bumlin, Lissonuffy and more recently in 1909, a section of Killukin. The present shape of Strokestown results from the re-organisations of the 1850s, when some of the above-mentioned parishes, which straddled Sliabh Bán, were divided up to form more natural divisions.

Doorway in the west wall of Lissonuffy church

The earliest reference to Christianity in this parish appears in Kiltrustan, Kildallogue and Bumlin. There is a very strong tradition of St Patrick's visit to Kiltrustan and how he appointed Trustan over his newly-founded church. Tober Patrick (Tobar Phádraig) also suggests St Patrick's association with this locality. While in Kildallogue (Cill Lallóg) St Patrick left St Lallog in charge of his church there. St Barry made his sister, St Midabaria, patron of Bumlin (Buimlinn). A stained glass window depicting St Midabaria is to be found in the sanctuary of St Mary's Church Carniska (Carrownaskeagh).

The *Papal Taxation List* of 1306 names the following churches: Kiltrustan, Kildallogue, Bumlin, Lissonuffy, Kilverdon, and describes Cloonfinlough church as being in ruins. There is no evidence of a church in Cloonfinlough today except for the cemetery, which identifies the site of the medieval church. However, Lissonuffy church ruin still stands. We learn from the *Annals of the Four Masters* that the original name of this place is Lios na nDubhthaigh. Some of its present ruins date from the twelfth century.

The Canons Regular of St Augustine ministered in this parish for a considerable period of time and were subject to Cloontuskert Abbey. King Turlough O'Conor granted a considerable area of land on the north western and southeastern slopes of Sliabh Bán in Lissonuffy parish to the Abbey of Cong as appears from the *Rental of Cong Abbey* and recorded in 1501 by Tadhg O'Duffy, Abbot of Cong. Lissonuffy suffered like all other churches during the suppression and subsequent penal laws. The remains of a Christian settlement recently discovered on the summit of Sliabh Bán would indicate that a place of refuge was established there where people worshipped during the persecution era. In the *Report on the State of Popery,* 1731, Mass

St Mary's Church, Carniska

Houses are listed for Lissonuffy, Cloonfinlough and one Mass House to serve Bumlin and Kiltrustan, while in 1824 churches are listed for Strokestown, Kiltrustan and Carniska.

St Mary's Church, Carniska, is the place of worship for the greater part of Lissonuffy and Cloonfinlough ancient parishes. In the late eighteenth century the first church built in Carniska was a thatched penal chapel, which subsequently became the old school house after 1841. The present church was built in 1840-41 and was called St Mary's after Lissonuffy medieval church. Originally a barn church, it was partly rebuilt and remodelled in 1909-10 with further improvements carried out in 1954-55 and also in the post-conciliar era. Until 1849, Carniska, along with Curraghroe, served the united parishes of Lissonnufy and Cloonfinlough, the two halves of the parish being separated by Sliabh Bán. Since that date it has been a curacy of Strokestown, with Curraghroe passing to Tarmonbarry and subsequently to Kilgefin.

The ancient parish of Bumlin is now divided between the present day parishes of Tarmonbarry and Strokestown but the site of the medieval parish church is in the Strokestown area. There is little trace of it left except for a few featureless walls

The west window of Urney church

in Bumlin cemetery. The Kildallogue church already referred to seems to be a late medieval church sometimes called Urney (Urnaidhe). Kilverdon (Cill Bhearnáin), on the eastern edge of the parish, was once part of the parish of Kilglass, and is reputed to be one of the oldest cemeteries in the diocese. In 1704 both Kiltrustan and Bumlin are listed as united parishes. Local tradition tells us that there was a Mass House in the Caslin Hills during the penal period.

Strokestown's modern parish church is today situated in the townland of Lisroyne on Elphin Street in the town of Strokestown. Maurice Mahon, on 24 Februrary 1795, gave the site for the church, for a lease period of 999 years. Consequently, the first church in the town of Strokestown was erected in 1797-1798. It was a thatched mud-wall cabin. However, the church, dedicated to St Mary, proved to be too small to accommodate the large numbers of worshippers. Due to its deplorable condition, it was decided to build a new church in the late 1850s. As there was no other site available, the renowned Dean Michael Mc Dermott had the present structure erected around the old church and people continued to worship there while the new church was being constructed. The well-known English architect, George Goldie, was responsible for designing and planning the construction of the church.

Church of the Immaculate Conception, Strokestown

The new church was opened for divine worship on 14 May 1863 but it took many years afterwards to have it completed. The spire-mounted tower as planned was never added. It wasn't until 26 May 1871 that the church was finally dedicated. However, the building once again proved to be too small for its large congregations and in 1959-60 it was extended and reconstructed. It was re-dedicated on 15 July 1960 in honour of the Immaculate Conception and underwent further sanctuary alterations in the 1990s. It was solemnly re-dedicated on 31 October 1993. The Rev James Egan's chalice of 1633 is a unique piece of church silverware, preserved in the parish and recorded by the National Museum as an important artefact

On the northeastern end of the parish is the Kiltrustan area. Its old cemetery with its badly dilapidated single wall church ruin marks the site of the earliest church in this area. The present church of St Patrick was originally erected around 1840 as a barn chapel, but was extensively remodelled in 1871.

Further major improvements were carried out in 1901 including the fitting of a new marble altar. The solemn dedication of the church took place on 12 May 1901.

Considerable alteration again took place in 1973 to comply with the new liturgical norms of the second Vatican Council. The church was re-dedicated on 8 December 1974.

The parish was fortunate also to have the Sisters of Mercy from 1891 until the present time. Down through the years they have provided both primary and secondary education to generations of young people. The convent and chapel dedicated in honour of Our Lady of Good Counsel was opened on 28 October 1897. The Marist Brothers were part of the parish from June 1928 until July 1974. The brothers played an active role in the life of the parish and rendered a significant contribution to the education of the young through their very commendable apostolate.

Scoil Mhuire secondary school in Bawn Street was opened in 1937 and was the first Catholic co-education school in the diocese. It provided secondary education for boys and girls until 1967 when both the Convent secondary and Scoil Mhuire were amalgamated under the title of Scoil Mhuire which survives to the present day.

St John's Church of Ireland, built in 1819 to the plan of a medieval chapter house, is the only octagonal church of its period in Ireland

The local Church of Ireland community erected their church at the west end of the town, dedicated to St John. It was built in 1819 to the design of a semi-medieval chapter house and stands on the site of an earlier eighteenth-century church. St John's church was closed in 1980 and is now the County Heritage and Genealogy Centre providing a worldwide service for people tracing their county Roscommon roots.

The James Egan Chalice, dated 1633

Key to the map

1.	Aghaclogher	32.	Cloonslanor	64.	Kilclogherna
2.	Aghadangan	33.	Cloonsreane	65.	Kildalloge
3.	Aghalard	34.	Cloonycarran Beg	66.	Killultagh
4.	Annaghabeg	35.	Cloonycarran More	67.	Kilmore
5.	Annaghmore	36.	Cloonlyon	68.	Kiltrustan
6.	Ballinafad	37.	Coggalfortyacres	69.	Lackan (Kilgefin ED)
7.	Ballintemple	38.	Coggalkeenagh	70.	Largan
8.	Bally Beg	39.	Coggalmore	71.	Lavally
9.	Bally More	40.	Coggalstack	72.	Lettreen
10.	Ballyduffy	41.	Coggaltonroe	73.	Lisduff
11.	Ballyhammon	42.	Corboghil	74.	Lisheen
12.	Bellmount or	43.	Cordrumman	75.	Lismeehy
	Cloggernagh		(Creeve ED)	76.	Lisnahirka
13.	Bumlin	44.	Corgarrow	77.	Lisroyne
14.	Bunnamucka	45.	Corhawny	78.	Lissaphobble
15.	Caldragh	46.	Corraslira	79.	Lissonuffy
16.	Carroward	47.	Corskeagh	80.	Luggs
17.	Carrowclogher	48.	Cregga	81.	Mihanagh
18.	Carrownagullagh	49.	Creta	82.	Moher
19.	Carrownaskeagh	50.	Cuilmore	83.	Moyglass
20.	Carrowntryla	51.	Cuilrevagh		(Ballygarden ED)
21.	Carrownvally	52.	Curaghduffy	84.	Newtown
22.	Castlenode	53.	Curry	85.	Oakfield
–	Cloghernagh or		(Annaghmore ED)	86.	Rathmore (Creeve ED)
	Bellmount (see 12)	54.	Derreen	87.	Rattinagh
23.	Clooncah	55.	Doon	88.	Reagh
24.	Cloonearagh	56.	Doonard Beg	89.	Telton
25.	Clooneen (Hartland)	57.	Doonard More	90.	Toberpatrick
26.	Cloonfinlough	58.	Doughloon	91.	Tullen
27.	Cloonfree	59.	Falsk	92.	Vesnoy
28.	Cloonrabrackan	60.	Farnbeg		
29.	Cloonradoon	61.	Farnmore		
30.	Cloonrane	62.	Grange		
31.	Cloonshannagh		(Ballygarden ED)		
	(Creeve ED)	63.	Kilcloghan		

Brown sandstone font from the ruins at Lissonuffy

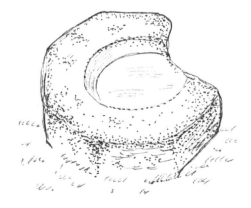

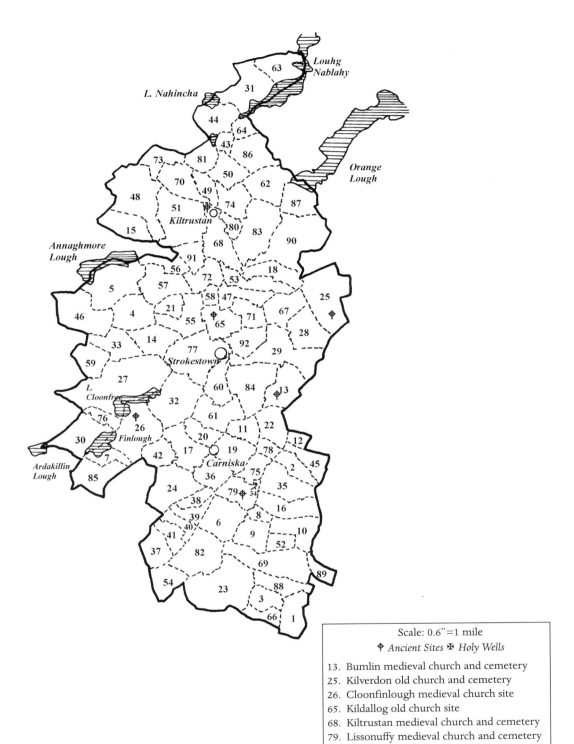

Louhg
Nablahy

L. Nahincha

63

31

44

64

43

86

73

81

50

70

49

62

48

51

74

Kiltrustan

80

83

15

68

90

Annaghmore
Lough

91

56

18

5

57

72

53

Orange
Lough

87

58

47

25

46

4

21

55

71

67

65

33

14

28

59

77

92

29

Strokestown

27

60

84

13

L.
Cloonfree

32

61

76

11

22

26

Finlough

20

12

30

17

19

78

7

42

36

75

45

Ardakillin
Lough

85

24

79

2

34

35

38

16

39

8

40

6

41

9

10

37

82

52

54

69

89

23

88

3

66

1

Scale: 0.6"=1 mile

✟ *Ancient Sites* ✠ *Holy Wells*

13. Bumlin medieval church and cemetery
25. Kilverdon old church and cemetery
26. Cloonfinlough medieval church site
65. Kildallog old church site
68. Kiltrustan medieval church and cemetery
79. Lissonuffy medieval church and cemetery

Parish of Tarmonbarry

(Kilbarry, Bumlin & Lissonuffy) County Roscommon
Churches: Whitehall & Scramogue

THE PARISH OF Tarmonbarry lies in northeastern Roscommon and is skirted by Ireland's major waterway, the River Shannon. This picturesque region of Roscommon is a haven for anglers, cruisers and seasonal tourists like its neighbouring parish of Kilglass. The bridge at Tarmonbarry village links the east with the west and Connacht with Leinster. The parish once formed part of the ancient political unit (tuath) called Cinéal Dubhthaigh, a territory which lay between Sliabh Bán and the River Shannon, and stretched from Carnadoe Bridge to Cloontuskert. O'Hanlys were the senior chieftains of this region and it was called Dúiche hAinlighe. The other parishes covered by this region were Kilglass and Lissonuffy.

The present parish of Tarmonbarry is bordered on the north by Strokestown and on the south by Kilgefin, and across the Shannon is the adjoining Diocese of Ardagh and Clonmacnoise. The parish has altered in shape following the re-organisation of parish boundaries implemented during the episcopate of Bishop Gillooly (1858-1895). The parish, under its ancient name of Kilbarry, reached from north of Rooskey to Tarmonbarry village. In 1879 the northern townlands in the Rooskey end of the parish were transferred from Tarmonbarry and assigned to Kilglass.

The ancient parish of Lissonuffy, lying south of Tarmonbarry, ceased to exist in November 1849 when its last parish priest, Fr Andrew Quinn, was transferred to Oran. Lissonuffy was divided in three and the southern portion of it was joined to Cloontuskert. However, the townlands of Derrycashel and Derryhanee were transferred to Tarmonbarry, with seven other townlands going to the new curacy of Scramogue, which had previously formed the greater part of the old parish of Bumlin. For some time Scramogue was joined to Kilglass, but has been attached to Tarmonbarry since 1879. Between 1880 and 1937 Curraghroe also formed part of Tarmonbarry, but was attached to Kilgefin after that date. Before these divisions, the old parishes of Lissonuffy, Bumlin, and Cloonfinlough straddled Sliabh Bán. Curraghroe chapel served the eastern end of Lissonuffy, and Carniska the western. In the old Bumlin parish, Scramogue served the eastern side, with Strokestown and Kiltrustan serving the west.

Stones from a Round Tower, in the cemetery wall at Kilbarry

328

Tarmonbarry derives its name from Termon or Sanctuary of St Berach (Barry). This sixth century saint, born at Cloone in county Leitrim, was of noble origin and descended from the race of Dobhtha. He was a disciple of St Dagaeus of Iniskeen (Iniscaoin) in county Louth, and for a time was under the care of St Kevin of Glendalough, from whom he received his staff (Bachall Gearr), as well as a bell called Clog Beraigh. There are a number of places where he is reputed to have established monastic cells, notably Kilbarrack (Cill Berach), the church of Berach, in county Dublin, and Díseart Beraigh or Berach's desert in Meath. It was from Meath that he came to Kilbarry where he established his principal foundation at Cluain Coirpthe. This important monastic site on the banks of the Shannon was an extensive foundation. It was a miniature of Clonmacnoise and must have looked quite impressive in early medieval times. According to John O'Donovan in 1837, 'This was St Berach's great monastery …. having been an ecclesiastical establishment of great importance.' The monastic foundations included Teampall Mór or Great Church, Teach Dorcha, Dir Teach, Teach Gael, Teampall Berach, as well as a round tower and a Tóchar or an ancient road which extended across the bog from Kilbarry to Newtown, the townland of the present church.

A short distance from this settlement was Tobar Beraigh, which was the focus of an annual pattern day on 15 August, although 15 February was the day of the saint's death, and is now his celebrated feastday. St Barry was renowned for his great holiness and charity which was his predominant virtue. People flocked to his monastery, especially those in need, and hospice care was provided for those sick in mind or body. In Teach Dorcha many people were cured of their mental ailments. St Barry is venerated as a missionary prophet and is depicted outside the present church of Whitehall standing in his boat.

While Barry died in the seventh century, his monastery continued to flourish for many centuries afterwards, and we learn that the settlement was plundered in 1238. The Comharba Beraigh, or successor-abbot of Cluain Coirpthe, was among those privileged to attend the inauguration of the Kings of Connacht. The 'Bachall Gearr Beraigh', or short crozier of St Berach, is preserved in the National Museum. It is the only relic linked to this early saint which has survived to the present day. The O'Hanlys, who were chieftains of this tuath or region, were the hereditary custodians of the Bachall Gearr until the Royal Irish Academy acquired it in 1863. There was much credence attached to the Bachall Gearr in former times and it was used for swearing upon in the settling of disputes.

Bachall Gearr Beraigh,
St Barry's crozier

There is very little left of the ancient monastic site today, and Kilbarry cemetery encloses the approximate extent of its foundation. There is evidence also of an ancient church at Cloonmore but nothing visible to the eye survives. In the *Papal Taxation List* of 1306, churches are listed for Kilbarry and Cloonmore, which were the sites of Patrician and medieval churches. There is no evidence of a Mass Rock in the parish during the penal period. However, according to the *Report on the State of Popery* in 1731, one Mass House existed, with Fr Hugh Cox as the parish priest, as well as one 'popish school'.

Tarmonbarry Parish Church, known as Whitehall Church *(Berna Chapman)*

In 1824, a parish chapel, known as Whitehall, was in existence in the townland of Newtown and was simultaneously used as a schoolhouse. In 1837, this church was still in place, but was replaced in 1896 by the present structure. This new church was designed by Patrick Kilgallen of Sligo, and constructed by Fees of Longford. Fr Eugene White PP (1886-1895) had worked hard to raise funds for the building of the new church in 1891, but was taken seriously ill, and the parish was administered by his brother, Fr William White (1891-1901), who was responsible for the erection of the church. This cruciform building consists of a chancel, nave and two transepts, and was solemnly dedicated in honour of the Sacred Heart and St Barry on 30 May 1897, by Bishop John Clancy of Elphin, assisted by Bishop John Healy of Clonfert and Bishop Joseph Hoare of Ardagh and Clonmacnoise.

At the other end of the parish in Scramogue is the Church of St Anne. This nineteenth-century church replaced an earlier one which stood three hundred yards northeast of the present building. While St Anne's Church was being erected in 1838-39, it was badly damaged during the Night of The Big Wind (6 Jan 1839). One of its walls had to be rebuilt, and an off-centre window in the transept is evidence of the reconstruction. The church, originally rectangular, was extended in 1885 to form the present cruciform design. It was solemnly blessed and re-opened for divine worship in 1886, and one hundred years later it was again extensively renovated and re-dedicated by Bishop Dominic Conway on 9 February 1986.

The parish, numerically the smallest in the diocese, is served by one priest, who resides in a presbytery erected in 1890, which stands about five hundred yards from the church at Whitehall. There are two schools in the parish, at Corraun and Cloonfower, both in the Tarmonbarry district.

Key to the map

01.	Aghamore
02.	Ashbrook or
	Knocknabarnaboy
03.	Ballyfeeny
04.	Ballygate
05.	Ballyhubert
06.	Ballymagrine
07.	Balytoohey
08.	Bellanamullia
09.	Bunnageddy (part of)
10.	Cloonfower
11.	Cloonmore
12.	Cloonshannagh
	(ED Bumlin)
13.	Cloonshannagh
	(ED Roosky)

14.	Cordrumman
15.	Coradrehid
16.	Corramagrine
17.	Corraun
18.	Cuilbeg
19.	Culliagh Lower
20.	Culliagh Upper
21.	Derrycashel
22.	Derryhanee
23.	Drinagh (part of)
24.	Garryglass
25.	Gortlustia
26.	Gorttoose
27.	Graffoge
28.	Kilbarry
29.	Killinordan

30.	Killinordanbeg
_.	Knocknabarnaboy
	(see 2)
31.	Lack
32.	Long Island
33.	Moneenacully
34.	Mongagh (part of)
35.	Newtown
36.	Northyard
37.	Pollymount
38.	Scramoge
39.	Tonycurneen
40.	Tooreen
41.	Treanacreeve

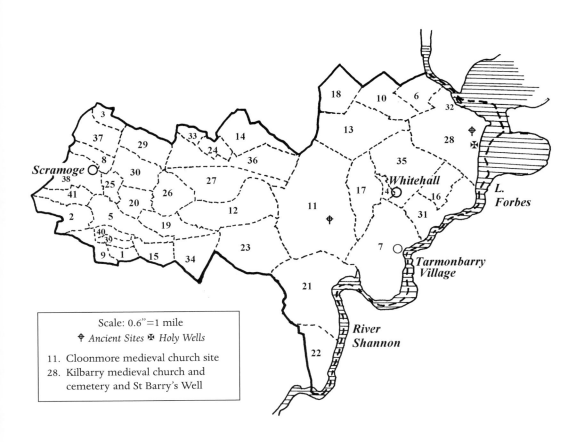

Scale: 0.6"=1 mile

✠ *Ancient Sites* ✠ *Holy Wells*

11. Cloonmore medieval church site
28. Kilbarry medieval church and
    cemetery and St Barry's Well

Parish of Tulsk

(Ogulla, Baslick, Killukin & Kilcooley) County Roscommon
Churches: Tulsk, Kilmurry & Killina

TULSK, formerly an incorporated market-town, a Parliamentary Borough, and the site of a strongly fortified castle erected by the O'Conors in 1406, is the name applied to the ancient parishes of Ogulla, Kilcooley, Killukin and Baslick. It is located in the centre of county Roscommon, at the junction of the main north-south route with the road from Castlebar to Dublin. Included within the parish boundaries is the ancient royal capital of Connacht at Rathcroghan (Cruachán), as well as the nearby coronation site at Carnfree, where the kings of Connacht were inaugurated. In pre-Christian times it was also a centre of druidic worship and a place of great assembly. In the village of Tulsk, the Cruachán Aí interpretative centre unfolds the unique storied past of the royal and druidic ceremonials associated with this national site. The name Tulsk comes from Tulach Uisce, the 'spring from the small hill', and refers to a stream issuing from a hill just north of the village.

Tulsk
Dominican
Abbey

In 1448 a Dominican abbey was founded at Tulsk by Phelim O'Conor who granted a quarter of land for that purpose. After its dissolution in the reign of Elizabeth, the lands were granted to one William Byrne, and in 1595 Sir Richard Bingham, Governor of Connacht, turned what remained of the conventual buildings into a fortification. The walls of the church and some of the dependencies of the abbey are still standing. The chief feature of what remains is a double-arched doorway, divided in the centre by a round pillar of elegant design. The east window is also partially intact. Both within and in the immediate vicinity of the church are a number of impressive tombs or mausoleums, notably those of the Plunkett, Grace, Kelly and Taaffe families. The parish today is dotted with the ruins of medieval churches which served as places of worship for many centuries. These include Baslick, Toberelva, Ogulla, Killynagh, Kilcooley, Rathmoyle and Killukin. While these churches are consigned to history, they have each contributed to the ecclesiastical heritage of the parish.

The first church built at Tulsk after the excesses of the seventeenth century was at Clooncullane (Kilcooley), about a mile from the village, on land given by the Plunketts of Ardkeenagh. It was a thatched building, and was demolished in the Night of the Big Wind in 1839. In response to this disaster, a new church, the present Church of Ss Eithne and Fidelma, was built in 1840-41. The foundation stone was laid on 20 April 1840 on a site provided by Daniel Kelly of Cargins, a 'highly respectable liberal Protestant', who also donated a church bell, and gave £50 to the building fund. Peter O'Conor of Toomona also donated £100 for the same purpose.

Tulsk church, which has the best examples of Irish stained glass artistry in the diocese

The church is in the Gothic revival style, cruciform in shape, with the altar in a columned recess. It is adorned in particular with two magnificent stained-glass windows. The chancel window, by Alfred E. Child (1875-1939), is regarded as one of his finest works, and was installed in 1914. It depicts the Baptism of Christ, Ecce Homo, the Resurrection, the Ascension and the four evangelists. The window in the north transcept was executed by artist Michael Healy (1855-1941), and commemorates the patronesses of the church, Ss Eithne and Fidelma, and their baptism at Ogulla well. There is also a memorial plaque to Fr Michael Lennon, parish priest of the united parishes of Ogulla, Kilcooley and Killukin from 1831 to 1871, and who was primarily responsible for having the church erected. Shortly before his death, the parish of Baslick, which forms the western end of the modern parish, was amalgamated with Ogulla. The church was extensively renovated in the late 1950s, following the building of a new parochial house in 1940. Foremost amongst the parish priests of

Tulsk was Monsignor James J. Kelly (1879-1888), a noted scholar and poet, and the author of *The Haunts of Goldsmith* and *Youthful Verses*.

The ancient parish of Baslick can claim historical associations dating back to the time of St Patrick, and the foundation of a church there in 433. A ruined church in the cemetery, which dates from the sixteenth or possibly seventeenth century, is believed to be on the same site as the Patrician foundation. The name Baslick is believed to have its origin in a tradition that Patrick brought relics there, and bestowed the name *Basilica Sanctorum* (Basilica of the Saints) on the site.

Fr Timothy O'Beirne was the last PP of Baslick before its union with Ogulla in 1868. He was buried in the old church in Kilmurry, and subsequently re-interred in the grounds of the new church. An attempt had been made to join Baslick with Kilcorkey (Ballinagare) in 1865, a move which encountered local opposition. The Bishop, Dr Browne, relented, and Baslick retained its own parish priest until the union with Ogulla three years later.

Kilmurry
church

According to tradition, the first church in Kilmurry (Cill Muire) was a thatched building in Glenvela. It was replaced in 1844 by a new building which was extended in 1860 and again at the end of the nineteenth century. A new church, designed by W. H. Byrne, was erected on an adjacent site in 1962, and took only fifteen months to complete. The foundation stone for this impressive church, with its free-standing bell-tower, was blessed in 1962. Five months later it was dedicated to St Paul by Bishop Hanly on 17 September 1962. The old church was renovated and converted to a Community Centre and opened for that purpose in 1976.

Killina
church

St Patrick's Church, Killina, in the townland of Cloony-quinn, was opened for divine worship in 1860, as its date-stone indicates. It replaced an earlier church in the townland of Flaskagh. Fr Joseph Egan, parish priest of Elphin, was responsible for its erection, as Killina was part of the parish of Elphin at that time. The church is called Killina after the ancient church of Killynaghmore, which is listed in the *Papal Taxation List* of 1306, and whose ruins survive in Killina old cemetery. Cloonyquinn, the birthplace of Percy French (1854-

1920), has been immortalised by Ireland's great troubadour. His eighteenth-century ancestral home is now demolished, but the site is commemorated by a sculptured memorial.

The parish church in Tulsk village gets its name from the two Celtic princesses, Eithne and Fidelma, daughters of the High King, whom St Patrick baptised at the fountain or well of Clebach, near Royal Rathcroghan. The sisters had the rather dubious reward of dying almost immediately after their conversion, and were buried near the well of Ogulla. It is thought that the name of the area comes from St Oigh-Ghiolla, (Servant of the Virgins), who ministered there in the sixth century. This would seem to suggest that a small monastic structure grew up near the graves of Eithne and Fidelma.

St Patrick baptising Eithne and Fidelma at Ogulla Well. *(From a stained glass window by Harry Clarke)*

There are several holy wells in the parish, notably St Patrick's Well, Corragreigh, St Brigid's Well, Cloonybeirne, St Colmcille's Well, Carrowbunnane and the widely known Ogulla Holy Well. A pilgrimage to the latter, on the last Sunday in July (Garland Sunday), was revived in 1974, and continues to the present time. The remains of a fragment of a decorated twelfth-century high cross was discovered at one of the stations at the site of the holy well at Ogulla which further confirms the importance of this ancient holy site.

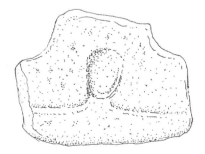 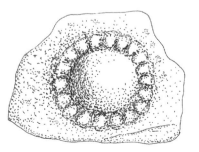

Fragments from the twelfth-century Ogulla High Cross, depicting Christ crucified on one side and a boss with floral petal elements on the other

Key to the map

01. Aghloonagh	42. Cloonkilly More	83. Killynagh More
02. Ardakillin	43. Cloonanart Beg	84. Kilmurry
03. Ardeevin	44. Cloonanart More	85. Kilnanooan
04. Ardkeenagh	45. Cloonastiallas	86. Kilree
05. Ardkeenagh (Plunkett)	46. Cloonbard	87. Knockalegan East
06. Attiballa	47. Clooncor	88. Knockalegan West
07. Ballaghabawbeg	48. Clooncullaan	89. Knockavurrea
08. Ballaghabawmore	49. Clooncunny	90. Laghtcausk
09. Ballindollaghan (Crumps)	50. Clooneigh	91. Lisheen
10. Ballindollaghan (Knox)	51. Cloonmahaan	92. Lismurtagh (Castlerea By)
11. Balloony	52. Cloonmurray	93. Lismurtagh (Roscommon By)
13. Ballybroghan	53. Cloonybeirne	94. Lisnaneane
14. Ballydaly	54. Cloonyogan	95. Lissacurkia
15. Ballyglass (Castlerea By)	55. Cloonyquin	96. Lissalway
16. Ballyglass (Roscommon By)	56. Corbally	97. Lissaphuca
17. Baslick	57. Corker	98. Lissawaddy
18. Bloomfield	58. Corlis	99. Manor
19. Boyanagh	59. Corrabaun	100. Milltown
20. Caddellbrook	60. Corrabeg	101. Moneyboy
21. Cammoge	61. Corracreigh	102. Mullygollan
22. Cargin Demense	62. Corragarve	103. Nadnaveagh
23. Carnkit	63. Correagh	104. Ogulla
24. Carns	64. Derryphatten	105. Pollranny
25. Carrigeennagappul	65. Derryquirk	106. Rahardagh
26. Carrowbaun	66. Drimnagh	107. Rathfuadagh
27. Carrowgarve	67. Drishaghaun East	108. Rathkeva
28. Carrowgobbagagh	68. Drishaghaun West	109. Rathmore
29. Carrowkeel (ED Castleplunkett)	69. Emlagh	110. Rathmoyle
30. Carrowkeel (ED Ogulla)	70. Farranawillin	111. Rathnagyle
31. Carrownageelaun	71. Flaskagh Beg	112. Rusheen
32. Carrownaskeagh	72. Flaskagh More	113. Sheegeeragh
33. Carrownrinny	73. Foxborough	114. Slevin
34. Carrowntoosan	74. Glenballythomas (part of)	115. Sroove
35. Cartron	75. Glenvela	116. Steill
36. Castleland	76. Gortnasillagh	117. Toberelva
37. Castleplunkett	77. Grange	118. Tonereagh
38. Castleruby	78. Heathfield	119. Tonroe
40. Clashaganny	79. Kanefield	120. Toomona
41. Cloonkilly Beg	80. Kilcooley	121. Tullintuppeen
	81. Killukin	122.
	82. Killynagh Beg	

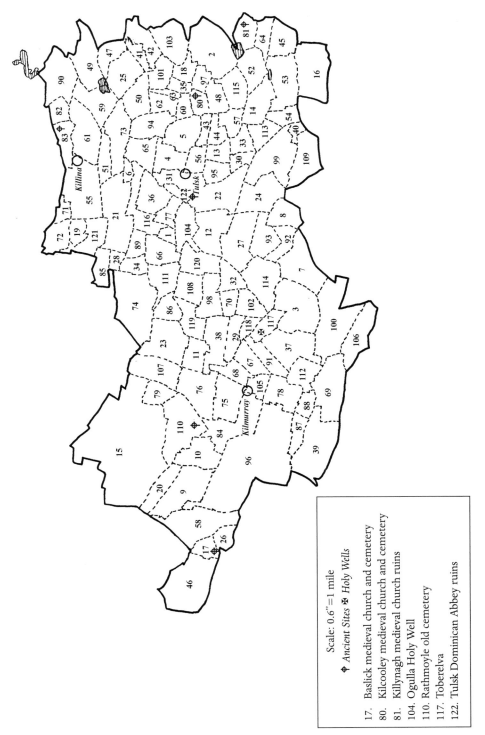

Scale: 0.6"=1 mile
✠ Ancient Sites ✠ Holy Wells

17. Baslick medieval church and cemetery
80. Kilcooley medieval church and cemetery
81. Killynagh medieval church ruins
104. Ogulla Holy Well
110. Rathmoyle old cemetery
117. Toberelva
122. Tulsk Dominican Abbey ruins

Patron Saints of the Parishes

Extracted from an article by Mgr J. J. Kelly, Athlone, and published in the *Irish Ecclesiastical Record, vol. xvi, 1904.*

Sligo Cathedral Parish (including Coolera & Calry)

8 Dec	Sligo Cathedral: The Immaculate Conception. The BVM under this title is also Patron of the diocese.
24 Jun	St John the Baptist.
8 Jun	Coolera: St Bron, or Bronus (Lat.), Bishop. His church still remaining is called Kilaspugbrone, i.e., the Church of Bishop Bron.
15 Jun	St Dermot of Kilmacowen, brother of St Evin.
4 Feb	Calry: St Loman (Lomanus) of Lough Gill.

Aghanagh Parish

24 Nov	Aghanagh (Ballinafad): St Maine, grandson of Eoghan. His holy well, Tuber Maine, is near the church of Aghanagh. In the *Naem Senchus* (versified genealogies of saints, *Book of Ballymote*, 230a, l. 45), Bishop Maine is given as son of Eichten, son of Eoghan.

Ahamlish Parish

12 Aug	Ahamlish: St Molaise or Laisren, son of Declan, was founder of Inismuireadhaigh, Innismurry. There is another St Molaise, of Devenish, son of Naitfraioch, whose festival is on the 12 Sept.
27 Oct	Dicuill, son of Menide, Abbot of Inishmurray, died AD 752.
1 Feb	Cliffoney: St Brigid.

Ahascragh Parish

15 Oct	Ahascragh: St Cuan, Cuanus (Lat.). The name of the place as given by the Four Masters is Áth Eascrath Cuain, the ford of (St) Cuan's sand-ridge. His well, near the town of Ahascragh, is still a holy well, where a pattern is held on 15 October, and where stations are still frequently performed. St Cuanna of Lismore, 4 Feb, seems to be different from St Cuan of Ahascragh.

Ardcarne Parish

8 Mar	Ardcarne: St Beoadh, bishop, Beoadus (Lat.). Died 524.

5 Jul   Tumna: St Etain of Tumna. This virgin is still vividly remembered at Tumna, now belonging to Croghan, and her grave is shown in the churchyard.

Athleague Parish

7 Feb   Athleague: St Maenucan. This parish was called Áth Liag Maenucain in his memory. It is to be distinguished from Áth Liag na Sinna (of the Shannon), now Ballyleague, at Lanesboro. Both places were in Hy-Many.

9 Sept   Fuerty: St Kieran of Clonmacnoise. There is still a vivid tradition of St Kieran who is reputed to have been born in this parish.

15 Jun   St Juis, or Justus, deacon, who baptised Kieran Mac an tSaoir (son of the wright), from Patrick's book.

Athlone Parish (St Peter's)

29 Jun   Athlone, St Peter's: St Peter, Apostle.

1 Feb   Drum: St Brigid. The church whose ruins still remain was dedicated to her. Her well is outside the churchyard wall. It was anciently called Drum Drestan, and also Drum na bhfeadh, i.e., the fayes or woods of O'Naughten's country. The church of St Brigid at Drum-Drestan had a right to one-third of the baptismal fees of the race of Hy-Maine.

1 Feb   Clonown: St Brigid. St Brigid's well is there. The Church of St Brigid at Cluain-Eamhain had one-third of the baptismal offerings of the O'Kellys of Hy-Many.

18 Feb   St Uidhrin of Drumdresna.

4 Jun   St Colum[ba], priest of Clonown.

1 Jul   St Ailill, bishop, Clonown.

Aughrim Parish

23 Feb   Aughrim and Clooncraff: St Finnian.

1 Feb   Kilmore: St Brigid and St Cocha. There are still traces of two churches there; one dedicated to St Brigid, the other, Kilcock, to St Cocha.

17 Mar   St Patrick, who founded the church of Kilmore.

10 Nov   St Loeghaire.

Ballinameen Parish

6 Feb   Kilnamanagh, Ballinameen, Kilcolagh: St Dabonna.

Ballintubber Parish

1st Feb   Ballintubber: St Brigid. In the ancient annals the place is called Baile

Tobar Brighde, i.e., the town of Brigid's well, which is still there. In the plain of Magh-Ai or Maghery-Connacht, Co Roscommon, St Brigid founded a monastery and dwelt for some considerable time. She also established different cells and convents in that district, according to the rule which she had formed. The plain of Magh-Ai extended from near the town of Roscommon to the verge of the barony of Boyle, and from Strokestown westward to Castlerea. In this territory, Kilbride, a parish adjoining that of Roscommon, perpetuates in its very name the memory of her church; and within its area, in the demesne of Holywell, St Brigid's Holy Well may still be seen.

27 Jan   St Crone, virgin. Kilcrone, now belonging to Ballymoe, was formerly part of the parish of Drumatemple. Kilcrone, the church of St Crone.

Ballyforan Parish

1 Feb   Dysart: St Brigid.

17 Sept   Dysart: St Grellan. Moy Senchenoil is situated on the banks of the river Suck, about half a mile south of Mount Talbot Bridge, in this parish.

Ballygar Parish

16 May   Killian, Killeroran, Ballygar: St Ita, the foster-mother of St Brendan. St Brendan's well has been a place of pilgrimage.

Boyle Parish

16 Jun   Boyle: St Cethec, or Cethiacus, bishop.

7 Jul   St Comgilla or Comgell, daughter of Dermot, placed there by St Patrick.

8 Mar   St Dachonna of Assylin, placed there by St Colmcille.

9 Feb   St Conell of Drum (Drumconnell, near Boyle).

9 Jun   St Colmcille.

Castlerea Parish

3 Nov   Kilkeevan: St Coemhan (Keevan). Kilkeevan, Coemhan's church, where St Patrick left Deacon Coemhan. St Coemhan is said to have been the chamberlain of St Patrick.

9 Sept   St Coelainn, Virgin. The Termon of [St] Coelain (Termon Coelaine) now called Tarmon, in this parish, a mile north-east of the town of Castlerea. Her holy well, Tober Coelain, is in the townland of Moore.

Croghan Parish

7 Jun   Killucan: St Lunicarnia.

19 Feb   Croghan, Eastersnow, Killumod: St Nuadha (pr. Nóah) of Lough
          Uama (Cavetown). (Disert Nuadhat, phonetically Ister Nuadhat =
          Eastersnow), Anchorite, also Abbot of Armagh.

Drumcliff Parish (including Rosses Point & Maugherow)

9 Jun   Drumcliff: St Colmcille. In the *Martyrology of Donegal*, it is related that
          St Colmcille founded the monastery of Drumcliffe, and placed there
          St Mothorian.

9 Jun   St Mothorac, its first abbot.

Elphin Parish

27 Apr   Elphin: St Asicus, first Bishop and Patron of the diocese.

17 Sept   Creeve: St Grellan, Patron of Hy-Many. From him the place was called
          Creeve-Grellan, branching tree of Grellan.

Fairymount Parish

          St Lalloc of Fairymount.

19 Feb   Tibohine: St Baoithine (Bohene). The place was called Teach Baoithine
          Airtigh, Tibohine Artagh, i.e., house (or church) of Baoithine, of the
          territory of Airteach.

Frenchpark Parish

26 Apr   Frenchpark: St Donaldus, son of Crimthan, Bishop of Ailech Airtig (in
          the demesne of Frenchpark), a disciple of St Patrick.

21 Jul   Kilcorkey: Church of St Curcach of Gregraighe (St Corcasia, Lat.).
          She was the sister of St Frigidian of Lucca.

5 Aug   St Comitius (Comedius) of Cloonshanville.

Geevagh Parish

1 Aug   Geevagh: St Ailbhe (Albaeus) priest, placed there (at Duma Graid) by
          St Patrick. In the *Annals of the Four Masters,* anno 545, is recorded the
          death of St Ailbe, of Seanchu-Ua-Oiliolla. His well, Tubber Elive, is in
          the townland of Killamey in Geevagh.

25 Jul   St James the Greater. His well, still called St James's Well, in Shancough,
          is held in veneration. A pattern was formerly held at it on St James's
          day, 25 July.

Kilbegnet Parish

9 Jun   Kilbegnet, Ballinakill, Kilcrone: St Colmcille.

4 Feb   Kilbegnet: St Begnata. In the *Life of St Cuan of Ahascragh* it is mentioned that he had a sister named St Begnata, who seems to be the patron of Kilbegnet.

Kilbride Parish

1 Feb   Kilbride: St Brigid's Church. She dwelt for some years in the plain of Roscommon, where she founded cells and convents. Within the parish of Kilbride her holy well may still be seen.

Kilgefin Parish

26 July   Cloontuskert: St Faithlec. His well is in the townland of Killaghy.

27 Jul   Kilgefin: St Diraidh, or Diradius, founder of Eadardruim, in Tuath Ainlighe, O'Hanly's Country, now called Drumdaff, in the parish of Kilbride.

Kilglass Parish

17 Mar   Kilglass and Rooskey: St Patrick. The church of Kilglass was founded by St Patrick.

Kiltoom & Cam Parish

5 Aug   Kiltoom: St Feith.

1st Feb   Cam: St Brigid. This parish was called Cammach Brighidi, now Camma or Cam, the winding or crooked glen. The old church of this parish, which, as its name imports, was dedicated to St Brigid, lies about six miles north-west from the town of Athlone. In the *Tribes and Customs of Hy-Many* it says: 'one of the seven principal Coarbs of Hy-Many, there enumerated, is the Coarb of Camach Brighdi, where the people of Hy-Many are baptised. St Brigid has the baptism of the race of Maine, and although the baptism may not be brought thither (to her church), her Coarb has the power of collecting the baptismal penny from these tribes; and it (the money thus obtained) is divided into three parts, of which one-third is given to herself (i.e., to her Coarb), one-third to Druim Drestan (Drum, near Athlone), and one-third to Cluain Eamhain (Cloonown).' The celebrated Holy Well of St Brigid, Tobar Brighde, now generally called in English, Brideswell, is there. This was one of the most famous shrines in ancient Ireland. Sir Randall Mac Donnell, the first Earl of Antrim, and his Countess, came there as pilgrims in 1625, as appears from an inscription left by him over the doorway of the old chapel. The well is still venerated. Pilgrimages are made, and patterns are held there.

31 Mar   St Colman of Camma, near Kiltomb.

Knockcroghery Parish

29 Aug   St John's, Kilmeane, Killinvoy, Rahara: St John. The priory of the Knights Hospitallers of St John was one of two religious establishments in the parish. The parish association with St John dates from its establishment.

Loughglynn Parish

30 Sept   Loughlin, Lisacull: St Mocona was placed over Clonard (Cluain Ardne) in this parish. He died in 713.

1 Feb   Kilsellagh was dedicated to St Brigid, according to Dr Beotius Egan, Bishop of Elphin. Her well is near the old ruin. The noble priest, Rodanus, was placed over the church of Senchell Dumaigi (Kilrodan) by St Patrick .

Oran Parish

16 Jun   Oran: St Cethec (Lat. Cethegus) buried there. The well was blessed by St Patrick, who founded at Oran a church called Cill-Garad, where Bishop Cethec was left and where he died. The Uarán or cold well from which the place takes its name, is still held holy and frequented by pilgrims.

Riverstown Parish

13 Jun   Riverstown, Tawnagh, Drumcolumb, Kilross, Ballinakill: St Cairell. St Patrick founded a church in Tawnagh, where he left St Cairell. St Patrick's well is in Tawnagh. A pattern is held there on 17 March.

9 June   St Colmcille. Drumcolumb church was founded by St Colmcille.

15 Feb   St Finnian, abbot. Kilross or Sooey was dedicated to St Finnian of Clonard, who visited this parish.

Roscommon Parish

26 Dec   Roscommon and Kilteevan: St Coman. Roscommon, Coman's Grove, (Ros Chomáin). His church and monastry were in Church Street where the Protestant church now stands. In 1170 his relics were placed in a splendid shrine, by O'Carmacan, his successor. St Coman's well, called Dábhach Chomáin (vat of Coman), is still in existence, and lies in a field to the east of the town, in the townland of Ballypheason (Baile an Phearsúin), still called the 'Hummaun Field', Coman's field.

1 Feb   Kilteevan: St Brigid. The old church of Kilteevan was dedicated to St Brigid. Her well is near the church.

Strokestown Parish

22 Feb   Bumlin (Buimlinn): St Midabaria, the sister of St Berach of Tarmonbarry, is the patron of this parish. Her old church of Bumlin and graveyard are part of the parish of Strokestown.

17 Mar   Kiltrustan: St Patrick. His well is Tober Patrick. The tradition is that St Patrick founded the church of Kiltrustan. These parishes were in the ancient territory of Corcoghlan. The parish and church of Bumlin were called the prebend of Kilcoghlan.

Tarmonbarry Parish

15 Feb   Tarmon Barry, the Termon or Sanctuary of St Berach or Barry, who lived about AD 580. He was of the tribe of O'Hanly or Kinel Dobhtha. The ruins of his church, Kilbarry, still remain.

Tulsk Parish

1 Aug   Baslic (from 'basilica'): St Sacel or Sacellus (Lat.) placed there by St Patrick.

26 Feb   Ogulla, Kilcooley, Killukin: St Ethnea and St Fidelm, or Fidelmia. Ogulla means the Tomb of the Virgins, Og-ullad, virgin tomb; so called from the saints Ethna and Fidelma, daughters of Laoghaire, monarch of Ireland, converted, instructed, and baptised by St Patrick, at the well of Ogulla, near Tulsk, beside the ruins and graveyard of Ogulla.

4 Jul   St Bolcanus of Kilcooley.

3 Apr   St Benatius of Kilcooley. The ruin and graveyard of Kilcooley are on the road between Tulsk and Strokestown. It was formerly a parish. St Felart, (Felartus, Lat.) bishop, on whose altar one of the patens made by St Asicus was used, was placed by St Patrick over the Domnach Mor of Magh Sealga, at Cams near Tulsk and Rathcroghan.

Saints from the region of Hy-Many

17 Sept   St Grellan. The inhabitants of those parts of Roscommon and Galway, which formerly comprised the territory of Hy-Many, or O'Kelly's Country, have always honoured St Grellan as the special patron of their race and country. Hy-Many comprised the baronies of Athlone, Moycarnan, and part of Kilian. It extended on the north from Bally-moe to Lanesboro, and through the barony of Athlone to Ahascragh and Caltra.

            The race of Maine, both women and men, pay a sgreaball caethrach (tribute in sheep) to St Grellan. St Grellan presides over their battles, i.e., the crozier of St Grellan is borne in the standard of the King of Hy-Many.

9 Feb   St Cairech or Cairigia, sister of St Enda of Arran, was regarded by the female branch of the O'Kellys as their special patron. Her monastery was at Cloonburren, on the banks of the Shannon, opposite Clonmacnoise. Seven garments are given by the queen to St Cairech Dergain yearly, and a penny by every Hy-Manian daughter, along with the tribute to St Ciaran.

9 Feb   Dairech of Dergan.

A sheet iron bell
found at St John's
c. 1861

345

A Bibliography
towards a history of the Diocese of Elphin

T HE DIOCESE, and its constituent parishes, have long been used as units of study by local historians. They both represent communities of interest which have endured over a long time span. The Diocese of Elphin as we know it today traces its origins from the twelfth century. While it covers a wide area of divergent geography from the Sligo coastline through the majestic Ben Bulben, the Curlew mountains, the limestone lowlands of Roscommon to the flood plains of the Shannon south of Athlone, it is united in its shared faith and its allegiance to its bishops over the centuries. The individual parishes, widely dispersed geographically, are united by the same faith and are interlinked by kindred ties at the micro level and by the constant movement of diocesan clergy at the macro level.

One of the principal tasks any historian has to undertake before writing a history is to survey the available sources. The study of any place or community over a time span of 1500 years presents particular problems with the availability of source material from the early period. The sources for the early period are for the most part available only in later collections and translations.

The purpose of this bibliography is to give the reader and future historians of the diocese a listing of sources which would be of use to them in writing a history of the diocese or any of its parishes. We do not presume this to be a complete bibliography of sources as such a compilation could not be completed in the time available to this group and new sources are coming on stream each year. There is, no doubt, a wealth of sources available in many repositories outside Ireland relating to the diocese, particularly in Rome, the investigation of which is beyond the scope of the present work. The majority of the sources listed here are secondary, but many will lead the enthusiast to the primary sources. Each source listed is followed by a short account of what will be found in that source. This is given as an aid to future historians in deciding on the appropriateness of any particular source for the task they may wish to undertake. It is hoped that the bibliography will be of benefit to students at both second and third level educational institutions in any research they undertake on the history of the diocese.

This bibliography is divided into three parts. The first part lists sources which are concerned with the diocese as a whole or with individual bishops. Some of the sources listed here are general works of reference which do contain references to the diocese but which were not collected with ecclesiastical history in mind, as is the case with some of the British Parliamentary Papers listed. The second part is a listing of sources concerned with the many foundations by religious orders in the diocese. These are mostly from the medieval and late medieval period. Also included here are sources on the history of the teaching and nursing orders of men and women who came to the diocese in the nineteenth and twentieth centuries. The third part of the bibliography deals with sources for individual parishes. This, it is hoped, will be of help to those whose interest is in their own particular parish. The amount of material available for parishes varies greatly but it should be borne in mind that many of the sources found in the other two parts of the bibliography are also appropriate for the study of particular parishes.

Abbreviations used:
R.H.S.A.J.: Roscommon Historical and Archaeological Society Journal
R.A.D.Y.: Roscommon Association Dublin Yearbook
E.D.A.: Elphin Diocesan Archive, St Mary's, Sligo

PART 1: DIOCESE

Angelus. The

Autumn 1959, VOL. 1, NO. 3: Pilgrimage to grave of St Asicus.

December 1959, VOL. 1, NO. 4 & March 1960, VOL. 2 , NO. 8: The cross of Roscommon.

October 1960, VOL. 2, NO. 7 and December 1960, VOL.2, NO. 8: St. Patrick in Caiseal Irra.

March 1961, VOL. 3, NO. 9: Education in the Diocese of Elphin.

October 1961, VOL. 3, NO. 10: St Patrick's churches in Elphin Diocese.

Spring 1963, VOL. 5, NO. 1: Mainchin Mac Collain of Kilmacallan.

Spring 1970, VOL. 1, NO. 3: Elphin bishops of the eighteenth and nineteenth centuries.

May 1974, VOL. 3, NO. 5: Homage to St Asicus: first diocesan pilgrimage.

December 1974, VOL. 3, NO. 12: A tribute to the late Bishop Hanly.

January 1975, VOL. 4, NO 1: Laurence Gillooly, Bishop of Elphin.

February 1975, VOL. 4, NO. 2: Diocesan Cathedral 100 years ago

March 1975, VOL. 4, NO. 3: Summaries of contributions and expenditure towards erection of a Cathedral of Elphin, 1876.

April 1975, VOL. 4, NO 4, pp. 8-9: Our diocesan heritage; Bishop Gillooly and the National Association.

Dr Gillooly's letter of convocation for aggregate meeting of the National Association, set up mainly to campaign for abolition of Church of Ireland Establishment, and his address on proposal of resolution on education to that meeting.

May 1975, VOL. 4, NO. 5: Bishop Gillooly and the temporal sovereignty of the Pope.

June 1975, VOL. 4, NO. 6: Opening of Cathedral 1874 (reprinted from *Sligo Chronicle*)

This article deals with the consecration of the altars and other religious objects in the cathedral together with the Episcopal High Mass for deceased benefactors. An excursion to Lough Gill by clergy and laity is described. This article is reprinted from *The Sligo Chronicle* 8 Aug 1874.

October 1975, VOL. 4, NO. 10, p. 9 and p. 11: John Brett Bishop of Elphin 1748-1756 by Rev John McGeevy.

A scholarly account of the life and times of Bishop Brett, the last Dominican Bishop of Elphin.

October 1975, VOL. 4, NO. 10, p. 1: St Oliver Plunkett – Pastoral letter of the Bishops of Ireland by Bishop Dominic Conway.

Refers to the times of Saint Oliver Plunkett in Ireland after his return from Rome in 1670.

December 1975, VOL. 4, NO. 12: Diocesan Cathedral reopened.

February 1979, VOL. 8, NO. 1: Father Michael O'Flanagan.

April 1982, VOL. 11, NO. 4: The story of old Summerhill.

Explains the role of Bishop Browne and of Bishop Gillooly in the development of educational facilities at Summerhill, Athlone, in the mid 1800s. It also follows the changes, which have taken place there from 1844 to the present second level college run by the Sisters of Mercy.

October 1983, VOL. 13, NO. 10: Elphin: Birth place of Diocese and site of first cathedral in the diocese.

Outlines the history of the cathedral until its demolition in 1964. The article was written to mark the completion of restoration work at the ruin in 1983.

November 1983, VOL. 13, NO. 11, p. 3: Topographical notes of the late Archdeacon Michael J. Connellan on Elphin Diocesan Chapter.

The origin of Elphin Diocesan Chapter and explanatory notes on the origin of the prebends.

January 1984, VOL. 14, NO 1: Topographical notes of the late Archdeacon Michael J. Connellan. This article gives a list of churches in Elphin from a taxation list of 1306 as well as some explanation of the placenames and the difficulties in interpreting them.

September 1986, VOL 17, NO 7: The work of Father Flanagan.

An article by Fr Val Peter, Director of Boystown, on Fr Flanagan.

September 1986, VOL. 17, NO. 7: Father Flanagan of Boystown by Fr Kevin Early.

July-August 1987, VOL. 18, NO. 6: Our Lady in Elphin Diocese.

March 1988, VOL. 19, NO. 2: Summerhill College prepares for centenary.

June 1990, VOL. 21, NO. 6: Stained glass windows in Elphin Diocese.

July-August 1994, VOL. 25, NO. 6: Ordination of Christopher Jones, Bishop of Elphin.

August-September 1996, VOL. 27, NO. 6: Death of Bishop Conway.

August-September 1997, VOL. 28, NO. 5: St. Columba: fourteenth century.

Sligo Champion

4 December 1858: Death of Dr Browne, Bishop of Elphin.

18 July 1874: Consecration of the Cathedral of Elphin, Sligo.

15 January 1895: Death of Most Rev Dr. Gillooly, Lord Bishop of Elphin.

30 March 1895: Consecration of Dr Clancy, Bishop of Elphin.

26 October 1912: Sligo's great loss: Most Rev Dr Clancy's death.

24 July 1926: The late Bishop Coyne: loss to Diocese of Elphin.

22 February 1930 and 23 March 1930: Lough Gill and St. Loman.

5 April 1930, Impressive ceremonies at Sligo Cathedral: formal opening of New Entrance, Photo included.

Report of High Mass of Thanksgiving Sunday 31 March 1930 and concert. Gives a description of architecture of the building.

26 March 1936: Bishop's Palace destroyed by fire.

Centenary No. 1936, p. 21: Six bishops of Elphin.

Biographical sketches of Bishops Burke, Browne, Gillooly, Clancy, Coyne and Doorly.

8 April 1950: Death of Elphin's well loved Bishop: priests and people mourn passing of Dr Doorly.

29 July 1950: New Bishop of Elphin appointed.

4 May 1957: Pilgrimage to the grave of St Asicus.

13 November 1970: Death of Bishop of Elphin: Vincent Hanly DD.

Roscommon Herald

26 October 1867: New Diocesan Cathedral.

1 August 1874: Consecration of Cathedral, Sligo.

10 September 1892: New College of the Immaculate Conception, Sligo formally opened.

26 October 1912: Death of Most Rev Dr Clancy.

24 July 1926: Death of Most Rev Dr Coyne.

26 December 1936: The late Bishop O'Doherty of Galway.

8 April 1950: West mourns death of great Bishop.

15 April 1950: Bishop Doorly laid to rest.

24 March 1962: Missionary Order's founder commemorated (Mgr Whitney).

16 May 1964: Cathedral demolished in Elphin.

20 November 1970: Bishop Hanly laid to rest.

   Consecration in Rome of Monsignor Conway.

23 April 1971: The enthronement of Bishop Conway.

12 December 1975: Impressive ceremony as Cathedral is re-opened.

17 July 1987: Roscommon born priest is bishop of Killala.

8 February 1991: George Thomas Plunkett, Bishop of Elphin 1814-1827.

Roscommon Journal

13 September 1856: Consecration of Dr Lawrence Gillooly.

2 February 1895: The late Bishop Gillooly, some interesting details.

5 April 1902: St Assicus.

Roscommon Messenger

4 December 1858: Death of Dr Browne, Bishop of Elphin.

15 February 1862: Pastoral of Most Rev Dr Gillooly.

19 January 1895: Bishop Gillooly's funeral, solemn and impressive cermonies.

Elphin Diocesan Archive, St Mary's Sligo

Correspondence of Bishops Lawrence Gillooly, John Clancy, Bernard Coyne, Edward Doorly and Vincent Hanly covering the period 1858 to 1970. An unpublished manuscript giving a biographical account of the priests who served in the diocese during the nineteenth century. Some historical data on parishes in Elphin Diocese.

National Archives

Religious census of the diocese of Elphin 1749, M. 2466 (copy in Roscommon County Library)

This manuscript census of the diocese undertaken under the auspices of the Church of Ireland bishop Edward Synge gives valuable information on the number of Catholics and some clergy names from the mid eighteenth century.

Parliamentary Papers

First Report of the Royal Commission on the state of Religious and other Public Instruction in Ireland. H.C. 1835, xxxiii, pp 15d-29d and xxxiv, pp. 16d-45d.

Second Report of the Commissioner of Irish Education Inquiry, H.C. 1826, xii.

First Report of the Commission of inquiry into the state of the poorer classes in Ireland, H.C. 1836, xxxi Supplement to Appendix D, xxxii, xxxiii Supplement to Appendix F, and xxxiv.

ARMSTRONG, E. C. R., *Irish seal-matrices and seals,* (Dublin, 1913), p. 45.
A description of the seal of Bishop Thomas Barret of Elphin (1372-1404).

BEIRNE, Rev Francis, *The Diocese of Elphin.* Typescript 4 pages. (copy in E.D.A.)
A short account of the diocese.

BEIRNE, Rev Francis, 'Events and changes in Sligo churches', in *Sligo Champion Sesquicentenary 1836-1986,* p. 69.
A detailed summary of events in Sligo and it's environs over fifty years.

BOURKE, Cormac, 'A crozier and bell from Inishmurray', in *Proceedings of the Royal Irish Academy,* VOL. 85, (1985), pp 145-168.
Descriptions of a crozier and bell from Inishmurray and their place in ninth century archaeology and the significance of the survival of two associated objects from the island monastery.

BRADY, John, *Catholics and Catholicism in the eighteenth century press,* (Maynooth, 1965).
References to people and events from Elphin Diocese from the eighteenth century.

BRADY, John, 'Father Flanagan of Boystown', in *R.H.A.S.J.,* VOL. I, (1986), p. 29.
A short account of the life and times of Fr Flanagan, a native of Elphin Diocese.

BRADY, W. M., *The Episcopal succession in England, Scotland and Ireland 1400-1875,* vol. ii, (Rome, 1876, Reprint London, 1971).
A complete list of the bishops of the diocese with some short biographical notes. Greater detail in later period. Up to 1545 some entries are in Latin.

BRADY, W. M., *The Irish Reformation or the alleged conversion of the Irish bishops at the accession of Queen Elizabeth,* (London, 1867), pp. 161-162.
Lists the Catholic bishops of Elphin from 1558 to 1858

BROWNE, Rev Raymond, *The destitution survey: reflection on the famine in the Diocese of Elphin,* (Boyle, 1997). 154 pages with illustrations.
Gives a detailed account of the suffering endured in Elphin Diocese during the Famine. Draws from newspapers and personal reminiscences to illustrate the story.

BROWNE, Rev Raymond, 'The paruchia of St. Brigid', in *R.H.A.S.J.,* VOL. VI, (1996), p. 88.
A list of various churches associated with St Brigid in the diocese.

BUCKLEY, J. J., 'Some Irish altar plate', in *Journal of the Royal Society of Antiquaries of Ireland,* VOL. LXIX, (1939), pp. 56, 58, 60, 62, 66-7.
Descriptions of various chalices associated with Elphin Diocese.

BURKE, W. P., *The Irish priests in the penal times 1660-1760,* with introduction by Mgr Patrick Corish, (Reprint, Shannon, 1969), pp. 412-53.
Detailed account of priests and leading Catholics in Connacht over this period drawn from a variety of sources, some no longer available.

BURKE, Rev Francis, *Loch Cé and its Annals: North Roscommon and the Diocese of Elphin in times of old,* (Dublin, 1895), 142 pages illus.

CANNING, Rev Bernard J., *Bishops of Ireland 1870-1987*, (Ballyshannon, 1987), pp. 340-46.
Gives a short biography and photograph of all Elphin bishops for the period 1870-1987.

CARRIGAN, Rev William, 'Catholic Episcopal Wills' in *Archivium Hibernicum*, II, (1912) pp. 235-40.
Two wills, the first of Bishop Carbery Kelly dated 1729, as well as details of how he proposed to dispose of his estate. It shows insight into his lifestyle. The second will is that of Bishop Patrick French dated 1748 and gives details of how he disposed of his estate.

CASEY, Rev M. T., 'The story of an island: Innismurry', in *Summerhill College Annual* (1950), pp.124-26.
An account of the island and its history.

COEN, Martin, 'George Joseph Plunkett Browne', in *Old Athlone Society Journal*, VOL. II, NO. 5 (1978), pp. 26-32
An account of the life of Bishop Browne from his youth through his time as Bishop of Galway to Elphin. Includes details on the election of his coadjutor and a photograph of the bishop's portrait.

CONNELLAN, Rev M. J., 'Our Lady in Elphin Diocese', in *Summerhill College Annual* 1953-54, pp. 7-11.
An account of the cathedral and other churches and institutions in the diocese dedicated to Our Lady.

CONNELLAN, Rev M. J., 'Sliabh Ua Nailealla and Bearnas Ua Nailealla', in *Journal of the Royal Society of Antiquaries of Ireland*, VOL. LXXX, (1950), pp. 237-241.
Travels of St Patrick in north Roscommon and east Sligo.

CONNELLAN, Rev M. J., 'Cill na Romhánach: An unrecorded patrician church', in *Summerhill College Annual* (1952), pp 35-37.
This article identifies this ancient church as being in the parish of Baslick.

CONNELLAN, Rev M. J., 'St Patrick's two crossings of the Shannon', in *Ardagh and Clonmacnoise Antiq. Society Journal*, VOL. XI, NO. 12, (1951), pp. 78-84.

CONNELLAN, Rev M. J., 'The See of Tuaim in Rathbreasail Synod', in *Galway Archaeological and Historical Society Journal*, (1951), pp. 19-26.
The extent of the proposed See of Tuaim is described, following the Synod in 1111 in Rathbreasail. The Synod wished to retain unpartitioned territorial units. Tuaim in Kilgefin parish was selected as the location of the see. The See of Tuaim as adumbrated in Rathbreasail was the nucleus of the See of Elphin inthe Synod of Kells.

CONNELLAN, Rev M. J., 'Archbishops Edmund MacGauran and Malachy O'Queely: some circumstances of their deaths', in *The Irish Ecclesiastical Record* 1948, pp. 48-59.
This article explains the circumstances surrounding the violent deaths of Archbishop Mac Gauran, Primate of All Ireland at Skeanavart near Elphin, county Roscommon in 1593 and of Archbishop O'Queely near Ballisodare, county Sligo in 1645.

CONNELLAN, Rev M. J., 'Clann Ceithearnaigh its whereabouts and extent', in *Galway Archaeological and Historical Society Journal* 1948, pp. 70-74.

A detailed article explaining the extent of Clann Ceithearnaigh in the Castlerea area of county Roscommon. St Patrick's links with the area are also explained.

CONNELLAN, Rev M. J., 'St Brocaidh of Imliuch Brocadha', in *Galway Archaeological and Historical Society Journal*, VOL. XXXII, NO. 3 AND 4, (1949), pp 138-146.
A discussion on various theories associating St Brocaidh with Emlagh in the parish of Kilkeevin.

CONNELLAN, Rev M. J., 'Three Patrician bishops and their seats in Airteach', in *Galway Archaeological and Historical Society Journal*, VOL. XX, NO. 3-4, (1951), pp. 125-29.
The writer explains why he thinks the three episcopal sees mentioned in the *Tripartite life of Saint Patrick* are in the old parish of Tibohine. Extensive references to placenames.

CONNELLAN, Rev M. J., 'St Patrick in Ardsenlis', in *Summerhill College Annual* 1953-4, pp. 61-3.
In this article the author identifies Strokestown as the location called Ardsenlis in early Irish writings where St Patrick left St Lalloc in charge of a church.

CONNELLAN, Rev M. J., 'St Muadhnat of Kill Muadhnat', in *Galway Archaeological and Historical Society Journal*, (1941) p. 56-62.
This article identifies a townland in Drumcliff parish as the site of the church of St Muadhnat, a sixth century saint.

CONNELLAN, Rev M. J., 'The implications of Rath Breasail Synod regarding Ardagh and adjacent diocese as then projected', in *Ardagh and Clonmacnois Antiquarian Society Journal* VOL. II, NO. 9, (1943), pp 18-21.
An account of proposed boundaries of the diocese about IIII containing some references to Elphin Diocese.

CONNOLLY, Padraig, 'Ballindrimley in the 1790s', in *R.H.A.S.J.*, VOL. V, (1994), pp. 97-8.
A commentary on a document from the O'Conor Papers at Clonalis House dated 1792 and concerning Mass attendance.

CONRY, Rev Michael, *The Faith of the Irish Exiles – The victims of the Famine Fever of 1847* (Dublin, no date) 34 pp.
The first lecture outlines the contribution of Irish exiles towards the propagation of the faith worldwide, particularly in America. The second lecture describes the horror of the Great Famine, and the work of priests and nurses in helping stricken victims on their arrival in Canada.

CONWAY, Rev Dominic, 'Guide to documents of Irish and British interest in Fondo Borghese: series I', in *Archivium Hibernicum*, XXIII (1960), series II-IV , ibid. XXIV (1961)
Contains some references concerning Elphin Diocese.

COUNTY SLIGO HERITAGE AND GENEALOGY SOCIETY, *Patron Saints of the parishes in the Diocese of Elphin,* unpublished typescript bound. (copy in E.D.A.)
Gives a list of saints, with notes, throughout the year. These are drawn from a number of sources but mostly John O'Hanlon's *Lives of the Irish Saints.*

CURRAN, Sr Loreto, 'Dr Laurence Gillooly CM DD, Bishop of Elphin 1856-1895, Founder of Summerhill College', in *St Joseph's Summerhill College Annual* 1991.
An abridged biography on the life and works of Dr Gillooly. references to his zealous and continuous efforts to create institutional and educational facilities for youth within the Diocese of Elphin. This article is based on an unpublished thesis by T. C. Griffin d ated *1984*.

CURRAN, Sr Loreto, 'Summerhill 1843-1980' in *Embers Summerhill College Magazine*, pp 16-19.
Chronicles the history of Summerhill Convent (Athlone) from the time it was left to Bishop Browne by the Gaynor family to 1980. It explains how different religious groups but particularly the Sisters of Mercy educated and cared for young people at this location.

D'ALTON, John, *The history of Ireland and the annals of Boyle,* (Dublin, 1845).
Historical notes on parishes in Boyle Barony including; Boyle Ardcarne, Easternsow, Tumna etc.

DELANEY, James, 'Two Holy Wells in county Roscommon', in *R.H.A.S.J.,* VOL. IV, (1992) pp. 56-9.
An examination of the pilgrimages to the wells at Brideswell and Oran, also a general discussion on christianising of the Lunasa festival with references to other assemblies in the diocese.

DOLAN, Rev Gerard, 'The Diocese of Elphin', in *Pioneer,* VOL. XLIX, NO. 10 (September 1997), pp. 24-5.
A short account of the diocese, with photographs.

DUNLEAVY, Gareth & DUNLEVY, Janet E, *The O'Conor papers. A descriptive catalogue and surname register of material at Clonalis House, Castlerea, county Roscommon,* (London, 1977)
A listing and brief description of various items in the O'Conor papers from the eighteenth to the twentieth century – some of religious interest.

EGAN, Joseph J. and EGAN, Mary J., *History of Clann Egan* (1979), pp. 29, 32, 95-97.
References to Bishop Boetius Egan, including a copy of his signature.

FAULKNER OFM, Anselm, 'Father O'Finaghty's miracles', in *The Irish Ecclesiastical Record,* NO. 104 (July-Dec 1965), pp. 349-362.
An account of the miracles of a seventeenth century Elphin priest drawn from contemporary sources. Fr. O'Finaghty was born c. 1614 and was later Vicar General of Elphin. He was still living in 1688.

FEENEY, O., The correspondence of the Rev Owen Feeney, Adm, Sligo, to Bishop Browne of Elphin, to Rev Mr Phillips and to the Ursuline Community, 1846-1850.

FENNING OP, Hugh, 'Clergy of Elphin Diocese 1810-1812 , in *Collectanea Hibernica,* NO. 34-35 (1992-93) pp. 139 -42.
Two lists of clergy from 1810 and 1812. Both lists quite similar.

FENNING OP, Hugh, 'The journey of James Lyons from Rome to Sligo 1763-65 , in *Collectanea Hibernica,* XI, (1968) pp. 91-110.
A series of letters written by James Lyons to his Alma Mater in Rome as he returned

and on his return to Elphin Diocese. They give a good account of social conditions of the times and the necessity for the clergy to speak Irish.

FENNING OP, Hugh, 'Two diocesan reports: Elphin (1753) and Killaloe (1792)', in *Archivium Hibernicum*, XXX, (1972) pp. 21-28.
The Elphin report deals with the spiritual state of the diocese. The number of parishes is reduced from 77 to 45. Gives an account of conditions of the laity.

FENNING OP, Hugh, 'Clergy lists of Elphin 1731-1818 , in *Collectanea Hibernica*, NO. 38 (1996), pp. 141-155.
Clergy lists from Elphin diocese from various sources mostly Roman, also from Religious Census of Elphin 1749. Some original documents including *relatio status* of Bishop Edmund French 1792, from Galway Diocesan Archive.

FENNING OP, Hugh, 'The Diocese of Elphin 1747-1802 documents from Roman Archives', in *Collectanea Hibernica*, NO. 36-37 (1994-95), pp. 159-173.
A number of clergy lists most drawn from postulations for new bishops made in 1748,1756 and 1786. There are also a number of letters concerning a school for girls in Athlone in 1748. Also a report on Elphin Diocese from Bishop Edmund French dated 1802 and a letter appointing a parish priest dated 1760.

FENNING OP, Hugh, 'Ambrose McDermott OP, Bishop of Elphin', in *Archivium Fratres Praedictorum*, XI, pp 267-8.
A brief account of Bishop Ambrose McDermott OP, including some original letters.

FINN, James, 'The Cross of Roscommon', in *Rosc Chomáin*, VOL. X, (1975), pp 9-11.
Gives an account of the twelfth-century Ceremonial Cross usually called the Cross of Cong and traces its connection with Roscommon.

FINN, John, 'Dry up your tears: Rev Henry 1854-1922 , in *Rosc Chomáin*, VOL. X, (1975), pp. 12-14.
A brief account of Fr Henry, a native of Roscommon parish. Ordained in New York he founded a mission for young female Irish emigrants there.

FITZMAURICE, Michael, 'The Holy Wells of Roscommon', in *R.A.D.Y.*, VOL. XI, (1985), p. 61.
A short list of some holy wells in county Roscommon.

FITZMAURICE, Michael, 'The Holy Wells of Roscommon', in *R.A.D.Y.*, VOL. IX, (1988), p. 29-30.
Similar to the 1985 article but some feast days are added and two maps.

FLYNN OP, Thomas S., 'Andrew O'Crean, Bishop of Elphin, 1562-1594: The conflict of ecclesiastical jurisdiction', in *The Irish Dominicans* (Dublin, 1993), pp. 63-7.
An account of Bishop O'Crean and his administration of Elphin.

FREEMAN, A. Martin, *The Annals of Connacht*, (Dublin, 1970).
Contains references to places in the Diocese of Elphin.

GACQUIN, William, 'Rev Dr James O'Fallon', in *A History of Tisrara*, (1997), pp. 76-81.
An account of Bishop O'Fallon 1709-1786 giving family background. Gives an account of some of his work in the diocese and the conditions of the clergy and people at that time.

GALLOWAY, Peter, *Cathedrals of Ireland* (Belfast, 1993), pp. 199-203.
A description of the two Cathedrals in Sligo: Cathedral of Immaculate Mary and Cathedral of St Mary the Virgin and St John the Baptist.

GIBLIN OFM, Cathaldus, 'Ten documents relating to Irish diocesan affairs', in *Collectanea Hibernica,* NO. 20 (1978), pp. 86-88.
A letter from Bishop James O'Fallon concerning the appointment of a parish priest of Kilkeevan in 1784.

GRATTAN-FLOOD, W. H., 'The episcopal succession in Elphin 1216-1539 , in *The Irish Ecclesiastical Record*, (Jan-June 1914), pp. 622-631.
A survey of the bishops of Elphin in the late medieval period up to 1539

GRIFFIN, Terrence, *Bishop Laurence Gillooly, educational issues in the Diocese of Elphin 1856-1894*, unpublished (M.A. Thesis, UCG, 1984).
This thesis deals with educational issues in the diocese of Elphin from 1832 up to the death of Bishop Gillooly.

GWYNN, Aubrey & HADCOCK, R. N,. *Medieval religious houses Ireland,* (London, 1970)
This book contains details on all medieval and early Christian foundations in the Diocese of Elphin.

HEALY, Rev John, *Maynooth College: its centenary history, 1795-1895,* (Dublin, 1895) XXIV, 770 pages, illus. ports. pp. 544-545.
A biographical note on Dr Healy and his editorship of *The Irish Ecclesiastical Record*.

HENNESSY, William (Editor). *The Annals of Loch Cé, a chronicle of Irish affairs from 1014–1590,* 2 vols. (London, 1871).
Many references to places and persons concerning ecclesiastical matters in Elphin Diocese.

HOBAN, James, 'From hedge school to National Board 1810-1861', in *R.H.A.S.J.,* VOL. I, (1986), pp. 10-13.
Article on education in county Roscommon between those dates with many references to parishes in Elphin Diocese.

HOBAN, James, 'Religious tensions in National Schools 1830-1861', in *R.H.A.S.J.,* VOL. VII, (1998), pp. 82-3.
A brief survey of some National Schools in the diocese between those dates.

JENNINGS, Rev Brendan, 'Florence Conry, Archbishop of Tuam, his death and transfer of his remains', in *Galway Archaeological and Historical Society Journal* , VOL. XXIII, NOS. 3 &4 (1949), pp. 83-93.
Details on the death in Madrid of Florence Conry, founder of the Irish Franciscan College in Louvain and the return of his remains to Louvain some years later.

JENNINGS, Joseph, 'Six bishops of Elphin', in *Summerhill College Annual 1952*, pp. 8-12.
Sketches of the bishops from Bishop Burke to Bishop Doorly.

JONES, W .A., 'Bishops of Elphin', in *Sligo Champion*, 7 June 1930.
A report from the *Irish World* New York gives sketches of Bishops De Burgo, MacDermott, O'Kelly and French.

JOYCE, P. J., *John Healy Archbishop of Tuam*. (Dublin, 1931), *330* pages, illus.
A full length biography of the Ballinafad born Maynooth Professor and historian who was Archbishop of Tuam from 1903 to 1918.

KAVANAGH, Brigid, 'St Asicus, patron of Elphin Diocese', in *R.A.D.Y.,* vol. XVII, (1996), pp. 42-3.
A brief outline of the life of the saint with a photograph of the interior of Elphin Cathedral.

KELLY, Rev J. J., 'St Patrick in Boyle', in *Irish Monthly,* vol. VII, (1879) pp. 482-92.

KELLY, Rev J. J., 'St Patrick's travels through Elphin', in *Irish Monthly,* vol. VII, (1879), pp. 576-84.

KELLY, Rev J. J., 'St Columba at Boyle', in *The Irish Ecclesiastical Record*, vol. I, (Aug. 1880), 3rd Series, pp. 391-401.
Places in the vacinity of Boyle and Lough Cé associated with St Columcille or Columba as recorded in Adamnan's life of the saint and other sources

KELLY, Rev J. J., 'The diocese of Elphin 1671-1717', in *The Irish Ecclesiastical Record*, XIV, (1893), pp 1086-95.
Gives an account of two Elphin bishops; Ambrose McDermott OP, 1707-1717, and Dominic Burke, 1671-1704.

KELLY, Rev J. J., 'Episcopal succession in the Diocese of Elphin in the Reformation period', in *The Irish Ecclesiastical Record,* XII, (Jan-June 1907), pp. 459-485.
A detailed account of the bishops of Elphin from 1244 to 1588. This article is concerned with the validity of succession of the bishops in the diocese.

KELLY, Rev J. J., 'Patron saints of the parishes of the Diocese of Elphin', in *The Irish Ecclesiastical Record,* vol. XVI, (July-Dec. 1904), pp. 43-58.
A long list of local saints as patrons for most parishes in the diocese. These are derived from various sources. Dates of feasts and short notes on each saint are given.

KELLY, Rev J. J., 'St Asicus, first Bishop and Patron of the Diocese of Elphin', in *The Irish Ecclesiastical Record,* vol. XVI, (3rd Ser.) (1895), pp. 727-734.
A short account on the patron saint of the diocese.

KELLY, Rev J. J., 'Martyr priests in the Diocese of Elphin', in *Summerhill College Annual* 1953-4, pp. 20-23
Lists chronoglically eight priests from Elphin martyred for the faith. Covers the period 1579 to 1707 and includes bibliographical notes in most cases.

LANNON, Rev P. D., 'Rt Rev Monsignor D. J. O'Doherty DD, D Litt, Rector Irish College, Salamanca', in *Summerhill College Annual* 1949.
A comprehensive survey of the life and times of Mgr O'Dogherty, a priest of Elphin Diocese, born in county Mayo in 1877, who was Rector of the Irish College Salamanca from 1911 to 1934. He compiled a history of the College, as yet unpublished.

LEWIS, Samuel, *A topographical dictionary of Ireland,* (London, 1837), 2 vols.
Contains references to all parishes and other places in the Diocese of Elphin.

MAC AODHA, Breandán S., 'Tobarainmneacha i gContae Ros Comáin: réamhshuirbhe', in *Journal of the Old Athlone Society,* VOL. II, NO. 6, (1985), pp. 136-38.
A list of sixty eight wells in county Roscommon, many associated with saints.

MACINERNEY OP, M. H., 'Maurice O'Connor, Bishop of Elphin 1266-1284', in *A History of the Irish Dominicans,* VOL. I (Dublin, 1916), pp. 271-284.
An account of the bishop and prevailing conditions in the diocese at the time.

MACLEOD, Catríona, 'Some medieval wooden figure sculptures in Ireland', in *Journal of the Royal Society of Antiquaries of Ireland,* VOL. LXXVI, (1946), pp. 153-61.
A detailed description of the statue of St Molaise of Innismurry with photographs.

MAC NIOCAILL, Gearóid, *Obligationes pro Annatio Diocesis Elphinensis.* In *Archivium Hibernicum,* XXII, (1959), pp. 1-27.
The text, in Latin, refers to a tax levied by the Holy See on parishes (some were exempt). Various records covering the period 1427 to 1548. The names of some priests are given.

MAG FHLOINN, Aodán, *Asicus.* Unpublished BA (Celtic Studies) thesis, St Patrick's College Maynooth, 1990, 32 pages in Irish with bibliography.
A detailed examination of early sources relating to St Asicus, with good bibilography.

MARTIN OSA, F. X., 'Confusion abounding: Bernard O'Higgins OSA, Bishop of Elphin 1542-1561, in *Studies in Irish history* (Dublin, 1980), pp. 38-83.
A very detailed and scholarly account of Elphin Diocese in the mid sixteenth century period. Deals with the question of reform within the Augustinian Order and the wider church. An account of Bishop O'Higgins' attempts to establish himself in Elphin. Fifteen original documents included.

MCGREEVY, Rev John J., 'The Diocese of Elphin in 1637', in *R.H.A.S.J.,* VOL. II, (1988), pp. 40-1.
A description of the life of Dr Boetius Egan, Bishop of Elphin 1625-1650. Dr. Egan was the only Catholic bishop in the Province of Connacht at the time of his consecration. A letter from Dr Egan to Pope Urban VIII translated from the Latin describes the persecution of the Catholic people. Dr Egan lists the priories, convents and nunneries in Elphin.

MCGREEVY, Rev John J., 'The Diocese of Elphin in 1637', in *Summerhill College Annual* (1950), pp. 107-110.
A description of the life of Dr Boetius Egan, Bishop of Elphin 1625-1650 is given. Dr Egan was the only Catholic bishop in the Province of Connacht at the time of his consecration. A letter from Dr Egan to Pope Urban VIII describes the persecution of the Catholic people. Dr Egan lists the priories, convents and nunneries in Elphin.

MCGREEVY, Rev John J., *Emigrant and Emigre: George Thomas Plunkett, Easpag Aill Finne 1814-1827,* (Boyle, 1992), 100 pages with illustrations.
Traces the career of a future bishop from his birth at Drumlion to his appointment as Bishop of Elphin in 1814 and the problems he encountered on his way.

McGreevy, Rev Sean, 'Archbishop Healy', in *Summerhill College Annual*, 1946, pp 25-28.
An outline of the life and career of Archbishop John Healy 1841-1918 an Elphin priest who had an illustrious career as an academic at Maynooth before becoming Bishop of Clonfert in 1884 and Archbishop of Tuam in 1903.

McManus, Sr M. Gabrielle, (Editor), *Community projects in action – north county Roscommon, Ireland*, (Boyle, 1984). 32 pages, photographs.
An account of various community projects in north Roscommon many of which are related to parish communities in Elphin Diocese.

McTernan, John C., 'In the footsteps of St Patrick', in *At the foot of Knocknarea*, (Sligo, 1990)
, illus. pp. 20-24.
Notes on early Christian foundations at Killaspugbrone, Kilmacowen and Templebree

Millett OFM, Benignus, 'Calendar of Volume II (1669-71) of *Scritture rifferite nei congressi Irlanda* in Propaganda Archive Part 1 ff 1-401', in *Collectanea Hibernica*, NO. 16, (1973), pp. 16-18.
A report on a visitation of Elphin Diocese in 1668 gives the names of all clergy, their parishes and a short note on each.

Millett OFM, Benignus, 'Calendar of Volume III (1672-75) of the *Scritture rifferite nei congressi Irlanda* in Propaganda Archive Part 1 ff 1-200', in *Collectanea Hibernica*, no. 18-19, (1976-77), pp. 66-67.
A report on Elphin Diocese in 1672 based on information from Bishop Dominic Burke OP. The bishop was trying to correct abuses etc which had occurred since the death of his predecessor.

Millett OFM, Benignus, 'Elphin and Ross seek Franciscans as bishops 1649-51', in *Collectanea Hibernica*, no. 34-35, (1992-93), pp. 18-21.
A letter from Roman Archives signed by eleven laymen recommending Boetius Egan OFM as bishop of the diocese. Short note in English on the bishop.

Mooney OFM, Canice, 'Bishop Boetius MacEgan of Elphin', in *The Franciscan College Annual*, 1952, pp. 142-5.
A detailed account of the life of Bishop MacEgan from his birth in 1580 through his education at Louvain and his episcopate at Elphin from 1625 until his death in 1650.

Mooney OFM, Canice, 'Boetius Mac Egan chalice 1634', in *The Franciscan College Annual* 1952, p. 55.
A brief account of the chalice.

Mooney OFM, Canice, 'Elphin', in *Dictionnaire d'histoire et de géographie ecclesiastique*, 15 (1963), pp 269-91. English translation, typescript, 25 pages. (copy in E.D.A.)
This scholarly article first published in French traces the history of the Diocese of Elphin from patrician times to 1950s.

Moran, Rev P. F., *Spicilegium Ossoriense*, Three volumes (Dublin, 1874, 1878, 1884)
A collection of original letters and papers on the history of the Irish church from the Reformation to 1800. All three volumes have references to Elphin Diocese.

MORAN, P. F., 'The See of Elphin in the sixteenth century', in *The Irish Ecclesiastical Record* (Jan 1866), pp. 149-156.
A survey of the sometimes overlapping appointments of bishops to the See of Elphin in the sixteenth century.

MORRIS, Henry, *St Patrick in county Sligo*, (Sligo, 1930), 28 pages, map.
The recorded acts and activities of Patrick in county Sligo from authentic sources supplemented by such traditions of the saint and his contemporaries as are still alive in the folklore of the people.

MURRAY, Patrick, *Monsignor John McCarthy 1908-1983*, (Athlone), 70 pages illus.
A biography of Mgr McCarthy, covering his family background and his years as a student, priest, professor, theological expert and educationalist.

NICHOLLS, K. W., 'Rectory, vicarage and parish', in *Journal of the Royal Society of Antiquities of Ireland*, VOL. 100, 1970, pp 75-6.
References to Elphin Diocese.

O'CALLAGHAN, Michael, 'Father Michael O'Flanagan', in *Summerhill College Annual*, (1979), pp. 19-21.
A short biographical note on Fr O'Flanagan.

O'CONNELL, Mary, 'An examination of how some county Roscommon Holy Wells feature in the cult of the Holy Well in Ireland', in *R.H.A.S.J.*, VOL. VI, (1998), pp. 58-65.
A scholarly article placing a number of holy wells in Elphin Diocese in a national context.

O'DONOVAN, John, *Annals of the kingdom of Ireland by the Four Masters from the earliest times to 1600*, (Dublin, 1856), 8 vols.
Has many references to various place in the Diocese of Elphin.

O'DONOVAN, John, *Ordnance Survey Letters, county Sligo*, (Bray, 1928), typescript 184 pages.
Information on churches and wells etc in most parishes.

O'DONOVAN, John, *Ordnance Survey Letters, county Roscommon*, (Bray, 1927), typescript 2 vols. 431 pages.
Information on churches and wells etc. in most parishes.

O'HANLON, Rev John, *Lives of the Irish Saints*, vols. 1-9 (Dublin, 1875).
Compiled from calendars, martyrologies and various ancient sources relating to early Christian period. Some Elphin saints mentioned: St Bron pp. 241-4, St Lomman, VOL. 2, pp 295-300.

Ó LAIMHÍN, T. S., *An tAthair Tomás Ó Ceallaigh agus a shaothar, maille le réamhrá, nótaí agus eile*, (Galway, 1943) 298 pages.
A detailed account of An tAthair Ó Ceallaigh and his work.

O'RORKE, T., *History of Sligo*, (Dublin, 1889), VOL. I, Reprint Sligo, 1986. pp. 226-240.
This extract entitled 'Depositions of non-juring Popish priests celebrating Mass in the town or county 1712' gives the depositions of Thomas Corkeran and other popish inhabitants of the town of Sligo dated 28 October 1712 and the depositions of Teig Mc Donagh of Shancough etc on 28 October and 11 November 1712.

OURSLER, Fulton and Will, *Father Flanagan of Boys Town,* (New York, 1949).
An account of the life faith and conviction of Father Edward J. Flanagan (1886-1948), a native of Ballymoe and founder of the celebrated boys home in Omaha, Nabraska, USA.

SHARKEY, Rev P. A., *The heart of Ireland,* (Boyle, 1927), 490 pages illus.
The antiquities of Boyle and surrounding areas, including Athleague, Castlerea, Kilglass, Loughglynn, Moylurg, Shancoe and Roscommon.

SIGGINS, Albert, 'Some late medieval crosses in county Roscommon', in *R.H.A.S.J.,* VOL. I, (1986), pp. 33-5.
A study of ten wayside crosses dated from 1623 to 1689. All but one is in Elphin Diocese.

SIGGINS, Albert, 'Some early Christian slabs from Fuerty and Cloontuskert', in *R.H.A.S.J.,* VOL. II, (1988), pp. 55-9.
A detailed account of early Christian slabs found at these sites with sketches and references.

SIGGINS, Albert, 'County Roscommon's Holy Wells', in *R.H.A.S.J.,* VOL. IV, (1992), p. 76-7.
A list of sixty eight wells with notes and some illustrations.

STOKES, Whitley (Editor), *The tripartite life of St Patrick, with other documents relating to that saint.* Two volumes. (London 1887).
Contains references to places in the diocese associated with St Patrick.

TIMONEY, Martin A., 'Roscommon Crucifixion Plaques, a detective story', in *R.A.D.Y.,* VOL. III, (1982), pp. 8-9.
References to two crucifixion plaques in Elphin Diocese at Cloonshanville and Ardcarne.

TIMONEY, Martin A., 'Two stone Crucifixion plaques from east Connacht', in *Irish Midland Studies: essays in commemoration of N. W. English,* (Athlone, 1980), pp. 142-146.
A detailed description of two crucifixion plaques, one from Roscommon town and a second from Castlegar townland in Ahascragh parish.

TIVNAN, Frank, 'An tAthair Tomás Ó Ceallaigh', in *R.H.A.S.J.,* VOL. V, (1994), p. 5.
A short account of Fr. Tomás Ó Ceallaigh 1879-1925, a priest of Elphin Diocese who became Professor of Education at NUI, Galway.

TONRA, Rev Henry, 'Sailing from the lowlands low', in *R.H.A.S.J.,* VOL. V, (1994), pp 90-3.
An account of Bishop Ambrose McDermott's attempt to reach Ireland after his appointment as Bishop of Elphin in 1707.

TYNDALL, Charles, *The ancient parish and church of St John the Baptist, Sligo* (Dublin, 1962), 44 pages, illustrated.
An historical account of St John's church from earliest times to disestablishment.

WARD, Catherine Coogan & WARD, Robert E., 'The ordeal of O'Conor of Ballanagare', in *Éire-Ireland: A journal of Irish Studies.* (Summer 1979).
Discusses the tensions between the government, the Catholic hierarchy and Charles O'Conor during the late eighteenth century and the movement for Catholic emancipation.

WILLIAMS, Jeremy, *A companion guide to architecture in Ireland 1837-1921* (Dublin, 1994), pp. 203-216, 329-339.
Contains architectural notes on some churches etc in the diocese.

— *Archdioceses and Dioceses of Ireland* (Dublin, 2000), pp. 60-63.
A brief historical account of the diocese, with photographs.

— 'Calendar of Papal Letters relating to Great Britain and Ireland', (Irish Mss. Commission, 1978-1998), VOLS., XIV, XV, XVII, and XIX, 1484-1513.
Contain numerous references to Elphin Diocese.

— 'Calendar of Volume XIV of the *Fondo di Vienna*', in *Collectanea Hibernica*, NO. 30 (1988), pp. 46-47.
A petition from the clergy of Elphin for a bishop in 1661. They asked for Dominic O'Kelly OP and give names of priests and their parishes as well as some information on O'Kelly.

— 'Some lists of priests in Ireland 1684-94', in *Collectanea Hibernica*, NO. 27-28 (1985-86), pp 100-102.
A petition of the clergy of Elphin Diocese (in Latin). Gives a list of the clergy and their parishes.

— 'Miscellaneous documents III', in *Archivium Hibernicum*, XV, (1972) pp 62-65.
A report (in Latin) on the diocese of Elphin 1675 addressed to Pope Clement X.

— '*Miscellanea Vaticano Hibernica*', in *Archivium Hibernicum*, V, (1916) pp 74-75 and 143-148.
A *Relatio Status* of Bishop James O'Fallon dated 1770. Also a *Relatio Status* of Elphin Diocese from Bishop Boetius Egan OFM dated 1637.

— 'Three new cross slabs and a Romanesque lintel from county Roscommon', in *R.H.A.S.J.*, VOL. VII, (1998), pp 137-8.
A list of recent findings of examples of early medieval ecclesiastical art in Fuerty and Ballinderry, county Roscommon.

— 'Bishop Laurence Gillooly: Roscommon town's greatest son', in *R.A.D.Y.*, VOL. VII, (1986), pp 84-5.
A short account of the life of Bishop Gillooly

— 'Letter from Ambrose MacDermott OP, Bishop of Elphin, to Grimaldi Rotterham dated June 25 1710', in *Collectanea Hibernica*, NO. 5, (1962), pp 25-6.
Deals with the state of the Irish church with references to religious orders in Elphin Diocese.

— 'State of Popery in the Diocese of Elphin', in *Archivium Hibernicum*, III, (1914), pp 136-40.
Dated 1731 this gives a list of the parishes in the diocese with the number of Mass Houses, schools, convents and friaries in each. The names of most of the priests of that time are included. It also gives dates for the building of some Mass Houses.

— 'A list of popish parish priests registered under an Act of Parliament 1704', in *Catholic Directory*, 1838.
There are lists from three counties Roscommon, Sligo and Galway. Gives the name of the priest, his parish, age, where ordained, ordaining prelate, date of ordination. Also given are the names of two guarantors for each priest.

— 'Miscellanea Vaticano-Hibernica, series I, VOL. 469, FOL. 332 , in *Archivium Hibernicum,* III, (1914), pp 359-365.
An account by James Fallon VG, Elphin of the 'desolation and sorrow everywhere' in the early years of the ministry of Bishop Boetius Egan and the steps taken towards renewal since his consecration.

— 'Papal taxation list 1306', in *Foundation of the parish of Kilkeevan,* pp. 430-38.
An annotated list of the churches in the Diocese of Elphin in the Papal Taxation List of Pope Clement V, to which is appended a list of the churches, compiled by Edward King, Protestant bishop in 1622.

— 'Irish Ecclesiastical register, Diocese of Elphin 1841-1858', in *Irish Catholic Directory* 1858
Extracts from Catholic Directories from 1841 to 1858 giving clergy lists for forty-three parishes, notes on state of religion and schools. An account of an appeal to Bishop Burke in 1841 to change residence from Sligo.

— *Centenary of the Cathedral of the Immaculate Conception, Sligo. Celebration Mass 8 December 1975,* (Boyle, 1975).
Prayers and readings of the celebration Mass.

— *Solemnity of Dedication of the Cathedral, 1 July 1983.*
A manuscript which outlines the various contributions to the construction and renovation of the Cathedral in Sligo. Gives dates for renovations.

— *Sligo Cathedral Yearbook 1951,* (Dublin, 1951), 114 pages, photographs.
A collection of articles, many relating to Elphin Diocese, with a supplement on the Holy Year of 1950. Articles on Bishop Doorly and Bishop Hanly.

— 'Letter of our Holy Father Pius IX to Most Rev Dr Gillooly', in *Irish Ecclesiastical Record* (1868) p. 410.

PART 2: RELIGIOUS FOUNDATIONS

Angelus, The
July 1962, VOL. 4, NO. 14: Sligo honours Marist Brothers.
September 1973, VOL. 2, NO. 9: Dominican Abbey's (Roscommon) first Mass in 400 years.
February 1977, VOL. 6, NO. 2: Sisters of St. Joseph, Gardenhill.
July-August 1978, VOL. 7, NO. 7 &8: When Nazareth came to Sligo.
March 1982, VOL. 11: Congregation of the Sisters of St Joseph of the Apparition.
May 1982, VOL. 11, NO. 5: Poor Sisters of Nazareth.
June 1982, VOL. 11, NO 6: Donamon: a brief history.
July-August 1982, VOL. 11, NO. 7: Institute of the Franciscan Missionaries of Mary.
December 1982, VOL. 11, NO. 12: Sisters of St Joseph celebrate twenty five years in Sligo.
January 1990, VOL. 21, NO. 1: Early days in Donamon.

Roscommon Herald

28 May 1859: New Convent of the Immaculate Conception, Roscommon.

13 April 1929: Boyle Convent Chapel dedicated.

7 January 1956: Bishop welcomes new Order to Sligo (La Sagesse).

30 June 1967: Donamon Castle past and present.

8 September 1972 p. 7: Franciscans are missed at Farragher.

15 September 1972 p. 8: Going of the Franciscans.

16 May 1975: The Boyle Convent centenary; major breakthrough in educational facilities.
An account of the work of the Sisters of Mercy in Boyle over 100 years.

4 July 1986: Elphin Convent was a great centre of education.

18 October 1991 p. 6: Strokestown and the Sisters of Mercy 100 years on.
An account of the century of work of the Sisters in Strokestown.

27 September 2000: Loughglynn Convent, home of the Franciscan Sisters.

Roscommon Journal

25 January 1896: New Convent, Strokestown

Roscommon Messenger

4 July 1857: New monastery, Parish of Oran.

Sligo Champion

8 January 1848: Opening of new Abbey of the Hole Cross.

24 February 1849: New Ursuline Convent.

16 April 1898: Extension to Holy Cross Church.

26 August 1899: Dedication of new Convent of Mercy chapel.

24 August 1946: Mercy Convent centenary.

2 June 1948: Holy Cross centenary 1848-1948.

3 June 1950: Centenary of Ursulines in Sligo.

27 September 1952: Foundation stone of new chapel at Nazareth House.

23 January 1970: Holy Cross for demolition.

24 November 1972: Foundation stone of new Holy Cross laid.

11 May and 18 May 1973: Opening of new Dominican church.

AHERNE, Daniel Martin, *Mainistir na Buaille/ Boyle Cistercian Abbey: an example study of Irish monastic architecture in the medieval period.* N.C.E.A. thesis, (Crawford Municipal College of Art, Cork ,1978). Unpublished typescript 46 pages.
A detailed study of the architecture of Boyle Abbey with illustrations.

BARRY, TERENCE B., *The Archaelogy of Medieval Ireland* (London, 1987), p. 175.
A map showing the location of Fratres Cruciferi Priory at Rindoon, St John's parish. This map differs from the evidence in John A. Claffey's article (see below).

BARTON, Roy L., 'Roscommon in history', in *R.H.A.S.J.,* VOL. V, (1994), pp 6-10.
An account of St Coman's monastery, Roscommon, from its foundation in c. 540 to its dissolution in 1578.

CAHILL, Rev Br Gerard, *Marist Brothers,* unpublished. (copy in E.D.A.)
Historical notes which trace the fortunes of the Marist Brothers in Strokestown from their coming in 1928 until their departure in 1978. It links the educational contribution of the Brothers with their involvement in parish affairs.

CARTY, Pierce A., 'Trinity Island: Lough Key', in *Boyle: the origins, the buildings, the times,* (Boyle, 1988), pp 31-35.
A short history of the Premonstratsianist Abbey on the island up to the death of the last abbot in 1585.

CLAFFEY, John A., 'Medieval Rindoon', in *Journal of the Old Athlone Society,* II (1978), pp 11-14.
References to the establishment of houses of the *Fratres Cruciferi* and the Premonstratensian canons at Rindoon on the shores of the Shannon in St John's parish in the thirteenth century.

CONLON OFM, Rev Patrick, 'The medieval priory of Saints Peter and Paul in Athlone', in *Irish Midland Studies: essays in commemoration of N. W. English,* (Athlone, 1980) pp 73-83.
A scholarly account of the Cluniac foundation in Athlone from 1150 to its dissolution in the late sixteenth century.

CONLON OFM, Rev Patrick, *Franciscan Ireland,* (Cork, 1978) pp. 88 & 101.
Brief account of the Franciscan houses at Elphin and Roscommon.

CONNELLAN, Rev M. J., 'Eglish Monastery, Ahascragh parish, county Galway', in *Journal of the Royal Society of Antiquaries of Ireland,* VOL. LXXIII, (Part March 1943).
Gives details of the monastery at Eglish from its foundation in 1436. This was a Carmelite monastery although some early official documents refer to it as Franciscan.

CONNELLAN, Rev M. J., 'Caldragh, a Franciscan Friary of the Third Order', in *Assisi, Irish Franciscan Monthly,* VOL. XV, NO. 8, (August 1943). pp 132-4.
An account of the Third Order of Franciscans reputed to have resided at a Convent at Caldragh near Elphin.

CRONIN, Timothy, 'The town of Roscommon', in *R.H.A.S.J.,* VOL. II, (1988), pp. 5-9.
Notes on the early and medieval Christian sites in the town.

CRONIN, Timothy, *Mainistreacha Chondae Ros Comáin/Monastic houses of county Roscommon,* (Dept of Education, Dublin, 1977). 24 pages.
A bilingual account of the monastic houses of county Roscommon. A film strip accompanies these notes.

CRYAN, James, 'Annals of Ballindoon Abbey', in *Roscommon Herald,* 3 June 1961.

COCKRANE, R. and LESK, H. G., *Ecclesiastical remains at Sligo Abbey,* (Dublin, 1928), 15 pages illus.
Official handbook containing historical and descriptive notes on the Dominican Priory.

CONBHUIDHE O Cist, Rev Colm Cille, *Boyle Abbey and the Cistercians in Boyle: the origins, the buildings, the times,* (Boyle, 1988) pp 10-21.

CRAWFORD, Henry S., 'O'Conor tomb in Roscommon Abbey', in *Journal of the Royal Society of Antiquaries of Ireland,* VOL. 54, (1925), pp. 89-90.

CRAWFORD, Henry S., 'Carved altar and mural monuments in Sligo Abbey', in *Journal of the Royal Society of Antiquaries of Ireland,* VOL. 51, (1921), pp 17-31.
Eight illustrations and very detailed text about the carved altar; sixteenth-century O'Crean altar and seventeenth-century mural monument of the O'Connor Sligo at the old Dominican Abbey in Sligo.

CURRAN, Rev B., *Ballindoon Abbey,* typescript unpublished. (copy in E.D.A.)
An outline of the history of Ballindoon Abbey from 1427 with a list of friars from 1507-1785 and short notes on Fr Michael McDonagh OP and on the Ballindoon chalice.

CURRAN, S. Loreto, 'New developments at St Joseph's College Summerhill', in *Summerhill College Magazine* 1989.
Gives an account of the developments at St Joseph's since becoming a secondary school in 1965. Description of school plans included.

DUFFY, Rev Br Declan, 'Should old acquaintance be forgot', in *R.A.D.Y.,* VOL. I, (1980), pp. 27-9.
An outline of the contribution of Religious Orders to county Roscommon.

DUFFY, Rev Joseph, 'An account of a Fermanagh man, Hugh Farmer, who became a Franciscan Brother in Galway and later superior of a House at Farragher, county Roscommon', in *Clogher Record,* VOL. VI, NO. I, (1966), p. 199.

ENRIGHT, Joyce, *Drumcliff: notes on the Monastic Enclosure, High Cross and Round Tower.*
20 pages, unpublished. (copy in E.D.A.)

FAHERTY, Sr Laurentia, *Sisters of Mercy, Diocese of Elphin 1846-1991,* typescript in Mercy Sisters Archive.
Details on the Mercy Convents and their various works throughout the Diocese of Elphin. Also their missionary activities in California and Kenya are recorded. Some of the developments which took place in the post Vatican II era are also outlined.

FINNEGAN SJ, Rev, 'The Jesuits and Athlone in the seventeenth and eighteenth centuries', in *Journal of the Old Athlone Society,* VOL.I, NO. 2 (1970-71), pp. 71-83.
An account of a short lived Jesuit presence at Athlone and an attempt to re-establish the community.

FITZGERALD, Walter, 'County Sligo: Sligo Abbey', in *Journal of the Association for the preservation of the memorials of the dead,* VOL. XII, 1914 pp. 156-62.
A detailed description and photographs of the pre-eighteenth century monuments, which still existed in the old Dominican Abbey Sligo.

FITZGERALD, Walter, 'Effigy of King Phelim O'Conor in Roscommon Abbey and the altar tomb it rests on', in *Journal of the Royal Society of Antiquaries of Ireland,* VOL. XXX, (1900), pp. 364-67, illus.

FLYNN, OP, T .S., *The Irish Dominicans 1536-1641*, (Dublin. 1993), pp. 40-67.
This extract has many references to the Dominican friars active in the diocese over this period.

GACQUIN, William, 'Mrs Julia Ann Conmee, c.1786-1860, Benefactress of CBS Roscommon', in *Rosc Chomáin*, (1997) pp. 9-11.
An account of Mrs Conmee and her part in the coming of the Christian Brothers to Roscommon.

GACQUIN, William, *Presentation foundation at Ballybay (Kiltoom and Cam parish) 1836-7*, unpublished. (copy in E.D.A.)
An account of the short lived Presentation Sisters foundation at Ballybay.

GAFFNEY OP, M. H., *Story of Sligo Abbey 1252-1952*, (Sligo, 1952), 24 pages.
The fortunes of the abbey from its rebuilding in 1414 to its sacking in 1642, together with sketches of illustrious sons, Fathers Cryan, MacDonagh O'Connor and O'Hart.

GANNON, Rev J. J., 'The Dominicans in Sligo', in *Sligo Champion*, 15 August 1953, p. 3.
An historical survey of the Dominicans in Sligo from 1253 to 1953.

GIBLIN OFM, Cathaldus, 'Franciscans in Elphin', 16 pages, bibl. typescript.
A well-documented article detailing the Franciscans in Elphin over four hundred years. Covers the period between 1450 and the death of Fr Anthony Garrahan PP, the last of the Elphin Franciscans, in 1835.

GRATTAN-FLOOD, W. H., 'The Cluniacs in Ireland', in *The Irish Ecclesiastical Record*, fifth series, I (1913), pp. 52-59.
An account of the only Cluniac foundation in Ireland at Athlone. Mentions many surrounding parishes in Elphin Diocese.

GRIFFIN, B. & HUNT, S., 'Fortunes of Coman's Abbey', in *Rosc Chomáin*, VOL. VII, (1972), pp. 24-28.
Notes on St Coman's Abbey with extracts from Annals and notes on holy wells in Roscommon parish.

GROSE, Daniel, 'Church of the Holy Trinity St Johns Randown Loughree, county Roscommon', in *The Antiquities of Ireland*, (Reprint 1991), p. 92.
Brief description of the church, locating it near the castle of Rindoon in St John's parish.

HEALY, Rev John, 'A pilgrimage to Inishmurray', in *Irish Monthly*, VOL. V, (1877) pp. 433-439.
An account of a visit in September 1876 with a description of the island and its monastic remains.

HERAUGHTY, Patrick, *Inishmurray: ancient monastic island*, (Dublin, 1982), Reprint 1996, 96 pages, illus., maps.
History of an early Christian monastic settlement (520-1170)

KELLY, Sr Geraldine, 'Sisters of Mercy Boyle 1875-1988', in *Boyle; the origins, the buildings, the times*, (Boyle, 1988), pp. 98-108.
A detailed account of the Mercy Sisters in Boyle and their work for the people of the district.

KELLY, Rev J. J., *An Abbey-town of Ireland*, (Catholic Truth Society of Ireland, 1901). 48 pages.
A study of monasteries as monuments and their origins in and about Boyle. In-depth coverage of the Cistercian Abbey in Boyle.

KELLY, M. J., 'An tAthair Peadar Mac Thomáis, Fr Peter Thompson 1893-1948', in *R.H.A.S.J.*, VOL. II, (1988), p. 36.
Short note on Fr Thompson and giving one of his poems.

KELLY, Sr M. St Dominic, *The Sligo Ursulines; the first fifty years 1826-1876*, (Sligo, 1987), 232 pages, illus. and bibl.
Traces the history of the Ursulines both before and after their arrival in Sligo. Appendices include a transcript of correspondence between Owen Feeney, Adm. Sligo and the Ursuline Order. Also a list of the Ursulines who joined the community 1850-1876.

KELLY, Sr M. St Dominic, *The Sligo Ursulines; ninety years of growth 1876-1966*, (Sligo, 1991), 96 pages, illus.
Traces the history of the building of the convent, the Secondary School, St Vincent's National School and educational issues in that period. Appendices include a list of Ursuline sisters professed in Sligo 1876-1966 and a list of the superiors for the same period.

— *Ursuline Convent Sligo, centenary souvenir 1850-1950*, (Sligo, 1950), 132 pages illus. and photographs.
A number of essays including 'Rise and growth of St Joseph's, Sligo'commencing in 1850 when the Ursulines left Athlone for Sligo. Also includes a list of past pupils.

MANNION, Rev P., 'The Franciscans in Elphin', in *Roscommon Messenger*, 3 Jan. 1903.
A newspaper account of a lecture given by Fr Mannion to the Gaelic League at Elphin on 26 December 1902 concerning the Franciscans in Elphin town from 1450. Contains references to St Patrick and St Asicus.

MATTIMOE, Cyril, *North Roscommon: its people past and present*, (Boyle, 1992) 214 pages, illus.
Comprehensive history of Boyle and Moylorg baronies in north Roscommon from earliest times to the late nineteenth century. Ecclesiastical history is covered in detail especially the arrival of the Cistercians in Boyle

McDERMOTT, Dermot, *MacDermots of Moylorg*, (Boyle , 1996), pp. 201-11.
This extract entitled 'Religious establishments in Moylorg' gives an account of the monasteries in North Roscommon area including Assylin, Ardcarn, Boyle, Loch Cé, Knockvicar and Tibohine.

McDONAGH OP, Patrick, *An account of the state and condition of the effects of the convent of Sligo*. Ms dated 1701 and written in Bilbao, Spain, now in Holy Cross, Sligo.
Gives a detailed record of the plate and vestments of the Dominican Priory in 1698 and contains names of a number of priests.

McGOWAN, Joseph, *Inishmurray: gale, stone and fire*, (Sligo, 1998), 64 pages, illus.
A portrait of the island with particular reference to its monastic buildings, stone altars, stations and other antiquities.

McGreevy, Rev John J., 'Atha Luain agus na hAgaistínigh', in *Roscommon Herald,* 6 September 1991, p. 9.
An account of the Augustinian friars in Athlone in the nineteenth century.

Meehan, Denis Molaise, *Molaise of Inishmurray,* (Tralee, 1989), 40 pages, illus. and maps.
Gives the origin of the saint's name and that of the bog-oak statue together with details of the sixth century monastic settlement. There are references to the 'Meehans' of Ballagh-ameehan (near Rossinver) 'the tribe who claim Molaise as there own'.

Meehan, Denis, 'The island of St Molaise', in *Sligo Champion* 16 July 1955.

(O'Brien, Gearóid) Oisín, 'The Augustinians in Athlone', in *Westmeath Independent* 22 February, 1 and 8 March 1996.
An account of the nineteenth-century Augustinian foundation in St Peter's, Athlone.

Ó Conchúir, An Br M. F., 'Roscommon CBS: a school with a tradition', in *R.A.D.Y.,* vol. i, (1980), pp. 85-7.
An outline of the Christian Brothers schools in Roscommon since 1937.

O'Connor, Kieran, Keegan, Mark & Tiernan, Padraig, 'Tulsk Abbey', in *R.H.A.S.J.,* vol. vi, 1996, pp. 67-9.
A detailed archaeological account of Tulsk Abbey from its foundation in 1446 to its dissolution and transformation of part into a tower house c. 1595.

O'Gorman, Thomas, 'Remarks on O'Conor's tomb in Roscommon', in *Journal of the Royal Society of Antiquaries of Ireland,* vol. viii, (1864-66), pp. 546-554. illus.

O'Heyne OP, John, 'Dominican Abbeys in the Diocese of Elphin', in *The Irish Dominicans of the Seventeenth Century* (Louvain, 1706, Reprint with appendix: *Ancient Dominican Foundations* by Ambrose Coleman OP, Dundalk 1902), pp. 96-111. In this extract there are chronological details about the following Dominican Abbeys: Sligo (1252-1865), Ballindoon (1507-1780s), Roscommon (1252-1844), Clonshanville (-1780s), and Tulsk (1448-1694), as well as information about Fr Thady O'Duane (-1608) and Fr Phelim O'Connor (-1679).

O'Heyne OP, John, 'The Friars of Sligo and Roscommon', in *Irish Dominicans of the Seventeenth Century* (Dundalk, 1902), pp. 231-273.
An account of the Dominican friaries at Roscommon and Sligo.

O'Nuallain, T., 'Carmelite Convent at Toghergar', in *Newbridge Ballygar Toghergar News* 1982, pp. 42-45.
Covers the history of the Carmelites at Toghergar from c. 1775 to 1873.

Ó Raghallaigh, Tomás, 'Duthaigh Thasmhar mar a raibh Ceitin', in *R.H.A.S.J.,* vol ii, (1988), p. 36.
A reprint in Irish of an essay in *The Irish Press,* June 1933 refers to the birth of Fearfeasa Ó Maolchonaire, one of the Four Masters, near Elphin.

O'Reilly, William, 'The McDermotts of Moylurg', in *R.H.A.S.J.,* vol. v, (1994), pp 32-35.
References to the Premonstratensian Abbey on Lough Key and the Cistercian Abbey at Boyle.

O'RORKE, T., *History of Sligo,* VOL. I (Dublin, 1889), Reprint Sligo, 1986, pp. 241-291.
This extract entitled 'Sligo Abbey' gives a description of the abbey, its cloisters and the
principal monuments.

SIGGINS, Albert, 'Birds and beasts', in *R.H.A.S.J.,* VOL. V, (1994), p. 72.
A description of two fifteenth century decorative slabs, from the Dominican Friaries at
Roscommon and Cloonshanville.

TAHENY OP, Luke, *The Dominicans in Roscommon,* (Tallaght, 1990) 63 pages.
An account of the Dominican Order in Roscommon town from the foundation of the
Abbey in 1153 until the death of the last Dominican friar in the area in 1872. Gives detailed
coverage to the period 1570 to 1820. Plans and sketches of the abbey included.

THOMAS, Avril, *The walled towns of Ireland,* VOL.2, (Dublin, 1992), pp. 185-189.
Contains references to the ecclesiastical foundations in Roscommon and Rindoon.

TOWEY FSC, Rev Br John, 'Summerhill 1880', in *Archivium Hibernicum* , XXXVI, pp. 26-33.
An account of a De La Salle Brothers foundation at Summerhill (St Peter's parish) from
July 1880 to January 1882. This was the first foundation of that Order in Ireland.

VALKENBURG OP, Fr, 'Dominican Priories of Roscommon', in *R.H.A.S.J.,* VOL. I, (1984), pp. 6-7.
An account of the foundation of Dominican priories in county Roscommon. Details
their struggle for survival during the years of suppression and persecution. Four members
of the Order were martyred during the Cromwellian period.

WAKEMAN, W. F., 'Notes on architectural peculiarities of some ancient churches in county
Sligo', in *Journal of the Royal Society of Antiquaries of Ireland,* NO. 17, (1886).
Notes on the churches at Aghanagh and Killaspugbrone.

WAKEMAN, W. F., 'Oaken statue of St Molaise on Inishmurry', in *Graves of illustrious Irishmen*
(Dublin,1880) pp. 13-14.
Theories as to the origin of the statue.

WAKEMAN, W. F., *A survey of the antiquarian remains on the island of Inishmurry,* (London,1893),
163 pages, illus.
A history of the island, its churches, altar stones, monumental stones and 'stations'.

WALSH SVD, Dermot, *Divine Word Missionaries in Ireland,* (Roscommon, 1995), 159 pages, photos.
A detailed history of the Divine Word Missionaries from their arrival in Donamon in
1939 to 1995. There are many references to the diocese throughout concluding with a
chapter on the Diocesan Pastoral Centre.

WALSH, Rev Thomas, *History of the Irish Hierarchy, with the monasteries of each county, biographical notices of the Irish Saints, etc.* (New York, 1854), pp. 622-57.
Notes on the monastic foundations of county Roscommon and county Sligo.

Irish Penny Journal
>   VOL.I, NO.10, 5 September 1840, pp. 73-5: The castle of Rinduin, or Randown, county Roscommon.
>   Contains references to the ecclesiastical foundations at Rindoon, St John's parish.

— *Marist Brothers Sligo Centenary 1862-1962*, (Sligo, 1962), 114 pages, illus.
>   A collection of essays, which chronicle the history of the Marist Brothers in Sligo from
>   their establishment as the first foundation of the Order in Ireland to 1962. Many
>   contributions from past pupils who reminisce on their schooldays and on aspects of
>   Sligo over the century.

— 'Roscommon Castle and Dominican Friary', in *Journal of the Royal Society of Antiquaries of
>   Ireland*, VOL. 37, (1907), pp. 341-48.

— *Sisters of Mercy Elphin Diocese 1846-1929*, (typescript in Mercy Sisters Archive).
>   This article outlines the work of the Mercy Sisters in Sligo from the time of their arrival
>   there in 1846 up to 1929. Also explains other Mercy Foundations as well as the Union of
>   several Convents into one Diocesan Congregation in 1871.

— *Convent of Mercy*. Typescript 3 pages.
>   Gives an account of the arrival of the Sisters of Mercy in Strokestowm in 1891. It details
>   the establishment of the convent and the various educational developments that
>   occurred at the instigation of the Sisters.

— 'The school', in *School record 1937-1952 Irish Christian Brothers*, (Roscommon. 1952).
>   A brief outline of the early days of the Christian Brothers' Schools in Roscommon.

— *Holy Cross Dominican Abbey Sligo Yearbook, 1956*. (Sligo, 1956), 15 pages

— *Holy Cross, Sligo, 1973: a commemorative brochure to mark opening of new Dominican Church,
>   13 May 1973*, (Sligo, 1973), 64 pages, illus.

PART 3: PARISHES

AGHANAGH PARISH

Angelus, The
>   April 1985, VOL. 16, NO. 3; Parish of Ballinafad.

Roscommon Journal
>   27 February 1858: Ballinafad new chapel.

HURLEY, Rev Timothy,. 'The parish and Diocese of Aughanagh', in *St Patrick and the parish of
>   Kilkeevan*, (Dublin, 1943), pp. 366-404.

LENNON, Rev Joseph, *History of the parish of Aughanagh*, dated 8 March 1941. (copy in E.D.A.)
>   A manuscript of twenty one pages. It gives details of the churches, schools and
>   cemeteries in the parish from earliest times. There is a clergy list from 1859.

AHAMLISH PARISH

Angelus, The

Summer 1965, VOL. 6, NO. 1: Cliffony: echoes of 1864.

January 1974, VOL. 3, NO. 1: When hunger stalked Ahamlish: extracts from letters of Malachi Brennan PP.

Sligo Champion

27 May 1837: letter from Dr Burke re Ahamlish Glebe.

14 June 1930: Dedication of Mullaghmore Convent chapel.

11 December 1948: Re-opening of St Molaise's Church, Cliffoney.

1 March 1958: Solemn blessing of Mary Immaculate Church, Grange.

McGOWAN, Joseph, *In the shadow of Benbulben*, (Mullaghmore, 1993), 336 pages, illus.
Aspects of the parish of Ahamlish.

O'RORKE, Rev T., *History of Sligo*, (Dublin,1889), Reprint Sligo, 1986, VOL. II, pp. 29-56.

QUINN, Rev Michael, *St Molaise's parish park Grange*, (Sligo, 1985), 16 pages, illus.
Outlines St Molaise's associations with that part of north Sligo and the island of Inishmurray in particular.

WAKEMAN, W. F., 'On certain wells in the north west of Ireland … St Brigid's Well, Cliffony', in *Journal of Royal Society of Antiquaries of Ireland*, VOL. XV, (1879-82), pp 365-84. illus.

AHASCRAGH PARISH

Connacht Tribune

26 August 1933: Ahascragh church dedicated.

1 July 1939: Caltra church dedicated.

BRENNAN, Rev Malachy, *Notes on parish of Ahascragh* (1941), typescript 6 pages. (copy in E.D.A.)
A general survey of the parish from 788 to 1941. Deals with churches and clergy mostly.

BRENNAN, Rev Malachy, 'The parish of Ahascragh', in *Summerhill College Annual* 1952, pp. 39-42.
An historical survey of the parish based on extracts from *Annals Of Ireland* and *Ordnance Survey Letters.*

GILMORE, Marty & KILROY, Mattie, *The history of Ahascragh and Caltra*, (Ballinasloe, 1993), 239 pages, photos.
A general history of the parish compiled under a FÁS. scheme. Details on all aspects of life over the centuries including religious sites. Many original sources reproduced, eg. Griffiths Valuation etc. Clergy lists also included.

MAC LOCHLAINN, Tadhg, *A historical summary on the parish of Ahascragh, Caltragh and Castleblakeney,* (Ballinasloe, 1979), 92 pages, photos.
A general survey of the parish covering religious, cultural, economic, educational, social and political affairs. Details on religious sites, churches etc. also clergy lists for the parish.

— *Eglish National School centenary 1899-1999,* (1999), 108 pages, photographs.
A history of the school with many articles on parish life and past pupils over the century.

ARDCARNE PARISH

Angelus, The

Spring 1963, VOL. 5, NO. 1: Ardcarne: once an ancient diocese.

June 1983, VOL. 13, NO. 10: Topographical notes on Ardcarne.

December 1984,VOL. 15, NO. 10, pp. 6-7: Ardcarne past and present.

Roscommon Herald

2 June 1906: Crossna new church dedicated.

25 June 1964: Ardcarne parish church re-dedicated.

29 August 1980: Drumboylan Jubilee celebrations.

Roscommon Messenger

17 May 1930: Laying foundation stone of Drumboylan new church.

GILLESPIE, Dorothy, 'St. Beaidh's Church, Ardcarne', in *Boyle places, people and pastimes,* (Boyle, 1993), pp. 27-29.

KELLY, M. J., 'Parish of Ardcarne', in *Boyle; the origins, the buildings the times,* (Boyle, 1988), pp. 22-3. A short history of the parish.

TONRA, Rev Henry, 'The famine in Ardcarne', in *R.H.A.S.J.,* VOL. VI, (1996), pp. 91-4. Notes and extracts from the parish register around the years of the famine.

TONRA, Rev Henry, 'Ardcarne', in *R.H.A.S.J.,* VOL. VII, (1998), pp. 55-7. A history of the church at Ardcarne before and after the Reformation down to 1997.

— *Parish of Ardcarne.* Typescript 13 pages. (copy in E.D.A.) Notes on the twelfth century history of Ardcarne as a diocese and the patron saints of Ardcarne and Tumma parishes. Details of the churches, schools and clergy of the late nineteenth and twentieth century.

ATHLEAGUE/FUERTY PARISH

Connacht Tribune

25 February 1933: Obituary of Canon M. J. Conry PP, Athleague.

Roscommon Champion

26 May 1944: St. Patrick's Church Athleague.

Roscommon Herald

11 August 1956: US Bishop dedicates new Fuerty Church.

CRAWFORD, Henry S., 'Two early cross slabs at Fuerty, county Roscommon', in *Journal of the Royal Society of Antiquaries of Ireland,* VOL. XVII, (1907), Series 5, pp. 417-19. An account of the early Christian cross slabs at Fuerty cemetery with sketches.

FLEMING, Rev John J., *Fuerty Parish,* manuscript 5 pages. (copy in E.D.A.) Notes on the parish mostly clergy list from 1806 to 1954. Fuerty united with Athleague from 1881.

KELLY, Denis H., 'An account of inscribed stones at Fuerty', in *Proceedings of the Royal Irish Academy,* VOL. VIII, (1861-4), Series 1, pp. 455-8.
: Notes on the early Christian tombstones at Fuerty.

KENNY, Maureen, 'The parish of Fuerty', in *R.H.A.S.J.,* VOL. V, (1994), p. 106-7.
: A short note on the parish.

MORAN, James M., *Stepping on stones,* (Roscommon, 1993), 146 pages, photographs, illus.
: A local history of the Ballinturly-Correal area of Athleague parish with many references and photographs of ecclesiastical interest, including a church at Clooneen.

MORAN, James M., *Vignettes, bicentennial commemoration, Fr James Curley SJ 1796-1889,* (Roscommon, 1996), 296 pages, photographs, illus., maps.
: A collection of local history, including a biography of Fr Curley SJ, a native of Athleague parish. Clergy lists and notes on Catholic and Church of Ireland clergy in Athleague and Fuerty. Photographs and details of churches and cemeteries in the parish.

SEANFHEAR. 'Abbeygrey (Mainistir na Léithe) or the ring', in *Newbridge Ballygar Toghergar News* 1984, p. 69.
: A short account of the remains of a religious site at Abbeygrey.

— *Parish of Athleague,* typescript undated 3 pages (copy in E.D.A.).
: Notes on the early history of the parish. Mentions a holy well.

ATHLONE (ST PETER'S) PARISH

Angelus, The
: July-August 1990, VOL. 21, NO 6: Restoration of Drum old Cemetery and Monastic site.

Roscommon Messenger
: 16 August 1930: New church for Athlone.

Roscommon Herald
: 5 June 1965: Drum Church conforms to modern requirements.

BRODERICK, John, 'Redeeming the times' in *Irish Midland Studies: essays in commemoration of N. W. English,* (Athlone, 1980), pp.
: Contains a description of the Old St Peter's Church c. 1790-1937.

CANAVAN, Kitty, 'Old St Peter's (Athlone) 1795-1937', in *R.H.A.S.J.* VOL. IV, (1992), p. 70.
: An account of the old parish church.

CROWE, Rev John, 'Athlone yesterday and today', in *Summerhill College Annual* 1952-3, pp. 24-7.
: An outline of the main developments in Athlone from 1922 to 1952 as well as a history of the Cluniac Monastery, founded there in 1150, and some other notable events since 1570.

EGAN, Edward (Editor), *Drum and its hinterland,* (Athlone, 1994), 368 pages, illus.
: A comprehensive history of Drum parish from earliest times. Includes tombstone

inscriptions from Drum Old Cemetery and Cloonakilla Cemetery. There are notes on the clergy of the parish and clergy and religious who were natives of the parish.

EGAN, Edward. 'Ancient funeral route to Clonmacnoise', in *R.H.A.S.J.*, VOL. VI, (1996), pp. 70-1.
An account of an ancient pilgrim or funeral route through Drum parish to Clonmacnoise.

EGAN, Edward, 'Thomastown cemetery', in *R.H.A.S.J.*, VOL. VII, (1998), pp. 102-104.
An account of the ancient cemetery at Thomastown, Drum parish, associated with the Naghten Family.

— *Clonown, the history, traditions and culture of a south Roscommon community,* (Athlone, 1989), 179 pages.
The humour, sadness, pastimes, industry, poetry and environment of the Clonown people are explained in words, pictures, charts and maps.

— *SS Peter & Paul, Athlone Golden Jubilee 1937-1987,* (Athlone, 1987) 24 pages.
An account of the Church of SS Peter & Paul. Short note on Dean Crowe, photographs included.

— *Churches of Athlone,* (A Student project).
Some information on churches in Athlone (mostly west side) from 1150 onward.

— 'New Church, Athlone ... an exemplar of Roman renaissance', in *The Irish Builder,* June 1936, 2 pages.
An architectural description of the new Church of Ss Peter and Paul, with names of the main contractors.

— *St Peter's, Athlone*
A booklet compiled by the Junior Praesidium of the Legion of Mary, Athlone, giving details on the planning and building of the Church of Ss Peter and Paul, and highlighting its unique architectural features and works of art. Published following the death of Dean Crowe in 1955.

AUGHRIM PARISH

Angelus, The
October 1985, VOL. 16, NO. 8: Re-dedication of Aughrim Church.

Roscommon Messenger
5 October 1907: Dedication of Aughrim church.

BEIRNE, Rev Francis, *Solemn rededication of Church of Our Lady of Perpetual Help,* (1985).
Gives a brief history of the parish.

BALLINAMEEN PARISH

Angelus, The
> September 1972, VOL. I, NO. 17: Blessing and opening of St. Attracta's Church, Ballinameen.

Roscommon Herald
> 17 August 1861: A new Catholic church for Breedogue.
> 20 February 1869: Dedication of St Brigid's Church, Kilnamanagh.
> 4 July 1903: Ballinameen new church dedicated.
> 13 June 1964: Bishop re-dedicates Breedogue Church.
> 1 September 1972: St Attracta's Church Ballinameen re-dedicated.

Roscommon Journal
> 28 June 1902: New church for Ballinameen.

DEVINE, Rev Michael, *Diocesan History: Breedogue/Kilnamanagh,* (1941). Typescript unpublished (copy in E.D.A.).
> Notes on the parish of Ballinameen and Breedogue mostly from late nineteenth century.

— *Kingsland, county Roscommon: its people past and present,* (1994), 88 pages, illus.
> Chronicles the history of Kingsland NS from its foundation in 1848. A number of articles on the educational, sporting and cultural contributions of the school to the people of the area.

— *Ballinameen,* (Boyle, 1999), 156 pages, photos. and illus.
> Gives a good account of the schools at Ballinameen from early nineteenth century and also short notes on some of the priests of the parish.

— 'Saint Attracta', in *R.A.D.Y.,* VOL. II, (1981), p. 9.
> Short note on the saint and some churches associated with her.

BALLINTUBBER PARISH

Roscommon Champion
> 18 June 1955: Beautiful new church opened at Ballymoe.
> 12 November 1999: Ballintubber church re-dedicated.

Roscommon Journal
> 22 May 1897: Foundation stone of Ballintubber new church.

Roscommon Messenger
> 15 April 1899: Ballintober new church solemn dedication.

Roscommon Herald
> 15 April 1899: Ballintubber new church dedicated.
> 18 June 1955: Bishop dedicates new Ballymoe church.

BRADY, John, 'A hundred years of St Bride's Church, Ballintober', in *R.H.A.S.J.,* VOL. VII, (1998), pp. 108-111.
> An account of the church from the laying of the foundation stone in 1897 to 1998, with photographs.

BRADY, John J., *A hundred years on: St Bride's Church, Ballintober, centenary celebration 1889-1999,* (Ballintober, 1999). 82 pages, photographs.
A detailed history of St Bride's Church, the parish of Balliontober-Ballymoe and its people. There is a clergy list from 1827.

BURNS, M. A. & FLANAGAN, J. A. (Eds.), *Souvenir of Ballymoe* (1955)
Contains history relating to the Church of St Croan.

BALLYFORAN / DYSART / TISRARA PARISH

Angelus, The
July-August 1973, VOL. 2, NO. 7 & 8: New church at Four Roads.

Roscommon Champion
22 March 1958: Re-dedication of St Patrick's Church, Dysart.

Roscommon Journal
19 May 1900: Dysart Church tenders to builders.

Roscommon Herald
21 October 1961: Ballyforan Parochial Hall.
6 July 1973: New church dedicated at Four Roads.

Roscommon Messenger
31 May 1862: Dysart Relief Committee.
25 February 1911: Four Roads Church tenders to builders.
5 November 1935: Unveiling ceremony at Four Roads Church.

HIGGINS, James, *Aspects of the archaeology and history of Dysart Church, Cummeen, county Roscommon,* (Dysart, 1994), 120 pages, illus.
An archaeological report on the excavation carried out by the author on the site of Dysart medieval church ruins and ancient graveyard. Also includes a list of memorial inscriptions for the cemetery.

HIGGINS, James, *The Tisrara medieval church, Carrowntemple, Four Roads, county Roscommon, its archaeology and history,* (Tisrara, 1995), 200 pages, illus.
An archaeological report of extensive excavation carried out by the author on the site of Tisrara medieval church ruin and the adjoining ancient graveyard. Also includes a list of the memorial inscriptions of those commemorated in the cemetery.

HIGGINS, James, *Taughboy medieval church and ancient cemetery, Ballyforan, county Roscommon.* Unpublished 1997.
An archaeological report of excavations carried out by the author on the site of Taughboy medieval church in 1996 and 1997 during restoration work. Contains a list of tombstone inscriptions.

— *A history of Tisrara,* (Tisrara, 1997), 220 pages, illus., photos.
A history of Tisrara parish but includes references to Dysart and Ballyforan. It deals

with the ecclesiastical, social, educational, sporting and community affairs of this compact but vibrant parish community. It covers from the pre-Christian to modern times. It relates the unique history of Tisrara

— *Mount Talbot school 1892-1992, A window on the past,* (Mt Talbot, 1992) 116 pages, illus., photos.
A chronicle of one hundred years of education in Mount Talbot school. The book is a compilation of articles by past pupils linking the past and the present. It contains a list of all pupils who attended the school in that period.

BALLYGAR PARISH

Roscommon Herald
14 December 1957: Beautiful extension to Ballygar church.
31 October 1980: Newbridge church re-dedicated.

Roscommon Messenger
11 September 1858: Consecration of new chapel at Ballygar.

BURKE, Jim,. 'Toghergar', in *Newbridge Ballygar Toghergar News 1984*, p. 105.
A short account of Toghergar district with clergy list from 1909 to 1984.

CREHAN, John Joe, 'Most Rev Patrick Delaney', in *Newbridge Ballygar Toghergar News 1982*, p. 53.
A short biographical note on Rev Patrick Delaney, a native of the parish who became Archbishop of Tasmania 1907-1926.

EGAN, P. E., 'Killeroran', in *Newbridge Ballygar Toghergar News 1982*, pp. 17-29.
Contains references to the churches at Killeroran and Ballygar both Catholic and Protestant.

— *Rolling back the years 1896-1996: Centenary celebration of St Patrick's NS, Ballaghlea,* (1996).
A history of the school with some information on the parish and clergy.

SEANFHEAR. 'Our Parish', in *Newbridge Ballygar Toghergar News 1989*, pp 5-9.
An outline of the parish from early Christian times, with references to a holy well.

SCALLY, Rev John, *Historical notes on the Parochial District of Newbridge, Parish of Ballygar, county Galway,* Manuscript dated November 1952, 22 pages. (copy in E.D.A.)
A general history of the parish with clergy list from 1861 to 1951. References to some parishioners who became bishops in other places.

BOYLE PARISH

Angelus. The
October 1960: Boyle Church seventy eight years ago.
June 1977: St Joseph's Church, Boyle.
January 1981, VOL. 10, NO. 1: Dedication of Boyle Church.
Roscommon Herald
1 May 1869: Meeting in Boyle parish church.

17 June 1876: Laying of foundation stone of Boyle new church.

23 September 1882: Consecration of St Joseph's Church, Boyle.

7 April 1883: Vincentian mission in Boyle.

1 June 1957: Boyle church gets new bell.

18 June 1966: Bishop re-dedicates Boyle's parish church.

9 May 1980: Foundation stone of Boyle new church.

Roscommon & Leitrim Gazette

17 June 1876: Laying of the foundation stone of Boyle church.

DODD, Rev Kevin, *Dedication of St Joseph's Church, Boyle,* (Boyle, 1980), 32 pages, illus.
A history of the parish and its religious houses as well as information on the new church. Includes clergy list from 1794.

DODD, Rev Kevin, 'Catholic worship in parish of Boyle from 1600', in *Boyle: the origins, the buildings, the times,* (Boyle, 1988), pp. 138-147.

LAHEEN, Rev Kevin, 'The missing Boyle Mission Cross', in *Boyle: Places, people and pastimes,* (Boyle, 1993), pp. 20-22.

WYNN, Christopher, 'Memories of Assylinn', in *Boyle: Places, people and pastimes,* (Boyle 1993), pp. 23-26.

— 'Roman Catholic church of St Joseph, Boyle consecrated', in *The Irish Builder,* VOL. XXIV, (1 October 1882), NO. 547, p. 280.

— 'Antiquities of Boyle: St Patrick's travels through Boyle', in *Irish Monthly,* VOL. 7 (1879), pp. 482-92.

CASTLEREA (KILKEEVIN) PARISH

Angelus, The

December 1984, VOL. 15, NO. 10, p. 1: Cloonbonniffe Church rededicated.

Sligo Champion

1 August 1896: Dedication of new Church of St Patrick, Castlerea.

Roscommon Herald

1 August & 22 August 1896: Dedication of Castlerea new church.

Roscommon Journal

22 August 1896: Dedication of Castlerea new church.

HURLEY, Rev Timothy, *St Patrick and the parish of Kilkeevan,* VOL. 1, (Dublin, 1943), 618 pages, illus.
A history of the parish of Kikeevan from earliest times with sections on early Irish church, the life and work of St. Patrick and considerable theological discourse. Includes episcopal succession in the Diocese of Elphin.

McDONAGH, Rev Oliver (Ed.), *St Patrick's Church Castlerea: Centenary 1896-1996,* (Boyle, 1996) 112 pp.
History of the parish and descriptions of the churches. Also included is information on

the topography and demography of the parish and a reprint of some recollections of Charles Owen O'Conor MP 1938-1906.

O'CALLAGHAN, Colm (Editor), *Cloonbonniffe school reunion, the Don National School 1875-1996*, (1997), 88 pages, illus.
Chronicles the history of Cloonbonniffe NS from its foundation in 1875 as well as Cloonsuck NS 1861 to 1875 when it was incorporated into the former. Articles on the impact of the school on the people in the social cultural and sporting areas.

WALL, Oliver, 'The foundation of Christianity in the parish of Kilkeevan', in *R.H.A.S.J.*, VOL. V, (1994), pp. 54-7.
A general survey of the churches in Kilkeevan parish from earliest times.

TUOHY, Anthony, 'St Joseph's Church', in *R.H.A.S.J.*, VOL. III, (1990), p .36.
A short note, with photograph, on St Joseph's Church Castlerea.

TUOHY, Anthony, 'Castlerea: history on your doorstep', in *R.H.A.S.J.*, VOL II, (1988), p. 47.
Short notes on Catholic and Protestant ecclesiastics with associations with the parish of Kilkeevin.

— *Rededication of Church of St Brigid, Cloonbonniffe, souvenir booklet*, (Boyle 1984), 48 pages, illus., photos.
Gives an account of the history of St Brigid's and other churches in Kilkeevan parish. Also contains information on social history of the parish.

— *Tarmon NS.Centenary 1890-1990*, (1990), 60 pages, illus., photos.
A history of the school over the one hundred years from it's foundation. Contains some information of ecclesiastical interest tracing the parish and its patrons from early Christian times.

COOLERA PARISH

Angelus, The
March 1960, VOL. 2 NO. 5, p. 3: Historic snippets on the churches of Coolera.
Notes on the ancient and modern churches of the parish with a clergy list from 1854.
August-September 1974, VOL. 3, NOS. 8 & 9: Consecration of Ransboro church.

Sligo Champion
20 August 1921: Dedication of St Patrick's Church, Strandhill.
9 June 1967: Blessing and formal opening of Star of the See Church, Ransboro.

CONWAY, Bishop Dominic, *Consecration of Our Lady Star of the Sea Church, Ransboro 8 Sept 1974* (Sligo, 1974) 16 pages.
This booklet gives a brief history of Ransboro as well as the Mass of dedication.

FINNEGAN, Bishop Thomas, *Rosses Point: Coney Island*, (Sligo, 1977), 21 pages.
General guide book with references to ruined church at Killaspugbrone.

FINNEGAN, Bishop Thomas, *Strandhill and its surroundings*, (Sligo, 1978), 13 pages.

General guide book with references to churches in the area.

HANLY, Bishop Vincent, *Souvenir of the official opening and Solemn Blessing of the new Church of Our Lady Star of the Sea, Ransboro, 4 June 1967.* (Sligo, 1967) 32 pages
This booklet gives a history of the church and the priests who ministered there.

MCTERNAN, John C., *At the foot of Knocknarea: a chronicle of Coolera in bygone days,* (Sligo, 1990), 188 pages, illus.

O'RORKE, Rev T., *History of Sligo,* (Dublin,1889), Reprint Sligo, 1986, VOL. I, pp. 417-439.

CROGHAN PARISH

Roscommon Messenger
22 March 1856: New chapel at Croghan.
12 July 1856: Dedication of Drumlion new church.
7 March 1857: Croghan Chapel.

Roscommon Herald
28 July 1945: New altars for Drumlion Church.
26 April 1952: Historic occasion for Croghan parish.
14 June 1968: Drumlion Church re-dedicated.

LEONARD, Rev R., *Croghan,* manuscript 5 pages dated 1984. (copy in E.D.A.)
A general account of the parish which outlines ancient parish names.

MCGREEVY, Sean, Notes from various sources on Drumlion district.
There is a clergy list added by Fr Michel Casey from 1854 to 1942.

MULLANEY, Thomas, *Shannon Gaels GAA Club 1884-1984, a history* (1984).
Contains some items of ecclesiastical interest.

— *Souvenir of ceremony in St Michael's Church, Drumlion 22 July 1945,* Pamphlet 4 pages.
Extract from *Leitrim Observer* on the occasion of the dedication of new altars at the church.

— *Drumlion Chalice centenary celebration 1884-1984,* Pamphlet 4 pages.
Gives clergy list for Croghan 1872-1980 and Drumlion 1869-1978.

DRUMCLIFF PARISH

Angelus, The
December 1963, VOL. 5, NO. 4: Rathcormac Church re-dedicated.

Sligo Champion
7 September 1963: Rathcormac Church re-dedicated.

DURAND, Rev Stella, *Drumcliffe: The Church of Ireland parish in its North Sligo setting* (Manorhamilton, 2000). 150 pp, illus.
The social, religious and political history from prehistoric times to the new millennium.

O'Rorke, Terrence, 'Parish of Drumcliff', in *History of Sligo,* (Dublin, 1889) Reprint Sligo 1986, vol. i, pp. 479-516 and vol. ii, pp. 1-28

Stokes, Margaret, 'Notes on the High Crosses of Drumcliff', in *Proceedings of the Royal Irish Academy,* vol. 31, (13), 1901.

Wood-Martin, W. G., 'The crosses of Drumcliff', in *History of Sligo,* vol. ii, (Dublin, 1889), Reprint Sligo 1986, pp. 299-306.

ELPHIN PARISH

Angelus, The
July 1961, vol. 3, no. 9: St Patrick in Elphin.
March 1984, vol. 15, no. 3: Topographical notes of the late Archdeacon Michael J. Connellan.
A brief outline of the three churches of Elphin town.

Roscommon Journal
27 October 1894: Dedication of new church of Elphin.

Brennan, Rev Malachy, 'Troubled Curate days', in *R.H.A.S.J.,* vol. vi, (1996), pp. 51-2.
Relates the experiences of Fr Brennan during the troubled years of the 1920s especially in Mantua, but also in Caltra, county Galway. (Reprinted from *Summerhill Annual* 1950).

Beirne, Rev Francis, 'A glance at Elphin in earlier times', in *R.H.A.S.J.,* vol. i, (1986), p. 30.
Four photographs of Elphin with detailed captions.

Connellan, Rev M. J., 'Elphin parish', in *Summerhill College Annual,* 1947, pp. 23-27.
Detailed article on the origin of the name Elphin with notes on the two churches at Elphin: the cathedral and St Patrick's and their decline.

Gormley, Mary, 'Elphin a proud past – a promising future', in *R.H.A.S.J.,* vol. iv, (1992), pp. 66-9.
A survey of the history of the town, it's cathedral and other religious foundations from earliest times.

Gormley, Mary, *St Patrick's Church Elphin 1894-1994,* (1994).
Gives a brief account of the history of the church and the parish.

Slack, Rev Canon W. Wynne, 'Footprints on the sand', in *R.H.A.S.J.,* vol. ii, (1988), p. 33-4.
A short account of the Bishop Hodson Grammar school in Elphin.

— *Mantua NS 1822-1997 Souvenir Book,* 96 pages, illus., photos.
A history of the school and its locality over 175 years. A description and history of Kilmaryal Church. Also contains a clergy list from 1822.

— *Bishop Hodson's Grammer School, Centenary magazine 1869-1969,* (Boyle, 1969), 57 pages, photos.
A collection of articles, on the school and Elphin, marking the centenary of the school.

FAIRYMOUNT PARISH

Roscommon Herald
> 11 May 1861: Tibohine new church opening.
> 15 June 1861: Opening of Tibohine new church.

GIBLIN, T., *Parish of Tibohine and Fairymount*. Manuscript 10 pages. (copy in E.D.A.)
> Notes on the history of the parish covering churches and clergy.

TIMON, Patrick, 'Tibohine (extracts from a talk to Lough Gara Historical Society 1969)', in *R.H.A.S.J.*, VOL. I, (1986), pp. 55-7.
> Notes on the Tibohine area in patrician times.

TIBOHINE COMMUNITY CENTRE COMMITTEE, *Tibohine Community Centre, a souvenir history*, (1987).
> Contains a short parish history especially pertaining to St Baethin.

— *Fairymount remembers the famine*, (Boyle, 1996).
> Records aspects of the Famine in the Fairymount area.

FRENCHPARK/BALLINAGARE PARISH

Roscommon Herald
> 11 June 1965: Foundation stone of Ballinagare church.
> 11 June 1966: New church to challenge the world: Historic cermony at Ballinagare.
> Centenary Edition 1959: Frenchpark (50 years ago)
> A general account of the parish from early twentieth century with some references to the clergy, churches and schools.
> 31 August 1979: Frenchpark church re-dedicated.

DWYER, Bernard, 'Midnight Mass in Ballinagare, 1726', in *R.A.D.Y.*, VOL. XVII, (1996), p. 78.
> A brief mention of Mass in Ballinagare in 1726.

MARTIN, Elain, 'Ballinagare', in *R.H.A.S.J.*, VOL. IV, (1992), pp. 18-19.
> A general article with some references to old churches.

GEEVAGH PARISH

Angelus, The
> April 1963, VOL. 5, NO. 2: Geevagh.
> June 1979, VOL. 8, NO. 6: Geevagh proud of its vocations.
> November 1995, VOL. 26, NO. 8: Dedication of Geevagh Church.

Sligo Champion
> 25 June 1898: Consecration of Altars and blessing of St Joseph's Church Geevagh.
> 6 August 1955 and 14 January 1956: Our Lady of Lourdes Church, Glenkillamey, Laying of foundation stone and dedication.
> 28 September 1957: Dedication of St Brigid's Church Highwood
> 25 October 1995: Dedication of Geevagh Church.

Roscommon Herald
> 23 June 1956: Bishop dedicates new church on mountain side-Glenkillamy.
> 28 September 1957: Highwood's new church blessed.

McGLOIN, Attracta & MOORE, Sam, 'Religious sites in Geevagh and Highwood', in *Aspects of Geevagh and Highwood,* (Sligo, 1996), pp. 49-69.
> Covers early Christian sites at Shancough, Carraig a Teampaill, Kilmactranny, etc.

O'RORKE, Rev T., *History of Sligo,* VOL. II, (Dublin ,1889) , Reprint Sligo, 1986, pp. 260-281.

— *Parish of Geevagh* (1995)
> A commemorative booklet published on the occasion of the dedication of St Joseph's Church, Geevagh, 22 October 1995. Contains a summary of the origins of Christianity in Geevagh and information on the parish church.

KILBEGNET PARISH

Roscommon Herald
> 14 August 1965: Kilbegnet church is re-dedicated.
> 30 July 1993 p. 3: Glinsk Church celebrates 150th anniversary.

Roscommon Champion
> 21 August 1965: Bishop re-dedicates Kilbegnet church.

CREHAN, Rev Bernard, *Kilbegnet, Ballinakill and Donamon,* manuscript 15 pages. (copy in E.D.A.)
> Notes on the history of the parish of Kilbegnet with details on churches, schools and holy wells, etc. Clergy lists from 1831 to c. 1940.

WARD, Martin. *The Church in Glinsk,* (1993).
> This publication celebrates the 150th anniversary of the church at Glinsk. Details given on holy wells, crucifixion plaques and old churches including the Abbey of Ballinakill. Includes a clergy list.

KILBRIDE PARISH

Roscommon Champion
> December 1995: Commemoration of Derrane Church 1845-1995.
> This article gives an outline history of the church at Derrane.

Roscommon Herald
> 11 April 1958; Century old Derrane Church for re-dedication.
> 16 May 1959: Re-dedication of Derrane Church.

Roscommon Messenger
> 10 April 1958: New chapel at Derrane.

BROWNE, Rev Raymond, *The parish of Kilbride,* typescript 2 pages. (Copy in E.D.A.)
> An outline history of the parish

— *Map of Derrane Abbey*, typescript 4 pages. (copy in E.D.A.)
Copy of a deed of lease of a site for a church in Derrane dated 1847.

KILGEFIN PARISH

Roscommon Champion
10 August 1959: Bishop will bless Ballagh new church.
24 March 1962: Re-dedication of Curraghroe church.
16 May 1969: Ballyleague church dedicated.

Roscommon Herald
17 December 1859: New Church of the Holy Rosary, Ballyleague.
13 October 1956: Foundation stone of Ballagh new church.

HURLEY, Rev Thomas P., *Annals of a parish: Parishes of Kilgefin, Clontuskert, Curraghroe, 1932.* (copy in E.D.A.)
Sixteen pages of newspaper cuttings relating to the history of these parishes from earliest times. Details on churches in the parishes from 520 to 1930.

KILGLASS PARISH

Angelus, The
November 1992, VOL. 23, NO. 9: Historic day for people of Kilglass.
April/May 1997, VOL. 28, NO. 3: Centenary of Kilglass church.

Roscommon Herald
4 February 1899: Mount Carmel Church, Rooskey.
28 November 1953: Dedication of Church at Rooskey.
An account of the dedication of Rooskey church on 22 November with some information on its past.

Roscommon Messenger
4 July 1896: Dedication of Kilglass Catholic church.

COYLE, Liam, *A history of Kilglass, Slatta, Ruskey , Kilglass; Kilglass Gales*, (1994), 559 pages, illus.
A comprehensive and lavishly illustrated history of Kilglass/Ruskey area. The emphasis is on Gaelic games but the ecclesiastical and social history of the area is also covered.

— *Solemn dedication of the Church of the Sacred Heart, Kilglass*, (1992).
Souvenir booklet giving a brief history of Kilglass church.

KILTOOM & CAM PARISH

Angelus, The
June-July 1974, VOL. 3, NO. 6 & 7: Dedication of the parish church Kiltoom.

Roscommon Herald
14 March 1967: Renovated Curraghboy church dedicated to St Brigid.

GACQUIN, William, *Roscommon before the the Famine, the parishes of Kiltoom and Cam 1749-1845*, (Dublin, 1996), 64 pages, maps.
> A general history of the parish of Kiltoom and Cam in the century before the famine. References to churches, schools and clergy for this period.

GACQUIN, William, *Tombstone Inscriptions: Cam Old Cemetery*, (1992)
> A list of tombstone inscriptions from Cam Old Cemetery with notes. Also includes general notes on parish history and clergy list from 1704 to 1992.

GACQUIN, William, *The history of Brideswell and the Celtic connection*, (1995) 14 pages typescript unpublished. (copy in E.D.A.)
> An account of the Pattern of Brideswell from the earliest time including the traditional stations performed at the Pattern

HAND, Teresa (Editor), *Scoil Náisiúnta na Carraige 1890-1990, Carrick National School, Curraghboy: A stroll down memory lane*, (1990), 80 pages, photos.
> A collection of articles on the one hundred years of the school and its influence on the area. Also a history of the introduction of the National Schools into the parish of Kiltoom and Cam

KELLY, M. K., *Cam of Saint Bride* (Athlone,1907) 13 pages.
> An account of Cam parish covering places of special importance such as Brideswell.

LONGFIELD, A. K., 'Some eighteenth century Irish tombstones VII: Clonmel, Kiltoom Ser Kieran, etc. with six plates', in *Journal of the Royal Society of Antiquaries of Ireland*, VOL. LXXXIV, 1954, PT. II, pp. 173-8.
> An account of two eighteenth-century tombstones in Kiltoom old cemetery.

MOORE, Arthur, 'A medieval charter relating to the townland of Cam', in *Journal of the Old Athlone Society*, VOL. I, (1970-71), p. 74.
> A brief account and translation of a grant of land from the Bishop of Elphin dated 1420.

RYAN, Hazel, 'Kiltoom church and graveyard', in *R.H.A.S.J.*, VOL. VII, (1998), pp. 27-33.
> A detailed survey of the old church and graveyard in Kiltoom with drawings and notes on its history from early Christian period.

— *Souvenir of the solemn blessing and re-opening of St Brigid's Church, Curraghboy* (1969) 4 pp.
> Outline history of Cam parish includes a list of parish priests of Kiltoom and Cam parish from 1771 to 1967.

— *Dedication of the Church of the Risen Christ, Ballybay* (1974) 20 pages.
> Outline history of Kiltoom parish including a list of parish priests from 1771 to 1974.

— *Ballybay's new church: unique link with the past.*
> Newspaper article from 1974 with photographs on the occasion of the dedication of 140 year old church.

KNOCKCROGHERY PARISH

Roscommon Journal

1886: Gives an account of the Blessing and opening of the Church of St Patrick Knock-croghery in that year.

Roscommon Herald

22 June 1957: Bishop blesses re-dedicated Lecarrow church.

15 December 1967: New church at Rahara opened.

Roscommon Messenger

24 October 1886: Consecration of St Patrick's Church at Knockcroghery.

COYNE, Ferdinand, 'St Patrick's church Knockcroghery', in *R.H.A.S.J.*, VOL. VIII (2000), pp 5-6.
An account of St Patrick's Church from it inception in 1870s to the opening in 1886 and final additions in 1950. Gives a description of the church and those it replaced.

COYNE, Ferdinand, 'The parochial hall', in *R.A.D.Y.*, VOL. XX, (1999), pp. 70-1.
An account of the converting of the old chapel at Cullen to a parish hall and the uses to which it was put.

COYNE, Ferdinand, 'They are all saints', in *R.A.D.Y.*, VOL. XVII, (1996), pp. 24-5.
A brief account of the old cemetery at Kilmaine describing some restoration work done in 1995 and some of the tombstones found there.

— *Souvenir of Solemn Blessing and opening of the new church Rahara, Friday 8 December 1967.* Typescript 3 pages. (copy in E.D.A.)
A short note on the new church and some prayers with order of ceremonies. One page on the history of the parish.

— *Diocesan History: St John's District.* Typescript 7 pages and 1 page manuscript. (copy in E.D.A.)
A survey of the history of St John's parish from earliest times. References to some priests who served there and to National Schools. Some sites in the surrounding districts are also mentioned.

— 'Rahara', in *R.H.A.S.J.*, VOL. V, (1994), p. 111.
A short note on Rahara parish with drawings.

LOUGHGLYNN PARISH

Roscommon Herald

31 October 1942: Lisacul new church dedicated.

25 Jan 1980: The village with a historic background.

Roscommon Messenger

3 June 1905: Laying foundation stone of Loughglynn new chruch.

20 Oct 1906: Dedication of Loughglynn church.

—— *Is this the right road to Gortaganny?* (1997).
    Gives a brief description of the parish as it was in the early nineteenth century.

McDermott, Vera, *The woodlands of Loughglynn,* (Manchester, 1998).
    Gives some information on the parish of Loughglynn.

MAUGHEROW PARISH

Angelus, The
    October 1991, VOL. 22, NO. 8: Maugherow church dedicated.

Sligo Champion
    14 December 1861: Appeal for funds for building of church.
    25 November 1882: Spire of church hit by lightning.
    31 March 1989: Lightning destroys Maugherow church.
    13 September 1991: Dedication of St Patrick's Maugherow

—— *Opening and Consecration of St Patrick's Church, Sept 1991,* (Sligo, 1991), 12 pages.

ORAN PARISH

Angelus, The
    March 1983, VOL.12, NO.3, p. 13: Dedication of Clooneycolgan church.
    December 1983, VOL. 13, NO. 12: Rededication of Cloverhill church.

Roscommon Herald
    9 May 1959: Ballinaheglish church renovated.

Roscommon Messenger
    28 July 1860: The chapel of Oran.
    27 August 1932: New church at Ballinaheglish.

Roscommon Journal
    9 June 1888: Cloonycolgan new church.

Hannon, Christopher, *The Parish of Oran,* (1999) typescript 3 pages. (copy in E.D.A.)
    An outline history of the parish, with clergy list from 1893 and a partial list from earlier
    times. Gives 'Station' used by pilgrims at St Patrick's Well, Oran.

Mullin, John, 'The Holy Well of Oran', in *R.A.D.Y.,* VOL. VIII, (1987), pp. 71-3.
    An account of the well at Oran and its association with StPatrick and importance for
    the parish of Oran.

White, James, *Oran parish.* Typescript two pages. (copy in E.D.A.)
    Brief account of the parish.

—— 'Early use of concrete in Ireland: Round Tower at Oran', in *The Irish Builder,* VOL. XII,
    (March 1870), NO. 246, p. 59.

RIVERSTOWN PARISH

Angelus, The

October 1983, VOL. 13, NO.10: Topographical notes on Ballinakill church.

Sligo Champion

1 January 1842 & 5 March 1842: Gallery collapses in Riverstown church and subsequent letter from Rev B. Hester PP.

29 June 1907: Dedication of St Colum's Church, Gleann.

13 December 1941: Dedication of the Church of the Sacred Heart, Riverstown.

19 August 1981: Re-dedication of Church of the Assumption, Sooey.

Roscommon Herald

26 August 1961: Reconstructed county Sligo church dedicated (Sooey).

MCGLOIN, A. & MOORE, S., *In the shadow of Carran Hill: historical perspectives of Gleann and its surroundings,* (Sligo, 1997), 196 pages, illus.

Includes a chapter on ecclesiastical sites and holy wells; viz St. James's Well, Drumcolumb, Ballinakill, Gleann Church and Templemore.

O'RORKE, Rev T., *History of Sligo,* (Dublin, 1889), Reprint, Sligo 1986, VOL. II, pp. 239-259.

ROSCOMMON PARISH

Angelus, The

December 1963, VOL. 5, NO. 4: Kilteevan's new church.

October 1981 & November 1981, VOL. 10, NOS. 10 & 11: Roscommon in history.

August-September 1997, VOL. 28. NO. 5: Sacred Heart Church, Roscommon: renovations.

Roscommon Messenger

6 July 1901: Roscommon new church.

18 April 1903: Forthcoming dedication of Roscommon new church.

20 June 1903: The Dr. Gillooly Memorial Church.

A detailed account of the Sacred Heart Church, its art and architecture.

26 June 1915: Silver Jubilee of Very Rev Canon Cummins DD PP VF.

21 March 1925: Church of the Sacred Heart Roscommon: Unveiling of decorated Sanctuary.

Roscommon Herald

11 July 1959: New church to be built (Kilteevan).

Roscommon Journal

11 March 1901: Roscommon new church.

FANNING, Thomas, 'An early Christian site at Ballinaboy, county Roscommon', in *Galway Archaeological and Historical Society Journal,* VOL. 37, (1979-80), pp. 90-93.

A description of an early Christian slab an possible religious site in Balliaboy townland.

GANNON, J. A., *Kilteevan church,* Typescript 5 pages, dated 1952 and based on notes by Rev John Finan dated 1912. (copy in E.D.A.)

A history of Kilteevan parish with many references to ancient religious sites.

GERAGHTY, Michael J., *Souvenir of the Church of the Sacred Heart of Jesus, Roscommon,* (Athlone, 1983) 79 pages, illus.
This book gives detailed information about the evolution of the Catholic church in Roscommon. An appraisal of the architectural features of the church and details about the religious significance of the various works of art which adorn the church.

KERRIGAN, John, 'An apologia for Church St Roscommon town sleepy valley', in *R.H.A.S.J.,* VOL. III, (1990), pp. 63-4.
References to the churches and Christian sites of Roscommon town.

KERRIGAN, John, 'Roscommon: an independent diocese and a separate kingdom', in *R.H.A.S.J.,* VOL. IV, (1992), pp. 51-3.
Short note on the Diocese of Roscommon.

KERRIGAN, John, 'Local priest averts panic', in *R.H.A.S.J.,* VOL. V, (1994), pp. 44-6.
An article on a Jesuit mission preached at Roscommon in 1857 and a short account of three nineteenth-century parish priests.

KERRIGAN, John, 'The Well of St Coman: the birthplace of our county', in *R.A.D.Y.,* VOL. XIV, (1993), pp. 54-5.
A brief description of the Well of St Coman in Roscommon parish.

MAHON, Rev T., *Roscommon in history,* dated 1935, typescript 10 pages. (copy in E.D.A.)
The text of a Radio Éireann broadcast in 1935, this general survey of the history of the county has many references to the church from earliest times to the seventeenth century.

MOLLOY, David, 'Dr Harrison and the Harrison Hall', in *R.H.A.S.J.,* VOL. III, (1990), pp. 3-6.
Contains references to the building which was the Catholic church in Roscommon town from 1829 to 1903.

MOONEY, M., 'The history of my home place', in *Rosc Chomáin,* 1980, pp. 21-23.
An account of the ecclesiastical history of the parish of Kilteevan.

RYAN, Hazel A., 'An ecclesiastical site at Cloontogher, Kilteevan', in *R.H.A.S.J.,* VOL. IV, (1992), pp. 45-47.
A detailed description of the medieval parish church and graveyard and an earlier Christian site.

RYAN, Hazel A. (Editor), *Kilteevan: a look at a school and its parish. A centenary publication of Kilteevan National School,* (Kilteevan, 1997), 248 pages, illus.
Detailed coverage of the history of Kilteevan NS from its foundation in 1897. The history of the area is also well documented.

SIGGINS, Albert, 'Romanesque graveslab from Roscommon town', in *R.H.A.S.J.,* VOL. VI, (1996), p. 11.
A description of an eleventh-century graveslab.

Siggins, Albert. 'An early Roscommon school foundation plaque', in *Rosc Chomáin*, vol. 1995, pp 27-9.
A short description of a plaque naming a Roscommon parish priest from late eighteenth to early nineteenth century.

— 'Roscommon (Friday, 5 July 1907)', in *Journal of the Royal Society of Antiquaries of Ireland*, vol. xxxvii, (1907), pp. 341-348.
This article gives an outline of the history of Roscommon from the earliest times. It gives considerable detail about the Dominican Abbey in the town.

ROSSES POINT PARISH

Finnegan, Bishop Thomas, *Rosses Point: Coney Island,* (Sligo, 1977), 21 pages.
General guide book with references to ruined church at Killaspugbrone.

McManus, Rev J,. *Rosses Point,* manuscript, 15 pages, c. 1940, unpublished.(copy in E.D.A.)
A short history of the church and schools in the parish with a clergy list from 1896.

SLIGO (ST ANNE'S) PARISH

Angelus, The
Spring 1959, vol. i, no. i: St Anne's Church, Sligo: Blessing and formal opening.
February 1981, vol. 10, no. 2: Sligo's Holy Well. …Tobernalt.

Sligo Champion
8 July 1896: Opening and dedication of St John's Church, Carraroe.
28 July 1956: Foundation stone laid 'St Anne's'.
2 August 1958 and 9 August 1958: Dedication and formal opening of St Anne's Church.
11 August 1962: Re-dedication of St John's Church, Carraroe.

Roscommon Herald
9 August 1958: Sligo's new church blessed by bishop (St Anne's).

Boylan, Eamon, *Tobernalt Holy Well: history and heritage,* (Sligo, 1997), 24 pages, illus.

Henry, Fergal, *Tobernalt: the well in the cliff,* (Sligo, 1985), 24 pages, illus.
The origins of the well are discussed with some of the customs and folklore associated with a place of ancient pilgrimage.

— *Our Parish: St Anne's,* (Sligo, 1991), 28 pages, illus.
An account of the parish of St. Anne's.

O'Mullane, M. J., 'Tobernault', in *Sligo Champion,* 25 July 1914.

SLIGO (ST MARY'S) PARISH

Sligo Champion
18 July 1874: Consecration of Cathedral of Immaculate Conception.
5 April 1930: Opening of new Entrance to Sligo Cathedral.
12 December 1975: Century old Cathedral gets overhall.

HARAN, Rev Cyril, *Sligo Cathedral 1875-1975*, (Sligo, 1975), 68 pages, illus.
The story of the building of the cathedral, with sketches of the diocese in the seventeenth and eighteenth centuries. Includes a list of bishops from IIII to 1975 and of administrators and curates of the parish from 1874 to 1975.

McTERNAN, John C., 'The mass house or parish chapel', in *Sligo long ago*, (Sligo, 1998) pp. 100-108.
This article gives an account of the parish chapel, Sligo, between 1776 and 1874 and the events and personalities associated with it.

TYNDALL, Charles, *The ancient parish and church of St John the Baptist, Sligo*, (Dublin, 1962), 44 pages, illus.
An historical account of St John's church from earliest times to Disestablishment.

SLIGO: ST JOSEPH'S / CALRY PARISH

Angelus, The
March 1981, VOL. 10, NO. 3: New church for Ballytivnan.
November 1983, VOL. 13, NO. 11, p. 6: St Joseph's Church, Ballytivnan.
Details on the dedication of the new church 30 Oct 1983 and an article on Ballytivnan past and present by Rev Francis Beirne.

Roscommon Herald
4 November 1983, p. 9: New community gets new church.
Information about the construction of the new church at Ballytivnan and its dedication.

O'RORKE, Rev T., *History of Sligo*, VOL. I, (Dublin, 1889, Reprint Sligo, 1986) pp. 440-478.

TRAVERS, Rev C., *Dedication of St Joseph's church , Ballytivnan, Sligo 30 October 1983*, (Boyle, 1983), 28 pages.
This booklet explains why the new church was built and gives information about the area past and present. Details of features of the church and its community centre.

STROKESTOWN PARISH

Angelus, The
January 1984, VOL. 14, NO.1, p. 1: Strokestown Presbytery – the old and the new.
July-August 1985, VOL. 16, NO.6: Church of Immaculate Conception, Strokestown.
Advent 1993, VOL. 24, NO. 10: Strokestown church reopened.

Roscommon Champion
16 July 1960: Strokestown Church re-dedicated.

Roscommon Herald
9 December 1871: Consecration of new church at Strokestown.
16 July 1960: Dedication of Strokestown parish church.

Roscommon Journal
13 June 1863: Dedication of new church at Strokestown.

Roscommon Messenger
   18 May 1901: Kiltrustan Chapel.

BEIRNE, Rev Francis, *Church of the Immaculate Conception, Strokestown,* Poster. (copy in E.D.A.)
   A description of the church in Strokestown highlighting some of its features. A clergy
   list from 1749 to 1981.

BEIRNE, Rev Francis, *St Mary's Catholic Church, Carniska.* Typescript 1 page. (copy in E.D.A.)
   An outline history of this church.

BEIRNE, Rev Francis, *The Parish of Strokestown (Bumlin, Lisonuffy, Cloonfinlough, Kiltrustan),*
   typescript dated 1981, 4 pages. (copy in E.D.A.)
   Historical notes on the Augustinian foundation at Lisonuffy and the modern church at
   Carniska.

BROWNE, Rev Raymond, 'The last priests of Lisanuffy', in *R.H.A.S.J.,* VOL. VI, (1996), pp. 51-2.
   An account of the famine in Lisanuffy and the efforts of the last parish priest, Fr John
   Boyd, to help his people. The article traces the fortunes of some Lisanuffy natives in the
   new world.

BROWNE, Rev Raymond, 'Part of original documentation re transfer of land as site for new
   church in Strokestown', in *R.H.A.S.J.,* VOL. VII, (1998), pp. 130-1.
   A letter dated 1795 re site for a church in Strokestown with others relating to the famine
   period. Also includes a threatening letter to the parish priest of Kilglass dated 1847.

MCDERMOTT, Rev Michael, *The denunciation calumny.* Typescript 3 pages dated 1847. (copy in
   E.D.A.)
   A copy of a letter to *The Evening Herald* protesting at the denunciation of the Strokes-
   town clergy following the murder of Major Mahon.

O'CALLAGHAN CM, Rev Malachy, 'Vincentian Mission in Strokestown', in *R.H.A.S.J.,* VOL. VII,
   (1998), p. 13.
   A short note on the first mission in Strokestown in 1867.

TARMONBARRY PARISH

Angelus, The
   March 1986, VOL.17, NO. 2: Dedication of Church of St Anne, Scramogue.
   October 1997, VOL. 28, NO. 6: Centenary of Church of Sacred Heart, Tarmonbarry.

Roscommon & Leitrim Gazette
6 September 1845: Tarmonbarry new chapel.

Roscommon Herald
   14 February 1986: Dedication ceremony at Scramogue century old church.

Roscommon Journal
   5 June 1897: Dedication of Tarmonbarry church.

FARRELL OSF, Rev Br Alan, 'Cluain Coirpthe and Kinel Dofa', in *R.H.A.S.J.*, VOL. VI, (1996),
pp. 89-90.
An account of the area about the present parish of Tarmonbarry with notes on St
Barry, its patron.

KELLY, Frank, *Whitehall National School 1892-1992 centenary history.* (1992) 68 pages.
Chronicles the history of Whitehall (Currawn) NS. Deals with the impact of the school
in a social, cultural, sporting context.

— *Church of the Sacred Heart, Whitehall, Tarmonbarry 1897-1997,* (1997).
Contains a brief history of the churches at Whitehall and Scramogue.

— *Solemn dedication of the Church of St Anne Scramogue,* (1986).
Contains a brief history of the church at Scramogue

— *Reply to queries on Diocesan history: Tarmonbarry,* Manuscript 4 pages. (copy in E.D.A.)
An outline of the parish from early Christian times with a clergy list from 1811.

TULSK PARISH

Angelus, The
October 1962, VOL. 4, NO. 15: New church at Kilmurry.

Roscommon Messenger
2 June 1857: Killina new chapel.

Roscommon Herald
21 April 1962: Blessing the foundation stone of new church for Kilmurry.

DE HORA, Kathy, *Archaeological report on Baslick graveyard, Tulsk.* (1993), unpublished.
An archaeological report on Baslick cemetery.

GORMLEY, Mary, *Tulsk Parish in Historic Maigh Ai,* (1989).
A detailed history of the parish giving an account on the Dominican Abbey, holy wells,
Mass Rocks, and also contains clergy lists.

MAC COLUIM, Fionn, 'Sgéal faoi Thobar Oilbhe, Co Ros Chomáin', in *Béaloideas* IML. I,
UIMH.I, Meitheamh 1929, pp. 56-7.
A story of the origin of the well of Oilbhe and a cure associated with it.

MANNION, Laurence & TIERNAN, Manus, *Rathmoyle cemetery.* (1996).
Includes items of parish history associated with the cemetery.

— 'The restoration of Rathmoyle ancient cemetery', in *R.H.A.S.J.*, VOL. VII, (1998), pp. 143-4.
An account of the restoration with notes on priests from the area and some of the local
landed families.

O'CONNELL, Mary, 'Urney Church', in *R.H.A.S.J.*, VOL. VIII, (2000), pp 140-1.
A description with sketches of a ruined church dedicated to a seventh-century saint at
Vesnoy townland.

Index

This index does not cover lists of people published within the book, lists of townlands accompanying maps, or bibliographical material.